8th Workshop on Argument Mining (ArgMining 2021)

Punta Cana, Dominican Republic and Online
10-11 November 2021

ISBN: 978-1-7138-9174-1

Printed from e-media with permission by:

Curran Associates, Inc.
57 Morehouse Lane
Red Hook, NY 12571

Some format issues inherent in the e-media version may also appear in this print version.

Printed with permission by Curran Associates, Inc. (2024)

For permission requests, please contact the Association for Computational Linguistics at the address below.

Association for Computational Linguistics
209 N. Eighth Street
Stroudsburg, Pennsylvania 18360

Phone: 1-570-476-8006
Fax: 1-570-476-0860

acl@aclweb.org

Additional copies of this publication are available from:

Curran Associates, Inc.
57 Morehouse Lane
Red Hook, NY 12571 USA
Phone: 845-758-0400
Fax: 845-758-2633
Email: curran@proceedings.com
Web: www.proceedings.com

EMNLP 2021

The 8th Workshop on Argument Mining (ArgMining 2021)

Proceedings of the Workshop

November 10 - 11, 2021
Online and in Punta Cana, Dominican Republic

Introduction

Argument mining (also known as "argumentation mining") is a young and gradually maturing research area within computational linguistics. At its heart, argument mining involves the automatic identification of argumentative structures in free text, such as the conclusions, premises, and inference schemes of arguments as well as their interrelations and counter-considerations. To date, researchers have investigated argument mining on genres such as legal documents, product reviews, news articles, online debates, user-generated web discourse, Wikipedia articles, academic literature, persuasive essays, tweets, and dialogues. Recently, also argument quality assessment and generation came into focus. In addition, argument mining is inherently tied to stance and sentiment analysis, since every argument carries a stance towards its topic, often expressed with sentiment.

Argument mining gives rise to various practical applications of great importance. In particular, it provides methods that can find and visualize the main pro and con arguments in a text corpus — or even on in an argument search on the web — towards a topic or query of interest. In instructional contexts, written and diagrammed arguments represent educational data that can be mined for conveying and assessing students' command of course material. In information retrieval, argument mining is expected to play a salient role in the emerging field of conversational search. And with the IBM Debater Project, technology based on argument mining recently received a lot of media attention.

While solutions to basic tasks such as component segmentation and classification slowly become mature, many tasks remain largely unsolved, particularly in more open genres and topical domains. Success in argument mining requires interdisciplinary approaches informed by NLP technology, theories of semantics, pragmatics and discourse, knowledge of discourse in application domains, artificial intelligence, information retrieval, argumentation theory, and computational models of argumentation.

The community around ArgMining is constantly growing. This year's edition of the workshop had 39 valid submissions (27 in 2017, 32 in 2018, 41 in 2019, and 30 in 2020). Among the submitted papers, there were 23 full papers, 9 short papers, and 7 shared-task papers. Out of the 39 papers, 11 full papers, 4 short papers, and 6 shared-task papers have been accepted, resulting in an overall acceptance rate of 54%. All the papers are included in the proceedings at hand.

Given the duration of the workshop (1.5 days) and its format (hybrid), we decided to give all the authors the possibility to present their work orally. Long papers were given 15 min for the talk and 5 min for the discussion, while the short papers were given 10 min for the talk and 2 min for discussion. We were delighted to have Professors Anthony Hunter from University College London and Lu Wang from the University of Michigan as keynote speakers. The speakers addressed interesting topics related to persuasion and argument generation.

The ArgMining 2021 workshop program covered the Quantitative Summarization–Key Point Analysis Shared Task, and also featured a best paper award, thankfully sponsored by IBM. Both the shared task and award are announced on the official workshop website chaired by Roxanne El Baff: `https://2021.argmining.org/`.

Khalid Al-Khatib, Yufang Hou, and Manfred Stede
(ArgMining 2021 co-chairs)

Organizers:

Khalid Al-Khatib, Bauhaus-Universität, Weimar (chair)
Yufang Hou, IBM Research Dublin (chair)
Manfred Stede, Universität Potsdam (chair)

Program Committee:

Stergos D. Afantenos, Université Paul Sabatier
Milad Alshomary, Paderborn University
Kevin Ashley, University of Pittsburgh
Roy Bar-Haim, IBM Research AI
Miriam Butt, University of Konstanz
Elena Cabrio, CNRS, Inria, I3S
Shohreh Haddadan, University of Luxembourg
Christopher Hidey, Google
Xinyu Hua, Bloomberg LP
Yohan Jo, Amazon
Christopher Klamm, Technische Universitat Darmstadt
Gabriella Lapesa, University of Stuttgart
Anne Lauscher, University of Mannheim
John Lawrence, University of Dundee
Diane Litman, University of Pittsburgh
Elena Musi, Columbia University
Alexis Palmer, University of Colorado
Joonsuk Park, University of Richmond
Simon Parsons, King's College London
Georgios Petasis, NCSR Demokritos
Olesya Razuvayevskaya, European Bioinformatics Institute
Chris Reed, University of Dundee
Patrick Saint-Dizier, IRIT - CNRS
Jodi Schneider, University of Illinois at Urbana Champaign
Benno Stein, Bauhaus-Universitat Weimar
Shahbaz Syed, Leipzig University
Nicolas Turenne, UMR LISIS (INRA,UPEM,CNRS)
Serena Villata, CNRS
Henning Wachsmuth, Paderborn University
Vern R. Walker, Maurice A. Hofstra University
Zhongyu Wei, Fudan University
Magdalena Wolska, Bauhaus-Universitat Weimar

Invited Speakers:

Anthony Hunter, University College London
Lu Wang, University of Michigan

Table of Contents

Long Papers

Short Papers

Shared-Task Papers

Workshop Program

November 10, 2021

09:00 – 09:30	***Opening Remarks***
09:30 – 10:30	**Invited Talk 1**
10:30 – 11:00	***Coffee Break***
	Session 1
11:00 – 11:20	*Argument Mining on Twitter: A Case Study on the Planned Parenthood Debate* Muhammad Mahad Afzal Bhatti, Ahsan Suheer Ahmad and Joonsuk Park
11:20 – 11:40	*Multi-task and Multi-corpora Training Strategies to Enhance Argumentative Sentence Linking Performance* Jan Wira Gotama Putra, Simone Teufel and Takenobu Tokunaga
11:40 – 12:00	*Explainable Unsupervised Argument Similarity Rating with Abstract Meaning Representation and Conclusion Generation* Juri Opitz, Philipp Heinisch, Philipp Wiesenbach, Philipp Cimiano and Anette Frank
12:00 – 13:00	***Lunch Break***
	Session 2
13:00 – 13:20	*Knowledge-Enhanced Evidence Retrieval for Counterargument Generation* Yohan Jo, Haneul Yoo, JinYeong Bak, Alice Oh, Chris Reed and Eduard Hovy
13:20 – 13:40	*On Classifying whether Two Texts are on the Same Side of an Argument* Erik Körner, Gregor Wiedemann, Ahmad Hakimi, Gerhard Heyer and Martin Potthast
13:40 – 13:52	*Multilingual Counter Narrative Type Classification* Yi-Ling Chung, Marco Guerini and Rodrigo Agerri
13:52 – 13:64	*Predicting Moderation of Deliberative Arguments: Is Argument Quality the Key?* Neele Falk, Iman Jundi, Eva Maria Vecchi and Gabriella Lapesa
14:04 – 14:16	*Self-trained Pretrained Language Models for Evidence Detection* Mohamed Elaraby and Diane Litman
14:16 – 14:28	*Multi-task Learning in Argument Mining for Persuasive Online Discussions* Nhat Tran and Diane Litman
14:30 – 14:45	***Coffee Break***
14:45 – 16:15	***Panel Talks and Discussion***
16:15 – 16:45	***Coffee Break***

November 10, 2021 (continued)

	Session 3
16:45 – 17:05	*Image Retrieval for Arguments Using Stance-Aware Query Expansion* Johannes Kiesel, Nico Reichenbach, Benno Stein and Martin Potthast
17:05 – 17:25	*Is Stance Detection Topic-Independent and Cross-topic Generalizable? - A Reproduction Study* Myrthe Reuver, Suzan Verberne, Roser Morante and Antske Fokkens
17:25 – 17:45	*Exploring Methodologies for Collecting High-Quality Implicit Reasoning in Arguments* Keshav Singh, Farjana Sultana Mim, Naoya Inoue, Shoichi Naito and Kentaro Inui

November 11, 2021

09:00 – 10:00	**Invited Talk 2**
	Session 4
10:00 – 10:20	*Assessing the Sufficiency of Arguments through Conclusion Generation* Timon Gurcke, Milad Alshomary and Henning Wachsmuth
10:20 – 10:40	*M-Arg: Multimodal Argument Mining Dataset for Political Debates with Audio and Transcripts* Rafael Mestre, Razvan Milicin, Stuart Middleton, Matt Ryan, Jiatong Zhu and Timothy J. Norman
10:40 – 11:00	***Coffee Break***
	Session 5
11:00 – 11:20	*Citizen Involvement in Urban Planning - How Can Municipalities Be Supported in Evaluating Public Participation Processes for Mobility Transitions?* Julia Romberg and Stefan Conrad
11:20 – 11:40	*Argumentation Mining in Scientific Literature for Sustainable Development* Aris Fergadis, Dimitris Pappas, Antonia Karamolegkou and Haris Papageorgiou
11:40 – 12:00	*Bayesian Argumentation-Scheme Networks: A Probabilistic Model of Argument Validity Facilitated by Argumentation Schemes* Takahiro Kondo, Koki Washio, Katsuhiko Hayashi and Yusuke Miyao
12:00 – 13:00	***Lunch Break***
13:00 – 14:30	***Shared Task Presentation***
14:30 – 14:45	***Break***
14:45 – 15:00	***Concluding Remarks***

Argument Mining on Twitter: A Case Study on the Planned Parenthood Debate

Muhammad Mahad Afzal Bhatti[*], **Ahsan Suheer Ahmad**[*], **and Joonsuk Park**[*†]
[*]Department of Math and Computer Science, University of Richmond
[†]NAVER AI Lab
{mahad.bhatti, ahsansuheer.ahmad}@richmond.edu
park@joonsuk.org

Abstract

Twitter is a popular platform to share opinions and claims, which may be accompanied by the underlying rationale. Such information can be invaluable to policy makers, marketers and social scientists, to name a few. However, the effort to mine arguments on Twitter has been limited, mainly because a tweet is typically too short to contain an argument—both a claim *and* a premise. In this paper, we propose a novel problem formulation to mine arguments from Twitter: We formulate argument mining on Twitter as a text classification task to identify tweets that serve as premises for a hashtag that represents a claim of interest. To demonstrate the efficacy of this formulation, we mine arguments for and against funding Planned Parenthood expressed in tweets. We first present a new dataset of 24,100 tweets containing hashtag #StandWithPP or #DefundPP, manually labeled as SUPPORT WITH REASON, SUPPORT WITHOUT REASON, and NO EXPLICIT SUPPORT. We then train classifiers to determine the types of tweets, achieving the best performance of 71% F_1. Our results manifest claim-specific keywords as the most informative features, which in turn reveal prominent arguments for and against funding Planned Parenthood.

1 Introduction

The goal of argument mining is to automatically extract arguments—typically defined as consisting of both a claim and at least one premise supporting the claim—from text in various domains. By analyzing the argumentative structure, we can not only identify claims, but also gain a deeper understanding of the evidence and reasons behind the claims (Rahwan et al., 2009; Mochales and Moens, 2011a; Peldszus and Stede, 2013; Lippi and Torroni, 2015; Budzynska and Villata, 2016; Lawrence and Reed, 2020). And the domains for argument mining have quickly expanded to include less formally written text on social media (Wyner et al., 2012; Goudas et al., 2014; Park and Cardie, 2014; Morio and Fujita, 2018; Chakrabarty et al., 2019).

Yet, the effort to mine arguments from Twitter has been limited due to a rather obvious reason—tweets are often too short to contain an entire argument, i.e., a claim and a premise (Dusmanu et al., 2017). For this reason, existing approaches to argument mining on Twitter typically focus on identifying claims, evidence, or either, but not both at the same time (Addawood and Bashir, 2016; Bosc et al., 2016a; Dusmanu et al., 2017; Wührl and Klinger, 2021). This is not ideal, since the underlying rationale can be as important as the claim.

To mine full arguments from Twitter, we propose a novel problem formulation based on an observation—some trendy hashtags serve as placeholders for claims, which may or may not be supported by the contents of the tweets containing them. In the case of the Planned Parenthood debate, the two opposing sides use hashtags #StandWithPP and #DefundPP to specify their respective claims; only a subset of the tweets serve as premises supporting the given claim. For instance, Example 3 in Table 1 can be interpreted as an argument in which the premise "#AllLivesMatter even the unborn." (= *all live matter, even the unborn*) supports the claim to "#DefundPP" (= *Planned Parenthood should not be funded by the government.*). In contrast, Example 6 cannot be considered a premise for the claim, as it does not provide a reason to "#StandWithPP"(= *Planned Parenthood should continue to be supported by the government*). In the case of Example 10, it is not even clear whether or not the user supports the claim #StandWithPP represents. Thus, the tweet cannot be considered a premise for the claim. (While both Examples 6 and 10 are not considered premises, distinguishing the two can be useful for compiling a quantitative summary, e.g. the number of tweets showing support—the former should count as a supporting tweet, unlike the latter.)

Proceedings of The 8th Workshop on Argument Mining, pages 1–11
Punta Cana, Dominican Republic, November 10–11, 2021.

2-class	3-class	#	Example Tweet
PREMISE	SUPPORT WITH REASON	1	I **#StandWithPP**. Routine healthcare shouldn't exist just for the rich.
		2	*@user* helps men too! **#StandWithPP**
		3	#AllLivesMatter even the unborn. **#DefundPP** #DefundPlannedParenthood
		4	God Has A Plan For Every Life #PraytoEndAbortion **#DefundPP** #DefendLife #innocent
NON-PREMISE	SUPPORT WITHOUT REASON	5	**#StandWithPP** now and forever.
		6	I wish everyone shouldn't hate on Planned Parenthood so fucking much **#StandWithPP**
		7	#YouHadMeAt I'll do everything in my power to ***#DefundPP***
		8	Tell your Senators to Defund Planned Parenthood SIGN & RT **#DefundPP** *[url]*
	NO EXPLICIT SUPPORT	9	Legal Troubles Continue for Group Attacking Planned Parenthood **#StandWithPP** *[url]*
		10	#SextaComMFSDV **#StandWithPP** Citizen Khan Grow your Twitter followers *[url]*
		11	*@user* Paid staffers? **#defundpp**
		12	Dont listen to the Daily Bugle . Spider-Man is a force for good .**#StandWithPP** #PeterParker

Table 1: Example Tweets for Each Class (2-class and 3-class setup). The user can show support with reason (SUPPORT WITH REASON), show support without providing a reason (SUPPORT WITHOUT REASON) or make their stance unclear through an irrelevant or overall confusing tweet (NO EXPLICIT SUPPORT).

Henceforth, we call a hashtag representing a claim a *claim-hashtag*, and a tweet serving as a premise a *premise-tweet*. From an argument mining perspective, the claim is already known for tweets containing a claim-hashtag, i.e., the claim represented by the claim-hashtag. And such tweets can be easily retrieved using the Twitter API or simple text matching. Thus, the main challenge is in determining whether a given tweet is a premise-tweet. In other words, we formulate argument mining on Twitter as a text classification task to identify premise-tweets for claim-hashtags of interest.

To demonstrate the efficacy of the proposed formulation, we mine arguments for and against funding Planned Parenthood expressed on Twitter: We first present a new dataset of 24,100 tweets containing hashtag #StandWithPP or #DefundPP, each manually labeled as SUPPORT WITH REASON, SUPPORT WITHOUT REASON, or NO EXPLICIT SUPPORT. We then train several classifiers and test them on 30% of the dataset held-out in advance. We find that fine-tuned BERT performs the best, achieving 71% F_1. We also show that claim-specific words serve as the most important features for this task, which in turn reveal important arguments for and against funding Planned Parenthood.

Why Planned Parenthood? The Planned Parenthood debate is multi-faceted, involving issues like the personhood of fetuses, women's rights, and health services to people of various socioeconomic status. A major benefit of automatically extracting arguments from Twitter is that it provides an easy access to arguments people have made. This is especially helpful for complex topics like Planned Parenthood, where unique but noteworthy arguments can be lost in the midst of others. From a practical perspective, each side of the Planned Parenthood debate has a dominantly used hashtag, allowing us to target two specific hashtags and gain a holistic view of the debate.

Our main contributions are threefold:

- We propose a novel problem formulation for mining full arguments—both a claim and a premise—on Twitter.
- We present a newly annotated dataset consisting of 24,100 tweets[1], which is 10 to 80 times bigger than existing datasets for mining arguments from Twitter.
- We identify prominent arguments for and against funding Planned Parenthood expressed on Twitter by analyzing the most informative features.

2 Related Work

2.1 Argument Mining

Argument mining has been used in various domains over the years. These include text written by professionals—such as legal documents (Moens et al., 2007; Wyner et al., 2010; Mochales and Moens, 2011b) and newspaper articles (Reed et al., 2008)—as well as student essays (Stab and Gurevych, 2014; Wachsmuth et al., 2016) and online user comments and reviews (Wyner et al., 2012; Goudas et al., 2014; Park and Cardie, 2014). In addition, researchers have tackled dialogues (Budzynska et al., 2014), political debates (Lippi and Torroni, 2016), clinical trials (Mayer et al., 2018), peer reviews (Hua et al., 2019) and news blogs (Basile et al., 2016). While

[1]Tweet IDs and labels are available at `joonsuk.org`

this is a diverse set of domains, they share a common trait that documents are long enough to contain full arguments, often multiple of them in a single document. Thus, argument mining involves identifying argumentative spans of text, determining argumentative units—e.g. premise and claim—within the arguments, and recognizing the argumentative structure connecting the units. However, tweets are typically too short to contain full arguments, preventing the use of standard argument mining approaches (Dusmanu et al., 2017).

There has been some pioneering work on mining arguments from tweets, as summarized by Schaefer and Stede (2021). To get around the issue of tweets being too short to contain an entire argument, researchers typically seek to identify argumentative tweets—tweets that contain an argumentative unit, e.g. claim *or* premise (Bosc et al., 2016a,b; Dusmanu et al., 2017; Wührl and Klinger, 2021). For instance, Bosc et al. (2016a,b) distinguish argumentative tweets from non-argumentative ones. For tweets containing a claim, they further distinguish opinion from factual tweets. For tweets containing evidence, they seek to identify the source. Addawood and Bashir (2016); Addawood et al. (2017) also identify argumentative tweets, which are further broken down into six different types, such as *expert opinion* and *blog*. Schaefer and Stede (2020) present several task formulations, where the closest one to ours is identifying evidence tweets (for a claim expressed in what they call a *context tweet* or a reply tweet).

Our work, however, specifically targets tweets containing both a claim (in the form of a hashtag) and a premise. This enables the full argument to be reconstructed for each argumentative tweet. In addition, our newly annotated dataset is significantly larger than the datasets used in previous tweet argument mining research, more than 10 to 80 times the size depending on the task (Dusmanu et al., 2017; Schaefer and Stede, 2020). This will enhance the reliability of the experiment results and analyses.

2.2 Planned Parenthood

Planned Parenthood is a non-profit organization that provides reproductive health services in the US and abroad.[2] Whether or not the US government should continue to fund Planned Parenthood has been the subject of ongoing debate, mainly due to the controversial practice of abortion (Halva-Neubauer and Zeigler, 2010; Devi, 2015; Silver and Kapadia, 2017); researchers have argued over the legality and subsequent funding for abortion (Primrose, 2012; Wharton et al., 2006). Supporters of Planned Parenthood have presented several arguments, including that it provides other medical services (Silver and Kapadia, 2017; Stevenson et al., 2016; House and Goldsmith, 1972). Those against Planned Parenthood also have expressed their position, mostly arguing against the practice of abortion (Halva-Neubauer and Zeigler, 2010; Ziegler, 2012; Devi, 2015).

The general public has also been voicing their opinions through various social media platforms such as Twitter. While Twitter provides a convenient means to express opinions, gathering such opinions for analysis is not as straight forward. This is unfortunate, as many arguments with compelling reasons and evidence are present in tweets; they are not used to further the discussion surrounding Planned Parenthood in a productive manner. Our work is a step toward addressing this issue by enhancing the efficiency of communication.

3 Data

#StandWithPP and #DefundPP represent the two opposing sides on the issue of the US federal government funding Planned Parenthood, or of Planned Parenthood itself. The claims represented by the hashtags can be stated as follows:

- **#StandWithPP:** Planned Parenthood should continue to receive federal funding.
- **#DefundPP:** Planned Parenthood should not receive federal funding.

Tweets containing either of these hashtags were collected over a span of two months. Prior to preprocessing, there were a total of 20,314 and 12,470 tweets containing #StandWithPP and #DefundPP, respectively.

3.1 Preprocessing

As part of the preprocessing, we first removed duplicate and otherwise uninformative tweets that can be easily identified[3]: tweets by the seven most frequently tweeting users (these are mostly auto-generated spams with repetitive content); tweets

[2] https://www.plannedparenthood.org/

[3] These were all NO EXPLICIT SUPPORT tweets, technically, but we removed them from the dataset, as they can be easily identified by pattern matching, without training a classifier.

Claim-Hashtag	PREMISE	NON-PREMISE		Total
	SUPPORT WITH REASON	SUPPORT WITHOUT REASON	NO EXPLICIT SUPPORT	
#StandWithPP (Training)	4,432 (35.9%)	2,940(23.8%)	4,962 (40.3%)	12,334
#StandWithPP (Test)	1,852 (35.0%)	1,316 (24.9%)	2,118 (40.1%)	5,286
#DefundPP (Training)	2,000 (44.1%)	486 (10.7%)	2,050 (45.2%)	4,536
#DefundPP (Test)	861 (44.3%)	193 (9.9%)	890 (45.8%)	1,944
Total	9,145 (37.9%)	4,935 (20.5%)	10,020(41.6%)	24,100

Table 2: Distribution of Classes in the Dataset. 30% of the tweets for each hashtag were randomly put in the held-out test set.

with a URL and two or more special character (this is a noticeable pattern for tweets in our dataset simply sharing URLs to news sites with random special characters to catch people's attention); tweets with fewer than 4 tokens; and tweets in which @-mentions, URLs, or hashtags make up more than 35% of the tokens.

The filtering process reduced the number of tweets to 16,870 and 7,230 for #StandWithPP and #DefundPP, respectively. Then, all @-mentions were masked to protect the users' privacy. Any URLs were also masked, as our goal is to recognize premises in the body of tweets.

3.2 Annotation

The dataset was then annotated using the Amazon Mechanical Turk[4] service. The annotators were asked to classify each tweet as one of the three possible classes:

- **SUPPORT WITH REASON:** The user supports the claim represented by the claim-hashtag and presents a reason, regardless of the validity and strength.
- **SUPPORT WITHOUT REASON:** The user supports the claim represented by the claim-hashtag, but does not provide a reason.
- **NO EXPLICIT SUPPORT:** All other tweets. Typically, the user has a neutral or unclear stance toward the claim represented by the claim-hashtag, such as news tweets. In some cases, the user uses a claim-hashtag to present a counter-argument to people supporting the claim, rather than to show support.

We ran a pilot study in which annotators were asked to annotate tweets for which we had the gold standard labels. Out of 100 annotators who participated, we identified 32 reliable annotators to annotate the dataset.

Then, each tweet was annotated by two annotators, where disagreements were resolved by an adjudicator. We observed a reasonable agreement, Krippendorff's α of 0.79. A common source of disagreement was incomplete information, e.g. "8 Unbelievably Heartbreaking Quotes From Women Who Aborted Their Own Babies | *[URL]*: *[URL]* #DefundPP." Depending on the quotes presented in the URL, this tweet can be for or against Planned Parenthood: What is heartbreaking could be abortion itself or the process of abortion due to the lack of access to adequate health services. (Given the presence of the hashtag #DefundPP, it is likely that the quote, and in turn this tweet, is against abortion and Planned Parenthood. However, the annotators were asked not to assume the presence of a hashtag as a sign of support, as it is not always true.)

Table 2 summarizes the resulting dataset. Note that this is after removing obvious spam tweets during preprocessing as described above. Thus, the percentage of NO EXPLICIT SUPPORT is higher in reality. Also, there is a noticeable difference between #StandWithPP and #DefundPP tweets in terms of the class distribution; a significantly smaller portion of the latter are SUPPORT WITHOUT REASON tweets. We suspect that this is because changing the status quo requires more convincing arguments. Thus, people arguing to defund Planned Parenthood are more likely to support their claim with a reason or evidence.

4 Premise-Tweet Identification

Argument mining consists of several subtasks, such as identifying argumentative spans of text, determining argumentative units—e.g. premise and claim—within the arguments, and recognizing the argumentative structure connecting the units. In this work, however, the claim is easily identifiable, as we assume that it takes the form of a hashtag, i.e., claim-hashtag, that is known in advance. Thus, the core of our approach to mining arguments on Twitter is deciding whether or not a given tweet is a premise-tweet for a given claim-hashtag. To tackle the task, we train fine-tuned BERT, CNN,

[4] http://www.mturk.com

Model	#StandWithPP				#DefundPP			
	Prec	Rec	F_1	Acc	Prec	Rec	F_1	Acc
Baseline approaches adopted from Schaefer and Stede (2020)								
- XGBoost with UNIGRAMS	.682	.676	.669	.676	.665	.682	.667	.682
- XGBoost with UNIGRAMS + BIGRAMS	.697	.686	.679	.686	.671	.686	.671	.686
- XGBoost with BERT Word Embedding	.542	.543	.528	.543	.534	.549	.532	.549
CNN with GloVe Word Embedding (CommonCrawl)	.675	.661	.650	.661	.607	.669	.634	.669
CNN with GloVe Word Embedding (Twitter)	.696	.689	.689	.689	.678	.685	.656	.685
Fine-tuned DistilBERT	.680	.675	.670	.675	.643	.683	.656	.683
Fine-tuned BERT	**.714**	**.714**	**.713**	**.714**	**.719**	**.728**	**.718**	**.728**

Table 3: Experiment Results for 3-Class Classification (SUPPORT WITH REASON vs SUPPORT WITHOUT REASON vs NO EXPLICIT SUPPORT). The experiments were conducted independently for #StandWithPP and #DefundPP tweets. Also, each entry in the table is the weighted average of the measures computed with respect to the classes.

and XGBoost classifiers as detailed in this section.

Note that we are also interested in distinguishing non-premise-tweets that support the claim (SUPPORT WITHOUT REASON) from those that do not (NO EXPLICIT SUPPORT); This is because the sheer number of tweets supporting a claim can be used to generate a statistical summary of people's support for the claim. Thus, we formulate argument mining on Twitter as a classification task with three classes: SUPPORT WITH REASON, SUPPORT WITHOUT REASON, and NO EXPLICIT SUPPORT.

4.1 Fine-tuned BERT

Given the successful use of fine-tuned BERT on various text classification tasks (Croce et al., 2020; Tian et al., 2020), we fine-tune a pre-trained BERT to premise-tweet classification task using our training set. For the experiments, we fine-tune the 'bert-base-uncased' pre-trained model (Wolf et al., 2020), which consists of 12 BERT attention layers, 768 hidden nodes, and 12 attention heads, with a total of 110M parameters. Using the BERT Tokenizer (Wolf et al., 2020), each tweet is represented by token, segment, and position embedding. Lastly, in order to classify tweets, the model is augmented with a fully-connected classification layer with ReLu activation on top of the pooled output from BERT. An AdamW optimizer is used for regularization (Loshchilov and Hutter, 2019).

In addition to BERT, we also test the efficacy of DistilBERT, which is a much simpler and faster model that can match the performance of BERT in some cases (Sanh et al., 2019).

4.2 Convolutional Neural Network (CNN)

While BERT's attention mechanism is shown to be effective for capturing both short and long distance relations between words in documents, a simple CNN may suffice given the brevity of tweets. Thus, we also experiment with CNN. Following the framework presented by Kim (2014), each tweet is represented as an $n \cdot k$ matrix, where n is the length of the tweet and k is the dimensionality of the word vectors. For word representation, we employ two versions of the GloVe word embedding (Pennington et al., 2014): A 200-d version trained on tweets, since we are working with tweets; and a 300-d version trained on Common Crawl, since a higher-dimensional embedding may be more effective. For both, we limit the size of the vocabulary to a million tokens.

4.3 eXtreme Gradient Boosting (XGBoost)

XGBoost is an extension to Gradient Boosting that has shown to be effective in several classification tasks (Stein et al., 2019; Qi, 2020). Schaefer and Stede (2020) show that using XGBoost to classify evidence tweets has promising results. Given the similarity of one of their setups to ours, we use as baselines the 3 variations they employed: XGBoost with UNIGRAMS, XGBoost with UNIGRAMS + BIGRAMS, and XGBoost with BERT word embeddings. The booster we use is a gradient boosting tree, with a standard max depth of 6 for a tree. The algorithm minimizes the multi-class log loss function, and applies a variation of softmax to get the predicted output probabilities.

5 Experiments

5.1 Setup

For each claim-hashtag in our dataset—#StandWithPP and #DefundPP—the classifiers were trained and tested on the respective training and held-out test sets (See Table 2). For optimizing hyper-parameters, 5-fold cross validation was done on the training set. The dropout rate was $p = 0.5$ for CNN and $p = 0.1$ for BERT. The learning rate was $lr = 0.001$ for CNN and $lr = 2e^{-}5$ for BERT.

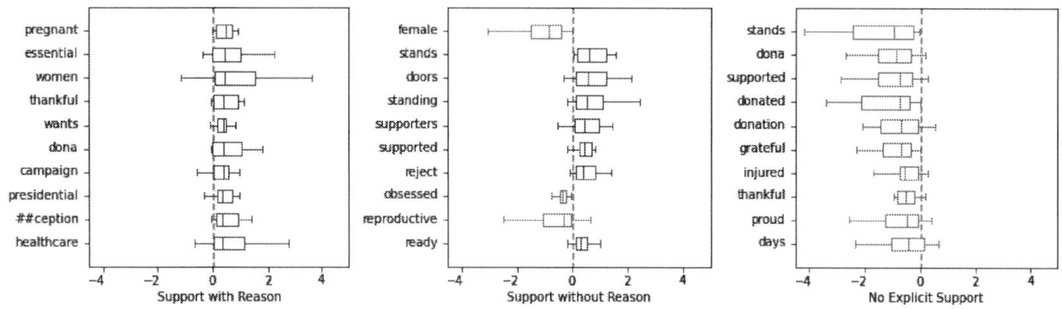

Figure 1: Words that had the biggest influence on the classification decision for BERT fine-tuned on **#StandWithPP** tweets, sorted by the median absolute SHAP value. Positive values are colored blue, and negative, red.

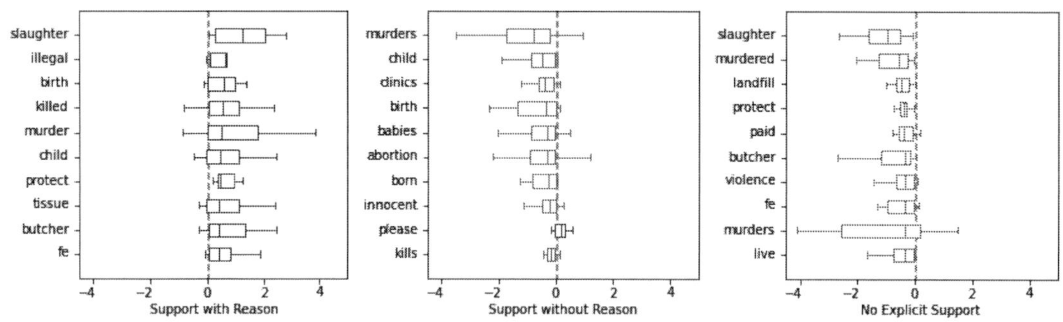

Figure 2: Words that had the biggest influence on the classification decision for BERT fine-tuned on **#DefundPP** tweets, sorted by the median absolute SHAP value. Positive values are colored blue, and negative, red.

Batch size was $b = 50$ for CNN and $b = 32$ for BERT. The number of epochs was 15 for CNN and 4 for BERT. For the XGBoost baselines, we used the same setup from Schaefer and Stede (2020), but the models were trained and tested on our training and test sets.

5.2 Results & Analysis

The experiment results are summarized in Table 3. Fine-tuned BERT outperformed the rest across the board. This is not surprising given the strong state-of-the-art performances of transformer-based models across various NLP tasks. DistilBERT, a much smaller and faster version of BERT, is noticeably worse than BERT, but is comparable to the CNNs. CNN with GloVe-Twitter performs slightly better than CNN with GloVe-Common Crawl; we suspect that the word embedding trained on tweets is more effective, since our dataset is also a collection of tweets. For the XGBoost baselines, using ngrams proved to be more effective than using BERT word embeddings. This is consistent with the results from Schaefer and Stede (2020), though the datasets are different, and thus a direct comparison cannot be made. We suspect that the straightforward mapping between dimensions and words in ngrams is better suited for XGBoost than multiple dimensions collectively representing a word in a word embedding; this is because XGBoost is a decision tree based approach that learns to weigh each feature (dimension) differently.

Figures 1 and 2 are the median SHAP (SHapley Additive exPlanations) (Lundberg and Lee, 2017) values of the top features for fine-tuned BERT, the best performing model. The SHAP value for a feature with respect to a class indicates the level of influence the given feature had in classifying a tweet as the given class. Here, the influence can be either positive or negative, indicated by the sign of the SHAP value. And the bigger the magnitude, the heavier the influence it had on the classification decision. The median for each word is calculated across all occurrences of the word in the test set. Note that words that occur fewer than 10 times in the test set were excluded from the plot.

Similar patterns are exhibited for both claim-hashtags. For SUPPORT WITH REASON, the words with large absolute SHAP values tend to be keywords for prominent arguments for the given claim.

#	Actual	Predicted	Tweet
1	S+R	S+R	[CLS] grateful to see judge po ##sner standing up for women ' s rights and calling out ridiculous restrictions on abortion providers . # stand ##with ##pp [SEP] [PAD] [PAD]
2	S+R	S+R	[CLS] for 100 years the brave people of planned parent ##hood have provided health care to women . here ' s to 100 more . # stand ##with ##pp [SEP]
3	S+R	S+R	[CLS] just when i think [UNK] can ' t get any lower they t ##wee ##t this , how about all those babies you butcher ##ed # def ##und [SEP]
4	S+R	S+R	[CLS] pp needs to be def ##und ##ed to the extent that un ##born baby slaughter can no longer be tolerated in america . # def ##und ##pp # [SEP]
5	S-R	S-R	[CLS] 1 just supported national day of solidarity on [UNK] / / [UNK] t _ ur ##l # stand ##with ##pp # investigate ##cl ##ini ##c ##vio ##lence [SEP] [PAD]
6	S-R	S-R	[CLS] please pray today that barack obama ' s veto to stop def ##und ##ing planned parent ##hood is thwarted . the u . s . senate voted in [SEP]
7	NES	NES	[CLS] 26 hours since a terrorist attacked a co [UNK] 3 civilians killed , 8 injured ##0 go ##p pre ##z hopeful ##s have mentioned the attack # stand [SEP]
8	NES	S+R	[CLS] so far state & amp ; fed investigation on the women ' s heath care provider turned up no evidence of wrong ##do ##ing # stand ##with ##pp [SEP]
9	S-R	S+R	[CLS] " your words and actions hurt women and create a climate of di ##sr ##es ##pe ##ct that makes violence possible . " # stand ##with ##pp [UNK] [SEP]

Table 4: Example tweets and classifications by fine-tuned BERT. Tokens are highlighted in blue if they have positive attribution scores with respect to the predicted class, and red if negative. The darker the color, the higher the absolute value of the score. The class names are abbreviated as follows: SUPPORT WITH REASON (S+R), SUPPORT WITHOUT REASON (S-R), and NO EXPLICIT SUPPORT (NES)

In the case of #StandWithPP, the words "women" and "healthcare" rank high; they typically appear in tweets that emphasize women's rights or the need for healthcare in general as reasons to support Planned Parenthood (See Examples 1 and 2 in Table 4). In the case of #DefundPP, words that emphasize babies and framing abortion as murder rank high (Examples 3 and 4).

For NO EXPLICIT SUPPORT, most of the words with large absolute SHAP values have negative values, meaning the existence of these words was taken as a sign that the given tweet is not NO EXPLICIT SUPPORT. In other words, lacking strong characteristics of the other classes is the characteristic of NO EXPLICIT SUPPORT(Example 7). This is partially due to our having removed spam tweets with obvious patterns during preprocessing. Otherwise, those patterns may have had positive SHAP values of large magnitudes.

For SUPPORT WITHOUT REASON, however, the two claim-hashtags exhibit some differences. For #StandWithPP, words that appear in clear statements of support, e.g. "support" and "stands [with Planned Parenthood]," have positive influence on classifying a tweet as SUPPORT WITHOUT REASON. The is because such tweets tend not to include a rationale (Example 5). However, similar words for #DefundPP, e.g. "defund" and "stop [funding Planned Parenthood]", do not have high SHAP values with respect to SUPPORT WITHOUT REASON, as they often appear with additional explanations (Example 4). Other than "please" (Example 6), there are not many indicators of SUPPORT WITHOUT REASON for #DefundPP. There are not many SUPPORT WITHOUT REASON tweets to begin with as shown in Table 2. Again, we suspect that non-NO EXPLICIT SUPPORT tweets for #DefundPP tend to contain a reason, as they have to be convincing enough to change the status quo.

Note that the informative features are not always helpful. Non-SUPPORT WITH REASON tweets that contain top feature words of SUPPORT WITH REASON can be incorrectly classified. For example, the tweet can be a news tweet reporting the state of affairs. Such tweet does not always reveal the stance of the user posting the tweet (Example 8). The tweet can also be part of a conversation where the reason for supporting the claim cannot be determined without knowing the tweet being replied to (Example 9).

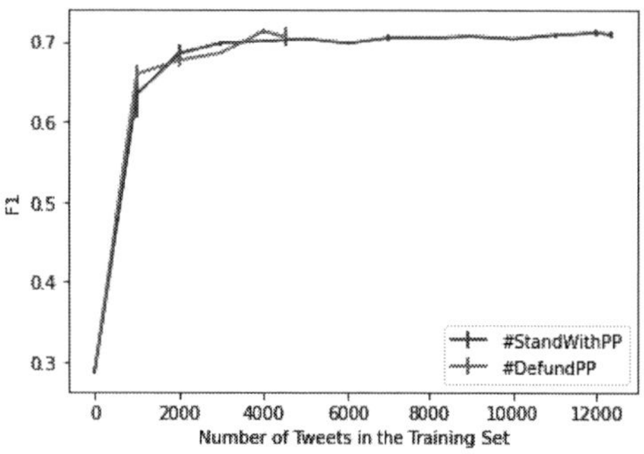

Figure 3: Impact of the training set size on the performance. Pre-trained BERT was fine-tuned on randomly subsampled training sets. Training set sizes in increments of 1,000 were tested and averaged over 3 runs.

6 Limitations and Implications

There are two main limitations of this work that need to be considered in future research. First, labeled training data is required to train a premise-tweet classifier for each claim of interest. The most informative features for our classifiers are specific to the claim-hashtag they are trained for; even though #StandWithPP and #DefundPP are on the same topic, the informative features are drastically different. This suggests that a classifier trained for a claim-hashtag likely is not effective for identifying premise-tweets for other claims-hashtags. In fact, this was confirmed through cross-domain testing, i.e., we fined-tuned BERT on the #StandWithPP training set and tested on the #DefundPP test set, and vice versa. There was a significant drop in the F1 score from 71% to 56% in both scenarios.

To determine how much training data is necessary, we fine-tuned BERT on randomly selected subsets of the training sets. We tested training set sizes in increments of 1k as shown in Figure 3. The same pattern can be observed for both claim-hashtags: There is a drastic improvement in performance after fine-tuning with even a small training set of size 1k; and the performance plateaus after increasing the size to about 3k to 4k. Based on the result, we suggest that a labeled dataset of at least 3k tweets is prepared to train a premise-tweet classifier for a claim-hashtag of your interest.

Second, our results are based on experiments with tweets containing two specific claim-hashtags. Future work should consider a more diverse set of claim-hashtags. It will not only test the generalizabilty of this approach, but may also reveal informative features that are claim-independent.

Manually compiling a list of diverse claim-hashtags can be laborious, however. To alleviate this issue, we have identified a class of claim-hashtags that can be automatically recognized. These hashtags represent so called *policy propositions*, meaning they suggest policies, or courses of action to be taken (Park et al., 2015). They typically take the form of an imperative—starting with a verb and ending with a noun, e.g. #StandWithPP, #DefundPP, #FightFor15, #LegalizeMarijuana, and #BanGuns. Hashtags do not contain spaces, but the *CamelCase* capitalization can be used for tokenization—a capitalized letter marks the beginning of a new word, unless several capitalized letters appear in succession to denote a proper noun. The repetitive use of hashtags in tweets is helpful in this regard, as it is very likely that at least one variation of a given hashtag is in CamelCase. Thus, to identify a diverse set of claim-hashtags, we suggest the method of identifying trending hashtags representing policy propositions.

7 Conclusion

Twitter is a popular platform to share opinions, which may be accompanied by the underlying rationale. However, the effort to automatically extract arguments from Twitter has been limited, mainly due to tweets typically not containing both a claim and a premise. The brevity renders it difficult to apply argument mining techniques designed for other domains, where claims and premises can be extracted together. In this paper, we proposed a novel problem formulation to mine arguments from Twitter: We formulated argument mining on Twitter as a text classification task to identify tweets serving as premises for hashtags that represent claims. We demonstrated the efficacy of this formulation by mining arguments for and against funding Planned Parenthood expressed on Twitter. We achieved the best performance of 71% F_1 with fine-tuned BERT. We also showed that domain specific words serve as the most important features, which in turn reveal prominent arguments in support of the given claim. In future work, we would like to continue the effort addressing the issues discussed in Section 6.

Acknowledgments

We thank the University of Richmond and the Thomas F. and Kate Miller Jeffress Memorial Trust, Bank of America, Trustee for their generous support for this project. We also thank Jamison Poland.

References

Aseel Addawood and Masooda Bashir. 2016. "what is your evidence?" a study of controversial topics on social media. In *Proceedings of the Third Workshop on Argument Mining (ArgMining2016)*, pages 1–11.

Aseel Addawood, Jodi Schneider, and Masooda Bashir. 2017. Stance classification of twitter debates: The encryption debate as a use case. In *Proceedings of the 8th International Conference on Social Media & Society*, pages 1–10.

Pierpaolo Basile, Valerio Basile, Elena Cabrio, and Serena Villata. 2016. Argument Mining on Italian News Blogs. In *Third Italian Conference on Computational Linguistics (CLiC-it 2016) & Fifth Evaluation Campaign of Natural Language Processing and Speech Tools for Italian. Final Workshop (EVALITA 2016)*, Naples, Italy.

Tom Bosc, Elena Cabrio, and Serena Villata. 2016a. DART: a dataset of arguments and their relations on Twitter. In *Proceedings of the Tenth International Conference on Language Resources and Evaluation (LREC'16)*, pages 1258–1263, Portorož, Slovenia. European Language Resources Association (ELRA).

Tom Bosc, Elena Cabrio, and Serena Villata. 2016b. Tweeties squabbling: Positive and negative results in applying argument mining on social media. *COMMA*, 2016:21–32.

Katarzyna Budzynska, Mathilde Janier, Juyeon Kang, Chris Reed, Patrick Saint-Dizier, Manfred Stede, and Olena Yaskorska. 2014. Towards argument mining from dialogue. In *COMMA*, pages 185–196.

Katarzyna Budzynska and Serena Villata. 2016. Argument mining. *IEEE Intell. Informatics Bull.*, 17(1):1–6.

Tuhin Chakrabarty, Christopher Hidey, Smaranda Muresan, Kathy McKeown, and Alyssa Hwang. 2019. AMPERSAND: Argument mining for PERSuAsive oNline discussions. In *Proceedings of the 2019 Conference on Empirical Methods in Natural Language Processing and the 9th International Joint Conference on Natural Language Processing (EMNLP-IJCNLP)*, pages 2933–2943, Hong Kong, China. Association for Computational Linguistics.

Danilo Croce, Giuseppe Castellucci, and Roberto Basili. 2020. Gan-bert: Generative adversarial learning for robust text classification with a bunch of labeled examples. In *Proceedings of the 58th Annual Meeting of the Association for Computational Linguistics*, pages 2114–2119.

Sharmila Devi. 2015. Anti-abortion groups target funding of planned parenthood. *The Lancet*, 386(9997):941.

Mihai Dusmanu, Elena Cabrio, and Serena Villata. 2017. Argument mining on twitter: Arguments, facts and sources. In *Proceedings of the 2017 Conference on Empirical Methods in Natural Language Processing*, pages 2317–2322.

Theodosis Goudas, Christos Louizos, Georgios Petasis, and Vangelis Karkaletsis. 2014. Argument extraction from news, blogs, and social media. In *Artificial Intelligence: Methods and Applications*, pages 287–299. Springer.

Glen A Halva-Neubauer and Sara L Zeigler. 2010. Promoting fetal personhood: The rhetorical and legislative strategies of the pro-life movement after planned parenthood v. casey. *Feminist Formations*, pages 101–123.

Elizabeth A. House and Sadja Goldsmith. 1972. Planned parenthood services for the young teenager. *Family Planning Perspectives*, 4(2):27–31.

Xinyu Hua, Mitko Nikolov, Nikhil Badugu, and Lu Wang. 2019. Argument mining for understanding peer reviews. In *Proceedings of the 2019 Conference of the North American Chapter of the Association for Computational Linguistics: Human Language Technologies, Volume 1 (Long and Short Papers)*, pages 2131–2137, Minneapolis, Minnesota. Association for Computational Linguistics.

Yoon Kim. 2014. Convolutional neural networks for sentence classification. In *Proceedings of the 2014 Conference on Empirical Methods in Natural Language Processing (EMNLP)*, pages 1746–1751, Doha, Qatar. Association for Computational Linguistics.

John Lawrence and Chris Reed. 2020. Argument mining: A survey. *Computational Linguistics*, 45(4):765–818.

Marco Lippi and Paolo Torroni. 2015. Argument mining: A machine learning perspective. In *International Workshop on Theory and Applications of Formal Argumentation*, pages 163–176. Springer.

Marco Lippi and Paolo Torroni. 2016. Argument mining from speech: Detecting claims in political debates. In *Thirtieth AAAI Conference on Artificial Intelligence*.

Ilya Loshchilov and Frank Hutter. 2019. Decoupled weight decay regularization. In *International Conference on Learning Representations*.

Scott M. Lundberg and Su-In Lee. 2017. A unified approach to interpreting model predictions. In *Proceedings of the 31st International Conference on Neural Information Processing Systems*, NIPS'17, page 4768–4777, Red Hook, NY, USA. Curran Associates Inc.

Tobias Mayer, Elena Cabrio, Marco Lippi, Paolo Torroni, and Serena Villata. 2018. Argument mining on clinical trials. In *COMMA*, pages 137–148.

Raquel Mochales and Marie-Francine Moens. 2011a. Argumentation mining. *Artificial Intelligence and Law*, 19(1):1–22.

Raquel Mochales and Marie-Francine Moens. 2011b. Argumentation mining. *Artif. Intell. Law*, 19(1):1–22.

Marie-Francine Moens, Erik Boiy, Raquel Mochales Palau, and Chris Reed. 2007. Automatic detection of arguments in legal texts. In *Proceedings of the 11th International Conference on Artificial Intelligence and Law*, ICAIL '07, pages 225–230, New York, NY, USA. ACM.

G. Morio and K. Fujita. 2018. Annotating online civic discussion threads for argument mining. In *2018 IEEE/WIC/ACM International Conference on Web Intelligence (WI)*, pages 546–553.

Joonsuk Park, Cheryl Blake, and Claire Cardie. 2015. Toward machine-assisted participation in erulemaking: An argumentation model of evaluability. In *Proceedings of the 15th International Conference on Artificial Intelligence and Law*, ICAIL '15, pages 206–210, New York, NY, USA. ACM.

Joonsuk Park and Claire Cardie. 2014. Identifying appropriate support for propositions in online user comments. In *Proceedings of the First Workshop on Argumentation Mining*, pages 29–38, Baltimore, Maryland. Association for Computational Linguistics.

Andreas Peldszus and Manfred Stede. 2013. From argument diagrams to argumentation mining in texts: A survey. *Int. J. Cogn. Inform. Nat. Intell.*, 7(1):1–31.

Jeffrey Pennington, Richard Socher, and Christopher Manning. 2014. GloVe: Global vectors for word representation. In *Proceedings of the 2014 Conference on Empirical Methods in Natural Language Processing (EMNLP)*, pages 1532–1543, Doha, Qatar. Association for Computational Linguistics.

Sarah Primrose. 2012. The attack on planned parenthood: A historical analysis. *UCLA Women's LJ*, 19:165.

Zhang Qi. 2020. The text classification of theft crime based on tf-idf and xgboost model. In *2020 IEEE International Conference on Artificial Intelligence and Computer Applications (ICAICA)*, pages 1241–1246. IEEE.

Iyad Rahwan, Guillermo R Simari, and Johan van Benthem. 2009. *Argumentation in artificial intelligence*, volume 47. Springer.

Chris Reed, Raquel Mochales Palau, Glenn Rowe, and Marie-Francine Moens. 2008. Language resources for studying argument. In *LREC*. European Language Resources Association.

Victor Sanh, Lysandre Debut, Julien Chaumond, and Thomas Wolf. 2019. Distilbert, a distilled version of BERT: smaller, faster, cheaper and lighter. *CoRR*, abs/1910.01108.

Robin Schaefer and Manfred Stede. 2020. Annotation and detection of arguments in tweets. In *Proceedings of the 7th Workshop on Argument Mining*, pages 53–58.

Robin Schaefer and Manfred Stede. 2021. Argument mining on twitter: A survey. *it-Information Technology*, 63(1):45–58.

Diana Silver and Farzana Kapadia. 2017. Planned parenthood is health care, and health care must defend it: a call to action.

Christian Stab and Iryna Gurevych. 2014. Annotating argument components and relations in persuasive essays. In *Proceedings of the 25th International Conference on Computational Linguistics (COLING 2014)*, pages 1501–1510, Dublin, Ireland. Dublin City University and Association for Computational Linguistics.

Roger Alan Stein, Patricia A Jaques, and Joao Francisco Valiati. 2019. An analysis of hierarchical text classification using word embeddings. *Information Sciences*, 471:216–232.

Amanda J Stevenson, Imelda M Flores-Vazquez, Richard L Allgeyer, Pete Schenkkan, and Joseph E Potter. 2016. Effect of removal of planned parenthood from the texas women's health program. *New England Journal of Medicine*, 374(9):853–860.

Lin Tian, Xiuzhen Zhang, Yan Wang, and Huan Liu. 2020. Early detection of rumours on twitter via stance transfer learning. In *European Conference on Information Retrieval*, pages 575–588. Springer.

Henning Wachsmuth, Khalid Al Khatib, and Benno Stein. 2016. Using argument mining to assess the argumentation quality of essays. In *Proceedings of COLING 2016, the 26th International Conference on Computational Linguistics: Technical Papers*, pages 1680–1691.

Linda J. Wharton, Susan Frietsche, and Kathryn Kolbert. 2006. Preserving the core of roe: Reflections on planned parenthood v. casey. *Yale Journal of Law and Feminism*, 18:2.

Thomas Wolf, Lysandre Debut, Victor Sanh, Julien Chaumond, Clement Delangue, Anthony Moi, Pierric Cistac, Tim Rault, Rémi Louf, Morgan Funtowicz, Joe Davison, Sam Shleifer, Patrick von Platen, Clara Ma, Yacine Jernite, Julien Plu, Canwen Xu, Teven Le Scao, Sylvain Gugger, Mariama Drame, Quentin Lhoest, and Alexander M. Rush. 2020. Transformers: State-of-the-art natural language processing. In *Proceedings of the 2020 Conference on Empirical Methods in Natural Language Processing: System Demonstrations*, pages 38–45, Online. Association for Computational Linguistics.

Amelie Wührl and Roman Klinger. 2021. Claim detection in biomedical Twitter posts. In *Proceedings of the 20th Workshop on Biomedical Language Processing*, pages 131–142, Online. Association for Computational Linguistics.

Adam Wyner, Raquel Mochales-Palau, Marie-Francine Moens, and David Milward. 2010. Semantic processing of legal texts. chapter Approaches to Text Mining Arguments from Legal Cases, pages 60–79. Springer-Verlag, Berlin, Heidelberg.

Adam Wyner, Jodi Schneider, Katie Atkinson, and Trevor JM Bench-Capon. 2012. Semi-automated argumentative analysis of online product reviews. *COMMA*, 245:43–50.

Mary Ziegler. 2012. Sexing harris: The law and politics of the movement to defund planned parenthood. *Buff. L. Rev.*, 60:701.

Multi-Task and Multi-Corpora Training Strategies to Enhance Argumentative Sentence Linking Performance

Jan Wira Gotama Putra[†], **Simone Teufel**[‡†], **Takenobu Tokunaga**[†]
[†]Tokyo Institute of Technology, Japan
[‡]University of Cambridge, United Kingdom
{gotama.w.aa@m, take@c}.titech.ac.jp, simone.teufel@cl.cam.ac.uk

Abstract

Argumentative structure prediction aims to establish links between textual units and label the relationship between them, forming a structured representation for a given input text. The former task, linking, has been identified by earlier works as particularly challenging, as it requires finding the most appropriate structure out of a very large search space of possible link combinations. In this paper, we improve a state-of-the-art linking model by using multi-task and multi-corpora training strategies. Our auxiliary tasks help the model to learn the role of each sentence in the argumentative structure. Combining multi-corpora training with a selective sampling strategy increases the training data size while ensuring that the model still learns the desired target distribution well. Experiments on essays written by English-as-a-foreign-language learners show that both strategies significantly improve the model's performance; for instance, we observe a 15.8% increase in the F1-macro for individual link predictions.

1 Introduction

Argument mining (AM) is an emerging area that addresses the automatic analysis of argumentation. Many recent studies commonly try to tackle two major tasks (Lawrence and Reed, 2020). The first of these is *argumentative component identification*, in which argumentative units (ACs) and non-argumentative components (non-ACs) including their boundaries are determined. ACs can be further classified according to their role in argumentation, e.g., *major claim*,[1] *claim* and *premise* (Stab and Gurevych, 2017). The second task is called *argumentative structure prediction*, which first establishes links from source to target ACs (this is called the *linking* task) and then labels the relationship between them, for instance using the *support* and *attack* relation labels (this is called the *relation labelling* task) (Stab and Gurevych, 2017).

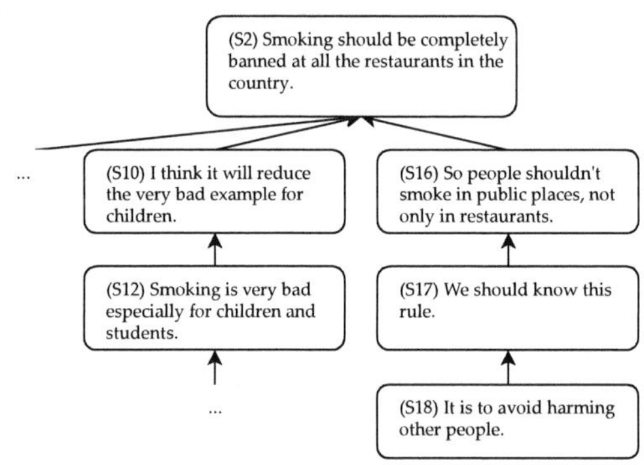

Figure 1: Illustration of linking task, using part of an essay discussing the topic "*Smoking should be banned at all restaurants in the country.*"

The linking task has been identified by earlier works as particularly challenging (Lippi and Torroni, 2016; Cabrio and Villata, 2018; Lawrence and Reed, 2020). There are many possible combinations of links between textual units, and a linking model has to find the most proper structure out of a very large search space. Another typical challenge in AM is the size of annotated corpora (Schulz et al., 2018). Corpus construction is a complex and time-consuming process; it also often requires a team of expert annotators. Existing corpora in AM are relatively "small" compared with more established fields, such as machine translation or document classification. This hinders training AM models when using a supervised machine learning framework.

In this paper, we perform the linking task for essays written by English-as-a-foreign-language (EFL) learners. Given an essay, we identify links between sentences, forming a tree-structured representation of argumentation in the text. Figure 1 illustrates the task. Our contributions are twofold. First, we propose two structural-modelling related

[1]The major claim is the statement expressing the writer's view on the discussion topic; also called *main stance* or *main claim*.

Proceedings of The 8th Workshop on Argument Mining, pages 12–23
Punta Cana, Dominican Republic, November 10–11, 2021.

auxiliary tasks to train our model in a multi-task learning (MTL) fashion. Past studies commonly executed several AM tasks or using discourse and rhetorical auxiliary tasks in the MTL setting (cf. Section 2). In comparison with other works, our auxiliary tasks are advantageous in that they do not require any additional annotation. Second, we combine multi-corpora training with a selective sampling strategy to increase the training data size. We explore the use of mixed training data of in-domain EFL and out-domain[2] student-essay corpora that were annotated using different schemes and of different quality, while ensuring that the model still learns the properties of the target in-domain data well.

The choice of EFL texts in this study aims to contribute to a less attended area. In AM, it is common to use well-written texts by proficient authors (e.g., Ashley, 1990; Peldszus and Stede, 2016). However, student texts often suffer from many problems because they are still in the learning phase. Even more, EFL texts are also less coherent and less lexically rich, and exhibit less natural lexical choices and collocations (Silva, 1993; Rabinovich et al., 2016). There are more non-native English speakers (Fujiwara, 2018), and yet, to the best of our knowledge, only one preceding study in AM concerned the EFL genre (Putra et al., 2021b). The codes accompanying this paper are publicly available.[3]

2 Related Work

2.1 Argumentative Structure Prediction

A variety of formulations have been proposed for the linking task. Traditional approaches formulated it as a pairwise classification task, predicting whether an argumentative link exists between a given pair of ACs (Stab and Gurevych, 2014). A further post-processing step can also be performed to combine the local predictions into an optimised global structure, e.g., using the minimum-spanning-tree algorithm (Peldszus and Stede, 2015). Recent studies proposed a more global approach instead, considering the entire input context. For instance, Potash et al. (2017) formulated the linking task as a sequence prediction problem. They jointly performed AC classification and AC linking at once, assuming that the segmentation and AC vs non-AC categorisation have been pre-completed. They experimented on the *microtext corpus* (Peldszus and Stede, 2016) and the *persuasive essay corpus* (PEC, Stab and Gurevych (2017)).

Eger et al. (2017) formulated argumentative structure parsing in three ways: as relation extraction, as sequence tagging and as dependency parsing tasks. They defined a BIO tagging scheme and performed end-to-end parsing at token-level, executing all subtasks (i.e., segmentation, unit type classification, linking and relation labelling) at once. Ye and Teufel (2021) also performed end-to-end parsing at the token-level. They proposed a more efficient representation for the dependency structure of arguments, and achieved the state-of-the-art performance for component and relation identifications on the PEC using a biaffine attention model (Dozat and Manning, 2017).

The biaffine attention model was originally designed to parse token-to-token dependency, but Morio et al. (2020) extended it to parse proposition (segment) level dependency. Their model dealt with graph-structured arguments in the Cornell eRulemaking corpus (Park and Cardie, 2018). Using the same architecture, Putra et al. (2021b) parsed tree-structured EFL essays in the ICNALE-AS2R corpus (Ishikawa, 2013, 2018; Putra et al., 2021a,b). In tree-structured argumentation, it is common for groups of sentences about the same sub-topic to operate as a unit, forming a sub-tree (sub-argument). Putra et al. (2021b) found that their linking model has problems in constructing sub-trees, that is, it splits a group of sentences that should belong together into separate sub-arguments (sub-trees) or, conversely, groups together sentences that do not belong together into the same sub-trees.

2.2 Low-Resource and Cross-Domain Argument Mining

Several approaches have been applied to alleviate the data sparsity problem in AM. Al-Khatib et al. (2016) used a distant supervision technique to acquire a huge amount of data without explicit annotation. Accuosto and Saggion (2019) pre-trained a discourse parsing model and then fine-tuned it on AM tasks. Lauscher et al. (2018) investigated the MTL setup of argumentative component identification and rhetorical classification tasks. Schulz et al. (2018) performed a cross-genre argumenta-

[2]Past studies used the term *domain* in a broad context. It has at least five different senses: text genre, text quality, annotation scheme, dataset and topic (or prompt). In the rest of this paper, we use the specific meaning whenever possible.

[3]`https://github.com/wiragotama/ArgMin2021`

tive component identification. They employed a sequence tagger model with a shared representation but different prediction layers for each genre.

Data augmentation can also be applied to mitigate the data sparsity problem. This aims to increase the amount of training data without directly collecting more data (Liu et al., 2020; Feng et al., 2021). A relatively straightforward strategy is to use multiple corpora when training models. For example, Chu et al. (2017) proposed a *mixed fine-tuning* approach for machine translation; they trained a model on an out-genre corpus and then fine-tune it on a dataset that is a mix of the target-genre and out-genre corpora. However, the use of multiple corpora of different genres is challenging in AM because argumentation is often modelled differently across genres (Lippi and Torroni, 2016; Lawrence and Reed, 2020). Daxenberger et al. (2017) found that training a claim identification model with mixed-genre corpora only perform as good as training on each specific corpus. The use of data augmentation may cause the distributional shift problem as well, where the augmented data alter the target distribution that should be learned by the model (Feng et al., 2021).

Putra et al. (2021b) provided some insights on the possible conditions for multi corpora training by experimenting using texts of different quality. They trained argumentative structure prediction models on EFL essays (in-domain) and parallel improved version of the texts (out-domain), and evaluated on the EFL texts. Their cross-domain system attained 94% accuracy of end-to-end in-domain performance. This signals the potential to use corpora of different text quality altogether to train a parsing model, as long as the text genre stays the same. However, mixed-quality corpora training has yet to be tried in practice.

In recent years, there has also been a growing interest towards more generic AM models. For example, Stab et al. (2018) proposed a simple annotation scheme for argument retrieval that is applicable in heterogeneous sources and can be performed by untrained annotators. Cocarascu et al. (2020) explored various deep learning architectures and features that work well across various datasets for the relation labelling task. They also provided a comparison of using contextualised and non-contextualised embeddings for the task. On the other hand, Ruiz-Dolz et al. (2021) compared the performance of transformer-based language models on the cross-topic relation labelling task.

3 Dataset

Our target texts are sourced from the ICNALE-AS2R, a corpus of 434 essays written by Asian college students with intermediate proficiency.[4] There are 6,021 sentences in total with 13.9 sentences on average per essay. To the best of our knowledge, this is the only currently publicly-available AM corpus focusing on EFL texts. The corpus is annotated at sentence-level, that is, a sentence corresponds to one argumentative unit. The corpus differentiates sentences as ACs (5,799 sents.) and non-ACs (222 sents.), without further classification of AC types. Links are established between ACs to form tree structure (avg. depth of 4.3, root at depth 0 in the corpus), where the *major claim* acts as the root. Four relation labels are employed to label the links: *support*, *attack*, *detail* and *restatement*.

4 Proposed Method

In this work, we experiment on the linking task. Given an entire essay of N sentences as input, $s_1, ..., s_N$, a linking model outputs the distance $d_1, ..., d_N$ between each sentence s_i to its target. For instance, if a sentence is connected to its preceding sentence, the distance is $d = -1$. We consider those sentences that have no explicitly annotated outgoing links as linked to themselves ($d = 0$); this concerns major claims (roots) and non-ACs. We do not consider labelling the links with their relationships in this paper.

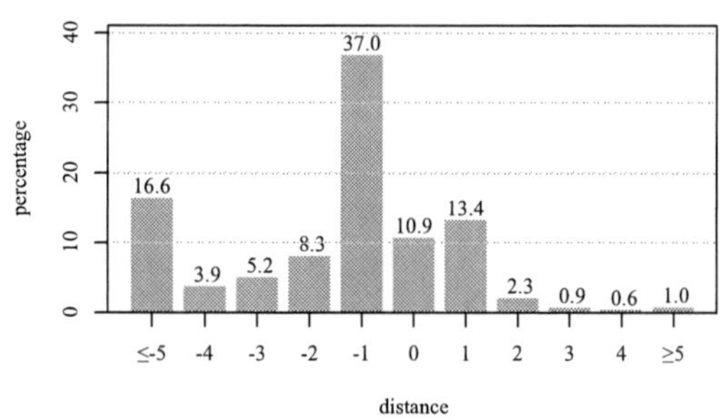

Figure 2: Distribution of distance (in percent) between related sentences in the ICNALE-AS2R corpus.

Figure 2 shows the distance distribution between the source and target sentences in the

[4] `https://www.gsk.or.jp/en/catalog/gsk2021-a`. The approximated CEFR level of the essay authors are A2 (94 essays), B1 (253) and B2 (87).

ICNALE-AS2R corpus, ranging $[-26, ..., +15]$. Adjacent links predominate (50.4%). Short distance links ($2 \leq |d| \leq 4$) make up 21.2% of the total. Backward long distance links at $d \leq -5$ are 16.6%, whereas forward long distance links are rare (1.0%). Self-loops make up 10.9% of the total. Following recent advances in AM, we approach the linking task as a sentence-to-sentence dependency parsing.

4.1 Baseline

We use Putra et al.'s (2021b) architecture as the state-of-the-art baseline ("BIAF" model, cf. Figure 3). In this architecture, input sentences are first encoded into their respective sentence embeddings using sentence-BERT encoder (Reimers and Gurevych, 2019). The resulting sentence embeddings are then passed into a dense layer for dimensionality reduction. The results are then fed into a bidirectional long-short-term memory network (BiLSTM) layer ($\#stack = 3$) to produce contextual sentence representations. These representations are then passed into two different dense layers to encode the corresponding sentence when it acts as a source $\left(h^{(source)}\right)$ or target $\left(h^{(target)}\right)$ in a relation.

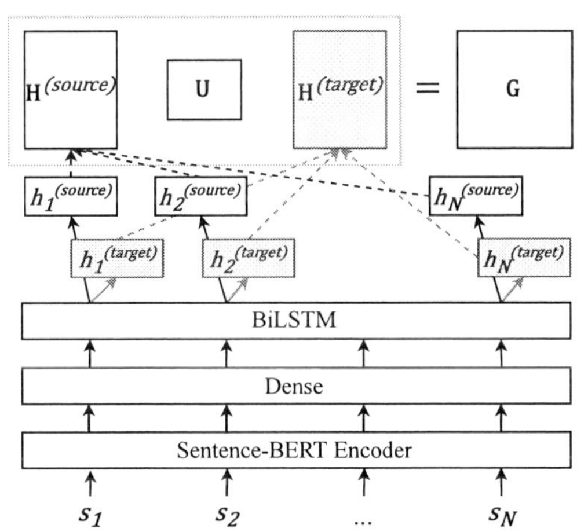

Figure 3: Biaffine attention model (BIAF).

Finally, a biaffine transformation (Dozat and Manning, 2017) is applied to all source and target representations to produce the final output matrix $\mathbf{G} \in \mathbb{R}^{N \times N}$, where each cell $g_{i,j}$ represents the probability (or score) of the source sentence s_i pointing to s_j. Equation (1) and (2) show the biaffine transformation (f), where $\mathbf{U}$ and W are weight matrices and b is bias.

$$f(x_1, x_2) = {x_1}^{\mathrm{T}}\mathbf{U}x_2 + \mathbf{W}(x_1 \oplus x_2) + b \quad (1)$$

$$g_{i,j} = f\left(h_i^{(source)}, h_j^{(target)}\right) \quad (2)$$

The Chu-Liu-Edmonds algorithm (Chu and Liu, 1965; Edmonds, 1967) is applied to create a minimum spanning tree out of the matrix $\mathbf{G}$. The links in the tree are then converted into distance predictions between source and target sentences for evaluation purpose.

4.2 Multi-Task Learning with Structural Signal

We propose to extend the BIAF model in an MTL setup using two novel structural-modelling-related auxiliary tasks.

The first auxiliary task is a *quasi* argumentative component type (QACT) prediction. ICNALE-AS2R corpus does not assign AC types per se, but we can compile the following four sentence types from the tree typology:

- *major claim (root)*: only incoming links,
- *AC (non-leaf)*: both outgoing and incoming links,
- *AC (leaf)*: only outgoing links and
- *non-AC*: neither incoming nor outgoing links.

For example, S2 is the major claim of Figure 1, S10 is AC (non-leaf) and S17 is AC (leaf). The QACT prediction task should help the linking model to learn the role of sentences in the argumentative structure, as well as the property of links for each sentence. This auxiliary task improved a sequence-tagger based linking model in Putra et al. (2021b), but it has not been applied to the BIAF model yet.

The second auxiliary task concerns node depth (ND) prediction. There are six depth categories employed in this paper: depth 0 to depth 4, and depth 5+. The argumentative structure in ICNALE-AS2R corpus is hierarchical, and there is no relations between nodes (sentences) at the same depth. The ND prediction task should help the model to learn the placement of sentences in the hierarchy and guide where each sentence should point at, that is, sentences at depth X point at sentences at depth $X - 1$.

We also propose to use sentence position (spos) embedding as an input feature because it has been proved to be useful in other studies (e.g., Song et al., 2020). The sentence position encoding is

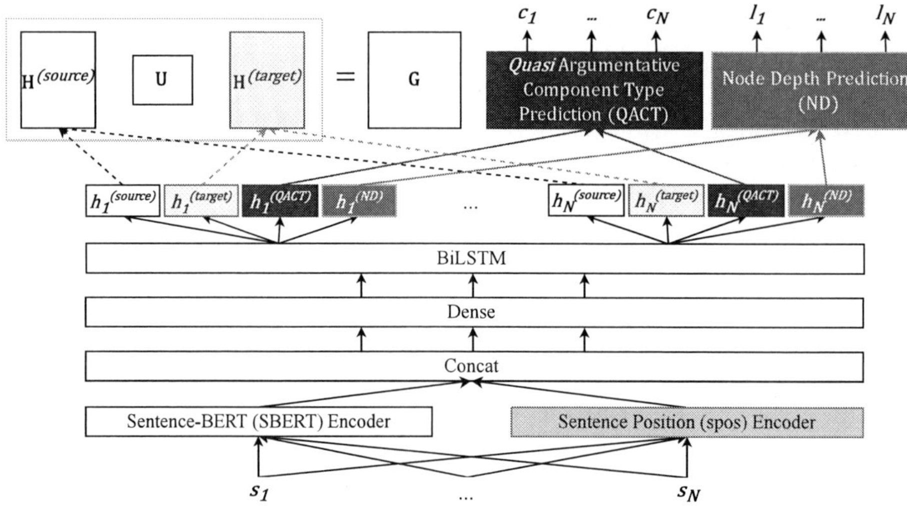

Figure 4: Our proposed extension for the BIAF model. Newly added modules are coloured.

calculated by dividing a sentence position by the essay length. When using this feature, sentence embeddings and spos encoding are concatenated before being passed to the first dense layer. Figure 4 illustrates our proposed architecture.

4.3 Multi-Corpora Training

In this paper, we also consider the use of multi-corpora training strategy, employing essays in the PEC as additional training data. Both ICNALE-AS2R and PEC provide argumentative essays written by students (in English) and represents argumentative structures as trees. However, there is no information on the essay authors proficiency (L1 or L2) nor the observed quality of the PEC. Hence, these two corpora might be of different quality. The writing prompts of ICNALE-AS2R and PEC essays are also different.

There are two settings when training using multiple corpora. The first is to use the entire 402 essays in the PEC on top of ICNALE-AS2R train set ("[P+I]" setting). However, PEC and ICNALE-AS2R are different in terms of length and annotation scheme. The PEC essays have 18.2 sentences on average (15.1 ACs and 3.1 non-ACs), while ICNALE-AS2R essays have 13.9 sentences on average (13.4 ACs and 0.5 non-ACs). The difference in non-ACs proportion between these corpora is likely caused by the difference in the set of relation labels employed. The essays in PEC were annotated using two relation types: *support* and *attack*, while ICNALE-AS2R additionally employed *detail* and *restatement*. Hence, there is arguably more information in the ICNALE-AS2R corpus. Particularly, some sentences that should have been annotated as non-ACs (hence not linked to other sentences) in the PEC's scheme might have been annotated as ACs in the ICNALE-AS2R's scheme by using the additional relations.

Due to the differences in annotation scheme and statistical properties, there is a possibility that the model might not properly learn the distribution of ICNALE-AS2R in the [P+I] setting. Therefore, we also propose a second *selective sampling* ("[SS]" setting) strategy to account for the differences between these two corpora. In this setting, we only use PEC essays that are somewhat similar to those of ICNALE-AS2R considering the following two criteria. First, we only use PEC essays having 17 sentences at maximum (ICNALE-AS2R avg. 13.9 + 3.3 SD). Second, the employed PEC essays contain two non-ACs at maximum (ICNALE-AS2R avg. 0.5 + 0.9 SD). There are 110 remaining PEC essays after the selective sampling procedure.

Note that ICNALE-AS2R was annotated at the sentence level while PEC was annotated at the segment level. Therefore, we convert the PEC annotation to the sentence level, following the strategy described by Song et al. (2020). If a sentence contains only one AC, we use the whole sentence as an AC; if a sentence contains two or more ACs, we split it into multiple sentences while including the preceding tokens into each AC. Figure 5 illustrates the splitting procedure, where a sentence contain-

(S1)*[To conclude,* ***art could play an active role in improving the quality of people's lives,****]* (S2)*[but I think that* ***governments should attach heavier weight to other social issues such as education and housing needs****]* (S3)*[because* ***those are the most essential ways enable to make people a decent life.****]*

Figure 5: Illustration of conversion of PEC's segment-level annotation to the sentence-level (essay075). Annotated AC segments are written in bold.

ing three ACs is split into three sentences.

5 Structural Metric

In this paper, we do not evaluate the model performance only on individual link predictions but also analyse the structural properties of the outputs, giving more insights into the models' ability to learn different aspects of the argumentative structure. We also investigate whether our proposed strategies improve the model performance concerning the grouping of related sentences into the same sub-tree, a challenge to linking models previously (manually) observed in Putra et al. (2021b) (cf. Section 2.1). A metric is needed to quantify the improvement on this aspect, and we propose to use a novel structural metric called **MAR^{dSet}**, that was developed by Putra et al. (2021a).[5]

Given two structures A and B (i.e., predicted and gold structures), we can quantify their similarity based on the presence of common substructures. We first define a *descendant set* (dSet) of a node X as the set consisting the node X itself and its descendants. Figure 6 shows examples of dSets (brackets given below the node ID).[6] For example, the dSet of node-2 in annotation A of Figure 6 is $\{2, 3, 4, 5\}$. Two corresponding nodes in A and B are required to have identical dSets in order to score a value of 1. For example, the matching score for node-2 between annotation A and B in Figure 6 is 0, while the matching score for node-3 is 1. Non-AC nodes are counted as a match if they are deemed non-argumentative in both structures.

With this formulation, we can get a vector v representing the matching scores for all nodes in the two structures. For example, $v = [0, 0, 1, 1, 0]$ for Figure 6. The similarity score between two structures are then calculated as MAR^{dSet}$= \frac{\sum_{i=1}^{N} v_i}{N}$, where N denotes the number of nodes; The MAR^{dSet} score for Figure 6 is 0.4.

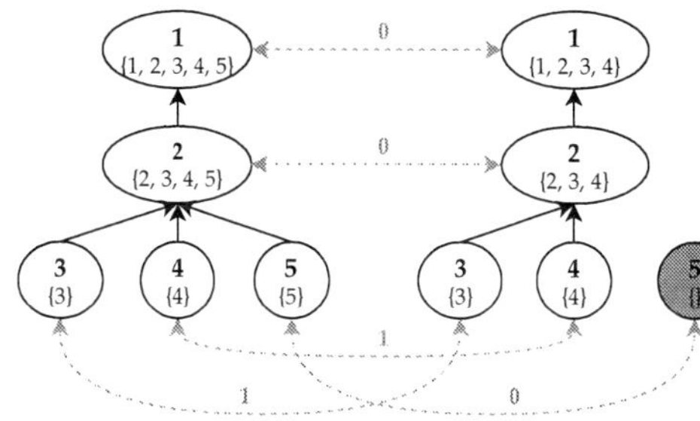

Figure 6: Example of descendant set matching between structure A (left) and B (right). Matching scores are written in red. Grey nodes represent non-AC.

6 Experiment and Discussion

6.1 Experimental Setting

In this experiment, the ICNALE-AS2R corpus is split into 80% train set (347 essays , 4,841 sents.) and 20% test set (87 essays, 1,180 sents.). We use the same splits as Putra et al. (2021b). The number of training essays for [P+I] and [SS] settings are 749 (12,162 sents.) and 457 (6,418 sents.), respectively. We run the experiment for 20 times[7] and report the average performance. Statistical testing, whenever possible, is conducted using the permutation test (Noreen, 1989) on the performance scores of the 20 runs with a significance level of $\alpha = .05$. Here, we also perform an ablation study. Appendix A shows some implementation notes.

6.2 Quantitative Analysis

Table 1 shows the experimental results on individual link predictions and MAR^{dSet}. Training the BIAF model using the QACT task improved the performance over the baseline, particularly in terms of F1-macro (non significant difference). In addition, using both QACT+ND auxiliary tasks significantly improved the performance over the baseline in terms of F1-macro. This signals that the proposed MTL setting benefits model performance.

We next look at how spos encoding affects the model performance. Introducing spos to the BIAF+QACT+ND model improves accuracy and MAR^{dSet}. However, the difference is not significant. Similarly, the difference between

[5]MAR stands for **M**ean **A**greement in **R**ecall. Descendant set (dSet) denotes the unit of analysis.

[6]In the implementation, we use sentence position in the input text as node ID.

[7]Twenty experiments were repeated on the same dataset splits to account for random initialisation in neural networks.

Model	Acc.	F1-macro	MAR^{dset}
Baseline			
BIAF	.471	.323	.419
MTL			
BIAF+QACT	.473	.333	422
BIAF+QACT+ND	.472	.338	423
Spos			
BIAF+QACT+spos	.472	.327	.421
BIAF+QACT+ND+spos	<u>.475</u>	.336	426
Multi-corpora Training			
BIAF+QACT+ND [P+I]	.468	<u>.360</u>	**.455**
BIAF+QACT+ND [SS]	**.489**†	**.374**†	<u>.452</u>

Table 1: Results of individual link predictions (Acc. and F1-macro) and MAR^{dSet}. The best result is shown in **bold-face**. The † symbol indicates that the difference to the second-best result (underlined) is significant.

BIAF+QACT+spos and BIAF+QACT is not significant. There are two possible explanations for this phenomenon. First, studies in *contrastive rhetoric* found that non-native speakers tend to structure and organise their texts differently from native speakers (Kaplan, 1966; Silva, 1993). Some students might have used the writing customs and rhetorical strategies of their first language instead of using the common English writing patterns. For example, Asian students sometimes put a claim after its reason, which is not common in Anglo-Saxon cultures (Silva, 1993; Johns, 1986). We observe that some texts in the ICNALE-AS2R corpus are written in the "claim-support" structure but some are written in the "support-claim" structure. Sentences on the same topic are sometimes distantly separated as well. These inconsistencies might have negated the effect of the spos encoding. Second, the output of the BIAF model is a graph **G** which considers the directed links between all pairs of sentences. The spos feature might not affect the biaffine transformation much in this context.

The models trained using multiple corpora attain the best performance for individual link and substructure (MAR) predictions. BIAF+QACT+ND [P+I] achieves the best performance of .455 in terms of MAR^{dSet}, and BIAF+QACT+ND [SS] achieves the best performance of .489 and .374 in terms of accuracy and F1-macro. The [SS] model also achieves the second-best performance of .452 in terms of MAR^{dSet}. These improvements are significant over the baseline and the BIAF+QACT+ND model. Note that when using the [SS] setting, the model performance is consistently improved with regard to all metrics, while the accuracy of the [P+I] model is lower than the baseline. In general, the [SS] model attains a better performance compared with the [P+I] model despite fewer training instances. This means that when training a model using multiple corpora, it is essential to consider training instances having the same properties as our goal. Simply having more training data does not guarantee improvement.

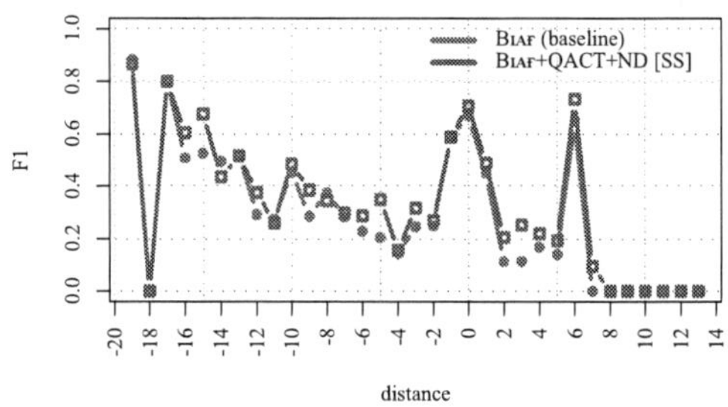

Figure 7: Model performance across distances.

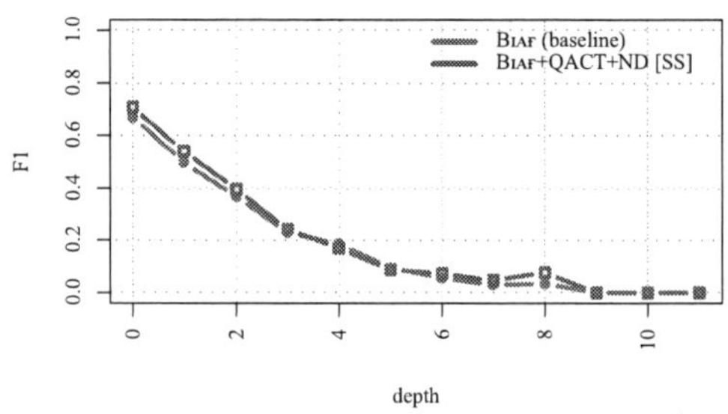

Figure 8: Model performance across depths.

To gain deeper insights into the individual link prediction improvement brought by the [SS] model over the baseline, Figure 7 shows F1 score per target linking distance. BIAF+QACT+ND [SS] is better than the baseline model, particularly at predicting short-distance links ($2 \leq |d| \leq 4$, avg. F1 = .24 vs .17), which is the weakest range of the baseline model. However, this is still the weakest range even for the [SS] model.

Figure 8 shows the performance across depths, that is, whether the model places each node at the proper depth in the predicted structure. BIAF+QACT+ND [SS] performs better than the baseline particularly in [0,3] and [6,8] ranges. This plot indicates that the model performance declines as one moves further down the tree.

We next look at the models' ability to predict the role of each node (QACT task) based on the predicted hierarchical structures. Table 2 shows

Model	Major Claim	AC (non-leaf)	AC (leaf)	Non-AC	F1-macro
Baseline					
BIAF	.730	.639	.599	.437	.601
MTL					
BIAF+QACT	.739	.639	.601	.453	.608
BIAF+QACT+ND	.734	.636	.601	.454	.606
Spos					
BIAF+QACT+spos	.725	**.641**	.602	.438	.602
BIAF+QACT+ND+spos	.738	.638	.603	.460	.610
Multi-corpora Training					
BIAF+QACT+ND [P+I]	748	.606	**.634**†	.420	.602
BIAF+QACT+ND [SS]	**.767**†	.633	.628	**.462**	**.622**†

Table 2: Results for the QACT prediction. Node labels are automatically identified from the predicted topology in the main task. This table shows F1 score per node label and F1-macro. **Bold-face**, † and underline as above.

the results. The MTL models perform better compared with the baseline model. Both BIAF+QACT and BIAF+QACT+ND achieve a significant improvement over the baseline in terms of non-AC prediction and F1-macro. This reconfirms that both of our proposed MTL tasks are useful to improve linking performance. Similar to the previous result on individual links, the spos feature does not provide much improvement. We notice that the BIAF+QACT+ND [P+I] model performs worse than the baseline in some aspects, particularly in terms of AC (non-leaf) and non-AC predictions. On the other hand, BIAF+QACT+ ND [SS] consistently achieves better performance compared with the baseline model. It attains the highest score of .622 in F1-macro, which is a significant improvement over other configurations. This confirms our hypothesis that the difference between annotation schemes and statistical properties between PEC and ICNALE-AS2R affects the model in terms of the distribution learned. The proposed selective sampling strategy helps to alleviate this problem.

We also analyse the overall shape of the predicted structures by all models, as shown in Table 3. The gold standard trees in ICNALE-AS2R have a particular shape, expressed as the average depth of 4.3 (SD = 1.4) and the leaf ratio of .439 (SD = 0.11). The baseline model tends to produce trees that are deeper and narrower than the ICNALE-AS2R gold trees. Our MTL auxiliary tasks help to improve the leaf ratio to become closer to the gold standard (significant difference between BIAF+QACT+ND and BIAF), while spos embedding does not provide additional improvement. When we introduce the multi-corpora training strategy, the predicted structures become shallower and wider compared with the baseline, particularly when using the [P+I] setting. We believe this is due to the shallower trees in the PEC compared with the ICNALE AS2R (i.e., the distributional shift problem). However, this is less of an issue for the [SS] model as it produces the most similar structure to the ICNALE-AS2R essays.

Model	Average Depth	Leaf Ratio
Dataset		
ICNALE-AS2R	4.3±1.4	.439±.11
PEC [all]	2.8±.63	.540±.09
PEC [after SS]	2.7±.53	.565±.08
Baseline		
BIAF	5.1	.404
MTL		
BIAF+QACT	5.1	.410
BIAF+QACT+ND	5.0	.418
Spos		
BIAF+QACT+spos	5.2	.407
BIAF+QACT+ND+spos	5.0	.412
Multi-corpora Training		
BIAF+QACT+ND [P+I]	4.1	.486
BIAF+QACT+ND [SS]	**4.5**†	**.446**†

Table 3: Structural-output qualities of linking models. **Bold-face**, † and underline as above.

We conclude BIAF+QACT+ND [SS] as the best model in this experiment, achieving the new state-of-the-art performance for the linking task. It consistently performs better compared with other configurations across all evaluation aspects.

6.3 Qualitative Analysis

We conducted a qualitative analysis on some random outputs of our best model, namely BIAF+QACT+ND [SS]. Some prediction errors are likely caused by the inability of the model to resolve anaphora. Figure 9 shows an output example. The model successfully groups sentences S5–S7 as a single sub-argument, as the gold annotation does. However, it connects S7 to S6, while the gold annotation connects S7 to S5 (with the *support* label). The link from S7 to S5 is the correct interpretation because the statement in S7 can be broadly applied to "*skills of working and cooperating*," not only to some specific instantiations mentioned in S6 ("*set the working agenda and get help from colleagues*"). A possible direction to alleviate this problem is to equip the model with a better ability to resolve anaphora. Another direction is to perform an anaphora resolution step before parsing the argumentative structure.

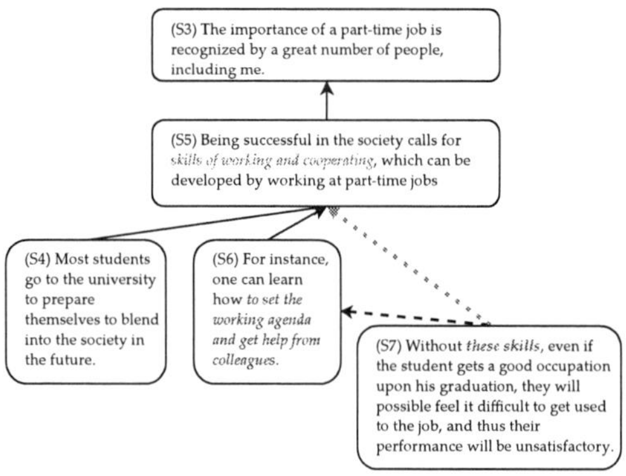

Figure 9: An excerpt of prediction for essay "W_HKG_PTJ0_029_B2_0_EDIT". The essay was written in response to a prompt "*It is important for college students to have a part-time job.*" The dashed line illustrates an erroneous link, while the dotted line (grey) illustrates the corresponding gold link.

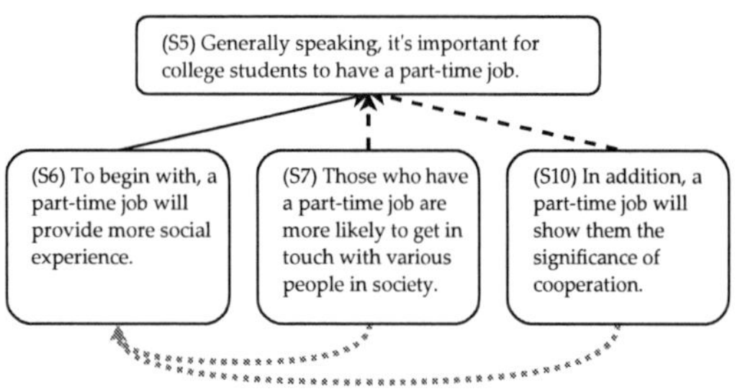

Figure 10: An excerpt of prediction for essay "W_CHN_PTJ0_242_B2_0_EDIT". The essay was written in response to a prompt "*It is important for college students to have a part-time job.*" Dashed lines and dotted lines as above.

Another source of error is the difficulty in judging whether two statements argue at the same conceptual level (hence the same depth in the tree). Figure 10 shows an illustration. S7 and S10 are exemplifications of S6, and therefore, they should be placed lower than S6. However, the model recognises S6, S7 and S10 arguing at the same conceptual level. The exemplifications are probably not obvious for the model because S7 is not accompanied by a discourse marker (e.g., "*for example*"). In general, EFL essays are often challenging to process due to improper use (can be excessive or limited too) of discourse markers.

7 Conclusion

In this paper, we presented a study on the argumentative linking task; given an essay as input, a linking model outputs the argumentative structure in a tree representation. We conducted experiments using an EFL corpus, namely ICNALE-AS2R. We extended the state-of-the-art biaffine attention model using a novel set of structural auxiliary tasks in the multi-task learning setup. Additionally, we also proposed a multi-corpora training strategy using the PEC to increase training instances. It has to be noted that simply increasing the training data size does not guarantee improvement. We need to ensure that the model still learns the desired target distribution as well. To this end, we filtered PEC essays using a selective sampling technique. These two strategies provided useful supervision signals to the biaffine model and significantly improved its performance. The F1-macro for individual link predictions was boosted to .374 from .323. Our strategies also improved the model performance on the structural aspects, achieving the MAR^{dset} of .452 from .419, and the F1-macro of .622 from .601 for the QACT task.

A possible future direction is to evaluate whether our proposed methods are beneficial for more complex discourses, such as scientific articles. It is also necessary to provide an even richer supervision signal to improve the linking performance. One possibility is to pre-train the model on the anaphora resolution task.

Acknowledgements

This work was partially supported by Tokyo Tech World Research Hub Initiative (WRHI), JSPS KAKENHI grant number 20J13239 and Support Centre for Advanced Telecommunication Technology Research. We would like to thank anonymous reviewers for their useful and detailed feedback.

References

Pablo Accuosto and Horacio Saggion. 2019. Transferring knowledge from discourse to arguments: A case study with scientific abstracts. In *Proceedings of the 6th Workshop on Argument Mining*, pages 41–51, Florence, Italy. Association for Computational Linguistics.

Khalid Al-Khatib, Henning Wachsmuth, Matthias Hagen, Jonas Köhler, and Benno Stein. 2016. Cross-domain mining of argumentative text through distant supervision. In *Proceedings of the 2016 Conference of the North American Chapter of the Association for Computational Linguistics: Human Language Technologies*, pages 1395–1404, San Diego, California. Association for Computational Linguistics.

Kevin D. Ashley. 1990. *Modeling legal argument - reasoning with cases and hypotheticals*. Artificial intelligence and legal reasoning. MIT Press.

Elena Cabrio and Serena Villata. 2018. Five years of argument mining: A data-driven analysis. In *Proceedings of the 27th International Joint Conference on Artificial Intelligence*, IJCAI'18, page 5427–5433. AAAI Press.

Chenhui Chu, Raj Dabre, and Sadao Kurohashi. 2017. An empirical comparison of domain adaptation methods for neural machine translation. In *Proceedings of the 55th Annual Meeting of the Association for Computational Linguistics (Volume 2: Short Papers)*, pages 385–391, Vancouver, Canada. Association for Computational Linguistics.

Y. Chu and T. Liu. 1965. On the shortest arborescence of a directed graph. *Science Sinica*, page 1396–1400.

Oana Cocarascu, Elena Cabrio, Serena Villata, and Francesca Toni. 2020. A dataset independent set of baselines for relation prediction in argument mining. In *Proceedings of Computational Models of Argument (COMMA)*, pages 45–52.

Johannes Daxenberger, Steffen Eger, Ivan Habernal, Christian Stab, and Iryna Gurevych. 2017. What is the essence of a claim? cross-domain claim identification. In *Proceedings of the 2017 Conference on Empirical Methods in Natural Language Processing*, pages 2055–2066, Copenhagen, Denmark. Association for Computational Linguistics.

Timothy Dozat and Christopher D. Manning. 2017. Deep biaffine attention for neural dependency parsing. In *Proceedings of the International Conference on Learning Representations (ICLR)*.

Jack Edmonds. 1967. Optimum branchings. *Journal of Research of the National Bureau of Standards - B. Mathematics and Mathematical Physics*, 71B:233–240.

Steffen Eger, Johannes Daxenberger, and Iryna Gurevych. 2017. Neural end-to-end learning for computational argumentation mining. In *Proceedings of the 55th Annual Meeting of the Association for Computational Linguistics (Volume 1: Long Papers)*, pages 11–22, Vancouver, Canada. Association for Computational Linguistics.

Steven Y. Feng, Varun Gangal, Jason Wei, Sarath Chandar, Soroush Vosoughi, Teruko Mitamura, and Eduard H. Hovy. 2021. A survey of data augmentation approaches for NLP. *CoRR*, abs/2105.03075.

Yumi Fujiwara. 2018. The role of grammar instruction in japanese efl context: Towards communicative language teaching. *Journal of the Academic Society for Quality of Life (JAS4QoL)*, 4(4):1–11.

Matt Gardner, Joel Grus, Mark Neumann, Oyvind Tafjord, Pradeep Dasigi, Nelson F. Liu, Matthew E. Peters, Michael Schmitz, and Luke Zettlemoyer. 2018. Allennlp: A deep semantic natural language processing platform. *CoRR*, abs/1803.07640.

Shinichiro Ishikawa. 2013. The icnale and sophisticated contrastive interlanguage analysis of asian learners of english. *Learner Corpus Studies in Asia and the World*, 1:91–118.

Shinichiro Ishikawa. 2018. The icnale edited essays: A dataset for analysis of l2 english learner essays based on a new integrative viewpoint. *English Corpus Linguistics*, 25:1–14.

Ann M. Johns. 1986. The esl student and the revision process: Some insights from scheme theory. *Journal of Basic Writing*, 5(2):70 – 80.

Robert B. Kaplan. 1966. Cultural thought patterns in inter-cultural education. *Language Learning*, 16(1-2):1–20.

Diederik P. Kingma and Jimmy Lei Ba. 2015. Adam: a method for stochastic optimization. In *Proceedings of International Conference on Learning Representations (ICLR)*.

Anne Lauscher, Goran Glavaš, Simone Paolo Ponzetto, and Kai Eckert. 2018. Investigating the role of argumentation in the rhetorical analysis of scientific publications with neural multi-task learning models. In *Proceedings of the 2018 Conference on Empirical Methods in Natural Language Processing*, pages 3326–3338, Brussels, Belgium. Association for Computational Linguistics.

John Lawrence and Chris Reed. 2020. Argument Mining: A Survey. *Computational Linguistics*, 45(4):765–818.

Marco Lippi and Paolo Torroni. 2016. Argumentation mining: State of the art and emerging trends. *ACM Trans. Internet Technol.*, 16(2).

Pei Liu, Xuemin Wang, Chao Xiang, and Weiye Meng. 2020. A survey of text data augmentation. In *2020 International Conference on Computer Communication and Network Security (CCNS)*, pages 191–195.

Gaku Morio, Hiroaki Ozaki, Terufumi Morishita, Yuta Koreeda, and Kohsuke Yanai. 2020. Towards better non-tree argument mining: Proposition-level biaffine parsing with task-specific parameterization. In *Proceedings of the 58th Annual Meeting of the Association for Computational Linguistics*, pages 3259–3266, Online. Association for Computational Linguistics.

Eric W. Noreen. 1989. *Computer Intensive Methods for Testing Hypotheses: An Introduction*. Wiley, New York.

Joonsuk Park and Claire Cardie. 2018. A corpus of eRulemaking user comments for measuring evaluability of arguments. In *Proceedings of the Eleventh International Conference on Language Resources and Evaluation (LREC 2018)*, Miyazaki, Japan. European Language Resources Association (ELRA).

Adam Paszke, Sam Gross, Francisco Massa, Adam Lerer, James Bradbury, Gregory Chanan, Trevor Killeen, Zeming Lin, Natalia Gimelshein, Luca Antiga, Alban Desmaison, Andreas Kopf, Edward Yang, Zachary DeVito, Martin Raison, Alykhan Tejani, Sasank Chilamkurthy, Benoit Steiner, Lu Fang, Junjie Bai, and Soumith Chintala. 2019. Pytorch: An imperative style, high-performance deep learning library. In H. Wallach, H. Larochelle, A. Beygelzimer, F. d'Alché-Buc, E. Fox, and R. Garnett, editors, *Advances in Neural Information Processing Systems 32*, pages 8024–8035. Curran Associates, Inc.

Andreas Peldszus and Manfred Stede. 2015. Joint prediction in MST-style discourse parsing for argumentation mining. In *Proceedings of the 2015 Conference on Empirical Methods in Natural Language Processing*, pages 938–948, Lisbon, Portugal. Association for Computational Linguistics.

Andreas Peldszus and Manfred Stede. 2016. An annotated corpus of argumentative microtexts. In *Argumentation and Reasoned Action - Proceedings of the 1st European Conference on Argumentation, Lisbon, 2015*.

Peter Potash, Alexey Romanov, and Anna Rumshisky. 2017. Here's my point: Joint pointer architecture for argument mining. In *Proceedings of the 2017 Conference on Empirical Methods in Natural Language Processing*, pages 1364–1373, Copenhagen, Denmark. Association for Computational Linguistics.

Jan Wira Gotama Putra, Simone Teufel, and Takenobu Tokunaga. 2021a. Annotating argumentative structure in english-as-foreign-language learner essays. *Natural Language Engineering*, pages 1–37.

Jan Wira Gotama Putra, Simone Teufel, and Takenobu Tokunaga. 2021b. Parsing argumentative structure in English-as-foreign-language essays. In *Proceedings of the 16th Workshop on Innovative Use of NLP for Building Educational Applications*, pages 97–109, Online. Association for Computational Linguistics.

Ella Rabinovich, Sergiu Nisioi, Noam Ordan, and Shuly Wintner. 2016. On the similarities between native, non-native and translated texts. In *Proceedings of the 54th Annual Meeting of the Association for Computational Linguistics (Volume 1: Long Papers)*, pages 1870–1881, Berlin, Germany. Association for Computational Linguistics.

Nils Reimers and Iryna Gurevych. 2019. Sentence-BERT: Sentence embeddings using Siamese BERT-networks. In *Proceedings of the 2019 Conference on Empirical Methods in Natural Language Processing and the 9th International Joint Conference on Natural Language Processing (EMNLP-IJCNLP)*, pages 3982–3992.

Ramon Ruiz-Dolz, Jose Alemany, Stella Heras, and Ana Garcia-Fornes. 2021. Transformer-based models for automatic identification of argument relations: A cross-domain evaluation. *IEEE Intelligent Systems*, pages 1–1.

Claudia Schulz, Steffen Eger, Johannes Daxenberger, Tobias Kahse, and Iryna Gurevych. 2018. Multi-task learning for argumentation mining in low-resource settings. In *Proceedings of the 2018 Conference of the North American Chapter of the Association for Computational Linguistics: Human Language Technologies, Volume 2 (Short Papers)*, pages 35–41, New Orleans, Louisiana. Association for Computational Linguistics.

Tony Silva. 1993. Toward an understanding of the distinct nature of l2 writing: The esl research and its implications. *TESOL Quarterly*, 27(4):657–677.

Wei Song, Ziyao Song, Ruiji Fu, Lizhen Liu, Miaomiao Cheng, and Ting Liu. 2020. Discourse self-attention for discourse element identification in argumentative student essays. In *Proceedings of the 2020 Conference on Empirical Methods in Natural Language Processing (EMNLP)*, pages 2820–2830, Online. Association for Computational Linguistics.

Christian Stab and Iryna Gurevych. 2014. Identifying argumentative discourse structures in persuasive essays. In *Proceedings of the 2014 Conference on Empirical Methods in Natural Language Processing (EMNLP)*, pages 46–56, Doha, Qatar. Association for Computational Linguistics.

Christian Stab and Iryna Gurevych. 2017. Parsing argumentation structures in persuasive essays. *Computational Linguistics*, 43(3):619–659.

Christian Stab, Tristan Miller, Benjamin Schiller, Pranav Rai, and Iryna Gurevych. 2018. Cross-topic argument mining from heterogeneous sources. In *Proceedings of the 2018 Conference on Empirical Methods in Natural Language Processing*, pages 3664–3674, Brussels, Belgium. Association for Computational Linguistics.

Yuxiao Ye and Simone Teufel. 2021. End-to-end argument mining as biaffine dependency parsing. In *Proceedings of the 16th Conference of the European Chapter of the Association for Computational Linguistics: Main Volume*, pages 669–678, Online. Association for Computational Linguistics.

A Implementation Notes

Hidden Units and Model Implementation 512 units for the first dense layer, 256 LSTM unit, and 256 units for the second dense layer after the BiLSTM layer. Dropout is applied between all layers. For a fair comparison, we follow Putra et al. (2021b) in using the sentence-BERT encoder fine-tuned on the NLI dataset ("bert-base-nli-mean-tokens", `https://github.com/UKPLab/sentence-transformers`). All models are trained using Adam optimiser (Kingma and Ba, 2015), and implemented in PyTorch (Paszke et al., 2019) and AllenNLP (Gardner et al., 2018).

Loss The MTL loss is defined as $L = \sum_t \frac{1}{2\sigma_t^2} L_t + \ln(\sigma_t)$, where the loss L_t of each task t is dynamically weighted, controlled by a learnable parameter σ_t. The loss for the main task (sentence linking) is computed using max-margin criterion, while losses for auxiliary tasks are computed using cross-entropy.

Explainable Unsupervised Argument Similarity Rating with Abstract Meaning Representation and Conclusion Generation

Juri Opitz[1] **Philipp Heinisch**[2] **Philipp Wiesenbach**[1] **Philipp Cimiano**[2] **Anette Frank**[1]

[1]Dept. of Computational Linguistics, Heidelberg University
[2]CITEC, Bielefeld University

[1]lastname@cl.uni-heidelberg.de,

[2]{pheinisch,cimiano}@techfak.uni-bielefeld.de

Abstract

When assessing the similarity of arguments, researchers typically use approaches that do not provide interpretable evidence or justifications for their ratings. Hence, the features that determine argument similarity remain elusive. We address this issue by introducing *novel argument similarity metrics* that aim at high performance and explainability. We show that Abstract Meaning Representation (AMR) graphs can be useful for representing arguments, and that novel AMR graph metrics can offer explanations for argument similarity ratings. We start from the hypothesis that *similar premises* often lead to *similar conclusions*—and extend an approach for *AMR-based argument similarity rating* by estimating, in addition, the similarity of *conclusions* that we automatically infer from the arguments used as premises. We show that AMR similarity metrics make argument similarity judgements more *interpretable* and may even support *argument quality judgements*. Our approach provides significant performance improvements over strong baselines in a *fully unsupervised* setting. Finally, we make first steps to address the problem of reference-less evaluation of argumentative conclusion generations.

1 Introduction

Rating the similarity of arguments (Reimers et al., 2019) is a core task in argument mining and argument search (Maturana, 1988; Wachsmuth et al., 2017; Ajjour et al., 2019). Argument similarity ratings are also needed for (case-based) argument retrieval (Rissland et al., 1993; Chesnevar and Maguitman, 2004), data exploration via argument clustering, and even automated debaters (Slonim et al., 2021): to counter an opponent's argument, one may retrieve an argument similar to theirs, but of opposite stance to the topic (Wachsmuth et al., 2018).

Typically, argument similarity ratings are computed over 'bag-of-word' argument representations, or else over argument representations inferred with language models such as BERT (Devlin et al., 2019) or InferSent (Conneau et al., 2017). Two key advantages of such approaches are due to their unsupervised setup: First, unsupervised methods do not rely on human annotations, which are expensive and can be subject to noise and biases. Second, it has been shown for previous supervised methods that they have learned less about argumentation tasks than had been assumed, by exploiting spurious clues and artifacts from manually created data (Opitz and Frank, 2019; Niven and Kao, 2019). This has led to a recent interest in solving argumentation tasks in an *unsupervised manner*, e.g., by logical reasoning (Jo et al., 2021).

In this paper we will highlight that previous methods for rating argument similarity suffer from a common flaw: beyond shallow statistics (word matches in bag-of-word models, or word similarities in distributional space), they do not provide any rationale for their predictions, and the prediction process is in general not transparent. Therefore, we know only little about the following question:

- *Which argument features correlate with human argument similarity decisions?*

In this work, we undertake a first attempt at answering this question, by testing two hypotheses:

i) Representing arguments with Abstract Meaning Representations (AMRs) and using AMR graph metrics improves argument similarity rating and provides explanatory information.
ii) Extending arguments with inferred conclusions can improve argument similarity rating.

In the following §2 we discuss related work. §3 introduces our two key hypotheses, and §4 presents our argument similarity rating model and its implementation. In §5 we compare our model against strong baselines from prior work. In §6 we conduct several analyses to show how our approach can contribute to a better understanding of arguments, their

Proceedings of The 8th Workshop on Argument Mining, pages 24–35
Punta Cana, Dominican Republic, November 10–11, 2021.

conclusions and argument similarity ratings: we i) assess predictors of human argument similarity ratings to investigate the criteria that correlate with human ratings of argument similarity; ii) discuss potential advantages of using AMR for graph-based argumentation tasks in a concrete example, and iii) investigate how interpretable argument similarity computation can help assess the quality and usefulness of conclusions drawn from arguments in a reference-less conclusion evaluation setup.[1]

2 Related work

Argument similarity and search Assessing argument similarity is a key task in argument mining (Reimers et al., 2019; Lenz et al., 2019) and can enhance argument search (Maturana, 1988; Rissland et al., 1993; Wachsmuth et al., 2017; Ajjour et al., 2019; Chesnevar and Maguitman, 2004). Yet, while delivering solid performance on benchmarks, current methods fail to provide any deeper rationale for their predictions. It is thus not clear whether and to what extent spurious clues or other artifacts may influence the similarity decision (Opitz and Frank, 2019; Niven and Kao, 2019). In this paper, we aim at alleviating these issues by i) representing arguments with Abstract Meaning Representation (Banarescu et al., 2013) and conducting similarity assessment using well-defined graph metrics that provide explanatory AMR structure alignments; and ii) by investigating to what extent argument similarity can be projected to inferred conclusions.

Explanations in argumentation Until recently, the quest for explanations in argumentation was mainly focused on theory development. The *Toulmin model*, e.g., offers a theory of what is needed to make an argument complete (Toulmin, 2003). *Argumentation schemes*, which develop taxonomies of argument types and argumentation fallacies (Walton, 2005; Walton et al., 2008) can be viewed as mechanisms for explaining functions, strengths and weaknesses of arguments. Other research aims at studying the computational and formal aspects of argumentation, e.g. abstract argumentation (Dung, 1995) and *Bayesian argumentation* (Zenker, 2013). Research in empirical *argument mining* led researchers to investigate practical methods for explanations (Lawrence, 2021; Becker et al., 2021; Gunning et al., 2019; Rago et al., 2021; Vassiliades et al., 2021). While most approaches focus on the analysis of linguistic aspects (Lauscher et al., 2021), e.g., by extracting selected features (Aker et al., 2017; Lugini and Litman, 2018) or leveraging discourse knowledge in language models (Opitz, 2019), others exploit large background knowledge graphs (Kobbe et al., 2019; Paul et al., 2020; Yuan et al., 2021) such as ConceptNet (Liu and Singh, 2004; Speer et al., 2017) or DBpedia (Mendes et al., 2012). An advantage of our approach is the explicit graph alignment between two arguments' meaning graphs that better marks related structures, and that can help explain argument similarity judgements.

Argument mining with graphs There is growing interest in extracting graph structures from natural language arguments. Lenz et al. (2020), e.g., propose a pipeline for detecting and linking argumentative discourse units (ADUs). Al-Khatib et al. (2020) detect textual phrases and link them with *POS/NEG* relations, where *POS* indicates a positive influence and *NEG* a negative influence (inhibition), e.g., *sports NEG health issues*. However, such approaches lack finer semantic assessment: they do not distinguish word senses, and the linked entities (phrases or ADUs) are taken as atoms, which hampers explainability: when linking *sports* and *health issues* with a *NEG* relation, we cannot differentiate *sports NEG issues* and *sports NEG health* (only the former is correct). We target a finer analysis of argumentative texts, by representing them with dense AMR graphs. Additionally, by aligning graph representations of several arguments, our work paves the way for improved argument knowledge graph construction, aided by, or based on, AMR.

Generation of argumentative conclusions The task of conclusion generation has been recently investigated by Alshomary et al. (2020, 2021), and allows us to infer conclusions from given premises. Conclusion generation can be seen as the inverse of argument generation (Sato et al., 2015; Schiller et al., 2020). In this work, we show that by considering conclusions inferred from pairs of arguments, we can improve our argument similarity ratings.

3 Hypotheses

We base our models for explanatory argument similarity assessment on two hypotheses.

Hypothesis I: Abstract Meaning Representation (Banarescu et al., 2013) of arguments supports explainable argument similarity assessment AMRs are directed, rooted and acyclic

[1]https://github.com/Heidelberg-nlp/amr-argument-sim

graphs that aim at capturing a sentence's meaning in a machine-readable format. Edges are labeled with semantic relation types (e.g., negation, cause, etc.) and vertices denote either variables or concepts (variables are instances of concepts and allow us to capture coreferences) Hence, the AMR formalism captures various semantic phenomena that can play a role when assessing argument similarity.

E.g., besides the obviously useful aspect of negation, AMR captures semantic roles and predicate senses (Kingsbury and Palmer, 2002). While it is clear that similar arguments tend to involve similar predicates and predicate senses, semantic structure and role assignment may also play a role. For instance, the claims: *consumption of alcohol leads to depression* vs. *depression leads to consumption of alcohol* are clearly distinct, while sharing the same concepts. Other AMR facets may also be useful. E.g., AMR captures coreferences and resolving them in different ways can induce significant meaning differences, Finally, AMR includes key semantic relations (location, cause, possession, etc.) that are often implicit or underspecified in language, hence their explicit representation in AMR provides a rich basis for assessing arguments.

Arguments represented with AMR can be compared with AMR graph metrics (Cai and Knight, 2013; Damonte et al., 2017; Opitz et al., 2020) that also induce an explicit alignment between two argument graphs.

Hypothesis II: similar arguments lead to similar conclusions We hypothesize that a key feature of similar arguments is that they invite for similar conclusions. Analogously, dissimilar arguments tend to lead to differing conclusions. Consider the following two arguments:

i) *Cannabis can have negative effects on brain development of teens.*
ii) *Smoking cannabis is harmful for the lungs.*

The arguments are *dissimilar*, even though they share the same (negative) stance and argue from a similar perspective (health). This dissimilarity is also reflected in the conclusions that can be inferred from them: from i) we can infer that, i.a., *Cannabis consumption should be strictly controlled for age* or *Cannabis can have a negative impact on the brain*—while from ii) we could infer that *Cannabis, if consumed, should not be smoked* or *Cannabis smokers should get their lungs checked.*

As a complementary example, the *similarity* of two arguments may be reinforced by the *similarity* of their inferred conclusions, as shown below:

i) *Fracking can contaminate water and water wells and suck towns dry.*
ii) *As a water-poor state, fracking and its toxic wastewater presents a serious danger to our communities and ecosystems.*

Arguments i) and ii) are rated as similar, presumably because they point at detrimental ramifications of fracking related to water issues. This similarity is likely to be reflected in conclusions drawn from them, such as: i) *Fracking can lead to water issues* or ii) *Fracking poses dangers for water-poor states.*

4 Argument Similarity via AMR Metrics

According **Hyp I**, we represent arguments with AMR graphs and rate their similarity with AMR metrics. To test **Hyp II** we infer conclusions from arguments with language models and compute similarity on arguments extended with their conclusion.

4.1 Models

We propose three model variants that aim at explaining argument similarity. Given two arguments a, a' and their *extrapolated* conclusions c = $conclusion(a)$, c' = $conclusion(a')$, we compute similarity in the space of abstract meaning representation using a similarity function f in three alternative ways: i) $f(a, a')$, between the two arguments, ii) $f(c, c')$ between their conclusions, iii) $f(a \oplus c, a' \oplus c')$, i.e., between the combinations of argument a and its derived conclusion c, where we use a simple decomposable weighting:

$$f(a \oplus c, a' \oplus c') = \lambda f(a, a') + (1-\lambda) f(c, c') \quad (1)$$

If not specified otherwise, λ is set to 0.95.[2] The AMR metric f will be described in the following.

4.2 Implementation

AMR parser We parse all arguments from the data with the parser from `amrlib`[3], a fine-tuned T5 sequence-to-sequence model that achieves high scores on AMR benchmarks.

[2]We choose a high value of λ since, clearly, the premises are bound to host the primary evidence for similarity, while a conclusion may serve as auxiliary information. In our experiments, we also consider extreme decompositions ($\lambda \in \{0, 1\}$).

[3]`https://github.com/bjascob/amrlib`

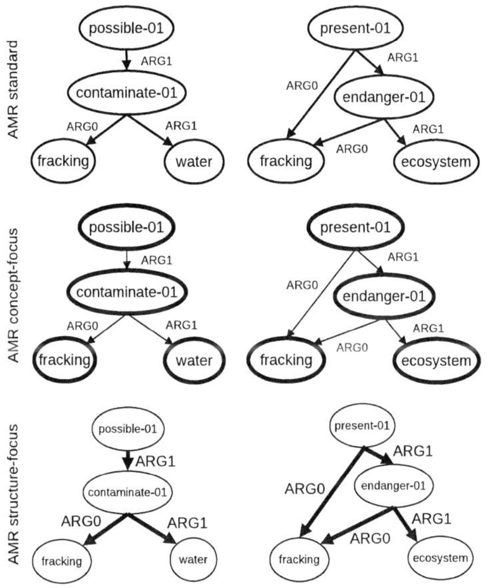

Figure 1: Standard, concept-focus and structure focus.

AMR metric We use S^2MATCH (Opitz et al., 2020), which is based on the AMR graph matching metric SMATCH (Cai and Knight, 2013), but admits graded concept similarity by matching concept nodes with GloVe embeddings (Pennington et al., 2014) and cosine similarity[4]. To find an optimal graph mapping, exactly like SMATCH, it leverages a hill-climber to approximate the NP-hard problem of aligning AMR graphs. Following the alignment step, the (soft) matching of propositions (triples) are scored with an F1 score. Since, so-far, little is known about the trade-off and interface between concrete and abstract semantics in human mental representations (Mkrtychian et al., 2019), we introduce two more variants that assess similarity from complementary perspectives: S2MATCH^{Concept} and S2MATCH^{Struct}. The first metric variant focuses on conceptual overlap (Fig. 1, middle), i.e. the more concrete semantic aspects, by putting a triple weight on concept matches. The second variant focuses on structural matches (Fig. 1, bottom), i.e., the more abstract semantic aspects, by putting triple weight on relation matches.

Conclusion generator We generate conclusions from arguments using the T5 model (Raffel et al., 2020) pre-trained on summarization tasks. To encourage the model to generate informative conclusions (as opposed to summaries), we further fine-tune it on premise-conclusion samples from Stab and Gurevych (2017), which contain intelligible and rational conclusions of high linguistic quality.[5]

5 Argument Similarity Prediction with AMR Metrics: Experiments

5.1 Setup

Data set and evaluation metric We use the UKP aspect corpus (Reimers et al., 2019), which contains 3,596 argument pairs on 28 topics that have been assigned a four-way similarity rating: highly similar (HS), somewhat similar (SS), not similar (NS), different topic/'can't decide' (DTORCD). Following Reimers et al. (2019), we frame the task as a binary prediction problem: *highly similar* (HS, SS) and *non-similar* (NS, DTORCD), and we conduct evaluation via cross validation with 4 folds. In every iteration, 7 topics serve as testing data, while the other 21 topics serve to tune a decision threshold of the metric score.[6] As in Reimers et al. (2019), we evaluate the F1 score for each of the two labels and the arithmetic F1 mean (macro F1).

Baselines We compare to previously established unsupervised baselines (Reimers et al., 2019): i) *Tfidf* calculates cosine similarity between Tfidf-weighted bag-of-word vectors; i) *InferSent-(FastText|Glove)* leverages sentence embeddings produced by the InferSent model (Conneau et al., 2017) based on either FastText (Bojanowski et al., 2016) or GloVe (Pennington et al., 2014) vectors, which are compared with cosine similarity; iii) *(GloVe|ELMo|BERT) Embedding* uses averaged GloVe embeddings or averaged contextualized embeddings from ELMo (Peters et al., 2018) and BERT (Devlin et al., 2019) language models.

5.2 Results

Best system Table 1 shows our main results. The AMR-based approach that is based on concept-focused S^2MATCH scores, taking both the argument and its inferred conclusion into account, obtains rank 1 (68.70 macro F1) and outperforms all baselines, including the BERT baseline. The difference is significant with $p < 0.005$ (Student t-test). This system is closely followed by other AMR-based systems, e.g., using concept-focused S^2MATCH that sees *only* the argument (68.17 macro

[4]If the cosine similarity exceeds $\tau = 0.95$.

[5]For further detail on this fine-tuning step see *Appendix*.

[6]Strictly speaking, this is not a fully unsupervised setup, however, we stick to this framing of the task to facilitate comparison to the previous work (Reimers et al., 2019).

	metric	model type	F1 score macro	F1 score sim	F1 score not sim	rank
	human	?	78.34	74.74	81.94	0
Baselines	random	-	48.01	34.31	61.71	16
Baselines	Tf-Idf	$f(a, a')$	61.18	52.30	70.07	10
Baselines	InfSnt-fText	$f(a, a')$	66.21	58.66	73.76	3/4
Baselines	InfSnt-GloVe	$f(a, a')$	64.94	54.72	75.17	9
Baselines	GloVe Emb.	$f(a, a')$	64.68	56.32	73.04	8
Baselines	ELMo Emb.	$f(a, a')$	64.47	53.55	75.38	7
Baselines	BERT Embe.	$f(a, a')$	65.39	52.32	**78.48**	6
Ours	AMR	$f(a, a')$	$65.44^{\pm 0.5}$	$55.23^{\pm 0.8}$	$75.66^{\pm 0.4}$	5
Ours	AMR	$f(c, c')$	$57.31^{\pm 0.6}$	$45.73^{\pm 1.2}$	$68.89^{\pm 0.4}$	14
Ours	AMR	$f(a \ominus c, a' \oplus c')$	$66.21^{\pm 0.3}$	$56.98^{\pm 0.6}$	$75.42^{\pm 0.1}$	3/4
Ours	AMR C-focus	$f(a, a')$	$68.17^{\pm 0.3}$	$59.2^{\pm 0.6}$	$77.14^{\pm 0.2}$	2 ◇♣
Ours	AMR C-focus	$f(c, c')$	$60.29^{\pm 0.5}$	$49.33^{\pm 0.4}$	$71.26^{\pm 0.8}$	13
Ours	AMR C-focus	$f(a \ominus c, a' \oplus c')$	$\mathbf{68.70}^{\pm 0.5}$	$\mathbf{60.35}^{\pm 1.0}$	$77.04^{\pm 0.1}$	**1** ◇♣
Ours	AMR S-focus	$f(a, a')$	$60.74^{\pm 0.5}$	$49.94^{\pm 0.8}$	$71.55^{\pm 0.5}$	12
Ours	AMR S-focus	$f(c, c')$	$56.48^{\pm 0.3}$	$44.96^{\pm 0.6}$	$67.99^{\pm 0.2}$	15
Ours	AMR S-focus	$f(a \ominus c, a' \oplus c')$	$61.14^{\pm 0.3}$	$49.74^{\pm 0.5}$	$72.55^{\pm 0.5}$	11

Table 1: Main results.

F1), and standard S²MATCH taking both argument and conclusion into account (66.21 macro F1).

Does incorporating conclusions help? Interestingly, assessing *only* conclusions *(rank 13/14/15)* outperforms the random baseline (rank 16). The low performance, in general, is expected, since clearly, argument similarity must be primarily determined based on the arguments, and hence, methods that rate the similarity of arguments only via a conclusion proxy have an obvious disadvantage. Hence, the more interesting question is: Do inferred conclusions provide complementary information for the task? Our results show a tendency that this is the case. All AMR-based models that take both conclusion and argument into account (model type $f(a \oplus c, a' \oplus c')$) outperform models that only see the arguments (AMR: +0.77; AMR concept-focus: +0.63; AMR struct-focus +0.40). At this point, however, we cannot explain whether this is due to useful reformulations or truly novel content that was generated, or a mix of both. We will investigate this question deeper in Section 6.

Argument similarity: driven by abstract or concrete semantics? The strong performance of the concept-focused AMR metric shows that a large overlap in concepts tends to correlate with human ratings more than an overlap in abstract semantic structure. The structure-focused AMR methods (last block in Table 1), while significantly outperforming the random baseline, lag behind all other baselines. Note, however, that the standard AMR-based model, which weights concept and structure overlap equally, provides strong performance, occupying rank 3-5 of all examined methods.[7]

predictor	Pearson's ρ $f(a, a)$	Pearson's ρ $f(c, c)$	Pearson's ρ $f(ac, a'c')$
Concepts	0.492‡	0.299‡	0.492‡
Sem. Role Labels (SRL)	0.400‡	0.185‡	0.402‡
Predicate Frames	0.355‡	0.232‡	0.357‡
Reentrancies (Coref.)	0.235‡	0.085‡	0.235‡
Named Entity (NER)	0.076‡	0.052‡	0.077‡
Negations	0.042†	-0.011	0.042†

Table 2: Semantic predictors of human argument similarity. †/‡: significant with p<0.05/p<0.005.

6 Analyses & Explainability

While these model ablations provide a global view of what matters in argument similarity rating, we now analyze the impact of finer semantic features.

6.1 Fine predictors of argument similarity

The previous experiment suggests that human argument similarity ratings can be modeled through a combination of different meaning facets, with a focus on concepts. We will now investigate how human argument similarity ratings correlate with specific meaning aspects represented in AMR graphs.

Setup For this we leverage fine-grained AMR metrics (Damonte et al., 2017) and compute semantic similarity with respect to 6 meaning aspects i) named entities (NER); ii) negation; iii) lexical concepts; iv) predicate frames; v) coreference and vi) semantic roles (SRL). Instead of merging the labels *somewhat similar* and *similar*, we keep them distinct and use a three-point Likert scale: 0 means *not similar* or *unrelated*, 0.5 means *somewhat similar*, and 1 means *highly similar*. To assess the correlation, we use **Pearson's correlation coefficient**.

Results of this univariate feature analysis are displayed in Table 2. As expected from the earlier experiment, shared concepts are strong predictors for argument similarity (Concepts, ρ=0.49). Also more abstract semantic features, such as similar semantic roles, have a solid signalling effect (SRL, ρ=0.40). Similarly, coreferences have predictive capacity, though at a lower range (ρ=0.23). On the other hand, negation or shared named entities do exhibit only small (yet still significant) predictive capacity (Negation, ρ=0.04 and NER, ρ=0.08).

[7]Motivated by this result, we conduct two extreme ablations: concept-only and structure-only metrics. While the structure-only variant shows worse results than AMR S-focus (macro F1 $\Delta f(a, a')$: -2.7), concept-only variant and concept-focused are more or less on par (macro F1 $\Delta f(a, a')$: -0.2).

The low correlation of NE overlap with human similarity ratings can in part be explained by the fact that we do not find many arguments where this could potentially matter (in our data, only 1 to 2 out of 1,000 nodes represent person NEs). However, if humans were to rate argument similarity in a dataset that features many *arguments from expert opinion* (Godden and Walton, 2006; Wagemans, 2011), named entity overlap may have a significant predictive capacity. Also negation might be more important than what we see in this analysis, since it can be expressed in alternative ways (e.g., through antonyms) that are not encoded as such in AMR.

6.2 Example case with alignment

To illustrate the potential of using AMR for connecting and assessing arguments, we study an example case in Fig. 2. It shows the graphs and graph alignments[8] that were found, for the actual arguments and their automatically induced conclusions, for our running example on fracking.

Observations about argument alignment The top figure shows the alignment of the two argument graphs, where important substructures have been linked. *Contamination of water and water wells* is linked to *endangering of our communities and ecosystems* (orange nodes and alignment). It is also appropriate that *towns that are sucked dry* is linked to *water poor state* (blue). This link is very valuable since these statements stand in a semantic EXACERBATE-relation that may be important for the arguments' similarity (the water-poverty of states is exacerbated if towns are sucked dry). Ideally, we would like such alignments to be labeled with a corresponding semantic relation. In future work, we plan to achieve this by leveraging commonsense knowledge graphs like ConceptNet.

Observations about conclusion alignment The bottom figure shows the alignment of the automatically deduced conclusions. For the left argument, the conclusion fails to produce an abstraction and more or less repeats the argument. For the argument on the right-hand side, however, the conclusion generator produced a more informative conclusion. From the input argument it concludes that *Fracking and its toxic wastewater are a threat to the environment*— focusing on the negative environmental impact of fracking. This triggers a graph alignment which adds valuable new information (see clouds with dotted margins). The alignment makes explicit that *water wells* and *toxic wastewater* stand in a correspondence in the context of *fracking*. Specifically, we see how the *contamination of wells* (left graphs) happens: wells are polluted with toxic wastewater (right graphs). Additionally, the left graph helps explain parts of the meaning of the right graph: Fracking and toxic wastewater are a threat *because* fracking *contaminates* water and water wells.

6.3 Investigations of conclusion quality

An inferred conclusion can be more or less abstract or dissimilar from the input argument. This raises the question of the *quality* of an inferred conclusion. In fact, we can apply our AMR similarity metrics to quantify the similarity of an argument and its inferred conclusion—formally: $f(a, c)$—which may be indicative of the *novelty* of a conclusion in relation to its premise. Hence, we investigate how AMR similarity metrics can be used to measure the *novelty* of a conclusion relative to its premise. Another aspect of conclusion quality is its *validity or justification*, i.e., to what extent it can be trusted. Clearly, a conclusion that is very similar to the premise has a high chance of being valid (as long as the premise is), whereas this is uncertain for parts of its meaning that do not match the premise.

In current research, not much is known about how to rate the quality of a conclusion drawn from an argument. We explore this question by performing a manual assessment of different quality aspects of conclusions, and investigate to what extent these can be assessed with our AMR similarty metrics.

We randomly sample 100 argument-conclusion pairs per topic. The pairs are given to two annotators whom we ask to assign binary ratings regarding two questions: i) Is the conclusion *justified* based on the premise? With this we aim to assess whether the argument legitimizes the conclusion; and ii) Does the conclusion introduce some *novelty* relative to the argument? This should be denied if, e.g., the conclusion repeats the premise.

As shown in Fig. 3, we measure moderate IAA, with slightly higher agreement for *novelty*. The results show that T5 often manages to produce either valid (*justification*, ≈65-75% of cases) or novel content (*novelty*, ≈ 50-60%), but struggles to produce conclusions that fulfill both criteria (*justification & novetly:* ≈ 25-35% of cases).

[8]The alignments were computed with S2M$^{Concept+Concl.}$

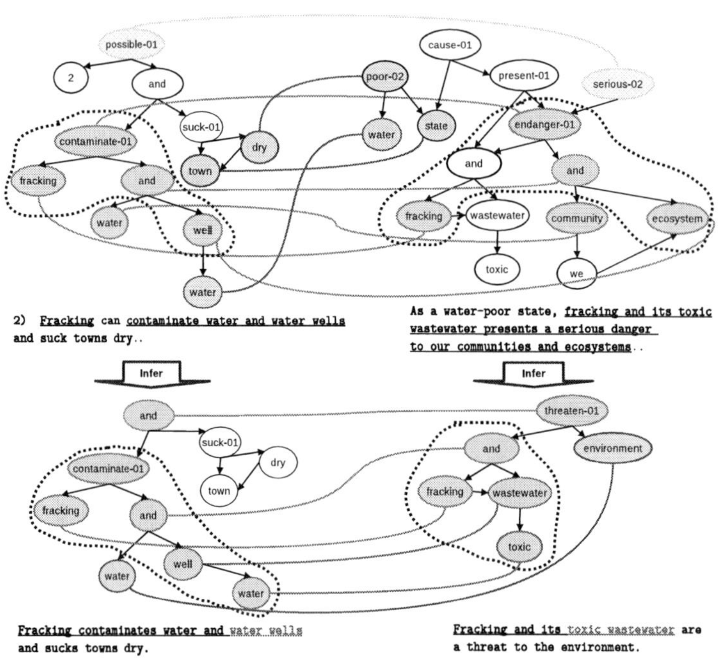

Figure 2: Full example (edge-labels omitted for simplified display) of explicit alignments between argument graphs (top) and automatically induced conclusions (bottom). Here, the conclusions help explaining argument similarity, since the alignment connects *fracking* in both graphs, as well as *water wells* and *toxic wastewater*, showing how *contaminating of the wells* (left graphs) actually happens: wells are polluted with toxic wastewater (right graphs).

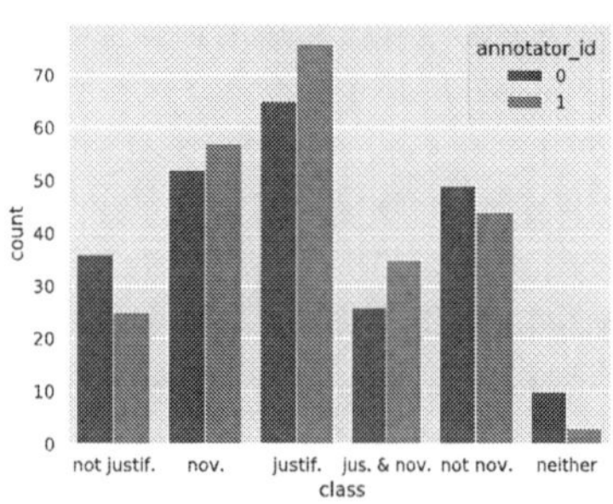

Figure 3: Annotation results of two quality aspects with IAA: $\mathcal{K}$=0.49 (*justification*) and $\mathcal{K}$=0.57 (*novelty*).

6.4 Can we predict conclusion quality?

We now extend the use of our metrics to assess conclusion quality by computing the similarity of argument and conclusion: $f(a, c)$.[9] We calculate six graph similarity statistics of their AMRs to finally produce an aggregate score assessment: i) $|a \cap c|/|a|$ measures the relative amount of premise content that is contained in the conclusion ('precision'); ii) $|a \cap c|/|c|$ measures the relative amount of conclusion content contained in the premise ('recall'); iii) the harmonic mean of i) and ii) corresponds to main metric $f(a, c)$; and features iv-vi) apply a non-linear function to i)-iii), measuring the proximity to the feature means[10], which expresses the idea that a conclusion that is both novel *and* justified may be situated at mean similarity of premise and conclusion, measured by $f(a, c)$.

We use a Linear SVM for predicting, in three binary classification tasks, either *justification*; *novelty* or *both*, using the feature set i)-vi).[11] Results are seen in Table 3. Despite the small training data, performance is good for predicting *justified* (max. 68.6 F1) or *novel* (max. 70.0 F1). But predicting a conclusion to be *novel & justified* yields substantially lower performance (max. 58.3 F1), while still above baseline. Feature correlations show that *novel* is negatively (-) associated with $f(a, c)$ (i-iii), while *justified* is positively (+) correlated with $f(a, c)$ (i-iii). We find much weaker correlation for *novel&justified*, tending to *mean* similarity (iv-vi).

[9] AMR metrics have been previously used in NLG evaluation by Opitz and Frank (2021).

[10] I.e., given the mean μ of a feature x, the new value x'_i of datum i is $x'_i = 1 - (\mu - x_i)^2$.

[11] We average all results over 25 runs of leave-one-out cross validations. When predicting either justification, or novelty, we average over the two annotators; when predicting justification *and* novelty, to increase the positive class labels slightly, the gold target are cases where one or two annotators annotated both *novel* and *justified*.

	justified	novel	both
random	0.5	0.5	0.5
i) $\|a \cap c\|/\|a\|$	59.0 ++	58.7 --	53.4
ii) $\|a \cap c\|/\|c\|$	**68.6** +++	64.3 ---	52.4
iii) harm. mean i), ii)	61.3 +++	61.9 ---	52.2
iv) proximity to mean i	49.8	55.1 --	56.5 +
v) proximity to mean ii	35.9	52.0	**58.3** +
vi) proximity to mean iii	30.5	54.4 -	58.1 +
i-vi combination	67.5	**70.0**	53.8

Table 3: Macro F1 scores for predicted conclusion quality using AMR-based models $f(a, c)$, assessing various aspects. For single features, + show positive correlation; - negative correlation (levels 0.05, 0.005, 0.0005).

	similarity (SIM) features				
feat. id	i	ii	iii	iv	v
	faa'	fcc'	$faa' - fcc'$	$(fac - fa'c')/2$	hum
P.'s ρ	0.83	**-22.81**	**26.6**	**-9.37**	**-14.72**
p-value	> 0.05	**1.2e^{-43}**	**2.8e^{-59}**	**1.8e^{-8}**	**7.3e^{-19}**

Table 4: Predictors of conclusion usefulness.

a)	*Because you may save up to eight lives through organ donation and enhance many others through tissue donation.*
c)	*organ donation is a great way to save up to eight lives.*
a')	*This medical research is important to understanding diseases in humans so that lives may be saved and improved.*
c')	*medical research is important to understand diseases in humans*

Table 5: AMR metrics detecting dissimilar arguments.

Our analyses support **Hyp1** in that AMR metrics are able to rate *similarity* of arguments, of conclusions and of argument-conclusion pairs, and this also allows us to determine if a conclusion is *novel* or *justified*. While many justified conclusions are highly similar to the premise, **deciding their justification is difficult if they involve novelty**. We argue this is because *justification* cannot be determined from premises alone, but requires external knowledge. We leave this issue for future work.

6.5 Conclusion usefulness

Finally, we revisit our **Hyp2**, that by extending arguments with inferred conclusions, we can support assessment of argument similarity. This raises the issue of the *usefulness* of a conclusion, in terms of achieving good performance and interpretability of an argument similarity method. The aspect of the *usefulness of a conclusion* clearly differs from the question of its *quality*. For one, it is possible that a good conclusion is not useful for argument similarity rating, simply because the assessment of the paired argument premises already provides a confident and precise similarity judgement. On the other hand, a mediocre conclusion could provide complementary indications that can support the similarity judgement. In this final section we aim to assess factors that can determine this usefulness.

Operationalizing conclusion usefulness We define a score $\mathcal{U}$ for the usefulness of a conclusion, based on a human rating y, the conclusion similarity $f(c, c')$ and argument similarity $f(a, a')$, as

$$\mathcal{U} = \frac{1}{1+(y-f(c,c'))^2} + (y - f(a, a'))^2, \quad (2)$$

where $\mathcal{U}$ is maximized *iff* the automatic similarity rating of the conclusions does not differ from the human rating, while the automatic similarity rating of the premises differs maximally from the human rating. It is in exactly these situations that a conclusion assessment will prove most useful.

Features for assessing conclusion usefulness $\mathcal{U}$ We assume the following features for modeling the usefulness of a conclusion, which we compute with our **similarity function** f: i) the similarity of the arguments $f(a, a')$; ii) the similarity of the conclusions $f(c, c')$; iii) the (signed) difference between the argument and the conclusion similarities $f(a, a') - f(c, c')$; iv) we compute the (signed) difference between the similarity of (a, c) and (a', c'): $\frac{f(a,c)-f(a',c')}{2}$; finally, v) y is the human rating.

Results Table 4 shows that the highest predictive power for conclusion *usefulness* is feature iii): the similarity of the two arguments *minus* the similarity of the two conclusions. It exhibits a highly significant positive correlation with conclusion usefulness, and relates to the following scenario: If two arguments are considered to be similar, *but* the conclusions as dissimilar, this may signal that the arguments are rated dissimilar by the human, and the high initial rating may be reconsidered.

Table 5 shows a data sample where the conclusions help to correct an initial, over-optimistic similarity rating of the premises. The premises are rated *dissimilar* by the human, but since they contain similar concepts, such as *saving lives*, the AMR metric assigns a high similarity rating (0.7) to the pair (a, a'). However, the automatically generated conclusions (c, c') are assigned low(er) similarity (0.2). The low rating can be explained by the fact that the conclusion generator has distilled different conclusions from the premises that reflect the different foci of the arguments: the first proposes that organ donations are good for saving lives, while the second argument proposes that generally more medical research should be conducted.

7 Discussion

Explanation dimensions Our argument similarity rating approach may provide explanations in various dimensions. i) First and foremost, the **explicit alignment and similarity computation based on AMR and AMR graph metrics**, by relating similar concepts between arguments and their conclusions, provides insight into which components of two argument AMRs relate to each other, with individual alignment scores, and to what extent they congtribute to the overall score. Especially in light of recent observations showing supervised models to be prone to superficial cues in data sets (Opitz and Frank, 2019; Niven and Kao, 2019; Heinzerling, 2020; Jo et al., 2021), this property is desirable. ii) We apply the fine-grained AMR decomposition of Damonte et al. (2017) in terms of semantic phenomena, such as negation or semantic roles. This can further **illuminate in which ways an argument pair is similar/dissimilar**. iii) By **taking into account the similarity of automatically inferred conclusions**, the similarity computed for premises may be re-adjusted in case the similarity of the inferred conclusions strongly differs.

On a related note, the AMR similarity statistics enabled us to **gain some first indications of what could be considered a good conclusion** (without even matching against a reference): e.g., our qualitative evaluations indicate that good conclusions tend to be neither very similar, nor very dissimilar to the premise. This seems plausible, since (too) high similarity may indicate a mere summary (reducing novelty), while (too) low similarity may indicate a lack of coherence (reducing validity).

Perspectives of improvement and future work A key component of our approach that influences all aspects of explainability described above, are the similarity metrics computed over AMRs. While we proposed one variant of S^{2}MATCH that focuses specifically on the similarity of concepts, further variations could be explored. We may also consider more recent AMR metrics that measure meaning similarity via graph kernels (Opitz et al., 2021).

Our approach also hinges on the quality of the inferred conclusions. The conclusions we obtained are often either *justified* or *novel*, but less often satisfy both conditions. In addition, we find that the degree of novelty is often rather small, perhaps reflecting that the T5 generator was pre-trained on summarization data and hence may tend to produce inferences that are *not* novel, since novelty is not a common characteristics of a summary. On the positive side, our approach can be fueled by an increasing amount of research on argument conclusion generation (Alshomary et al., 2020, 2021). In general, and particularly for our approach, it will be interesting to work with systems that produce not only a single, but multiple valid conclusions. Considering relations *across and within two conclusion sets* inferred from two premises may provide key information on argument similarity.

Finally, by measuring the similarity of premises and their conclusions, our approach could shed light on another important question: ***how to assess novelty and justification of a conclusion without a reference***? This is an important question for research on argument conclusion generation since it lacks methods that can judge the quality of conclusions in the absence of (costly) references.

8 Conclusion

In this paper, we investigated two hypotheses: i) **AMR meaning representation and graph metrics help in assessing argument similarity**, ii) **automatically inferred conclusions can aid or reinforce the similarity assessment of arguments**. We find solid evidence for the first hypothesis, especially when slightly adapting AMR metrics to focus more on concrete concepts found in arguments. We find weak evidence that supports the second hypothesis, i.e., metrics improve consistently, but by small margins, when they are allowed to additionally consider the AMRs of automatically inferred conclusions. We believe, however, that more substantial gains may be obtained in future work, by improving conclusion generation models such that they produce content that is both *valid and novel*. Finally, we have made first steps towards a *reference-less* metric for assessing novelty and justification of generated conclusions.

Acknowledgements

We are grateful to the anonymous reviewers for their valuable comments. This work has been partially funded by the DFG through the project ACCEPT as part of the Priority Program "Robust Argumentation Machines" (SPP1999).

References

Yamen Ajjour, Henning Wachsmuth, Johannes Kiesel, Martin Potthast, Matthias Hagen, and Benno Stein. 2019. Data acquisition for argument search: The args. me corpus. In *Joint German/Austrian Conference on Artificial Intelligence (Künstliche Intelligenz)*, pages 48–59. Springer.

Ahmet Aker, Alfred Sliwa, Yuan Ma, Ruishen Lui, Niravkumar Borad, Seyedeh Ziyaei, and Mina Ghobadi. 2017. What works and what does not: Classifier and feature analysis for argument mining. In *Proceedings of the 4th Workshop on Argument Mining*, pages 91–96, Copenhagen, Denmark. Association for Computational Linguistics.

Khalid Al-Khatib, Yufang Hou, Henning Wachsmuth, Charles Jochim, Francesca Bonin, and Benno Stein. 2020. End-to-end argumentation knowledge graph construction. In *Proceedings of the AAAI Conference on Artificial Intelligence*, volume 34, pages 7367–7374.

Milad Alshomary, Wei-Fan Chen, Timon Gurcke, and Henning Wachsmuth. 2021. Belief-based generation of argumentative claims. In *Proceedings of the 16th Conference of the European Chapter of the Association for Computational Linguistics: Main Volume*, pages 224–233, Online. Association for Computational Linguistics.

Milad Alshomary, Shahbaz Syed, Martin Potthast, and Henning Wachsmuth. 2020. Target inference in argument conclusion generation. In *Proceedings of the 58th Annual Meeting of the Association for Computational Linguistics*, pages 4334–4345, Online. Association for Computational Linguistics.

Laura Banarescu, Claire Bonial, Shu Cai, Madalina Georgescu, Kira Griffitt, Ulf Hermjakob, Kevin Knight, Philipp Koehn, Martha Palmer, and Nathan Schneider. 2013. Abstract Meaning Representation for sembanking. In *Proceedings of the 7th Linguistic Annotation Workshop and Interoperability with Discourse*, pages 178–186, Sofia, Bulgaria. Association for Computational Linguistics.

Maria Becker, Siting Liang, and Anette Frank. 2021. Reconstructing implicit knowledge with language models. In *Proceedings of Deep Learning Inside Out (DeeLIO): The 2nd Workshop on Knowledge Extraction and Integration for Deep Learning Architectures*, pages 11–24, Online. Association for Computational Linguistics.

Piotr Bojanowski, Edouard Grave, Armand Joulin, and Tomas Mikolov. 2016. Enriching word vectors with subword information. *arXiv preprint arXiv:1607.04606*.

Shu Cai and Kevin Knight. 2013. Smatch: an evaluation metric for semantic feature structures. In *Proceedings of the 51st Annual Meeting of the Association for Computational Linguistics (Volume 2: Short Papers)*, pages 748–752, Sofia, Bulgaria. Association for Computational Linguistics.

Carlos Iván Chesnevar and Ana G Maguitman. 2004. Arguenet: An argument-based recommender system for solving web search queries. In *2004 2nd International IEEE Conference on'Intelligent Systems'. Proceedings (IEEE Cat. No. 04EX791)*, volume 1, pages 282–287. IEEE.

Alexis Conneau, Douwe Kiela, Holger Schwenk, Loïc Barrault, and Antoine Bordes. 2017. Supervised learning of universal sentence representations from natural language inference data. In *Proceedings of the 2017 Conference on Empirical Methods in Natural Language Processing*, pages 670–680, Copenhagen, Denmark. Association for Computational Linguistics.

Marco Damonte, Shay B. Cohen, and Giorgio Satta. 2017. An incremental parser for Abstract Meaning Representation. In *Proceedings of the 15th Conference of the European Chapter of the Association for Computational Linguistics: Volume 1, Long Papers*, pages 536–546, Valencia, Spain. Association for Computational Linguistics.

Jacob Devlin, Ming-Wei Chang, Kenton Lee, and Kristina Toutanova. 2019. BERT: Pre-training of deep bidirectional transformers for language understanding. In *Proceedings of the 2019 Conference of the North American Chapter of the Association for Computational Linguistics: Human Language Technologies, Volume 1 (Long and Short Papers)*, pages 4171–4186, Minneapolis, Minnesota. Association for Computational Linguistics.

Phan Minh Dung. 1995. On the acceptability of arguments and its fundamental role in nonmonotonic reasoning, logic programming and n-person games. *Artificial intelligence*, 77(2):321–357.

David M Godden and Douglas Walton. 2006. Argument from expert opinion as legal evidence: Critical questions and admissibility criteria of expert testimony in the american legal system. *Ratio Juris*, 19(3):261–286.

David Gunning, Mark Stefik, Jaesik Choi, Timothy Miller, Simone Stumpf, and Guang-Zhong Yang. 2019. Xai—explainable artificial intelligence. *Science Robotics*, 4(37).

Benjamin Heinzerling. 2020. Nlp's clever hans moment has arrived. *Journal of Cognitive Science*, 21(1):159–168.

Yohan Jo, Seojin Bang, Chris Reed, and Eduard H. Hovy. 2021. Classifying argumentative relations using logical mechanisms and argumentation schemes. *CoRR*, abs/2105.07571.

Paul Kingsbury and Martha Palmer. 2002. From treebank to propbank. In *Proceedings of the Third International Conference on Language Resources and Evaluation (LREC'02)*.

Jonathan Kobbe, Juri Opitz, Maria Becker, Ioana Hulpus, Heiner Stuckenschmidt, and Anette Frank. 2019. Exploiting Background Knowledge for Argumentative Relation Classification. In *2nd Conference on Language, Data and Knowledge (LDK 2019)*, volume 70 of *OpenAccess Series in Informatics (OASIcs)*, pages 8:1–8:14, Dagstuhl, Germany. Schloss Dagstuhl–Leibniz-Zentrum fuer Informatik.

Anne Lauscher, Henning Wachsmuth, Iryna Gurevych, and Goran Glavaš. 2021. Scientia potentia est – on the role of knowledge in computational argumentation.

John Lawrence. 2021. *Explainable argument mining*. Ph.D. thesis, University of Dundee.

Mirko Lenz, Stefan Ollinger, Premtim Sahitaj, and Ralph Bergmann. 2019. Semantic textual similarity measures for case-based retrieval of argument graphs. In *International Conference on Case-Based Reasoning*, pages 219–234. Springer.

Mirko Lenz, Premtim Sahitaj, Sean Kallenberg, Christopher Coors, Lorik Dumani, Ralf Schenkel, and Ralph Bergmann. 2020. Towards an argument mining pipeline transforming texts to argument graphs. *Computational Models of Argument: Proceedings of COMMA 2020*, 326:263.

Hugo Liu and Push Singh. 2004. Conceptnet—a practical commonsense reasoning tool-kit. *BT technology journal*, 22(4):211–226.

Luca Lugini and Diane Litman. 2018. Argument component classification for classroom discussions. In *Proceedings of the 5th Workshop on Argument Mining*, pages 57–67, Brussels, Belgium. Association for Computational Linguistics.

Humberto R Maturana. 1988. Reality: The search for objectivity or the quest for a compelling argument. *The Irish journal of psychology*, 9(1):25–82.

Pablo Mendes, Max Jakob, and Christian Bizer. 2012. DBpedia: A multilingual cross-domain knowledge base. In *Proceedings of the Eighth International Conference on Language Resources and Evaluation (LREC'12)*, pages 1813–1817, Istanbul, Turkey. European Language Resources Association (ELRA).

Nadezhda Mkrtychian, Evgeny Blagovechtchenski, Diana Kurmakaeva, Daria Gnedykh, Svetlana Kostromina, and Yury Shtyrov. 2019. Concrete vs. abstract semantics: from mental representations to functional brain mapping. *Frontiers in human neuroscience*, 13:267.

Timothy Niven and Hung-Yu Kao. 2019. Probing neural network comprehension of natural language arguments. In *Proceedings of the 57th Annual Meeting of the Association for Computational Linguistics*, pages 4658–4664, Florence, Italy. Association for Computational Linguistics.

Juri Opitz. 2019. Argumentative relation classification as plausibility ranking. In *Proceedings of the 15th Conference on Natural Language Processing (KONVENS 2019): Long Papers*, pages 193–202, Erlangen, Germany. German Society for Computational Linguistics & Language Technology.

Juri Opitz, Angel Daza, and Anette Frank. 2021. Weisfeiler-leman in the bamboo: Novel amr graph metrics and a benchmark for amr graph similarity. *arXiv preprint arXiv:2108.11949*.

Juri Opitz and Anette Frank. 2019. Dissecting content and context in argumentative relation analysis. In *Proceedings of the 6th Workshop on Argument Mining*, pages 25–34, Florence, Italy. Association for Computational Linguistics.

Juri Opitz and Anette Frank. 2021. Towards a decomposable metric for explainable evaluation of text generation from AMR. In *Proceedings of the 16th Conference of the European Chapter of the Association for Computational Linguistics: Main Volume*, pages 1504–1518, Online. Association for Computational Linguistics.

Juri Opitz, Letitia Parcalabescu, and Anette Frank. 2020. AMR similarity metrics from principles. *Transactions of the Association for Computational Linguistics*, 8:522–538.

Debjit Paul, Juri Opitz, Maria Becker, Jonathan Kobbe, Graeme Hirst, and Anette Frank. 2020. Argumentative relation classification with background knowledge. In *Computational Models of Argument*, pages 319–330. IOS Press.

Jeffrey Pennington, Richard Socher, and Christopher Manning. 2014. GloVe: Global vectors for word representation. In *Proceedings of the 2014 Conference on Empirical Methods in Natural Language Processing (EMNLP)*, pages 1532–1543, Doha, Qatar. Association for Computational Linguistics.

Matthew E. Peters, Mark Neumann, Mohit Iyyer, Matt Gardner, Christopher Clark, Kenton Lee, and Luke Zettlemoyer. 2018. Deep contextualized word representations. In *Proceedings of the 2018 Conference of the North American Chapter of the Association for Computational Linguistics: Human Language Technologies, Volume 1 (Long Papers)*, pages 2227–2237, New Orleans, Louisiana. Association for Computational Linguistics.

Colin Raffel, Noam Shazeer, Adam Roberts, Katherine Lee, Sharan Narang, Michael Matena, Yanqi Zhou, Wei Li, and Peter J. Liu. 2020. Exploring the limits of transfer learning with a unified text-to-text transformer. *Journal of Machine Learning Research*, 21(140):1–67.

A Rago, O Cocarascu, C Bechlivanidis, D Lagnado, and F Toni. 2021. Argumentative explanations for interactive recommendations. *Artificial Intelligence*, 296:1–22.

Nils Reimers, Benjamin Schiller, Tilman Beck, Johannes Daxenberger, Christian Stab, and Iryna Gurevych. 2019. Classification and clustering of arguments with contextualized word embeddings. In *Proceedings of the 57th Annual Meeting of the Association for Computational Linguistics*, pages 567–578, Florence, Italy. Association for Computational Linguistics.

Edwina L Rissland, David B Skalak, and M Timur Friedman. 1993. Bankxx: a program to generate argument through case-base search. In *Proceedings of the 4th international conference on Artificial intelligence and law*, pages 117–124.

Misa Sato, Kohsuke Yanai, Toshinori Miyoshi, Toshihiko Yanase, Makoto Iwayama, Qinghua Sun, and Yoshiki Niwa. 2015. End-to-end argument generation system in debating. In *Proceedings of ACL-IJCNLP 2015 System Demonstrations*, pages 109–114.

Benjamin Schiller, Johannes Daxenberger, and Iryna Gurevych. 2020. Aspect-controlled neural argument generation. *arXiv preprint arXiv:2005.00084*.

Noam Slonim, Yonatan Bilu, Carlos Alzate, Roy Bar-Haim, Ben Bogin, Francesca Bonin, Leshem Choshen, Edo Cohen-Karlik, Lena Dankin, Lilach Edelstein, et al. 2021. An autonomous debating system. *Nature*, 591(7850):379–384.

Robyn Speer, Joshua Chin, and Catherine Havasi. 2017. Conceptnet 5.5: An open multilingual graph of general knowledge. In *Thirty-first AAAI conference on artificial intelligence*.

Christian Stab and Iryna Gurevych. 2017. Parsing argumentation structures in persuasive essays. *Computational Linguistics*, 43(3):619–659.

Stephen E Toulmin. 2003. *The uses of argument*. Cambridge university press.

Alexandros Vassiliades, Nick Bassiliades, and Theodore Patkos. 2021. Argumentation and explainable artificial intelligence: a survey. *The Knowledge Engineering Review*, 36.

Henning Wachsmuth, Martin Potthast, Khalid Al Khatib, Yamen Ajjour, Jana Puschmann, Jiani Qu, Jonas Dorsch, Viorel Morari, Janek Bevendorff, and Benno Stein. 2017. Building an argument search engine for the web. In *Proceedings of the 4th Workshop on Argument Mining*, pages 49–59.

Henning Wachsmuth, Shahbaz Syed, and Benno Stein. 2018. Retrieval of the best counterargument without prior topic knowledge. In *Proceedings of the 56th Annual Meeting of the Association for Computational Linguistics (Volume 1: Long Papers)*, pages 241–251, Melbourne, Australia. Association for Computational Linguistics.

Jean HM Wagemans. 2011. The assessment of argumentation from expert opinion. *Argumentation*, 25(3):329–339.

Douglas Walton. 2005. Justification of argumentation schemes. *The Australasian Journal of Logic*, 3.

Douglas Walton, Christopher Reed, and Fabrizio Macagno. 2008. *Argumentation schemes*. Cambridge University Press.

Jian Yuan, Zhongyu Wei, Donghua Zhao, Qi Zhang, and Changjian Jiang. 2021. Leveraging argumentation knowledge graph for interactive argument pair identification. In *Findings of the Association for Computational Linguistics: ACL-IJCNLP 2021*, pages 2310–2319, Online. Association for Computational Linguistics.

Frank Zenker. 2013. Bayesian argumentation: The practical side of probability. In *Bayesian Argumentation*, pages 1–11. Springer.

A Appendix

A.1 Fine-tuning the conclusion generator

To fine-tune the sequence to sequence language model T5 for conclusion generation, we create training data from the the persuasive essays dataset of Stab and Gurevych (2017) as follows: From all premise-conclusion-pairs annotated in this dataset, we retrieved all claims with their annotated premises. In addition, we employ all annotated major claims with their supportive claims as premise-conclusion-pairs.[12] We discarded samples for which we cannot retrieve any premise. Each resulting premises-conclusion-sample has 3.1 premises on average.

We split the data into 80% instances for training, and 10% for validation and testing, each. For each sample, we input the concatenated premises by encoding `summarize:<premises>` and train with the conclusion as a target by applying a cross-entropy loss for each token. We guide the training process with an early stopping mechanism to ensure the best accuracy (ignoring padding tokens) on our validation dataset. In inference, we apply a 5-beam-search in combination with sampling over the 20 most probable tokens per inference step.

To assess the quality and relatedness of the generated conclusions, we manually compared the predicted conclusions with their premises in our test split. Since we observed promising and appropriate conclusion generations, we were encouraged to utilize the learned capabilities of the fine-tuned language model to generate conclusions for the argumentative sentences in the UKP aspect corpus.

[12] Whenever we encounter multiple premises or supportive claims of a single claim, we concatenate them in document order.

Image Retrieval for Arguments Using Stance-Aware Query Expansion

Johannes Kiesel
Bauhaus-Universität Weimar
johannes.kiesel@uni-weimar.de

Nico Reichenbach
Leipzig University
nico.reichenbach@posteo.de

Benno Stein
Bauhaus-Universität Weimar
benno.stein@uni-weimar.de

Martin Potthast
Leipzig University
martin.potthast@uni-leipzig.de

Abstract

Many forms of argumentation employ images as persuasive means, but research in argument mining has been focused on verbal argumentation so far. This paper shows how to integrate images into argument mining research, specifically into argument retrieval. By exploiting the sophisticated image representations of keyword-based image search, we propose to use semantic query expansion for both the pro and the con stance to retrieve "argumentative images" for the respective stance. Our results indicate that even simple expansions provide a strong baseline, reaching a precision@10 of 0.49 for images being (1) on-topic, (2) argumentative, and (3) on-stance. An in-depth analysis reveals a high topic dependence of the retrieval performance and shows the need to further investigate on images providing contextual information.

Figure 1: Mock-up of an image search engine for arguments, featuring a query box, checkboxes to filter, and results categorized as pro (left) and con (right) images.

1 Introduction

Images are a prominent form of non-verbal communication. Images convey messages in diverse ways including scribbles, concept drawings, (produced) photos, data visualizations, or internet memes. Moreover, images can serve as an inspiration or an overview of the topic at hand. They play a key role in public discourse (Woods and Hahner, 2019) and in expressing personal opinion (Heiskanen, 2017), e.g., in the form of political memes. Spread "virally," they can gain a large followership on social media and influence political decision-making (Watt, 2015) or serve as a form of evidence for troublesome events. For example, about 150,000 images are uploaded to Facebook every minute.[1] All of these uses often form an integral part of argumentative writing or speechmaking. Composing an argumentative text or speech hence does not only include the retrieval and arrangement of written arguments, but also that of relevant "argumentative images" to go along with them.

However, though the retrieval of written arguments has become a well-established line of research, the paper at hand is the first of its kind to define and tackle the task of retrieving "argumentative images." Inspired by existing argument search interfaces, Figure 1 illustrates how an image search engine for arguments might look.

By proposing stance-aware query expansion, this paper shows how to harness existing keyword-based image retrieval technology for the task of retrieving images for arguments. The key assumption of this expansion is that adding terms to the user's query that indicate a stance (i.e., pro or con the query's underlying issue), then images retrieved for the expanded queries support that stance. Figure 1 illustrates the desired effect: the shown images stem from Google's image search after having expanded the query `nuclear energy` with either the term `good` (images on the left-hand side) or the term `anti` (right-hand side).

[1] https://www.domo.com/learn/data-never-sleeps-8

Proceedings of The 8th Workshop on Argument Mining, pages 36–45
Punta Cana, Dominican Republic, November 10–11, 2021. ©2021 Association for Computational Linguistics

In what follows, Section 3 introduces the task of "argumentative image" retrieval, Section 4 outlines our approach to this task—stance-aware query expansion—including three methodological variants, and the Sections 5 and 6 detail important elements of our experimental setting as well as evaluation results for the three proposed methods.

2 Related Work

Al-Khatib, 2019 defines an argumentation strategy as "a set of principles that guides the selection and arrangement of arguments (plus contextual information) in an argumentative discourse." While research in computational argumentation has so far focused on verbal argumentation, real-world discourse often integrates images to great effect, ranging from memes emerging on the spur of of a moment to figures summarizing months of research. Discourse analyses thus often include images (e.g., Frohmann, 1992; Farkas and Bene, 2020).

Images for Arguments Images can provide contextual information and express, underline, or popularize an opinion (Dove, 2012), thereby taking the form of subjective statements (Dunaway, 2018). Some images express both a premise and a conclusion, making them full arguments (Roque, 2012; Grancea, 2017). Other images may provide contextual information only and need to be combined with a conclusion to form an argument. In this regard, a recent SemEval task distinguished a total of 22 persuasion techniques in memes alone (Dimitrov et al., 2021). Moreover, argument quality dimensions like acceptability, credibility, emotional appeal, and sufficiency (Wachsmuth et al., 2017a) all apply to arguments that include images as well. And as a kind of visual argumentation scheme (a "stereotypical pattern of human reasoning"; Walton et al., 2008), some images are frequently adapted to different topics (Heiskanen, 2017). Social groups even create their own symbolisms and use them to express opinions (e.g., fringe web communities; Zannettou et al., 2018). The potentially high emotional impact of images to a vast audience (Adler-Nissen et al., 2020) can cause changes in the social discourse and eventually politics (Woods and Hahner, 2019). Examples include photos of a drowned refugee child (Barnard and Shoumali, 2015; D'Orazio, 2015), police violence (Berger, 2010), or the recent departure of Western military forces from Afghanistan.

Image search Keyword-based image search analyzing the content of images or videos has been studied for decades (Aigrain et al., 1996), pre-dated only by approaches relying on metadata and similarity measures (Chang and Fu, 1980). In a recent survey, Latif et al. (2019) categorize image features into color, texture, shape, and spatial features. Current commercial search engines also index text found in images, surrounding text, alternative texts displayed when an image is unavailable, and their URLs (Wu, 2020; Google, 2021). Also related to the retrieval of argumentative images is that of "emotional images", which relies on image features like color and composition (Wang and He, 2008; Solli and Lenz, 2011). Argumentation goes hand in hand with emotions, so that emotional features may be promising for retrieving images for arguments in the future. For lack of labeled data (argumentativeness plus emotionality), we start by exploiting keyword-based web search to retrieve images for arguments from the web, as did the earliest image search approaches (e.g., Yanai, 2001).

Argument search Based on argument mining from texts (cf. Peldszus and Stede, 2013), argument search engines aim to support decision-making and persuasion. Conceptually, a query to an argument search engine may either name an issue without a stance (Stab et al., 2018) (e.g., `nuclear energy`), or represent a conclusion for which supporting and attacking premises are to be retrieved (e.g., `nuclear energy mitigates climate change`). The first collection of arguments from the web is the Internet Argument Corpus (Walker et al., 2012), containing 400,000 posts from an online debate portal. The first argument search engine, args.me, indexes a similar dataset of arguments (Wachsmuth et al., 2017b). Not relying on retrieval in collections of arguments, ArgumenText (Stab et al., 2018) first searches for documents relevant to a user's query in generic web crawls, and then mines arguments on the fly within retrieved documents. Regarding the evaluation of argument search engines, judging the topic relevance of a retrieved text alone is insufficient, it must also be argumentative (Potthast et al., 2019; Bondarenko et al., 2021). Research on argumentation has identified many further quality criteria for arguments (Wachsmuth et al., 2017a), yet few have been investigated for argument retrieval, and hardly anything has been said on the argumentative quality of images.

3 Image Retrieval for Arguments

Similar to textual argument retrieval, we define the task of retrieving images for arguments as follows:

> Given a keyword query suggesting an issue or a claim for a topic, retrieve as two ranked lists those and only those images that can assist someone in (1) supporting and (2) attacking it.

This definition presumes that a given user intends to search for images suitable to assist in persuading others, an intent that encompasses a diversity of real-life scenarios, such as sending a pertinent image to a friend, using it as a cover for a news article or blog post, or on a slide in a presentation. Furthermore, it encompasses deliberation scenarios, such as forming an own opinion, and creating a collage for a school project. We expect search engines for argumentative images to offer facets as shown in Figure 1 to meet such needs.

To assess the relevance of an image to a given query, a three-fold judgment is required:

Topic relevance The image content is related to the query topic. This criterion corresponds to the notion of relevance in keyword-based image retrieval (Shanbehzadeh et al., 2000).

Argumentativeness The image can be used to support a stance regarding the query topic. This criterion corresponds to the notion of a context-dependent claim in textual argument mining (Aharoni et al., 2014).

Stance relevance The image can be used to support the predicted stance within the query topic. This criterion corresponds to the categorization into pros and cons in standard argument search (Wachsmuth et al., 2017b).

Since stance relevance entails argumentativeness, which in turn entails topic relevance, we refer to these three as "levels" of relevance.

Though previous work focused on stance relevance only (e.g., Stab et al., 2018), an analysis on all three levels provides more insight into the errors made and is especially warranted for "argumentative images." Figure 2 illustrates the different levels for the example query `nuclear energy`, showing images that fail (a) topic-relevance, (b) argumentativeness, and (c) stance-relevance (provided the image is categorized as a con). Though also many textual arguments appeal to emotion rather than logic, images are especially suited for such an appeal. However, as the emotions invoked can depend on both the viewer and context, it can be surprisingly unclear whether an image is argumentative or to which stance it is relevant. Consider Figure 2d. The meme image mixes the question of nuclear energy with the emotions towards a certain political moment (US president Trump's 2020 State of the Union Address, where, at its conclusion, the Speaker of the House of Representatives Pelosi tore up its official copy as a symbolic comment on its contents, Stewart, 2020). Depending on the own emotions towards the shown politicians and statement, one can read the image as pro nuclear energy ("society" not caring for facts) or against ("society" ripping up lies). In the case of such images with ambiguous stance, the definition of stance relevance above suggests listing the image both as a pro and a con. In the future, however, additional considerations of argumentative quality (especially in terms of clarity) might suggest to omit such images completely, or to show them separately.

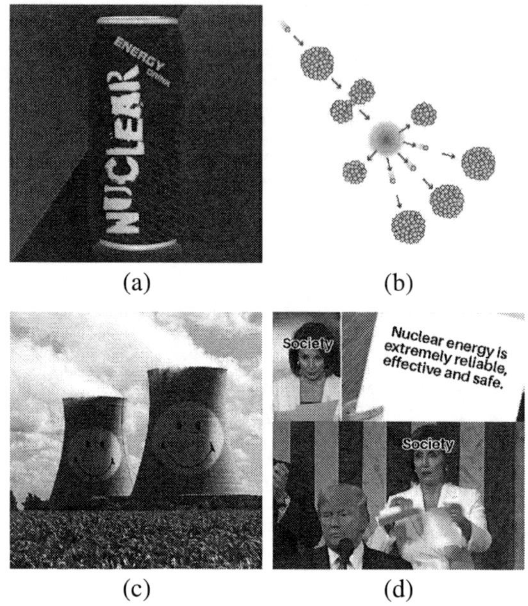

Figure 2: Example results for the query `nuclear energy` that are (a) off-topic, (b) not argumentative, (c) supportive, and (d) with ambiguous stance.

4 Stance-Aware Query Expansion

The basic hypothesis of our approach is that the task of image retrieval for arguments can be tackled effectively by the structure shown in Figure 3a,

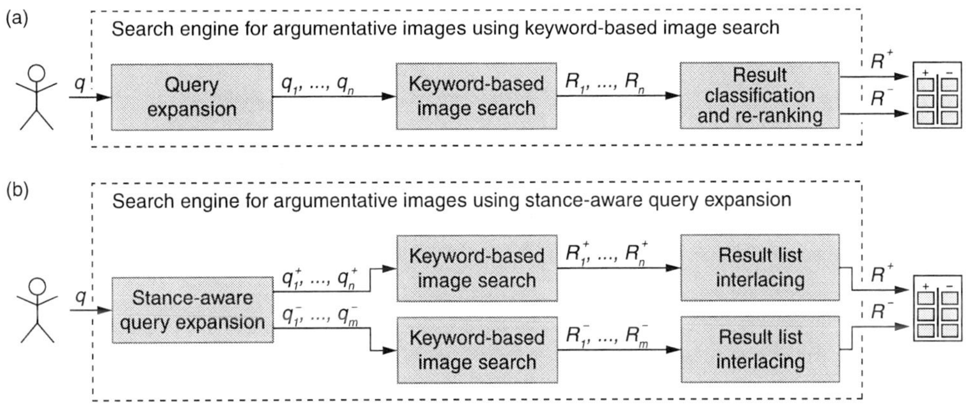

Figure 3: (a) Generic structure of an image search engine for arguments using a keyword-based image search engine and (b) the more specific structure of stance-aware query expansion employed in this paper. In the generic structure, the user's query q is expanded to n queries $q_1, \ldots, q_n$, a result list R_i is retrieved for each q_i, which are classified and re-ranked to create the lists of pro (R^+) and con images (R^-). Structure (b) corresponds to a particular case without classification and re-ranking, where different sets of expanded queries, $q_1^+, \ldots, q_n^+$ and $q_1^-, \ldots, q_m^-$, are used to independently create R^+ and R^-.

which issues for a user's query several expanded queries to a keyword-based image search engine and then fuses the result lists to a list of pro and con images. However, we assume that the semantic capabilities of modern keyword-based image search engines can be harnessed further to already provide a classification of the images, thus separating pro and con images as well as omitting neutral ones.

In particular we propose a stance-aware query expansion as depicted in Figure 3b. It generates focused queries for both relevant stances (superscript $+$ for pro and $-$ for con), which are processed independently of each other, presuming that a sufficient diversity of expanded stance-aware queries recalls relevant images for each stance on the top ranks. In that case, the development of a post-retrieval image stance classifier can be omitted. The result lists of each stance are interlaced, i.e., composed by taking the first result of each list for a stance, then the second of each, and so on.

We devise three methods: (1) appending always the same stance-indicating terms to the user's query, (2) appending sentiment-indicating terms that co-occur with the query's terms, and (3) appending topic-specific stance-indicating terms obtained from a text argument search engine.

(1) Good-Anti Conceivably the single most basic method is to expand the user's query with one term per stance. After some manual experiments, we opted for `good` as a pro term and `anti` as a con term. Another option for the latter was `bad`, but for some topics this term is more associated with "doing it poorly" than with "being against it."

(2) Positive-Negative This method exploits the fact that stance is often reflected through expressions of sentiment, for example, as used in counterargument retrieval (Wachsmuth et al., 2018). For each stance, we generate up to five queries by appending the top positive (for pro) or negative terms (for con) of the 8000 entries in the MPQA subjectivity lexicon (Wilson et al., 2005) as ranked by their co-occurrence with the query according to the Leipzig Corpora Collection's English corpus (120 million sentences, Goldhahn et al., 2012).

(3) Pros-Cons This method employs argument search engines to identify terms typical for certain topic-stance-combinations. E.g., in arguments retrieved for `nuclear energy`, "CO2 neutrality" occurs more often in pro arguments than in con ones, whereas "radiation" occurs more often in con arguments than in pro ones. Based on work in anomaly detection (Afgani et al., 2008), this method calculates the specificity of a term t to a stance s, $\delta(t, s)$, as their contribution to the Kullback-Leibler divergence of the term distributions between the two stances:

$$\delta(t, s) = \mathrm{P}(T{=}t|S{=}s) \cdot \log \frac{\mathrm{P}(T{=}t|S{=}s)}{\mathrm{P}(T{=}t|S{\neq}s)},$$

where $P(T = t|S = s)$ is the probability of observing t given the stance s. This probability is estimated by word frequencies[2] in all arguments that an argument search engine—`args.me`[3] in our case (Wachsmuth et al., 2017b)—retrieves for the query and s. For preprocessing, we lemmatize both arguments and the query. Furthermore, we filter out all arguments from the website *debate.org*, as we found that its debate structure encourages to reference opposing points in arguments to counter them, which diminishes the δ of the respective terms. The method generates up to five queries for each stance by appending the top terms as ranked by δ.

5 Crowdsourcing Relevance Judgements

In retrieval tasks, human relevance judgments of retrieval results for a fixed set of topics allows for evaluating the effectiveness of competing retrieval models. Known as the Cranfield paradigm or TREC-style evaluation (Voorhees, 2001), it is also employed in textual argument retrieval within the Touché shared tasks (Bondarenko et al., 2020). All our expansion methods retrieve results for the same set of queries, which are then pooled and manually judged with respect to their relevance to a given query's information need.

To evaluate the methods presented in Section 4, we employ a sample of 20 controversial questions from the Touché 2020 Task 1 test set (Bondarenko et al., 2020), from which we derive one query each.[4] We calculate the number of relevant images in the methods' ten top-ranked images (precision@10) for both rankings of pro and con images (thus actually for 20 images), which is straightforward to interpret for multiple relevance levels. To ensure state-of-the-art keyword-based retrieval and a large image index, all methods retrieve images using the Google image search.

Figure 4 shows the annotation interface for gathering relevance judgments. As described in Section 3, we distinguish relevance on three levels: topic, argumentativeness, and stance. The first three options, the image being able to support the pro, contra, or both stances, indicate the image stance(s) and that it is argumentative and on topic. The fourth option, the image not being able to support a stance, indicates that the image is on-topic

Figure 4: Annotation interface, showing (from top to bottom) the current topic, question, and image, as well as the generic annotation options and comment box.

only. The final option indicates that the image has no stance and is neither argumentative nor on-topic.

Using the annotation interface of Figure 4, we collected 2988 annotations on 993 images[5] and 20 topics from 12 layperson annotators: three annotators per image and topic. The images' order was randomized for each annotator within a topic to avoid order biases. The annotator agreement is fair to moderate (Fleiss' κ of 0.39; Fleiss, 1981; Figure 7 shows κ per topic). We compute a single label for each image and topic pair as per majority vote (two out of three), treating an annotation *both* as a vote for both *pro* and *con*, and assigning the ground-truth label *both* if there are at least two votes for both *pro* and *con*.[6] To ensure consistency in the face of difficulties reported by the annotators, we reviewed the ground-truth and changed the label for 223 images. The vast majority of changes (85%) were due to vagueness in our instructions: Annotators labeled images that can introduce the topic or question but have no argumentative value otherwise (see Figure 5 for examples) often as being able to support *both* stances though they should have labeled them as non-argumentative (*neither*).

[2]To avoid zero probabilities, we employ standard add-one smoothing (Jurafsky and Martin, 2009).

[3]API: `https://www.args.me/api-en.html`

[4]From the original 49 topics, 13 were omitted for which one or more methods found no expansion terms, sampling 20 at random from the remainder to meet our labeling budget. Questions, queries, retrieved images, and annotations are available at `https://doi.org/10.5281/zenodo.5202934`.

[5]Three images were retrieved for two topics.

[6]E.g., if votes are *off-topic*, *neither*, *pro*, the result would be *neither* as two voted for on-topic but only one for a stance.

Figure 5: Examples of images annotated as being able to support *both* stances but corrected to *neither*.

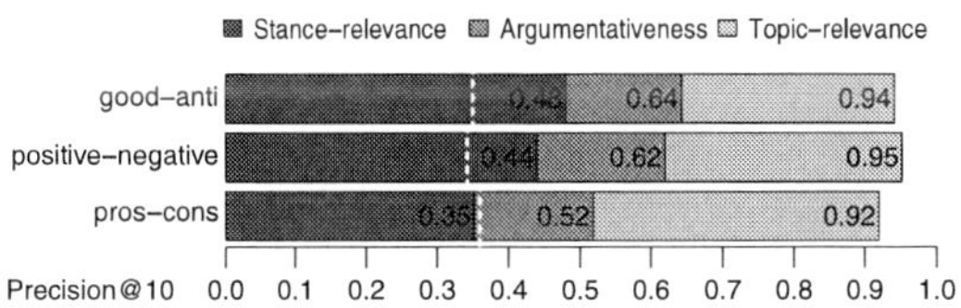

Figure 6: Precision@10 achieved by the three query expansion methods at three relevance levels, averaged across 20 topics and each topic's individual pro and con rankings. The dashed lines indicate the expected precision@10 of a random image stance classifier dividing the retrieved images into the pro and con rankings. The bars are overlaid, not stacked.

6 Evaluation

This section reports on a comparative evaluation of the three query expansions methods by their retrieval effectiveness, followed by a topic-wise error analysis. Last, we also carried out an investigation into the counterintuitive case of ambiguous images that can support both stances.

6.1 Overall Retrieval Effectiveness

Figure 6 shows the precision@10 for the three query expansion methods introduced in Section 4 with respect to the three levels of relevance assessed. Nearly all retrieved images can be expected to be relevant to the topic (92% to 95%). This being testimony to the effectiveness of Google's image search, it also indicates that the query expansion methods do not impair the keyword-based image search.

The basic good-anti heuristic performs best, achieving an argumentative precision@10 of 0.64 and outperforming the pros-cons method by 0.12. An inspection of the pros-cons method's expanded terms reveals that they lack the stance-specificity of the other methods' terms. For example, the expansions `money` and `person` (pros-cons) are less specific than the expansions `cheap` and `harm` (positive-negative), as only the latter terms intrinsically convey a preference or stance.

All methods lose 16 to 18 percentage points when being judged for stance-relevance, showing that 25% (good-anti) to 33% (pros-cons) of the retrieved images that are argumentative do support the opposite stance as intended. While for two of the three methods their stance precision@10 is better than a random stance assignment (dashed lines in Figure 6), it is far from perfect. Since Google image search is not public, it is challenging to pinpoint the source of the stance errors. A possible explanation may be that expansion terms found on an image's web page do not refer to being pro or con a given topic, but are used in a different context or even to convey the opposite stance.

6.2 Topic-wise Error Analysis

We analyzed the retrieval effectiveness on a per-topic basis to learn which are the most challenging ones for retrieving argumentative images. It turns out that some topics are less well-suited to a keyword-based image retrieval (or to our query expansion methods). Moreover, some arguments are not suited to being illustrated or are for other reasons not found through image search. Figure 7 shows the retrieval effectiveness as precision@10 and the image stance distribution per topic.

As the average precision@10 scores show, topic precision is high overall, except for the query `standardized tests education` (for issue: "Do standardized tests improve education?"). On closer inspection, we found that many off-topic images were either on education or standardized tests, possibly hinting at a lack of images that combine both.

Average argumentativeness precision@10, however, varies a great deal between 0.18 and 0.87. As an inspection of topics with low precision reveals, many of the retrieved images are well-suited to introducing the topic, but not as argument support. For example, most images for `body cameras police` ("Should body cameras be mandatory for police?") show a police officer wearing a body camera. Similarly, many of the images for `performance-enhancing drugs in sports` ("Should performance-enhancing drugs be accepted in sports?") show sports equipment and syringes. For queries related to commercial products, like `e-cigarettes` ("Is vaping with e-cigarettes safe?"), `bottled water` ("Should bottled water be banned?"), or `school uniforms` ("Should students have to wear school uniforms?"), many of the images are product photos from shopping or review pages and merely display the prod-

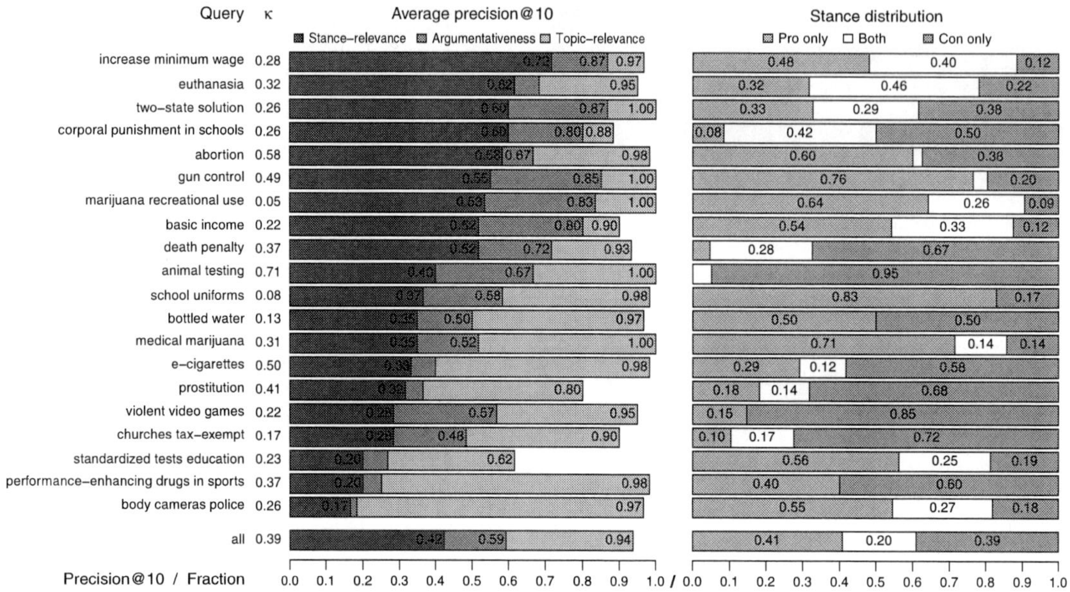

Figure 7: Topic-wise analysis depicting Fleiss' κ, precision@10 per relevance level averaged across expansion methods and stances, and the stance distribution for the retrieved images as judged by our annotators.

uct. We assume that in these cases the expansion methods cannot sufficiently counter the search engine optimization (SEO) done by companies working in that domain, suggesting a pre-filtering by web document and/or image genre.

Similarly, average stance precision@10 varies a lot between topics, ranging from 0.17 to 0.72. This variation is partly due to the large differences in the stance of the retrieved images, as illustrated in the right plot of Figure 7. For some topics, argumentative precision and stance precision differ by as much as 0.30 (`gun control` and `marijuana recreational use`). Upon inspection, we noticed that the errors in the stance assignment dominantly occur in a single direction per topic. Though our setup intends to retrieve an equal amount of pros and cons per topic, the right plot of Figure 7 shows that the result set is often skewed in one direction. In the extreme, 95% of the retrieved argumentative images for `animal testing` are con only—which is plausible, as illustrating the benefits of animal testing is much more complex than showing animals being treated poorly. On the other hand, an unexpectedly high fraction of images are ambiguous and can be used to support both stances. For example, this is the case for nearly half of the retrieved argumentative images for `euthanasia`. Figure 8c shows one example for the topic.

6.3 On Images with Ambiguous Stance

When 46% of the retrieved images can provide support for both stances, as for `euthanasia`, should an image search engine for arguments separate pro and con images in its search results as in Figure 1? To investigate this question, we inspected all 111 images that were judged ambiguous. Figure 8 exemplifies the image categories we identified. We found that most of the 111 images provide contextual information (78 images, 70%) in the form of geographic comparisons as in Figure 8a, statistics (especially polls), or forecasts. Similar categories include sources on the topic (10 images, 9%) and definitions (11 images, 10%). Images from these three categories (89% total) can strongly support an argumentation, even though different pieces of information they entail might lend support to different stances. Due to the benefits of such images, it thus makes sense to display them separately in a search interface, either on-demand or up front. As outliers, two other images contrast key points for pro and con, supporting mostly deliberation tasks. The remaining images were ambiguous in the way hypothesized before in that their stance changes depending on how one interprets them. Images of this kind will be a challenge to image retrieval for arguments, since their interpretation requires common sense and/or domain knowledge.

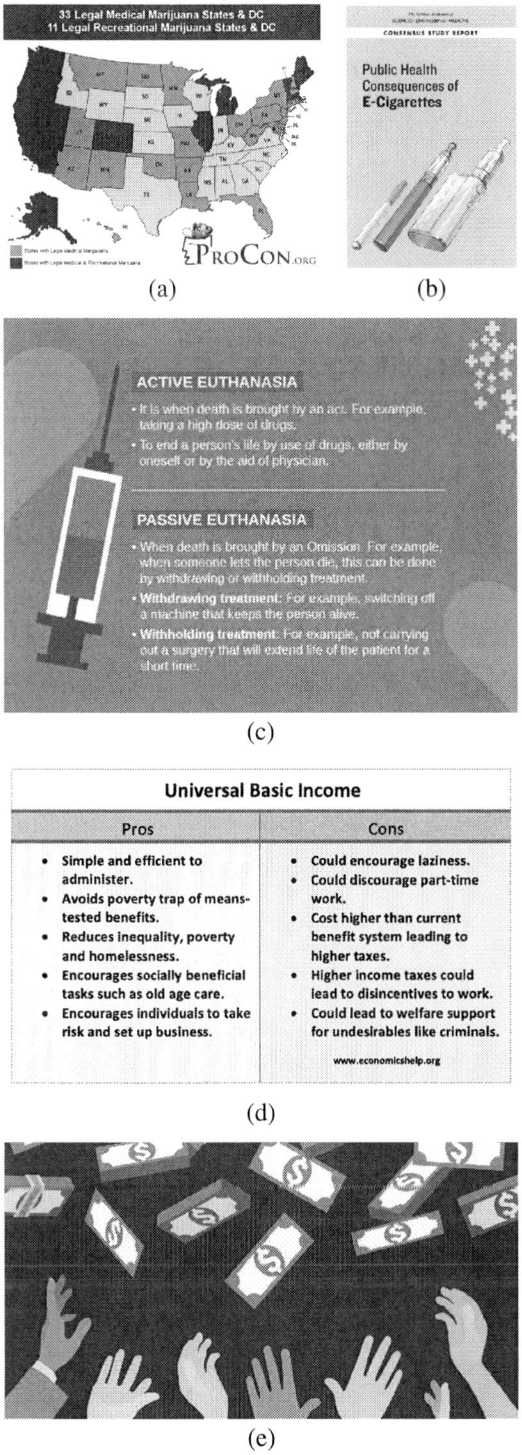

Figure 8: Example images representing different categories of images that are able to support both stances: (a) contextual information: 70% of 111 analyzed images, (b) sources: 9%, (c) definitions: 10%, (d) key point tables: 2%, and (e) ambiguous messages: 9%.

7 Conclusion

This paper introduces the task of image retrieval for arguments, proposes with stance-aware query expansion a family of methods to tackle the task that exploits existing keyword-based image search technology, and carries out a first empirical analysis for the task using human annotations on 993 images and 20 topics. In the experiments, the basic good-anti heuristic, which expands a user query with the same two terms (`good` for pro images, `anti` for con ones), outperforms more sophisticated query expansion approaches that employ terms specific to the query's topic. An error analysis unveils a high topic-dependence of the retrieval effectiveness. Finally, the paper investigates ambiguous images labeled as supporting both the pro and con stances. In cases where many neutral images are found, we suggest displaying them separately.

Relying on Google's image search engine ensures a state-of-the-art retrieval model at the price of exact replicability. Since commercial image search engines are subject to frequent changes it must be investigated how reproducible our results are. Developing an open image retrieval system for arguments would enable laboratory evaluation. It would also allow for creating image representations tailored to argumentation, but requires creating and labeling an extensive image collection that covers a manifold of controversial topics.

There is a lot of room to improve precision. Filtering images by analyzing their web pages may avoid ones that merely show a product or otherwise fail to make a point. Further analyses of the web pages with argument mining technologies could provide for a better stance classification of the images. Also images search engine feature to retrieve similar images may be helpful in this regard. Moreover, classifiers to identify persuasion techniques or emotions in images may prove beneficial to identify images for arguments. Assessing the quality of argumentative images could improve the imagined search engine's evaluation and utility to users. To foster research, we run a corresponding shared task to be held as part of the Touché 2022 lab.[7]

This paper seeks to extend argument mining in general and argument retrieval in particular to considering images. Other argument mining tasks (e.g., relation extraction in articles) could similarly be extended to account for the widespread use of images in argumentative texts or speechmaking.

[7] `https://webis.de/events?q=touche#touche-2022`

References

Rebecca Adler-Nissen, Katrine Emilie Andersen, and Lene Hansen. 2020. Images, emotions, and international politics: the death of Alan Kurdi. *Review of International Studies*, 46(1):75–95.

M. Afgani, S. Sinanovic, and H. Haas. 2008. Anomaly detection using the kullback-leibler divergence metric. In *1st International Symposium on Applied Sciences on Biomedical and Communication Technologies (ISABEL 2008)*, pages 1–5. ISSN: 2325-5331.

Ehud Aharoni, Anatoly Polnarov, Tamar Lavee, Daniel Hershcovich, Ran Levy, Ruty Rinott, Dan Gutfreund, and Noam Slonim. 2014. A benchmark dataset for automatic detection of claims and evidence in the context of controversial topics. In *1st Workshop on Argument Mining (ArgMining 2014)*, pages 64–68. ACL.

Philippe Aigrain, Hongjiang Zhang, and Dragutin Petkovic. 1996. Content-based representation and retrieval of visual media: A state-of-the-art review. *Multimedia Tools and Applications*, 3(3):179–202.

Khalid Al-Khatib. 2019. *Computational Analysis of Argumentation Strategies*. Dissertation, Bauhaus-Universität Weimar.

Anne Barnard and Karam Shoumali. 2015. Image of drowned syrian, aylan kurdi, 3, brings migrant crisis into focus. The New York Times.

Martin A. Berger. 2010. Fixing images: Civil rights photography and the struggle over representation. *RIHA Journal*, 10.

Alexander Bondarenko, Maik Fröbe, Meriem Beloucif, Lukas Gienapp, Yamen Ajjour, Alexander Panchenko, Chris Biemann, Benno Stein, Henning Wachsmuth, Martin Potthast, and Matthias Hagen. 2020. Overview of touché 2020: Argument retrieval. In *Working Notes Papers of the CLEF 2020 Evaluation Labs*, volume 2696 of *CEUR Workshop Proceedings*.

Alexander Bondarenko, Lukas Gienapp, Maik Fröbe, Meriem Beloucif, Yamen Ajjour, Alexander Panchenko, Chris Biemann, Benno Stein, Henning Wachsmuth, Martin Potthast, and Matthias Hagen. 2021. Overview of touché 2021: Argument retrieval. In *Advances in Information Retrieval. 43rd European Conference on IR Research (ECIR 2021)*, volume 12036 of *Lecture Notes in Computer Science*, pages 574–582, Berlin Heidelberg New York. Springer.

Ning-San Chang and King-sun Fu. 1980. Query-by-pictorial-example. *IEEE Transactions on Software Engineering*, 6(6):519–524.

Dimitar Dimitrov, Bishr Bin Ali, Shaden Shaar, Firoj Alam, Fabrizio Silvestri, Hamed Firooz, Preslav Nakov, and Giovanni Da San Martino. 2021. SemEval-2021 task 6: Detection of persuasion techniques in texts and images. In *15th International Workshop on Semantic Evaluation (SemEval'2021)*, pages 70–98, Online. Association for Computational Linguistics.

Francesco D'Orazio. 2015. Journey of an image: from a beach in Bodrum to twenty million screens across the world. In *The Iconic Image on Social Media: A Rapid Research Response to the Death of Aylan Kurdi*. Visual Social Media Lab.

Ian J. Dove. 2012. On images as evidence and arguments. In Frans H. van Eemeren and Bart Garssen, editors, *Topical Themes in Argumentation Theory: Twenty Exploratory Studies*, Argumentation Library, pages 223–238. Springer Netherlands, Dordrecht.

Finis Dunaway. 2018. Images, emotions, politics. *Modern American History*, 1(3):369–376.

Xénia Farkas and Márton Bene. 2020. Images, politicians, and social media: Patterns and effects of politicians' image-based political communication strategies on social media. *The International Journal of Press/Politics*.

J. L. Fleiss. 1981. The measurement of interrater agreement. In *Statistical methods for rates and proportions*, 2 edition, pages 212–236. John Wiley & Sons, New York.

Bernd Frohmann. 1992. The power of images: A discourse analysis of the cognitive viewpoint. *Journal of Documentation*, 48(4):365–386.

Dirk Goldhahn, Thomas Eckart, and Uwe Quasthoff. 2012. Building large monolingual dictionaries at the leipzig corpora collection: From 100 to 200 languages. In *Eighth International Conference on Language Resources and Evaluation (LREC 2012)*, pages 759–765. European Language Resources Association (ELRA).

Google. 2021. Google images best practices. Google Developers.

Ioana Grancea. 2017. Types of visual arguments. *Argumentum. Journal of the Seminar of Discursive Logic, Argumentation Theory and Rhetoric*, 15(2):16–34.

Benita Heiskanen. 2017. Meme-ing electoral participation. *European journal of American studies*, 12(2).

Dan Jurafsky and James H. Martin. 2009. *Speech and language processing: an introduction to natural language processing, computational linguistics, and speech recognition*, 2 edition. Prentice Hall series in artificial intelligence. Prentice Hall.

Afshan Latif, Aqsa Rasheed, Umer Sajid, Jameel Ahmed, Nouman Ali, Naeem Iqbal Ratyal, Bushra Zafar, Saadat Hanif Dar, Muhammad Sajid, and Tehmina Khalil. 2019. Content-based image retrieval and feature extraction: A comprehensive review. *Mathematical Problems in Engineering*, 2019:21.

Andreas Peldszus and Manfred Stede. 2013. From argument diagrams to argumentation mining in texts: A survey. *International Journal of Cognitive Informatics and Natural Intelligence*, 7(1):1–31.

Martin Potthast, Lukas Gienapp, Florian Euchner, Nick Heilenkötter, Nico Weidmann, Henning Wachsmuth, Benno Stein, and Matthias Hagen. 2019. Argument search: Assessing argument relevance. In *42nd International ACM Conference on Research and Development in Information Retrieval (SIGIR 2019)*. ACM.

Georges Roque. 2012. Visual argumentation: A further reappraisal. In Frans H. van Eemeren and Bart Garssen, editors, *Topical Themes in Argumentation Theory*, volume 22, pages 273–288. Springer Netherlands, Dordrecht. Series Title: Argumentation Library.

Jamshid Shanbehzadeh, Amir-Masoud Eftekhari-Moghadam, and Fariborz Mahmoudi. 2000. Image indexing and retrieval techniques: past, present, and next. In *Storage and Retrieval for Media Databases 2000*, volume 3972 of *SPIE Proceedings*, pages 461–470. SPIE.

Martin Solli and Reiner Lenz. 2011. Color emotions for multi-colored images. *Color Research & Application*, 36(3):210–221.

Christian Stab, Johannes Daxenberger, Chris Stahlhut, Tristan Miller, Benjamin Schiller, Christopher Tauchmann, Steffen Eger, and Iryna Gurevych. 2018. ArgumenText: Searching for arguments in heterogeneous sources. In *Conference of the North American Chapter of the Association for Computational Linguistics (NAACL-HLT 2018)*, pages 21–25. ACL.

Emily Stewart. 2020. Why nancy pelosi ripping up some papers has set the internet on fire. Vox.

Ellen M. Voorhees. 2001. The philosophy of information retrieval evaluation. In *Second Workshop of the Cross-Language Evaluation Forum, CLEF 2001*, volume 2406 of *Lecture Notes in Computer Science*, pages 355–370. Springer.

Henning Wachsmuth, Nona Naderi, Yufang Hou, Yonatan Bilu, Vinodkumar Prabhakaran, Tim Alberdingk Thijm, Graeme Hirst, and Benno Stein. 2017a. Computational argumentation quality assessment in natural language. In *15th Conference of the European Chapter of the Association for Computational Linguistics (EACL 2017)*, pages 176–187.

Henning Wachsmuth, Martin Potthast, Khalid Al Khatib, Yamen Ajjour, Jana Puschmann, Jiani Qu, Jonas Dorsch, Viorel Morari, Janek Bevendorff, and Benno Stein. 2017b. Building an argument search engine for the web. In *4th Workshop on Argument Mining (ArgMining 2017)*, pages 49–59, Copenhagen, Denmark. Association for Computational Linguistics.

Henning Wachsmuth, Shahbaz Syed, and Benno Stein. 2018. Retrieval of the best counterargument without prior topic knowledge. In *56th Annual Meeting of the Association for Computational Linguistics (ACL 2018)*, pages 241–251. Association for Computational Linguistics.

Marilyn A Walker, Pranav Anand, Jean E Fox Tree, Rob Abbott, and Joseph King. 2012. A corpus for research on deliberation and debate. In *8th International Conference on Language Resources and Evaluation (LREC 2012)*, pages 812–817, Istanbul.

Douglas Walton, Chris Reed, and Fabrizio Macagno. 2008. *Argumentation Schemes*. Cambridge University Press.

Weining Wang and Qianhua He. 2008. A survey on emotional semantic image retrieval. In *International Conference on Image Processing (ICIP 2008)*, pages 117–120. IEEE.

Nicholas Watt. 2015. David Cameron says UK will take thousands more Syrian refugees. *The Guardian*.

Theresa Wilson, Janyce Wiebe, and Paul Hoffmann. 2005. Recognizing contextual polarity in phrase-level sentiment analysis. In *Human Language Technology Conference and Conference on Empirical Methods in Natural Language Processing (HLT/EMNLP 2005)*, pages 347–354. ACL.

Heather Suzanne Woods and Leslie Ann Hahner. 2019. *Make America meme again: the rhetoric of the alt-right*, volume 45 of *Frontiers in political communication*. Peter Lang, New York.

Angela Wu. 2020. Learn more about what you see on google images. Google Blog.

Keiji Yanai. 2001. Image collector: An image-gathering system from the world-wide web employing keyword-based search engines. In *International Conference on Multimedia and Expo, (ICME 2001)*. IEEE.

Savvas Zannettou, Tristan Caulfield, Jeremy Blackburn, Emiliano De Cristofaro, Michael Sirivianos, Gianluca Stringhini, and Guillermo Suarez-Tangil. 2018. On the origins of memes by means of fringe web communities. In *Proceedings of the Internet Measurement Conference (IMC 2018)*, pages 188–202. ACM.

Is Stance Detection Topic-Independent and Cross-topic Generalizable? – A Reproduction Study

Myrthe Reuver[1] **Suzan Verberne**[3] **Roser Morante**[1] **Antske Fokkens**[1,2]
[1]Computation Linguistics and Text Mining Lab, Vrije Universiteit Amsterdam
[2] Dept. of Mathematics and Computer Science, Eindhoven University of Technology
[3] Leiden Institute of Advanced Computer Science, Leiden University
{myrthe.reuver,antske.fokkens,r.morantevallejo}@vu.nl
s.verberne@liacs.leidenuniv.nl

Abstract

Cross-topic stance detection is the task to automatically detect stances (pro, against, or neutral) on unseen topics. We successfully reproduce state-of-the-art cross-topic stance detection work (Reimers et al., 2019), and systematically analyze its reproducibility. Our attention then turns to the cross-topic aspect of this work, and the specificity of topics in terms of vocabulary and socio-cultural context. We ask: To what extent is stance detection topic-independent and generalizable across topics? We compare the model's performance on various unseen topics, and find topic (e.g. abortion, cloning), class (e.g. pro, con), and their interaction affecting the model's performance. We conclude that investigating performance on different topics, and addressing topic-specific vocabulary and context, is a future avenue for cross-topic stance detection.

1 Introduction

(Online) debate has long been studied and modelled by computational linguistics with argument mining tasks such as stance detection. Stance detection is the task of automatically identifying the stance (agreeing, disagreeing, and/or neutral) of a text towards a debated topic or issue (Küçük and Can, 2020; Schiller et al., 2021).[1] Its use-cases increasingly relate to online information environments and societal challenges, such as argument search (Stab et al., 2018), fake news identification (Hanselowski et al., 2018), or diversifying stances in a news recommender (Reuver et al., 2021).

Cross-topic stance detection models should thus be able to deal with the quickly changing landscape of (online) public debate, where new topics and issues appear all the time. As Schlangen (2021) described in his recent paper on natural language processing (NLP) methodology, generalization is a main goal of computational linguistics. A computational model (e.g. a stance detection model) should learn task capabilities beyond one set of datapoints, in our case: beyond one debate topic.

Cross-topic stance detection is especially challenging because generalization to a new discussion topic is not trivial. Expressing stances is inherently socio-cultural behavior (Du Bois, 2007), where social actors place themselves and targets on dimensions in the socio-cultural field. This also comes with very topic-specific word use (Somasundaran and Wiebe, 2009; Wei and Mao, 2019). For instance, an *against* abortion argument might be expressed indirectly with a 'pro-life' expression, and someone aware of the socio-cultural context of this debate will be able to recognize this. Knowledge from other debate topics such as *gun control* may not be useful, since the debate strategies might change per topic. Despite these fundamental challenges, pre-trained Transformer models show promising results on cross-topic argument classification (Reimers et al., 2019; Schiller et al., 2021).

In this paper, we investigate the ability of cross-topic stance detection approaches to generalize to different debate topics. Our question is: *To what extent is stance detection topic-independent and generalizable across topics?*

Our contributions are threefold. We first complete a reproduction of state-of-the-art cross-topic stance detection work (Reimers et al., 2019), as reproduction has repeatedly shown to be relevant for NLP (Fokkens et al., 2013; Cohen et al., 2018; Belz et al., 2021). The reproduction is largely successful: we obtain similar numeric results. Secondly, we investigate the topic-specific performance of this model, and conclude that BERT's performance fluctuates on different topics. Additionally, we find that a bag-of-words-based SVM model can rival its performance for some topics. Thirdly, we relate this to the nature of the stance detection modelling

[1]There is a wide array of datasets, definitions, and operationalizations of stance detection and classification, and recently Schiller et al. (2021) gave a great overview in their Section 2, as do Küçük and Can (2020) in their survey.

Proceedings of The 8th Workshop on Argument Mining, pages 46–56
Punta Cana, Dominican Republic, November 10–11, 2021.

task, which is inherently more connected to sociocultural aspects and topic-specific differences than related tasks such as sentiment analysis.

This paper is organized as follows. Section 2 discusses earlier work on stance detection, and specifically generalizability across topics. Section 3 presents the reproduction results. Section 4 adds additional, topic-specific analyses of the classification performance and a bag-of-words-based model to find topic-(in)dependent features. This is followed by our conclusions in Section 5.

2 Background

2.1 Definition of Stance Detection

Stance detection is a long-established task in computational linguistics. Küçük and Can (2020) identify its most commonly used task definition: "For an input in the form of a piece of text and a target pair, stance detection is a classification problem where the stance of the author of the text is sought in the form of a category label from this set: Favor, Against, Neither." (Küçük and Can, 2020, p. 2).[2] The number of stance classes can vary from 2 to 4, e.g. by adding 'comment' and 'query' next to 'for' and 'against' (Schiller et al., 2021). Küçük and Can (2020) emphasize that this computational definition is built upon the linguistic phenomenon of actors communicating their evaluation of targets, by which they place themselves and their targets on "dimensions in the sociocultural field" (Du Bois, 2007, p. 163). Current work focuses mostly on debates deemed controversial in the U.S. sociopolitical domain, such as abortion and gun control.

2.2 Prior work

Early work on stance detection focused on parliamentary debates and longer texts (Thomas et al., 2006). Since Mohammad et al. (2016)'s stance detection shared task, Twitter has attracted a lot of attention in NLP work on stance detection (Zhu et al., 2019; Darwish et al., 2020; Hossain et al., 2020). Others addressed stance detection in the news domain, with (fake) news headlines (Ferreira and Vlachos, 2016; Hanselowski et al., 2018), disinformation (Hardalov et al., 2021) and user comments on news websites (Bošnjak and Karan, 2019).

Feature-based approaches have largely been replaced by end-to-end neural models. Stance detection has seen a performance increase due to pre-trained Transformer models such as BERT (Devlin et al., 2019). Reimers et al. (2019) reported .20 point F1 improvement over an LSTM baseline with a pre-trained BERT model. Combining multiple stance detection datasets in fine-tuning such a pre-trained Transformer again led to a performance increase, though this model lacks robustness against slight test set manipulations (Schiller et al., 2021).

2.3 Generalization to new topics

Recent work has specifically worked on identifying stances on topics not seen in training. Reimers et al. (2019) train their model on detecting stances and arguments for unseen topics. In their approach however, they treat all topics and stances on these topics as similar and comparable, and report one averaged evaluation metric over topics.

Earlier work (Somasundaran and Wiebe, 2009) already established that ideological stances on topics deemed controversial, such as gay rights, are expressed in a topic-specific manner. Topic-specific features were more informative for SVM models than more topic-independent features.

In more recent work, Wei and Mao (2019) instead specifically focus on how generalizable certain topics are for transferring knowledge to new topics on stance detection. Some Twitter discussion topics seem to share a latent, underlying topic (e.g. both feminism and abortion have the latent topic of equality). In a (latent) topic-enhanced multi-layer perceptron (MLP) model with RNN representation of the tweet, the model indeed uses shared vocabulary between the related topics.

Allaway et al. (2021) notice that earlier work, when considering training on some topics and testing on others, incorporates topic-relatedness. Unlike these other studies however, Allaway et al. (2021, p. 4756) "do not assume a relationship between training and test topics" as a fairer test of robustness. Results they present do show that stance detection is related to topic, but their efforts go to finding topic-invariant stance representations, which improves the generalizability of their model. Their consideration of topic similarity shows that topic difference is very relevant to stance detection.

ALDayel and Magdy (2021) describe in their survey how several studies (Klebanov et al., 2010; Zhu et al., 2019; Darwish et al., 2020) show that texts pro or against an issue use different vocabularies (e.g. using 'pro-life' when expressing a stance

[2] We would like to note that the stance expressed in a text unit does not have to be the stance of an author, e.g. in cases where someone is writing a piece in which they express or quote someone else's opinion.

against abortion). Some of these studies attempt to leverage these vocabularies to generalize across similar topics. Recent work has looked into generalizing stance detection across datasets, task definitions, and domains (Schiller et al., 2021), in which topic-specific performance is not mentioned.

A recent approach to topic-specificity in stance detection is task adaptation. Stein et al. (2021) acknowledge that stance detection usually requires knowledge about the topic of discussion, which is not available for unseen topics. They approach this problem by changing the task to "same-side stance classification", in which a model is trained to classify whether two arguments either have the same or a different stance. This reduces the model's leaning on topic-specific pro- and con-vocabulary, while still being able to separate different stances on the same topic. The best approach to this adapted task on a dedicated leaderboard[3] receives an F1 of .72 in the cross-topic setting with a fine-tuned BERT model (Ollinger et al., 2020).

Our current work adds the discussion of topic difference and topic specificity to state-of-the-art stance detection results. That is, earlier bag-of-words-based work considered lexical specificity of different topics for stance detection, and we add that into the discussion for the current state of the art: pre-trained, end-to-end neural models.

3 Reproduction Experiments

Reimers et al. (2019) apply their approach of cross-topic claim classification to two datasets: the *UKP Sentential Argument Mining Corpus* (Stab et al., 2018) ('the UKP dataset') and the *IBM Debater: Evidence Sentences* dataset (Shnarch et al., 2018) ('the IBM dataset'). We focus on the UKP Dataset, since the IBM Debater dataset has no 'pro' and 'con' class, but rather 'evidence' and 'no evidence' (and our focus is on stance detection). As a second step after stance classification, the authors also attempt to cluster similar arguments within the same topic in a cross-topic training setting. We do not replicate this component, but instead dive deeper into the classification results.

We adopt the definition of reproduction by Belz et al. (2021): repeating the experiments as described in the earlier study, with the exact same data and software. We analyze our reproduced results according to the three dimensions of reproduction proposed by Cohen et al. (2018): whether we find either the same or different (1) (numeric) values, (2) findings, and (3) conclusions as the earlier study.[4] Reproducing the same **values** means obtaining the same numeric results from a specific experiment. Experiments involving fine-tuning on BERT are non-deterministic. We therefore consider the metric fully reproduced if the original result lies within two standard deviations (stdevs) from our result, obtained from 10 random seeds.[5] The same **finding** means that the relation between the values associated with two or more dependent variables is the same, i.e. a system that outperformed another in the original study also does this in the reproduced study. The **conclusion** is the same when the broader implication of findings and values is the same. Conclusions are thus a matter of interpretation. As such, the same findings can lead to different conclusions and conclusions are, contrary to findings, not repeatable (Cohen et al., 2018). This section focuses on the repeatable components of reproducing a study: the values and the findings. We address the conclusions using our more detailed analyses in Section 4.

3.1 Dataset Description

The UKP dataset (Stab et al., 2018) consists of 25,492 argument sentences from 400 Internet texts (from essays to news texts) on 8 topics. The dataset designer's definition of claim is "a span of text expressing evidence or reasoning that can be used to either support or oppose a given topic" (Stab et al., 2018, p. 3665). They define topic as "some matter of controversy for which there is an obvious polarity for possible outcomes" (Stab et al., 2018, p. 3665), and map this polarity to a text expressing one of two classes: for or against the use, adoption, or idea of the topic under discussion. A third class is 'no argument' to the topic under discussion, i.e. the text span falls outside of this polarity.

The 8 topics in the dataset were randomly chosen from online lists of controversial topics on discussion websites (Stab et al., 2018, p. 3666). Specifically, these topics are *abortion*, *cloning*, *death penalty*, *gun control*, *marijuana legalization*, *minimum wage*, *nuclear energy* and *school uniforms*. The stance classes (pro, con, and no argument) were annotated by two argument mining experts

[3] `https://webis.de/events/sameside-19/`, Accessed on the 22th of September 2021.

[4] For reasons of clarity, we present these dimensions in reverse order compared to Cohen et al. (2018).

[5] The paper we reproduce, Reimers et al. (2019), does not provide model performance standard deviation over seeds.

and seven U.S. crowdworkers. The distribution of the dataset for different topics is shown in Table 1.

In Stab et al. (2018) we see a difference in agreement on stance classes in different topics, especially between expert and crowd. The topic achieving the highest agreement between crowd worker and expert is *school uniforms* ($\kappa = .889$), and the lowest is *death penalty* ($\kappa = .576$). The standard deviation over topics is .08 for expert–expert coded data and .16 for expert–crowd coded, both with a mean of $\kappa = .72$.

3.2 Obtaining the Data

The UKP Dataset is not available online due to copyright concerns, but there is a scraping script with archived hyperlinks available on Reimers et al. (2019)'s GitHub page. We ran this script with all specifications given. The scraping script was able to return all claims on 6 of the 8 topics. The topics for which not all claims were detected were *nuclear energy* and *minimum wage*. We then instead obtained the complete datafiles from the authors.[6]

3.3 Training and Evaluation Method

Reimers et al. (2019) use the training method described in Stab et al. (2018). Each topic is split into a training (70%), development (10%), and test split (20%). Training is done on the training splits of 7 topics, tuned on the development split (10%) of these 7 topics, and finally evaluated on the test split (20%) of the held-out 8th topic. They do this for each of the 8 topics (holding out a different topic each time), then apply this procedure for 10 different random seeds on a GPU. Evaluation is assessed with macro F1, averaged over all topics and all random seeds. Their best performing model is a fine-tuned BERT-large model (Devlin et al., 2019), but with only minor improvement over BERT-base.

We use the same training set-up and BERT models for our reproduction. For training, we use the author's code with Python3.8 on a single NVIDIA GeForce RTX 2080 Ti GPU. Our learning rate is 2e-5 for both models, as in Reimers et al. (2019).[7]

We additionally train a non-BERT model (a Support Vector Machine (SVM) with tf-idf features) in the same hold-one-topic-out manner. Tf-idf-based approaches have shown quite solid performance on stance detection in prior work (Riedel et al., 2017). This model is deterministic and is thus not run with multiple seeds. It is run with Python3.9 and the sklearn package. The SVM is intended for the feature analysis in Section 4.3, but we present the performance of this model also in Table 2 and the following section.

3.4 Results of Reproduction

BERT-base Table 2 shows that mean performance over the 3 classes ('pro', 'con', or 'no argument') is F1 = .617 (stdev over 10 seeds = .006). Reimers et al. (2019)'s reported result (F1 = .613) lies within 1 stdev from this result.

BERT-large Mean performance over all topics and stance classes is F1 = .596 (stdev over 10 seeds = .043). The performance reported in Reimers et al. (2019) is F1 = .633, which lies within 2 stdev of our result. However, our stdev is relatively high due to high variance of performance over different seeds, with half of our seeds performing noticeably lower than even BERT-base.[8] For the other 5 seeds, the model performed better (F1 = .636, stdev = .007), and within one (much smaller) stdev of the performance reported in Reimers et al. (2019).

SVM+tf-idf (non-BERT model) This model performs at F1 = .517 averaged over the held-out topics and three classes ('pro', 'con', and 'no argument'), see Table 2. This outperforms by .10 points in F1 the best performing LSTM-based architecture presented in Stab et al. (2018) (F1 = .424), a baseline in Reimers et al. (2019). Their performance improvement of the BERT model over LSTM was .20 in F1. Comparing our SVM model to BERT, we find a smaller improvement over a non-BERT model: .10 F1 improvement for BERT-base (F1 = .617). Our BERT models still outperform our

[6]These files revealed that the scraping script broke down in the *minimum wage* topic due to one specific claim that was archived, but could not be retrieved. "Despite the inevitable negative outcomes that will surely result from a $ 15 minimum wage – we 've already seen negative effects in Seattle 's restaurant industry – politicians and unions seem intent on engaging in an activity that could be described as an "economic death wish." We speculate this claim could possibly not be retrieved due to it containing the dollar sign, `https://web.archive.org/web/20160217041546/http://www.aei.org:80/publication/ten-reasons-economists-object-to-the-minimum-wage/`

[7]All our code can be found in the following GitHub repository: `https://github.com/myrthereuver/claims-reproduction`.

[8]Our large variance in performance over seeds is due to each seed fine-tuning the model 8 times (once for each topic). The 5 unevenly performing seeds each under-perform on a different topic (F1 < .50) due to only assigning the majority class ('no argument'). Other topics in these 5 seeds do outperform BERT-base.

		abortion	cloning	death penalty	gun control	marijuana legalization	minimum wage	nuclear energy	school uniform	all
train	*pro*	490	508	316	566	422	414	436	392	3.544
	con	591	604	789	479	450	396	613	525	4.447
	no arg	1.746	1.075	1.522	1.359	908	968	1.524	1.248	10.350
dev	*pro*	54	56	38	63	47	46	48	44	396
	con	66	67	90	53	50	44	68	58	496
	no arg	195	120	165	152	101	108	170	139	1.150
test	*pro*	136	142	103	158	118	116	122	109	1.004
	con	165	168	232	133	126	111	171	146	1.252
	no arg	486	299	396	378	253	270	424	347	2.853

Table 1: Distribution of the UKP data over topics and over training (70%), test (20%), and validation (10%) sets.

Model	**UKP Dataset**				
mean (stdev) 10 seeds	F1	P pro	P con	R pro	R con
Reimers et al. (2019) biclstm+BERT	.424	.267	.389	.281	.403
Reimers et al. (2019) BERT base	.613 (-)	.505 (-)	.531 (-)	.470 (-)	.576 (-)
Reimers et al. (2019) BERT large	**.633** (-)	.554 (-)	.584 (-)	.505 (-)	.560 (-)
SVM+tf-idf	.517	.418	.460	.414	.423
Reproduction BERT-base	**.617 (.006)**	.519 (.011)	.538 (.007)	.464 (.029)	.581 (.019)
Repr. BERT-large - all seeds	.596 (.043)	.483 (.057)	.527 (.057)	.464 (.058)	.516 (.063)
Repr. BERT-large - 5 evenly performing seeds	.636 (.007)	.532 (.014)	.578 (.016)	.515 (.016)	.567 (.022)

Table 2: Reproduction results Reimers et al. (2019). The fourth row shows our non-BERT model (an SVM) beating their LSTM baseline, and the fourth and fifth row show the results of our BERT reproductions. The sixth row shows an average BERT-large performance without the 5 seeds that considerably under-performed for one topic.

non-BERT model, as in Reimers et al. (2019). Our SVM result does fall within 2 stdevs of BERT-large, but this is due to BERT-large's substantial stdev due to a steep drop in performance for half of the seeds.

3.5 Conclusion of reproduction

Reimers et al. (2019)'s results are reproducible in the sense the first dimension of reproducibility (Cohen et al., 2018): the originally reported numeric **values** fell within 2 stdevs of our reproduced results for both BERT-base and BERT-large. For BERT-base and 5 of the 10 seeds in BERT-large, we obtained a precision, recall, and F1 that are very similar to the original study.

The results are also reproducible in four of the five reproducibility aspects identified by Fokkens et al. (2013): under-descriptions of preprocessing, experimental set-up, versioning, and system output. These were described in either the paper, on the author's GitHub page, or in code documentation. We do observe differences in relation to 'system variation' which is inherent to training neural networks, where identical results are seldom obtained. These variations were small for most experiments, except for the 5 random seeds that led to substantial under-performing on one topic for BERT-large.

When looking at the second dimension of reproducibility defined by Cohen et al. (2018) (**findings**), we observe that BERT-base and BERT-large indeed clearly outperform the LSTM baselines from Stab et al. (2018) as well as our own stronger SVM+tf-idf non-BERT model on the stance detection task. We were able to reproduce the reported increase in performance of BERT-large over BERT-base and non-BERT models. However, BERT-large also showed considerable under-performance on one topic in 5 out of 10 seeds. We see this outcome as a confirmation that it is important to look at different seeds, and that care should be taken when drawing conclusions based on minor differences when working with neural models.

The third dimension of reproducibility is that of **conclusions**. Reimers et al. (2019) conclude that BERT strongly outperforms previous results on identifying arguments for unseen topics, which we confirm, and that these results are "very encouraging and stress the feasibility of the task" (Reimers et al., 2019, p. 575). The remainder of this paper provides further analyses to investigate whether our results also lead to this overall conclusion. In particular, we investigate how our models perform on individual topics (Section 4) and generic topic-independent signals in the data (Section 4.3).

4 Topic Specifics in Classification

To support the conclusions in Reimers et al. (2019) on the success of cross-topic stance detection, we expect a relative stability of performance over topics. The following sections go into some details not explored in Reimers et al. (2019), specifically the cross-topic performance of different topics, and the interaction between topic and class and its influence on performance.

4.1 Variance over (classes in) topics

Table 3 presents the performance of the models on individual topics. The results show that some topics perform considerably worse than others with the cross-topic training method (training on seven topics and testing on the held-out eighth topic). The *cloning* topic performs more than .07 F1 higher than the averaged model performance (F1 = .693 vs F1 = .617). The *abortion* and *gun control* topics perform almost .09 lower than the averaged model performance (F1 = .533 & .530 vs F1 = .617). Note that a difference nearing .10 in F1 score is relatively large, as it is comparable to the difference between the SVM performance and the state-of-the-art BERT models in the previous section.

A per-topic analysis in Table 3 shows that the SVM+tf-idf model performs within .10 points of the BERT-base model for seven of the eight topics, with some performing less than .3 points lower than BERT. The only exception is the topic *marijuana legalization*, which performs .28 points lower than the BERT model. The large average performance increase (+.11 in F1) over SVM comes from BERT-base improving performance on this one topic.

Figure 1 presents the BERT-base in-class F1 score of the three classes ('pro', 'con', 'no argument'), and in-topic averaged F1. The red line indicates the average model performance of .617. We see some consistency, e.g. the 'no argument' class consistently scoring around F1 = .80, but we also see some topic-specific behavior. *Cloning*, *minimum wage*, and *school uniforms* obtain higher F1 performance than average for all classes. In contrast, *death penalty*, *gun control*, and *abortion* perform considerably lower than the average F1 performance in the 'pro' and 'con' classes. These topics see in-class performance of even F1 < .50.

Each cross-topic model is trained by removing one topic from the training data. In this way, we remove a different number of training examples each time. The topics with the most training examples for a class (e.g. 'pro' in the *gun control* topic) therefore have a smaller training set for this class when training a cross-topic model. If there were a linear relationship between dataset size and performance, one would expect that topics with *fewer* training examples (and therefore more training examples left when this topic is left out of training) to do better than topics with *more* training examples (whose cross-topic models lose more training examples).

Table 1 does show that the 'no argument' class has a three times larger proportion of the training set than the 'pro' and 'con' classes, which could explain the better performance of this class in all topics, but training set size difference does not account for the between-topic variation in the 'pro' and 'con' classes. Instead, Table 1 shows that topics with the most training examples (that means, the largest set of examples removed in a cross-topic model) do not have the worst performing cross-topic models in Figure 1. For example, the *abortion* topic has relatively few 'con' examples removed (591) compared to other classes such as *cloning*, *death penalty*, and *nuclear energy*, and yet has the lowest in-class F1 for the 'con' class (in-class F1 = .40). Performance thus appears to be less related to the number of training examples.

We investigated the source of low performance on the 'pro' and 'con' class in the *abortion* topic with confusion matrices, and compared this to a topic where pro and against did not under-perform (*minimum wage*). We did not pick one specific seed, but calculated the mean percentage of 'true' examples in each confusion matrix cell over all 10 seeds. In the *abortion* topic, 44 % of 'pro' arguments get classified as 'against', and only 33% get correctly classified as 'pro'. The *minimum wage* topic shows no discernible pro/against classification confusion, and 60% of all true 'pro' and 'against' arguments are correctly classified. The section below analyzes the misclassifications in low-performing topics.

4.2 Qualitative Analysis of Misclassification

The low performance of 'pro' and 'con' in some topics (*abortion*, *gun control*, and *death penalty*) warrants some further investigation. Table 5 shows four example misclassifications between 'pro' and 'con' by BERT-large in the test examples the model encountered on these topics.[9]

[9] To ensure we are not cherry-picking examples, we looked at errors that were not unique to just one seed, and identified these examples as salient examples of a general trend.

held-out topic	abortion	cloning	death penalty	gun control	marijuana legalization	minimum wage	nuclear energy	school uniform
SVM+tf-idf	.463	.585	.482	.515	.323	.615	.598	.576
BERT-base	.533 (.011)	.693 (.013)	.562 (.012)	.530 (.013)	.607 (.016)	.670 (.009)	.660 (.011)	.678 (.016)
diff.	+.070	+.108	+.080	+.*028*	**+.283**	+.055	+.0850	+.102

Table 3: BERT-base's performance in F1 (macro) on different held-out topics. The *italicized* difference shows the smallest difference between the SVM model and the BERT-base model (on the gun control topic), while the **bolded** difference shows the largest difference (on the marijuana topic).

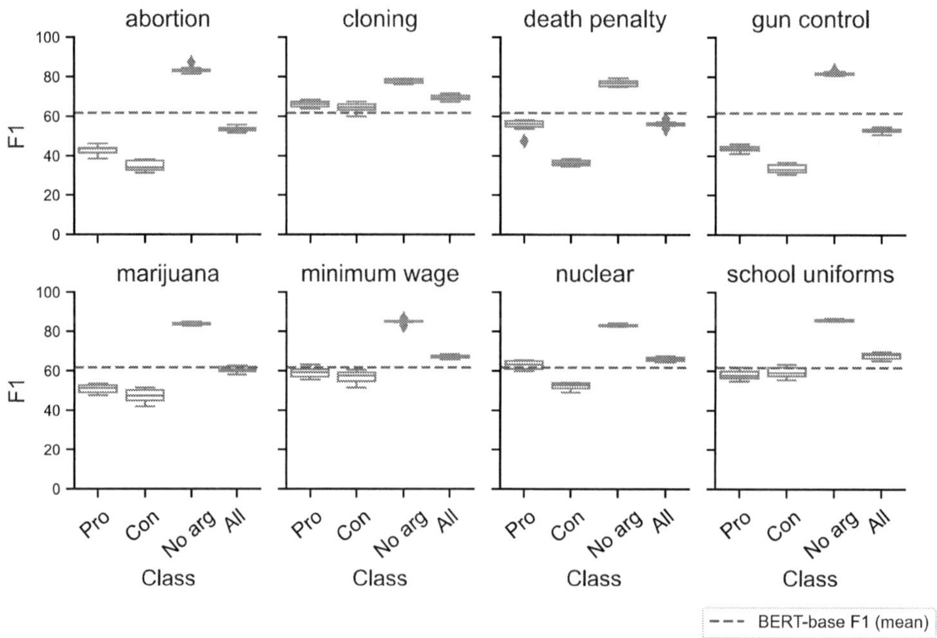

Figure 1: BERT-base's performance on different topics plotted in a boxplot, with on the y-axis the F1 score of the 4 categories plotted on the x-axis: 'pro', 'con', 'no argument', and overall. A longer boxplots means more variability over seeds in score. The red line represent the averaged F1 score of the same model (BERT-base), presented as model performance in Reimers et al. (2019).

We find two types of misclassifications, each related to topic-specific differences to stance classes. The first type is **misclassification due to the socio-cultural background knowledge and context** of a specific topic's arguments. The second type is related to a model taking the **stance towards a subcomponent of a topic** and confusing it for the text's overall stance on the topic, e.g. statements in the 'pro' class mostly expressing views *against* something else related to the argument (unwanted pregnancies, gun violence, innocents dying).

Examples of both issues are arguments centering around "many innocents (babies, children, mentally ill) will die". There are 5 variations of this argument in these 3 topics: row 1 and row 3 (*gun control*), row 8 (*abortion*), and rows 9 and 12 (*death penalty*) in Table 5. Not only is one usage of this argument traditionally connected to the 'pro' class of one topic (*gun control*), and the 'con' class of another (*abortion*), the implication is: innocents dying is bad. The model seems to lack this world knowledge, and for instance classifies this argument as 'pro' *death penalty*.

Another salient example is row 2 of Table 5. This argument argues *in favor* of gun rights for self-defense, but the model misclassifies this as *against* gun control. The model also fails to connect the second amendment discussion to the *against gun control* class. This is the same mistake made by the LSTM-model in Stab et al. (2018, p.3671), showing that BERT appears to not improve over LSTM on the topic-specific nuances here. In other words, it fails to correctly identify the socio-cultural dimensions (Du Bois, 2007) of this debate.

all topics				abortion topic			
Pro (vs Con)	Con (vs Pro)	No Argument		Pro (vs Con)	Con (vs Pro)	No Argument	
		vs Pro	vs Con			vs Pro	vs Con
pejorative	*morality*	basic	pronounced	seek	babies	way	anti
pronounced	format	section	threatens	illegal	abortion	against	ways
activity	*bill*	take	additional	reproductive	life	we	over
relations	workshop	**robert**	revolt	simply	conception	side	always
additional	workers	introduced	now	humane	simply	justify	thing
unexceptional	*sources*	unquestioned	proper	bear	risks	experience	question
threatens	*philosophical*	revolt	typical	lifers	abortions	held	performed
variable	coincidentally	scientifically	mentor	mother	complications	tell	debate
39th	*statutes*	**lifenews**	sharing	healthy	birth	single	illegal
where	phrases	individuals	denuded	lives	kill	had	equal

Table 4: Top-features for different topics according to SVM, Pairwise F-based feature analysis. We see potentially meaningful words in *italics* (the 'con' class has features based on morality and legality, e.g. bills and statutes), and potential spurious features in **bold** (such as names websites and even of individuals).

Topic	True	Pred	Sentence	Frequency in seeds
gun contr.	pro	con	"When high-capacity magazines were used in mass shootings, the death rate rose 63 % and the injury rate rose 156 % ."	9/10
gun contr.	con	pro	"[..] The Second Amendment protects an individual right to possess a firearm unconnected with service in a militia , and to use that arm for traditionally lawful purposes , such as self-defense within the home . "	7/10
gun contr.	pro	con	"In this crossfire , bullets would likely hit civilians (imagine a room filled with a crowd and three people shooting at each other) and the casualty count would increase."	9/10
gun contr.	con	pro	"Gun enthusiasts understand the benefit of large ammo feeders and wish to defend them because they recognize the advantage that such feeders give."	7/10
abortion	pro	con	"Not only has the biological development not yet occurred to support pain experience , but the environment after birth , so necessary to the development of pain experience , is also yet to occur ."	4/10
abortion	pro	con	"Warren concludes that as the fetus satisfies only one criterion, consciousness (and this only after it becomes susceptible to pain) , the fetus is not a person and abortion is therefore morally permissible ."	5/10
abortion	con	pro	It is argued that just as it would not be permissible to refuse temporary accommodation for the guest to protect him from physical harm , it would not be permissible to refuse temporary accommodation of a fetus .	2/10
abortion	con	pro	"92 % of abortions in America are purely elective – done on healthy women to end the lives of healthy children."	3/10
death pen.	con	pro	Mentally ill patients may be put to death .	2/10
death pen.	con	pro	Evidence shows execution does not act as a deterrent to capital punishment.	9/10
death pen.	pro	con	A system in place for the purpose of granting justice can not do so for the surviving victims , unless the murderer himself is put to death .	8/10
death pen.	con	pro	CON : " ... Since the reinstatement of the modern death pen. , 87 people have been freed from death row because they were later proven innocent .	9 /10

Table 5: Misclassifications on political topics with considerable 'pro' and 'con' confusion

4.3 SVM and Lexical Features

To analyze which words are used in relation to specific stances and topics, we trained an SVM model with tf-idf features on stance detection on all topics (F1 = .573). For each class pair ('pro' vs 'con', 'pro' vs 'no-argument', etc.), we extracted top-10 features with the highest coefficient for that specific class.

Table 4 presents the most important features of the topic-agnostic model trained on all topics. Some unigrams appear meaningful for the class. For instance, in the cross-topic setting, the word "morality" is a feature for the 'con' class. In contrast, the 'no argument' class is often identified with words that appear to have little content-relationship to the class identity: a topic-specific pro-life website (lifenews) or someone's name ('robert').

We also trained within-topic models to find whether there is topic-specific vocabulary related to stance that differs from the topic-agnostic model. Table 4 also presents the 10 most informative features for a model trained on only the abortion topic (F1 = .595). Immediately we see that there is only limited overlap with the lexical features used to decide between 'pro' and 'con' in a multi-topic scenario. Within only the abortion topic, the 'pro' and 'con' class are defined by concepts related to the lexical content of this specific discussion: babies, life, and birth. We also see the contrast between 'pro' arguments talking about reproduction and the mother, while the 'con' arguments mention life, conception, and babies. This lexical feature analysis shows no apparent overlap between the topic-specific features in the abortion model and the topic-independent features in the topic-agnostic model. This might indicate that vocabulary is quite specifically related to topics in stance detection.

5 Conclusion: Topic Matters

Stance detection is a difficult NLP task. Despite recent advances by pre-trained Transformers, these models have similar issues in a cross-topic setting as earlier models. This paper reproduced stance detection experiments with pre-trained Transformers by Reimers et al. (2019), training on seven topics and testing on an eighth topic. We found similar results, but also both class and topic influencing performance. Cross-topic BERT models perform below mean model performance in some topics (*abortion, gun control*) on the pro and con classes.

This makes us pause about Reimers et al. (2019)'s main claim: does BERT improve cross-topic stance detection over non-Transformer models? We argue this claim needs an asterisk: this cross-topic approach does not work as well for all topics. Different topics show specific vocabularies and socio-cultural contexts, and especially these specific contexts BERT cannot navigate. BERT models still make similar mistakes on gun control as the LSTM-based models in Stab et al. (2018).

These findings lead us to two take-aways. Firstly, we hypothesize that models like BERT rely more on topic-specific features for stance detection than topic-independent lexical words related to argumentation. Thorn Jakobsen et al. (2021) also recently found this, and connected BERT's cross-topic stance detection performance to its focus on spurious topic-specific lexical features ("gun", "criminal") rather than words related to argumentation. They also conclude a fair real-world evaluation of cross-topic stance detection means reporting the worst performing cross-topic pair rather than average performance over topics.

Secondly, we also think it is necessary to analyze the context of topics, and its relation to other debate topics within and outside the dataset. Most topics in stance detection studies are currently U.S. socio-political issues. This goes beyond a limitation of language, such as a focus on English without specifying this (Bender, 2019), since the same socio-cultural topics are not even universally relevant in the English-speaking world (gun control is not a salient discussion in Scotland). Such a focus on topic diversity is also important for use-cases. For diversity of viewpoints in search (Draws et al., 2021) or news recommendation (Reuver et al., 2021), stance detection needs to work on many different topics.

Schlangen (2021) states that we need to carefully define specific NLP tasks and capabilities needed to solve them. Modelling cross-topic stance detection in a topic-agnostic manner, while divorcing it from socio-cultural context, might not do justice to stance detection. Future work might focus on the specifics of topics: analyzing similarity between discussions (Wei and Mao, 2019), or modelling required socio-cultural contextual knowledge ('second amendment is related to gun control'). Models able to deal with topic-specific vocabulary and socio-cultural context of debates might improve on the state-of-the-art of cross-topic stance detection.

Acknowledgments

This research is funded through Open Competition Digitalization Humanities and Social Science grant nr 406.D1.19.073 awarded by the Netherlands Organization of Scientific Research (NWO). Our computing was done through SURF Research Cloud, a national supercomputer infrastructure in the Netherlands also funded by the NWO. We would like to thank dr. Nils Reimers for sending us their paper's data. We would also like to thank the anonymous reviewers, whose very helpful comments improved the paper. All opinions and remaining errors are our own.

References

Abeer ALDayel and Walid Magdy. 2021. Stance detection on social media: State of the art and trends. *Information Processing & Management*, 58(4):102597.

Emily Allaway, Malavika Srikanth, and Kathleen McKeown. 2021. Adversarial learning for zero-shot stance detection on social media. In *Proceedings of the 2021 Conference of the North American Chapter of the Association for Computational Linguistics: Human Language Technologies*, pages 4756–4767, Online. Association for Computational Linguistics.

Anya Belz, Shubham Agarwal, Anastasia Shimorina, and Ehud Reiter. 2021. A systematic review of reproducibility research in natural language processing. In *Proceedings of the 16th Conference of the European Chapter of the Association for Computational Linguistics: Main Volume*, pages 381–393, Online. Association for Computational Linguistics.

Emily Bender. 2019. The #benderrule: On naming the languages we study and why it matters. *The Gradient.*

Mihaela Bošnjak and Mladen Karan. 2019. Data set for stance and sentiment analysis from user comments on croatian news. In *Proceedings of the 7th Workshop on Balto-Slavic Natural Language Processing*, pages 50–55.

K Bretonnel Cohen, Jingbo Xia, Pierre Zweigenbaum, Tiffany J Callahan, Orin Hargraves, Foster Goss, Nancy Ide, Aurélie Névéol, Cyril Grouin, and Lawrence E Hunter. 2018. Three dimensions of reproducibility in natural language processing. In *LREC... International Conference on Language Resources & Evaluation:[proceedings]. International Conference on Language Resources and Evaluation*, volume 2018, page 156. NIH Public Access.

Kareem Darwish, Peter Stefanov, Michaël Aupetit, and Preslav Nakov. 2020. Unsupervised user stance detection on twitter. In *Proceedings of the International AAAI Conference on Web and Social Media*, volume 14, pages 141–152.

Jacob Devlin, Ming-Wei Chang, Kenton Lee, and Kristina Toutanova. 2019. BERT: Pre-training of deep bidirectional transformers for language understanding. In *Proceedings of the 2019 Conference of the North American Chapter of the Association for Computational Linguistics: Human Language Technologies, Volume 1 (Long and Short Papers)*, pages 4171–4186, Minneapolis, Minnesota. Association for Computational Linguistics.

Tim Draws, Nava Tintarev, and Ujwal Gadiraju. 2021. Assessing viewpoint diversity in search results using ranking fairness metrics. *ACM SIGKDD Explorations Newsletter*, 23(1):50–58.

John W Du Bois. 2007. The stance triangle. *Stancetaking in discourse: Subjectivity, evaluation, interaction*, 164(3):139–182.

William Ferreira and Andreas Vlachos. 2016. Emergent: a novel data-set for stance classification. In *Proceedings of the 2016 conference of the North American chapter of the association for computational linguistics: Human language technologies*, pages 1163–1168.

Antske Fokkens, Marieke Van Erp, Marten Postma, Ted Pedersen, Piek Vossen, and Nuno Freire. 2013. Offspring from reproduction problems: What replication failure teaches us. In *Proceedings of the 51st Annual Meeting of the Association for Computational Linguistics (Volume 1: Long Papers)*, pages 1691–1701.

Andreas Hanselowski, PVS Avinesh, Benjamin Schiller, Felix Caspelherr, Debanjan Chaudhuri, Christian M Meyer, and Iryna Gurevych. 2018. A retrospective analysis of the fake news challenge stance-detection task. In *Proceedings of the 27th International Conference on Computational Linguistics*, pages 1859–1874.

Momchil Hardalov, Arnav Arora, Preslav Nakov, and Isabelle Augenstein. 2021. A survey on stance detection for mis-and disinformation identification. *arXiv preprint arXiv:2103.00242.*

Tamanna Hossain, Robert L Logan IV, Arjuna Ugarte, Yoshitomo Matsubara, Sean Young, and Sameer Singh. 2020. Covidlies: Detecting covid-19 misinformation on social media. In *Proceedings of the 1st Workshop on NLP for COVID-19 (Part 2) at EMNLP 2020.*

Beata Beigman Klebanov, Eyal Beigman, and Daniel Diermeier. 2010. Vocabulary choice as an indicator of perspective. In *Proceedings of the ACL 2010 conference short papers*, pages 253–257.

Dilek Küçük and Fazli Can. 2020. Stance detection: A survey. *ACM Comput. Surv.*, 53(1).

Saif Mohammad, Svetlana Kiritchenko, Parinaz Sobhani, Xiaodan Zhu, and Colin Cherry. 2016. SemEval-2016 task 6: Detecting stance in tweets. In *Proceedings of the 10th International Workshop on Semantic Evaluation (SemEval-2016)*, pages 31–41, San Diego, California. Association for Computational Linguistics.

Stefan Ollinger, Lorik Dumani, Premtim Sahitaj, Ralph Bergmann, and Ralf Schenkel. 2020. Same Side Stance Classification Task: Facilitating Argument Stance Classification by Fine-tuning a BERT Model. *arXiv:2004.11163 [cs]*. ArXiv: 2004.11163.

Nils Reimers, Benjamin Schiller, Tilman Beck, Johannes Daxenberger, Christian Stab, and Iryna Gurevych. 2019. Classification and Clustering of Arguments with Contextualized Word Embeddings. In *Proceedings of the 57th Annual Meeting of the Association for Computational Linguistics*, pages 567–578, Florence, Italy. Association for Computational Linguistics.

Myrthe Reuver, Antske Fokkens, and Suzan Verberne. 2021. No NLP task should be an island: Multidisciplinarity for diversity in news recommender systems. In *Proceedings of the EACL Hackashop on News Media Content Analysis and Automated Report Generation*, pages 45–55, Online. Association for Computational Linguistics.

Benjamin Riedel, Isabelle Augenstein, Georgios P Spithourakis, and Sebastian Riedel. 2017. A simple but tough-to-beat baseline for the fake news challenge stance detection task. *arXiv preprint arXiv:1707.03264*.

Benjamin Schiller, Johannes Daxenberger, and Iryna Gurevych. 2021. Stance Detection Benchmark: How Robust is Your Stance Detection? *KI - Künstliche Intelligenz*.

David Schlangen. 2021. Targeting the benchmark: On methodology in current natural language processing research. In *Proceedings of the 59th Annual Meeting of the Association for Computational Linguistics and the 11th International Joint Conference on Natural Language Processing (Volume 2: Short Papers)*, pages 670–674, Online. Association for Computational Linguistics.

Eyal Shnarch, Carlos Alzate, Lena Dankin, Martin Gleize, Yufang Hou, Leshem Choshen, Ranit Aharonov, and Noam Slonim. 2018. Will it blend? blending weak and strong labeled data in a neural network for argumentation mining. In *Proceedings of the 56th Annual Meeting of the Association for Computational Linguistics (Volume 2: Short Papers)*, pages 599–605, Melbourne, Australia. Association for Computational Linguistics.

Swapna Somasundaran and Janyce Wiebe. 2009. Recognizing stances in online debates. In *Proceedings of the Joint Conference of the 47th Annual Meeting of the ACL and the 4th International Joint Conference on Natural Language Processing of the AFNLP*, pages 226–234, Suntec, Singapore. Association for Computational Linguistics.

Christian Stab, Tristan Miller, Benjamin Schiller, Pranav Rai, and Iryna Gurevych. 2018. Cross-topic argument mining from heterogeneous sources. In *Proceedings of the 2018 Conference on Empirical Methods in Natural Language Processing*, pages 3664–3674, Brussels, Belgium. Association for Computational Linguistics.

Benno Stein, Yamen Ajjour, Roxanne El Baff, Khalid Al-Khatib, Philipp Cimiano, AG Semantic Computing, and Henning Wachsmuth. 2021. Same side stance classification. Preprint.

Matt Thomas, Bo Pang, and Lillian Lee. 2006. Get out the vote: Determining support or opposition from congressional floor-debate transcripts. In *Proceedings of the 2006 Conference on Empirical Methods in Natural Language Processing*, EMNLP '06, page 327–335, USA. Association for Computational Linguistics.

Terne Sasha Thorn Jakobsen, Maria Barrett, and Anders Søgaard. 2021. Spurious correlations in cross-topic argument mining. In *Proceedings of *SEM 2021: The Tenth Joint Conference on Lexical and Computational Semantics*, pages 263–277, Online. Association for Computational Linguistics.

Penghui Wei and Wenji Mao. 2019. Modeling transferable topics for cross-target stance detection. In *Proceedings of the 42nd International ACM SIGIR Conference on Research and Development in Information Retrieval*, pages 1173–1176.

Lixing Zhu, Yulan He, and Deyu Zhou. 2019. Hierarchical viewpoint discovery from tweets using bayesian modelling. *Expert Systems with Applications*, 116:430–438.

Exploring Methodologies for Collecting High-Quality Implicit Reasoning in Arguments

Keshav Singh[‡] **Farjana Sultana Mim**[‡] **Naoya Inoue**[⋆,†]
Shoichi Naito[‡,†,◇] **Kentaro Inui**[‡,†]

[‡] Tohoku University [†] RIKEN [⋆] Stony Brook University [◇] Ricoh Company, Ltd.
{keshav.singh29,naoya.inoue.lab}@gmail.com
{mim.farjana.sultana.t3,naito.shoichi.t1}@dc.tohoku.ac.jp
inui@tohoku.ac.jp

Abstract

Annotation of implicit reasoning (i.e., warrant) in arguments is a critical resource to train models in gaining deeper understanding and correct interpretation of arguments. However, warrants are usually annotated in unstructured form, having no restriction on their lexical structure which sometimes makes it difficult to interpret how warrants relate to any of the information given in claim and premise. Moreover, assessing and determining better warrants from the large variety of reasoning patterns of unstructured warrants becomes a formidable task. Therefore, in order to annotate warrants in a more interpretative and restrictive way, we propose two methodologies to annotate warrants in a semi-structured form. To the best of our knowledge, we are the first to show how such semi-structured warrants can be annotated on a large scale via crowdsourcing. We demonstrate through extensive quality evaluation that our methodologies enable collecting better quality warrants in comparison to unstructured annotations. To further facilitate research towards the task of explicating warrants in arguments, we release our materials publicly (i.e., crowdsourcing guidelines and collected warrants).

1 Introduction

Implicit reasonings, commonly referred to as *warrants* (Toulmin, 1958), have long been studied to understand the grounds on which a premise lends support to the claim (Freeman, 1992). In other words, a warrant, when made explicit, clearly shows the inferential link between claim and premise (Pineau, 2013). As depicted in Figure 1, identification of such warrants by students has been shown to aid them in making better arguments (Erduran et al., 2004), as well as improving their critical thinking skills (von der Mühlen et al., 2019) and argument comprehension process (Hitchcock and Verheij, 2006).

While explication of warrants with assistance from teachers has been shown to be useful for improving students' argumentation skills, automating this explication process would not only help students to be less dependent on teachers, but it can also be beneficial for different downstream educational applications such as argument analysis (Becker et al., 2020), enthymeme reconstruction (Razuvayevskaya and Teufel, 2017; Hulpus et al., 2019) and essay scoring (Williamson, 2013). However, building an automated warrant explication system has been a challenge due to the difficulty of collecting warrants in a form that explicitly manifests the way a warrant relates the information between claim and premise. Generally, warrants are annotated in an unstructured (i.e., free-text) format which lays no restriction on its lexical structure (Boltužić and Šnajder, 2016). As a result, sometimes the warrant consist of no information that overlaps with claim or premise which makes it difficult to understand how the warrant connects the claim to its premise. Furthermore, for a given argument, unstructured warrants can be framed in diverse ways that would have a wide variety of reasoning patterns (Kock, 2006) (given no restriction on the lexical structure), and identifying the correct ones from this large pool of warrants can be a preposterous task.

In order to annotate warrants on a large-scale and in a way that overcomes the aforementioned challenges, we propose two novel warrant annotation methodologies: Pre-defined Keyword-based Warrant (PKW) and User-defined Keyword-based Warrant (UKW), which restrict a warrant's lexical structure to a semi-structured form. In contrast to approaches that crowdsource unstructured warrants, these methodologies explicate warrant by enforcing it to have the key information (i.e., keywords) from both claim and premise. The intuition behind our semi-structured approach is to restrict the structure of warrants to specific keyword-based

Proceedings of The 8th Workshop on Argument Mining, pages 57–66
Punta Cana, Dominican Republic, November 10–11, 2021.

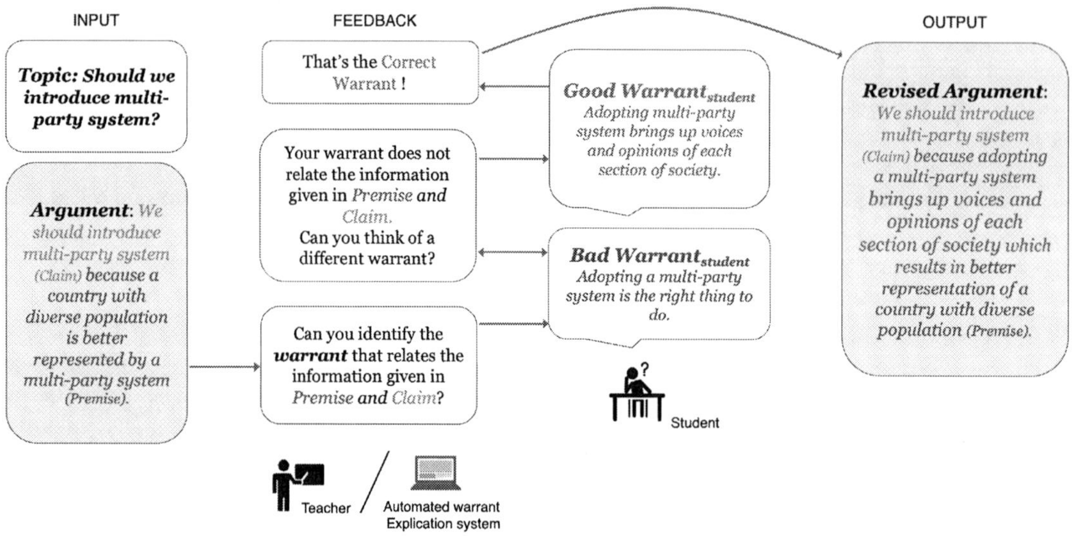

Figure 1: A typical example of warrant explication. Feedback provided by teachers or automated warrant explication system can help students identify correct warrants and leverage it in their revised argument to make the argument more reasonable.

reasoning patterns. We hypothesize that leveraging such keyword-based pattern could assist in collecting high quality warrants, where keywords are derived from the original argument (i.e., claim and premise). Our assumption follows the formal definition of warrants in the sense that warrants act as a inferential link between the contents of claim and its premise (Toulmin, 1958; Freeman, 1992).

Many previous work demonstrated different strategies of collecting high quality warrants (Becker et al., 2017; Habernal et al., 2018; Becker et al., 2020), but did not apply any restriction on the structure of warrants to handle the variety of reasoning patterns in which warrants can be explicated. In contrast, our annotation methodologies are designed to restrict the reasoning pattern and ensure that warrant explicates the reasoning link between claim and premise.

In order to evaluate the warrants annotated via our proposed UKW and PKW methodologies, we devise specific guidelines to judge their quality through scoring. We also collect unstructured warrants (i.e., Natural Language Warrants (NLW)) and perform quality evaluation on them in order to compare with our annotated warrants. Our results suggest that in comparison to NLW, high quality warrants can be annotated via our proposed UKW methodology. To the best of our knowledge, this is the first study which targets large scale annotation of warrants in semi-structured form. To facilitate further research in warrant explication, we publish our crowdsourcing guidelines and the preliminary corpus of around 1700 warrants that are annotated via UKW methodology, covering over 600 arguments [1].

2 Related Work

Explication of warrants in arguments has already been approached in many previous researches. In an initial attempt, Feng and Hirst (2011) proposed leveraging argumentation schemes (Walton et al., 2008) as a means to automatically reconstruct warrant, but did not approach the task due to the absence of training datasets. To overcome the unavailability of dataset, Boltužić and Šnajder (2016) leverage crowdsourcing and ask non-expert workers to annotate all possible variations of warrants for a given claim-premise pair. However, they concluded that the annotation of warrants varied both in number annotated per argument and in content due to no restrictions imposed on in the annotation process.

In order to overcome the prior difficulties, recent approaches leverage crowdsourcing to restrict the number of warrants collected per argument and either employ a step by step filtering process to weed out bad warrants (Habernal et al., 2018) or hire ex-

[1] Our crowdsourcing guidelines and annotated warrants are publicly available at `https://github.com/cl-tohoku/ukw-warrants`

	Argument	Warrant
1.	Claim: We should abolish zoos. Premise: Zoos are notorious for animal abuse.	Abolishing zoos *leads to animals being in their natural habitat which results in no* animal abuse.
2.	Claim: We should ban whaling. Premise: Whaling is considered to be unacceptable cruelty towards animals.	Banning whaling *would stop the inhumane methods of stabbing whales which is* unacceptable cruelty towards animals.
3.	Claim: We should introduce compulsory voting. Premise: Compulsory voting can help obtain better results during elections.	Introducing compulsory voting *leads to every citizen exercising the right to vote which can help* obtain better results during elections.

Table 1: Example warrants demonstrating the semi-structured form used for annotation.

perts who iteratively converge to a single warrant annotation (Becker et al., 2017). In an advanced attempt, Razuvayevskaya and Teufel (2017) explored whether it is feasible for human annotators to explicate warrants in arguments. They propose the idea of template-based warrant reconstruction using information from premise and claim, and employ experts to perform the task. In contrast, our annotation methodology is designed for expert as well as non-expert workers. Additionally, our annotation aims to restrict the warrant's structure to semi-structured format such that it comprises knowledge that is necessary to form an inferential link between the key contents of claim and premise. Furthermore, we do not restrict the number of warrants to one, but collect set of warrants per argument that fulfill the criteria of qualifying as a high quality warrant.

3 Warrant Desiderata

We define warrant that we want to annotate by characterizing its desired properties. Properties such as structure of warrant, quality in terms of how well a warrant links claim and premise, and feasibility of annotating warrant for an argument. In this work, we define this feasibility in terms of whether a warrant can be annotated for an argument, regardless of whether it is good or bad. We assume that explication of a warrant might not be possible if the argument is too good (i.e., warrant is explicated in the premise) or if the argument is too bad (i.e., no warrant can explicate the link between claim and premise).

Structure Warrants are implicit reasoning that logically link the contents of claim and premise (Toulmin, 1958; Freeman, 1992). Therefore, we hypothesize that a warrant should have a structure that (a) comprises the key information given in claim and premise, and (b) explicates logical connection between the aforementioned key information with some implicit knowledge that is relevant to the argument. We define the warrants framed in such a way as semi-structured warrants. Examples of such semi-structured warrants are provided in Table 1, where key information or keywords from claim and premise is linked with relevant implicit knowledge which all together forms a semi-structured warrant.

Feasibility Warrants may not be explicable for all the arguments. Specifically, for an argument with bad premise there may be no feasible way to explicate the logical link between claim and premise. For example, the warrant for the argument *"We should introduce multi-party system because it's the right thing to do"* is not feasible, since the argument is a fallacy (i.e. begging the question) where the premise: *"it's the right thing to do"* provides no adequate support to the claim: *"We should introduce multi-party system"*. Similarly, for arguments with very good premise, it might not be necessary to explicate the warrant since the warrant might already be explicated in the premise. In contrast, as shown in Table 1, for arguments with moderately good/bad premise, we assume that one can frame a warrant by leveraging argument relevant external knowledge. [2].

[2]The arguments shown in Table 1 were already annotated with moderate quality scores in a larger study (Gretz et al., 2019)

Quality A key factor distinguishing warrants from any other type of implicit knowledge or statement (e.g., commonsense knowledge) is their ability to justify the flow of reasoning between claim and premise. For example, in Table 1, warrant (3) explicitly answers how introducing compulsory voting can help obtain better results in elections. These are the type of warrants we would like to annotate. Conversely, statements which do not serve this purpose cannot be qualified as a warrant. For example, given argument (3) from Table 1, the statement *"Introducing compulsory voting enables people to freely choose their favourite candidate which results in encouraging better results during elections"* cannot be labeled as a warrant because it offers little to no help in bridging the implicit reasoning link between claim and premise.

4 Annotation Methodologies

In this section, we discuss the development and design of our proposed semi-structured annotation methodologies. In particular, we consider two methodologies for annotating warrants: *Pre-defined Keyword-based Warrant* and *User-defined Keyword-based Warrants*.

Pre-defined Keyword-based Warrants (PKW) In order to annotate semi-structured warrants that encompass information from claim and premise, we propose using keywords which encode the key information given in claim and premise. As shown in Table 1, the purpose of these keywords is to create a semi-structured format for completing a warrant annotation such that keywords from claim form the initial (shown in red) and keywords from premise (shown in blue) form the latter part of the warrant. The keywords are linked by implicit knowledge that is necessary to connect the keywords in a meaningful way. Example annotation and task design of PKW annotation is shown in Figure 2. For PKW methodology, the annotator is initially provided with keywords and is tasked to explain the flow of reasoning between them by writing implicit knowledge (i.e., hidden reasoning).

In order to provide pre-defining keywords to the annotator, we employ spaCy (Honnibal et al., 2020) and automatically extract the key information from claim and premise by parsing the sentence into verb/noun phrases. For example, for claim *"We should ban whaling"*, the verb phrase *"Banning whaling"* and for premise *"Whales are necessary for ecological sustainability of the oceans"*, the noun phrase *"ecological sustainability of the oceans"* is extracted. To ensure the feasibility of framing a warrant with extracted keywords, we perform a manual check and if needed, make minimal changes to its tense or word-order.

User-defined Keyword-based Warrants (UKW) While PKW methodology introduces restrictions on warrant annotation via pre-defined keywords, they might be too restrictive or not provide sufficient flexibility for annotators to annotate the warrant. Moreover, automatically extracting keywords from claim and premise can be sometimes challenging due to varied syntactic structure of the argument. Therefore as an alternate approach, we ask the annotators to derive their own keywords from claim and premise. To do this, we provide detailed guidelines and concrete examples in our interface for annotators so that they can correctly understand the process of deriving keywords.

The annotation design and example annotation is shown in Figure 3 , where for the given claim and premise, the keywords from claim can be a verb phrase: *"Introducing compulsory voting"*, and keywords from premise can be verb phrase: *"obtain better results during elections"*. To avoid annotations where annotator might write keywords with information from outside claim/premise, annotators were strictly advised not to use any external knowledge when writing the keywords, although the use of external knowledge was permitted for writing the hidden reasoning.

5 Warrant Collection Procedure

Our goal is to establish a procedure for collecting semi-structured warrants and their annotations at large-scale. In order to collect such warrants from each methodology, we build a multi-step crowdsourcing process designed for encouraging annotator's creativity, while preventing biases in the annotations.

In general, we break the warrant collection procedure into three steps of simple tasks: (i) Deriving keywords, (ii) Judging feasibility and (iii) Framing warrant. In addition, we implement several mechanisms for quality assurance and employ manual checks to ensure annotators understand and perform the final task correctly.

(i) Deriving keywords In order to collect semi-structured warrants, we require keywords derived from each of claim and premise. These keywords

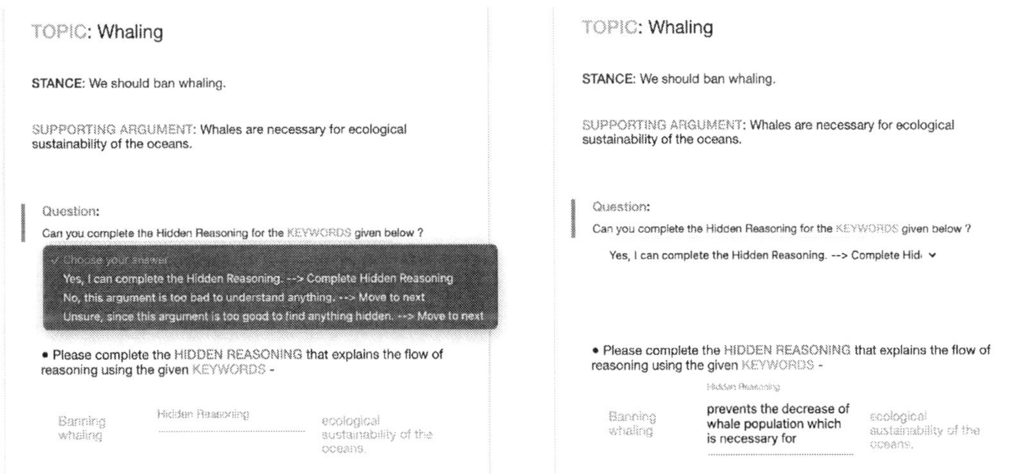

Figure 2: The interface used for warrant annotations, along with an example of a annotator's annotation for Pre-defined Keyword-based Warrant. To avoid using complicated terminology, we used the terms *stance*, *supporting statement* and *hidden reasoning* to convey the notion of claim, premise and warrant respectively.

act as the skeleton of the final annotated warrant. For example, as shown on the left side of Figure 3, *"Introducing compulsory voting"* and *"obtain better results during elections"* are keywords derived from claim and premise respectively. To derive these keywords, annotators are instructed to strictly include only key information conveyed in their respective counterparts and no external information. For PKW methodology, keywords in this step are already derived as shown in Figure 2. To ensure annotators understand the notion of keywords, we provide sufficient variety of examples for them to get used to this sub-task.

(b) Judging feasibility Since warrants may not be explicable for all the arguments, i.e., if a premise is very bad or contrastingly very good, we explicitly ask annotators to judge the feasibility of writing a warrant by asking if they can complete the hidden reasoning. This step is rather tricky since annotators may be biased to answer "No" or "Unsure" (See Question in Figure 2 and 3) to avoid doing the task and finish the task quickly. To avoid this, we treat this step as bonus question and depending on majority response i.e., if majority of annotators believe a warrant can be explicated for the given argument, then the majority annotators get bonus. Similarly, if majority of annotators believe a warrant cannot be explicated for a given argument, then again majority annotators get bonus. We keep a high bonus for this step in order to compel annotators to do task as instructed instead of providing low quality response. This step helps us get a better judgement of feasibility of warrants and also identify annotators who are not doing the task properly.

(c) Framing Warrant The last step in warrant collection procedure is for the annotators to frame the hidden reasoning to complete the warrant. This step is the most challenging since it requires the annotator to be logical and use his background knowledge to complete warrant annotation. To complete this via PKW methodology, annotator's are restricted in terms of pre-defined keywords, while for UKW methodology the annotator can annotate the warrant by minimally changing the keywords as well as hidden reasoning.

Auxiliary verification measures For each task, we hold preliminary qualification test that consists of several basic questions to judge the understanding of annotator's reasoning skills. Annotators who score more than a pre-defined threshold ($\geq 80\%$) are granted access to the main task. Our qualifications are open to annotators from major English speaking countries, namely USA, UK, New Zealand and Canada. Additionally, to address any ethical issues (Adda et al., 2011) raised by our task, we actively monitored multiple pilot tests to ensure annotators were satisfied with our task. Simultaneously, we corresponded directly to annotators that had questions/comments on our task. Annotators were paid in accordance with the minimum wage

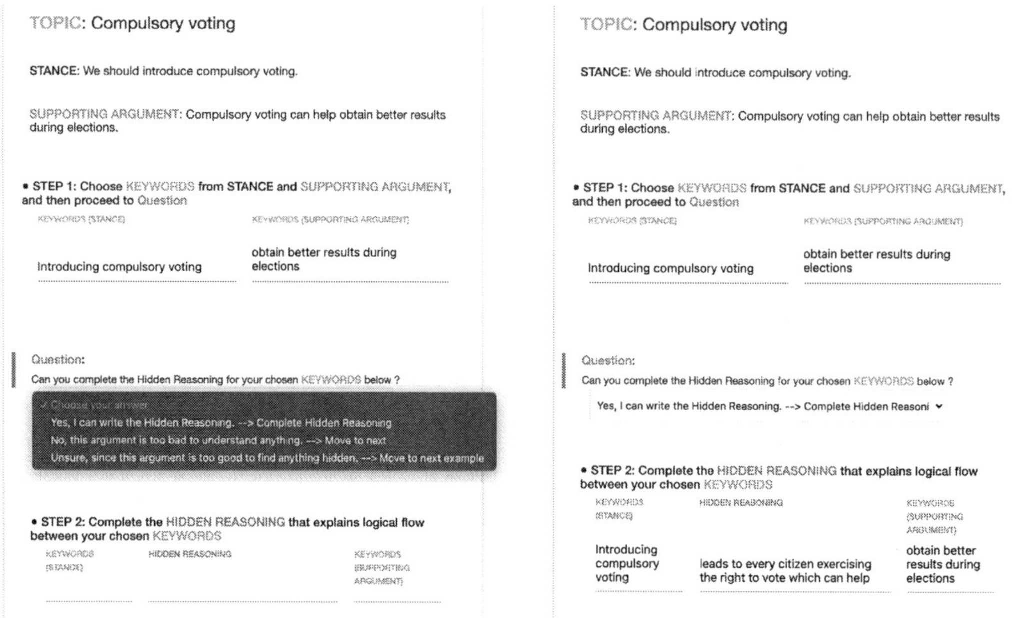

Figure 3: The interface used for our warrant annotations, along with an example of a annotator's annotation for User-defined Keyword-based Warrant.

calculated by conducting many trials and based on average work-time. Additional bonus was paid to annotators that provided quality annotations.

6 Crowdsourcing

We choose Amazon Mechanical Turk (AMT)[3] as our crowdsourcing platform due to its success in previous argumentation mining tasks (Habernal et al., 2018). As an initial step, we only allowed annotators who had $\geq$ 98% acceptance rate and $\geq$ 5,000 approved Human Intelligence Tasks (HITs). Each annotator was paid \$0.30 for doing the task and workers who qualified for bonus were paid an additional \$0.25 per HIT. For the task involving UKW annotations, the payment was increased to \$0.40 for doing the task and \$0.35 as bonus.

Source data For the purpose of annotating warrants for a given set of arguments, we utilize a well-known argumentation dataset, IBM-Rank-30K corpus (Gretz et al., 2019), which already consists arguments in the form of claim and premise. The dataset contains around 15K crowd-sourced arguments covering 71 topics, annotated for supporting as well as opposing stance.[4] The arguments were collected with strict length limitations and accompanied by extensive quality control measures. Our inspection of arguments from IBM-Rank-30k revealed that a for large proportion of the arguments we can explicate warrants. To proceed with our warrant annotation, we selected a subset of three 3 well-known debatable topics: *We should abolish zoos*, *We should ban whaling* and *We should introduce compulsory voting*.

Annotations In addition to warrants annotated via PKW and UKW methodologies, we also annotated unstructured warrants via crowdsourcing to compare the quality of annotated warrants across different methodologies. We followed similar crowdsourcing procedure as employed by Habernal et al. (2018) and refer to the warrants annotated via this process as *Natural language Warrants (NLW)*. For each methodology, we annotate 40 unique claim and premise pairs, randomly chosen from the three pre-selected topics. Each argument was annotated by 5 annotators resulting in a total of 200 annotations per methodology and all warrants were limited to have a length between 60 and 200 characters excluding keywords.

Filtering For each methodology, it is possible to collect at most 200 warrants (given 40 arguments and 5 annotators). However, not all annotators

[3] www.mturk.com

[4] In our work we only focus on arguments with supporting stance.

Methodology	Natural Language		User-defined		Pre-defined	
Topic	α	Avg.	α	Avg.	α	Avg.
Abolish zoos	0.64	1.55	0.67	1.60	0.62	1.57
Intro. compulsory voting	0.45	1.50	0.51	1.55	0.53	1.47
Ban whaling	0.63	1.37	0.61	1.61	0.58	1.59
Overall	0.57	1.46	0.56	**1.59**	0.53	1.55

Table 2: Comparison between the different warrant crowdsourcing methodologies. Avg. corresponds to the average score given by both expert annotators.

Score	Explanation
0	Warrant is unrelated to the claim and its premise.
1	Warrant is related to the claim and premise but does not make the relationship between them easy to understand and/or strengthen the argument. In addition, the warrant may overlap or be a paraphrase of the premise.
2	The relationship between the claim and premise is easier to understand and/or strengthened because of the warrant.

Table 3: Guidelines used by our expert annotators for scoring the quality of warrants on a scale of 0-2.

chose "Yes" when they were asked to judge if they can write a warrant. After filtering the negative responses at this step, we discover that, in total, annotators wrote 155, 101 and 65 warrants out of possible 200 warrants for Natural language Warrant, PKW and UKW methodologies respectively. We utilize these 321 collected warrants for further analysis.

7 Results

In order to analyze the quality of the annotated warrants, we hired two annotators who are experts in the field of argumentation to score the crowdsourced warrants. To frame quality scoring guidelines for judging warrants, we ran several pilot tests and take expert advice to make our guidelines easier to interpret. Our final quality annotation guidelines are shown in Table 3. The experts were asked to score a given warrant on a scale of (0-2), with 0 being the lowest and 2 being the highest. Both annotators were given 50 warrants randomly chosen from the pool of collected warrants for each methodology. Each topic was represented fairly in the quality annotation step with each topic having at least 15 warrants. In total, our experts annotated 150 warrants out of a total 321 annotated warrants. As shown in Table 2, the agreement between both experts as judged by Krippendorff's alpha α (Krippendorff, 2011) was found to be fairly good. We find that the average scores given by two expert annotators (Avg.) on a scale of (0-2) indicated user-defined and pre-defined methodologies with overall higher quality warrants as compared to natural language warrants. We also measure the combined average score given to the warrants for each topic to measure if the warrants belonging to one topic was of higher quality. We find that on average warrants annotated for *Introducing compulsory voting* were scored the lowest while for other topics was fairly high.

7.1 Qualitative Analysis

To further analyze the quality of warrants and the quality of the entire crowdsourcing process, we analyze sample of the warrants collected via each methodology and which were annotated by experts.

In Table 4, we can see that the warrants that were scored the highest by experts have fair amount of keyword overlap with the claim/premise. This follows from our initial motivation for using semi-structured annotation methodology where we hypothesized that the inclusion of keyword information from the claim and premise can assist in framing better quality warrants. As shown in Table 4, warrants UKW (1) and PKW (1) have similar keywords *"Banning whaling"* and *"ecological sustainability of the oceans"*, hence the annotated implicit knowledge is also same. This indicates that our keyword-based PKW and UKW methodologies restrict the diverse ways in which warrants can be explicated. On the contrary, for NLW (1) the warrant is analogous to a general statement yet has

1.	Claim: We should ban whaling. Premise: Whales are necessary for ecological sustainability of the oceans.
NLW:	Marine life in the ocean cannot survive without ecological sustainability.
PKW:	Banning whaling would prevent the decreasing of whale population on which marine life thrives which will result in ecological sustainability of the oceans.
UKW:	Banning whaling prevents the decreasing of whale population which is necessary for ecological sustainability of the oceans.
2.	Claim: We should abolish zoos. Premise: We should abolish zoos to prevent the cruel confinement of wild animals.
NLW:	Animals in confinement suffer physically and emotionally.
PKW:	Abolishing zoos enables animals to live a more stimulating and fulfilling life in the wild which prevents the cruel confinement of wild animals.
UKW:	Zoos force many animals to live in prison-like environment with unhygienic conditions which is a cruel way of confining wild animals.
3.	Claim: We should introduce compulsory voting. Premise: Compulsory voting can help encourage better results during elections.
NLW:	Mandatory voting will reflect people's actual preferences in election results.
PKW:	Compulsory voting produces a winning candidate that is more accurately representative of all the voters which ensures better election results.
UKW:	Introducing compulsory voting stops one side from rigging the process by canvasing more people which results in better elections.

Table 4: Examples of warrants scored 2 by both experts. Majority of warrant belonging to UKW methodology were found to be of good quality.

1.	Claim: We should ban whaling. Premise: Whaling has led to a major decrease in whale populations over the years.
NLW:	Whales could soon die off completely. It is our duty to ban whaling.
PKW:	Banning whaling leads to whales not dying which has cause decrease in whale population over the years.
UKW:	Banning whaling is a harmful practice which results in decrease in whale population over the years.
2.	Claim: We should abolish zoos. Premise:It is unfair to trap animals from their natural habitat and confine them to small spaces for human entertainment.
NLW:	Zoos keep animals captive where where they cannot run free and thrive.
PKW:	Abolishing zoos is a bad practice because it is unfair to trap animals from their natural habitat and confine them to small spaces for human entertainment.
UKW:	Abolishing zoos makes sure that animals are not being treated unfair and in small spaces.
3.	Claim: We should introduce compulsory voting. Premise: Compulsive voting is a patriotic act that must be fully complied with.
NLW:	We enjoy the freedom and liberty enjoyed by expressing our opinions. We should take advantage of such compulsion.
PKW:	Introducing compulsory voting makes you feel that you belong to your country which is a patriotic act.
UKW:	Compulsory voting will force people to engage in politics and choose a right leader that can lead their country in the future.

Table 5: Examples of warrants scored 0 or 1 by both experts. Low scored warrants were mainly paraphrased (Scored 1) from the premise or did not relate to the given topic (Scored 0).

similar implicit knowledge explicated in UKW (1) and PKW (1) warrants. This hints that NLW can also be of higher quality but its quality can vary to a larger extent due to no restrictions.

In Table 5, we can see that even though the warrants encode claim-premise information, the quality of the warrant can essentially be bad. For example, the warrants PLW (1) and UKW (1) explicate implicit knowledge which does not make the inferential link between claim and premise clear. Additionally, we note that while keyword-based methods restrict most warrants to a single sentence, natural language warrants often consist of shorter yet multiple sentences. Overall, we found that 23% of natural language warrants were composed of more than one sentences. Besides, such warrants were scored low and were often found to be paraphrased from the information in the premise or annotators rephrased previous premise in place of the warrant. Although this was mostly observed in natural language warrants, we found few such instances in our keyword-based collected warrants (See UKW (1) in

Table 5). This suggests that while keyword-based methods assist in collecting warrants that explicate the inferential link between claim and premise, it still does not guarantee high quality warrant annotations and might require further adjustments.

7.2 Preliminary large-scale corpus

Based on our finding that user-defined keyword-based warrant methodology comparatively results in better warrants, we follow this method to collect a total of 1700 warrants across 3 topics, annotated for 600 claim-premise pairs. All warrants are limited to have a length between 60 and 200 characters. Since this is an ongoing work, we plan to make further analysis on our preliminary dataset in future.

8 Conclusion and Future work

In this work, we tackle the difficult task of explicating warrants in arguments and propose two novel methodologies to annotate warrants in semi-structured format. We conduct extensive analysis and perform annotation study for determining the appropriate methodology for collecting warrants and show that user-defined keyword based approach produces the highest quality warrants as compared to pre-defined keyword-based warrant and natural language warrants. In future, we plan to extend the annotation of warrants for more diverse topics. Moreover, we plan to cover warrant annotations for claim-premise pairs with premises attacking the claim in addition to premises supporting the original claim. We would also like to test the usefulness of our annotations for constructing a model for automatic warrant explication which can be used to explicate warrant for any given argument. We believe that such a model can be useful in a pedagogical setting to perform downstream tasks such as argument analysis or giving constructive feedback to students.

Acknowledgements

This work was partially supported by JST CREST Grant Number JPMJCR20D2 and NEDO Grant Number J200001946. The authors would like to thank Paul Reisert, other members of the Tohoku NLP Lab, and the anonymous reviewers for their insightful feedback.

References

Gilles Adda, Benoît Sagot, Karën Fort, and Joseph Mariani. 2011. Crowdsourcing for language resource development: Critical analysis of amazon mechanical turk overpowering use. In *5th Language and Technology Conference*.

Maria Becker, Ioana Hulpuş, Juri Opitz, Debjit Paul, Jonathan Kobbe, Heiner Stuckenschmidt, and Anette Frank. 2020. Explaining arguments with background knowledge. *Datenbank-Spektrum*, 20(2):131–141.

Maria Becker, Michael Staniek, Vivi Nastase, and Anette Frank. 2017. Enriching argumentative texts with implicit knowledge. In *International Conference on Applications of Natural Language to Information Systems*, pages 84–96. Springer.

Filip Boltužić and Jan Šnajder. 2016. Fill the gap! analyzing implicit premises between claims from online debates. In *Proceedings of the Third Workshop on Argument Mining (ArgMining2016)*, pages 124–133, Berlin, Germany. Association for Computational Linguistics.

Sibel Erduran, Shirley Simon, and Jonathan Osborne. 2004. Tapping into argumentation: Developments in the application of toulmin's argument pattern for studying science discourse. *Science education*, 88(6):915–933.

Vanessa Wei Feng and Graeme Hirst. 2011. Classifying arguments by scheme. In *Proceedings of the 49th Annual Meeting of the Association for Computational Linguistics: Human Language Technologies*, pages 987–996, Portland, Oregon, USA. Association for Computational Linguistics.

James B Freeman. 1992. Relevance, warrants, backing, inductive support. *Argumentation*, 6(2):219–275.

Shai Gretz, Roni Friedman, Edo Cohen-Karlik, Assaf Toledo, Dan Lahav, Ranit Aharonov, and Noam Slonim. 2019. A large-scale dataset for argument quality ranking: Construction and analysis. *arXiv preprint arXiv:1911.11408*.

Ivan Habernal, Henning Wachsmuth, Iryna Gurevych, and Benno Stein. 2018. SemEval-2018 task 12: The argument reasoning comprehension task. In *Proceedings of The 12th International Workshop on Semantic Evaluation*, New Orleans, Louisiana. Association for Computational Linguistics.

David Hitchcock and Bart Verheij. 2006. *Arguing on the Toulmin model*, volume 10. Springer.

Matthew Honnibal, Ines Montani, Sofie Van Landeghem, and Adriane Boyd. 2020. spaCy: Industrial-strength Natural Language Processing in Python.

Ioana Hulpus, Jonathan Kobbe, Christian Meilicke, Heiner Stuckenschmidt, Maria Becker, Juri Opitz, Vivi Nastase, and Anette Frank. 2019. Towards explaining natural language arguments with background knowledge. In *PROFILES/SEMEX@ ISWC*, pages 62–77.

Christian Kock. 2006. Multiple warrants in practical reasoning. In *Arguing on the Toulmin model*, pages 247–259. Springer.

Klaus Krippendorff. 2011. Computing krippendorff's alpha-reliability.

Andrew Pineau. 2013. The abuses of argument: Understanding fallacies on toulmin's layout of argument. *Informal Logic*, 33(4):531–546.

Olesya Razuvayevskaya and Simone Teufel. 2017. Finding enthymemes in real-world texts: A feasibility study. *Argument & computation*, 8(2):113–129.

Stephen Edelston Toulmin. 1958. *The use of argument*. Cambridge University Press.

Sarah von der Mühlen, Tobias Richter, Sebastian Schmid, and Kirsten Berthold. 2019. How to improve argumentation comprehension in university students: Experimental test of a training approach. *Instructional Science*, 47(2):215–237.

Douglas Walton, Christopher Reed, and Fabrizio Macagno. 2008. *Argumentation schemes*. Cambridge University Press.

David M Williamson. 2013. Probable cause: Developing warrants for automated scoring of essays. In *Handbook of automated essay evaluation*, pages 175–202. Routledge.

Assessing the Sufficiency of Arguments through Conclusion Generation

Timon Gurcke **Milad Alshomary** **Henning Wachsmuth**
Department of Computer Science
Paderborn University, Paderborn, Germany
<first name>.<last name>@uni-paderborn.de

Abstract

The premises of an argument give evidence or other reasons to support a conclusion. However, the amount of support required depends on the generality of a conclusion, the nature of the individual premises, and similar. An argument whose premises make its conclusion rationally worthy to be drawn is called *sufficient* in argument quality research. Previous work tackled sufficiency assessment as a standard text classification problem, not modeling the inherent relation of premises and conclusion. In this paper, we hypothesize that the conclusion of a sufficient argument can be *generated* from its premises. To study this hypothesis, we explore the potential of assessing sufficiency based on the output of large-scale pre-trained language models. Our best model variant achieves an F_1-score of .885, outperforming the previous state-of-the-art and being on par with human experts. While manual evaluation reveals the quality of the generated conclusions, their impact remains low ultimately.

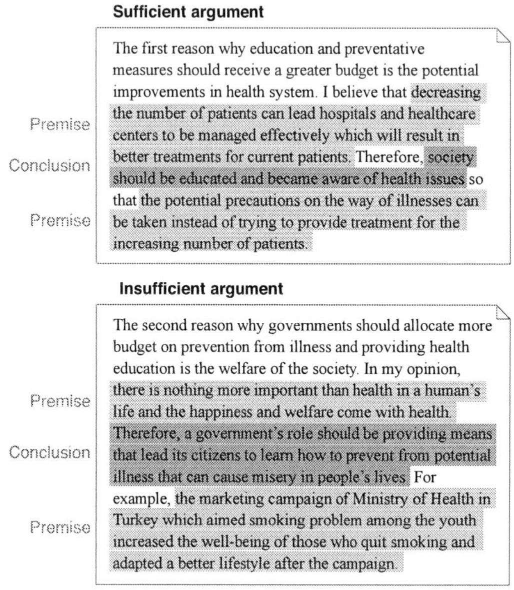

Figure 1: Two example arguments from a persuasive student essay, one classified as *sufficient*, the other as *insufficient* in the corpus of Stab and Gurevych (2017b).

1 Introduction

The quality assessment of natural language argumentation is nowadays studied extensively for various genres and text granularities, from entire news editorials (El Baff et al., 2020) to arguments in online forums (Lauscher et al., 2020) to single claims in social media discussions (Skitalinskaya et al., 2021). The reason lies in its importance for driving downstream applications such as writing support (Stab, 2017), argument search (Wachsmuth et al., 2017b), and debating technologies (Slonim et al., 2021). Wachsmuth et al. (2017a) organized quality dimensions of arguments into three complementary aspects: logic, rhetoric, and dialectic. Logical quality refers to the actual argument structure, that is, how strong an argument is in terms of the support of a claim (the argument's *conclusion*) by evidence and other reasons (the *premises*).

A key dimension of logical quality is *sufficiency*, capturing whether an argument's premises together make it rationally worthy of drawing its conclusion (Johnson and Blair, 2006). Consider, for example, the two arguments on health education in Figure 1, taken from the argument-annotated essay corpus of Stab and Gurevych (2017a). While the upper one was deemed sufficient by human experts (Stab and Gurevych, 2017b), the lower one was not, likely because the second premise tries to reason from a single example. A reliable computational assessment of argument sufficiency would allow systems to determine those arguments that are well-reasoned.

As detailed in Section 2, previous approaches to argument sufficiency assessment model the task as a standard text classification problem and tackle it with convolutional neural networks (Stab and Gurevych, 2017b) or traditional feature engineer-

Proceedings of The 8th Workshop on Argument Mining, pages 67–77
Punta Cana, Dominican Republic, November 10–11, 2021.

ing (Wachsmuth and Werner, 2020). In the focused domain of persuasive student essays, Stab and Gurevych (2017b) obtained a macro F_1-score of .827, not far away from human performance in their setting (.887). However, to further improve the state of the art, we expect the integration of knowledge beyond what is directly available in the text at hand is needed. In particular, we observe that existing work neither explicitly considers an argument's premises and conclusions, nor a property of their relationship. We hypothesize that only a sufficient argument makes it possible to infer the conclusion from the premises. Consequently, comparing the stated conclusion of an argument with one that is (automatically) *generated* from the premises could help the model to distinguish sufficient arguments from insufficient ones. This hypothesis raises the question of whether the knowledge encoded in large-scale pre-trained language models can be leveraged, a direction nearly unexplored so far in argument quality assessment.

In this paper, we study whether generating a conclusion from an argument's premises benefits the computational assessment of the argument's sufficiency. In particular, we first enrich the argument with structural annotations, highlighting which parts are the premises and which part is the conclusion. We propose in Section 4 to then mask the conclusion in order to learn to re-generate it using fine-tuned BART (Lewis et al., 2020). Combining the generated conclusion with the original argument and its annotations, our approach learns to distinguish sufficient from insufficient arguments using a modified RoBERTa model (Liu et al., 2019).

Starting from ground-truth argument structure, we subsequently evaluate conclusion generation and sufficiency assessment on the merged annotations of the corpora of Stab and Gurevych (2017a) and Stab and Gurevych (2017b), as described in Section 3. Our generation experiments indicate that fine-tuning BART leads to better conclusions, which are on par with human-written conclusions in terms of sufficiency, likeliness, and novelty (Section 5). To quantify the impact on sufficiency assessment, we explore various combinations of premises, original conclusion, and generated conclusion in systematic ablation tests, and we compare them to the state of the art and a human upper bound (Section 6). Our sufficiency experiments reveal that, even on the plain input text of an argument, RoBERTa already improves significantly over the state of the art. The addition of structural annotations and the generated conclusion lead to further improvements, although the benefit of generation ultimately remains limited, possibly due to the generally limited importance of knowing the conclusion on the given data. Finally, we discuss the results of our approaches in Section 7 in light of their implications for the field.

The main contributions of this paper are:[1]

- A language model that can generate human-like argument conclusions.
- The new state-of-the-art approach to argument sufficiency assessment.
- Insights into the importance of mined and generated structure within argument assessment.

2 Related Work

Computational argumentation research has assessed various dimensions of argument quality. Wachsmuth et al. (2017a) provide a theory-based taxonomy of 15 logical, rhetorical, and dialectical quality dimensions and of the work in natural language processing done in these directions. We focus on the (local) *sufficiency* dimension, which is key to logical cogency, representing that an argument's conclusion can rationally be drawn from its premises, given that these are acceptable and relevant (Johnson and Blair, 2006).

Few approaches tackled sufficiency computationally so far. Aside from Wachsmuth and Werner (2020) who assess it as one of the 15 dimensions above using traditional text-focused feature engineering, we are only aware of the work of Stab and Gurevych (2017b) who extend the argument-annotated essay corpus of Stab and Gurevych (2017a) with binary sufficiency annotations. On this basis, the authors compare a support vector machine using lexical, syntactic, and length features to a convolutional neural network (CNN) with word vectors, the latter achieving the best result with a macro F_1-score of .827. In our experiments, we use their dataset and replicate their experiment settings, in order to compare to the CNN.

Unlike Stab and Gurevych (2017a), we rely on a transformer-based architecture, namely we adapt RoBERTa (Liu et al., 2019) to assess sufficiency. Approaches to argument quality assessment using such architectures are still limited, mostly focusing

[1]The experiment code can be found under: https://github.com/webis-de/ArgMining-21

on a holistic view of quality (Gretz et al., 2020; Toledo et al., 2019), although a few approaches used transformers for some of the dimensions of Wachsmuth et al. (2017a), such as Lauscher et al. (2020), or somewhat related dimensions in light of quality improvement (Skitalinskaya et al., 2021).

In contrast to the standard use of transformers for text classification, we leverage the structure of arguments for their assessment. Wachsmuth et al. (2016) provided evidence that mining the argumentative structure of persuasive essays helps to better assess four essay-level quality dimensions of argumentation. Similarly, we use annotations of the premises and conclusions of arguments for the sufficiency assessment, but we target the arguments. Moreover, we explore to benefit of conclusion *generation* for the assessment.

The idea of reconstructing an argument's conclusion from its premises was introduced by Alshomary et al. (2020), but their approach focused on the inference of a conclusion's target. The actual generation of entire conclusions has so far only been studied by Syed et al. (2021). The authors presented the first corpus for this task along with experiments where they adapted BART (Lewis et al., 2020) from summarization to conclusion generation. While they trained BART to directly generate a conclusion based on premises, we generate conclusions that fit the context of an entire argument. To this end, we leverage and finetune BART's inherent denoising capabilities obtained during pretraining to replace a mask token in an argument.

3 Data

To study our hypothesis that a sufficient argument's conclusion can be generated from its premises, we need data that is annotated for both argument structure and sufficiency. In this section, we describe how we employ existing corpora for this purpose.

3.1 Data for Conclusion Generation

The argument-annotated essay (AAE-v2) corpus (Stab and Gurevych, 2017a) contains structural annotations for 402 complete persuasive student essays. For conclusion generation (as well as for structure-based sufficiency assessment), we only need annotations of single arguments.

Our instance creation procedure resembles the one of Alshomary et al. (2020), but we work on argument level rather than conclusion level, since we approach conclusion generation as a language model denoising task (Lewis et al., 2020). Concretely, instead of using premises-conclusion training pairs where the conclusion shall be generated given the premises, we rely on argument-argument pairs. The first argument here is a modified version of the second argument where the conclusion is masked. This way, we avoid conflicts with the argument-level sufficiency annotations of Stab and Gurevych (2017b) (see below). In total, we obtain 1506 argument-argument pairs relating to 1506 unique conclusions matched with 1029 unique arguments. On average, each argument has a length of 4.5 sentences and contains 94.6 tokens.

For training, we rely on 5-fold cross-validation, ensuring that the argument-argument pairs from one essay are never split between training, validation, and test data. This prevents possible data leakage that could artificially improve the final evaluation scores. For each folding, we use 70% training, 10% validation, and 20% test data.

3.2 Data for Sufficiency Assessment

Stab and Gurevych (2017b) further classified each argument in the 402 essays of the AAE-v2 corpus as being sufficient or not. Following Johnson and Blair (2006), the authors defined that an "argument complies with the sufficiency criterion if its premises provide enough evidence for accepting or rejecting the claim" (we speak of "conclusion" here instead of "claim"). All 1029 arguments were labeled, of which 681 (66.2%) were considered sufficient and 348 (33.8%) insufficient.

We use the provided corpus both in its original form and in a modified version where we replace the conclusion of an argument with two separator tokens, "</s></s>". This allows us to study a wide range of different approaches for sufficiency assessment by placing text in-between the two tokens as a replacement for the original conclusion.

For training, we replicate the original 20-times 5-fold cross-validation setup of Stab and Gurevych (2017b), with 70% training, 10% validation, and 20% test data, in order to ensure comparability.

4 Approach

This section describes our two-step approach to assess the sufficiency of a given argument through conclusion generation. First, we generate a conclusion from the argument's premises using a pretrained language model finetuned on the task of replacing the masked conclusion of an argument.

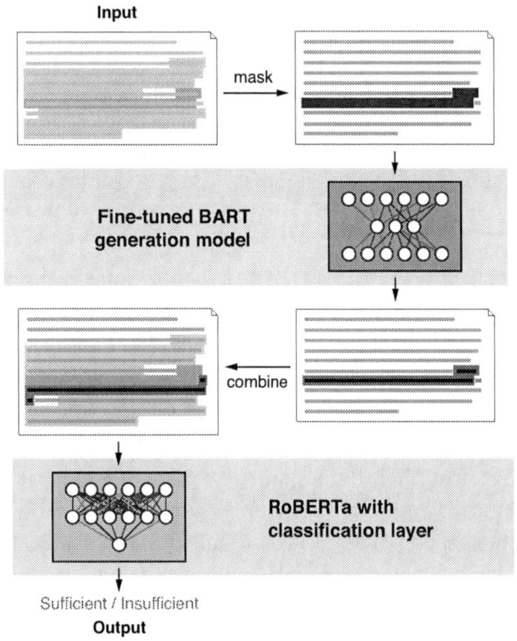

Figure 2: Illustration of our sufficiency assessment approach through generation: (1) BART is used to generate the masked conclusion in an argument. (2) The generated conclusion is combined with the ground truth annotation of the argument. (3) RoBERTa classifies the enriched argument as sufficient/insufficient. Several ablations of the annotations are tested in our experiments.

Second, the generated conclusion is used to assess the argument's sufficiency by experimenting with eight modified versions of the original input argument (Section 6). An overview of the approach is shown in Figure 2. In the following, we detail how we train the models for the two steps.

4.1 Conclusion Generation using Denoising

Given an argument with a masked conclusion, the first task is to re-generate the conclusion. To tackle this task, we use BART-large (Lewis et al., 2020) and treat generation as a denoising task. We explore two model variants:

BART-unsupervised In this variant, we do not finetune BART on any data, but we use its vanilla denoising capabilities obtained in its pre-training procedure. Note that the masked conclusions usually do not represent entire sentences, thus leaving textual markers which trigger BART to generate a logical conclusion, for example, "Thus, <mask>" or "This makes it clear that <mask>." We consider this model as a baseline.

BART-supervised In this variant, we finetune BART on the data from Section 3, in order to tailor its denoising capabilities towards conclusion generation. In particular, we thereby adjust the language model towards the given domain and teach the model to replace the mask token with a conclusion (instead of just generating text that fits the context). We finetune BART using cross-entropy loss, as commonly done in text generation.

The proper training settings of the two models are found via a hyperparameter search. For the evaluation described below, we ran 10 trials for each fold, testing batch sizes between 4 and 8 and learning rates between $5 \cdot 10^{-6}$ and $5 \cdot 10^{-5}$. We fixed the number of epochs to 3 per fold, as we did not observe any improvements afterwards, and we used a cosine learning rate scheduler with 50 warm-up steps to stabilize the training. At inference time, we employed a beam size of 5 to obtain the final generated conclusions. We considered the epoch out of three, which performs best on the validation data in terms of BERTScore (Zhang* et al., 2020).

4.2 Sufficiency Assessment using Structure

Given a modified argument, the second task is to predict whether the premises in the argument are rationally worth drawing the conclusion. We use RoBERTa (Liu et al., 2019) for this task by adding a linear layer on top of the pooled output of the original model (Devlin et al., 2019).

Successfully optimizing RoBERTa using mean squared error (MSE) or cross-entropy loss functions would be difficult, as both of them do not align well with the target metric of sufficiency assessment (macro F_1-score). We therefore follow ideas of Puthiya Parambath et al. (2014) and Eban et al. (2017) who propose to optimize machine learning models on the F_1-score directly. Accordingly, we allow the model to output probabilities instead of interpreting a single binary value. Analogous to Stab and Gurevych (2017b), we allow our model to adjust hyperparameters between folds. In our experiments, we followed the same hyperparameter optimization procedure as before but for different parameters and ranges. In total, we ran 10 trials for each fold, and we adjusted the batch size to be between 16 and 32 and the learning rate between 10^{-6} and $5 \cdot 10^{-5}$. We selected the epoch for each trial out of three, which performed best on the validation data in terms of macro F_1-score.

Model	BERTScore	ROU.-1	ROU.-2	ROU.-L
BART-unsupervised	0.14	19.69	4.05	16.40
BART-supervised	**0.25**	**20.97**	**4.79**	**17.49**

Table 1: Automatic evaluation results of concluion generation: Rescaled F1-BERTScore and ROUGE-1/-2/-L scores of the two considered models on the full corpus.

5 Evaluation of Conclusion Generation

To study our hypothesis, we need to ensure that the generated conclusions are meaningful and fit in the context of a given argument, so they can be helpful in sufficiency assessment. In this section, we therefore evaluate the quality of the generated conclusions, both automatically and manually.

5.1 Automatic Evaluation

As indicated in Section 4, we compare two approaches: (1) *BART-unsupervised*, which replaces the mask token in an argument (denoising) with fitting text, as it is part of BART's training procedure (Lewis et al., 2020); and (2) *BART-supervised*, which finetunes BART on the argument-argument pairs from Section 3. For both approaches, we obtained the complete set of generated conclusions using the cross-validation setup described in Section 4. Matching these with the corresponding ground-truth conclusion, we then computed their quality in terms of BERTScore as well as ROUGE-1, ROUGE-2, and ROUGE-L.

Results Table 1 lists the results of the approaches. BART-unsupervised is a strong baseline in terms of lexical accuracy: Values such as 19.69 (ROUGE-1) and 16.40 (ROUGE-L) are comparable to those that Syed et al. (2021) achieved in similar domains with sophisticated approaches. However, finetuning on the argument-argument pairs does not only significantly increase the semantic similarity between generated and ground truth conclusions from 0.14 to 0.25 in terms of BERTScore, but it also leads to a slight increase in lexical accuracy.

5.2 Manual Evaluation

The metrics used to automatically evaluate conclusion generation are not ideal, since they expect a single correct result. The task of conclusion generation, in contrast, allows for multiple, possibly very different correct conclusions, for example, a different conclusion target may be derived from a single set of premises (Alshomary et al., 2020). We thus conducted an additional manual annotation study to evaluate the quality of the conclusions generated by the two approaches in comparison to the human ground truth.

We randomly chose 100 arguments from the given corpus, 50 labeled as sufficient and 50 labeled as insufficient. For each arguments, we additionally created two variants, replacing the original conclusion with the generated conclusion of either approach. In each case, we then presented the three arguments with their premises and conclusions highlighted to five annotators of different academic backgrounds (economics, computer science, health/medicine), none being an author of this paper. We asked each annotator three questions, Q1–Q3, on each argument, resulting 300 annotations for each model and 900 annotations in total. For consistency reasons, we used a 5-point Likert scale for each question:

- Q1: Are the premises sufficient to draw the conclusion? This question referred to the *sufficiency* of arguments, from "not sufficient" (score 1) to "sufficient" (score 5). We asked this question to see how the sufficiency of generated and human-written conclusions differs, thus directly evaluating our hypothesis.
- Q2: How likely is it that the conclusion will be inferred from the context? This question referred to the *likelihood* of a conclusion, from "very unlikely" (score 1) to " very likely" (score 5). We asked this question as an internal quality assurance, ruling out the possibility that our models generate conclusions unrelated to the given context of the argument.
- Q3: How can the conclusion be composed from the context? This question, finally, referred to the *novelty* of the generated conclusions in light of their context. The score range here is more complex; inspired by Syed et al. (2021), who also ask annotators about the novelty of generated conclusions, it reflects the cognitive load required to infer the conclusions from the context of the argument: "verbatim copying" (1), "synonymous copying" (2), "copying + fusion" (3), "inference" (4), and "can not be composed" (5).

Results For each question, Table 2 shows the inter-annotator agreement, the distribution of majority scores, and the resulting mean score of the three compared approaches (including the ground truth), and the mean rank. We obtained the rank by

#	Question	Approach	(a) Agreement		(b) Majority Scores					(c) Mean Results	
			α	Majority	1	2	3	4	5	Score ↑	Rank ↓
Q1	Are the premises sufficient to draw the conclusion?	Ground Truth	.23	**63%**	7	24	39	30	0	**2.92**	1.43
		BART-unsupervised	**.43**	**63%**	14	19	34	32	1	2.87	1.40
		BART-supervised	.35	60%	14	21	30	34	1	2.87	**1.37**
Q2	How likely is it that the conclusion will be inferred from the context?	Ground Truth	.19	57%	4	18	54	24	0	**2.98**	1.42
		BART-unsupervised	**.32**	**64%**	16	15	46	23	0	2.76	1.54
		BART-supervised	.28	**64%**	12	15	38	35	0	2.96	**1.39**
Q3	How can the conclusion be composed from the context?	Ground Truth	.19	72%	0	4	18	73	5	**3.79**	**1.39**
		BART-unsupervised	**.50**	80%	14	11	15	47	13	3.34	1.54
		BART-supervised	.32	**82%**	8	8	22	53	9	3.47	1.54

Table 2: Manual evaluation results of conclusion generation on the 100 arguments of each of the three approaches: (a) Agreement of all five annotators in terms of Krippendorff's α and majority. (b) Distribution of majority scores. For Q1/Q2, higher scores mean more sufficient/likely. For Q3, they mean less "copying" (see text for details). (c) Mean score of each approach and rank obtained by comparing the majority score for each argument in isolation.

treating each question as a ranking task where, for each argument, the approaches are ranked from 1 to 3 by decreasing highest majority score.

We find that the general *agreement* for the questions in terms of Krippendorff's α is low, with values between .19 and .50, but comparable to other tasks in the realm of argumentation (Wachsmuth et al., 2017a). On all three questions, the annotators agreed mostly for BART-unsupervised, followed by the BART-supervised, while having the least agreement for the ground truth. This may indicate a more apparent connection of the generated conclusions to the premises. In 57% to 64% of the cases, we observe majority agreement of the annotators for the first two questions, whereas this value goes up to 72%–78% for the last question.

The ranking for Q1 shows that conclusions generated by our BART-supervised model overall ranked best in *sufficiency* (mean rank 1.37), even though the mean score is slightly better for the ground truth. While the differences are small, this behavior is expected as half of the provided arguments were initially labeled as insufficient.

Considering the *likelihood* of the premises (Q2), we see that conclusions of BART-supervised are on par with the ground truth conclusions (score rank 2.96 vs. 2.98, rank 1.39 vs. 1.42) and better than those generated by the baseline BART-unsupervised (1.54). This suggests that the conclusions generated by our model both fit the context of the argument and are at least as likely to be drawn as the ones written by humans. This property is essential for our approach to sufficiency assessment to rule out the possibility of failure due to a low quality of the generated conclusions in general.

Finally, we consider the cognitive load that is required to compose a conclusion given its context, as reflected by *novelty* (Q3). This information is vital to rule out that the generated conclusions are copied from the context of an argument instead of being inferred. We find the ground-truth conclusions to require the most cognitive load in this regard, having a clearly better mean rank (1.39) than the others (both 1.54). Thus, they potentially provide the most novelty to the context. The mean scores indicate an increase of novelty from BART-unsupervised (3.34) to BART-supervised (3.47) though.

The scores and ranks can be interpreted more easily when looking at the *majority scores* for the two BART models and the ground truth. As expected, we find that the amount of conclusions considered to be sufficient is approximately the same to those considered insufficient. The annotators did not agree on the highest sufficiency rank, which may be due to subjectivity in the perception of "full" sufficiency. We observe an analog behavior for score 5 for the likelihood of conclusions (Q2). Here, this may imply that, rarely, only a single conclusion would fit the premises of an argument. Regarding the novelty of the generated conclusions, Q3 reveals that the ground truth annotations are mostly inferences (score 4) and only rarely copied from the context (scores 1 and 2). While BART-unsupervised only somewhat follows this distribution, our BART-supervised model shows a similar behavior to the ground truth, though in less clear form. This is another indication that BART-supervised has learned to generate conclusions from premises.

# Label	Part	Text
(a) Sufficient	Argument	Second, <MASK>. Averagely, public transports use much less gasoline to carry people than private cars. It means that by using public transports, the less gas exhaust is pumped to the air and people will no longer have to bear the stuffy situation on the roads, which is always full of fumes.
	Ground truth	public transportation helps to solve the air pollution problems
	BART-unsupervised	public transport is more efficient than private cars
	BART-supervised	using public transports will help to reduce the amount of pollution in the air
(b) Insufficient	Argument	Last, <MASK>. Playing musical instrument is a good way, I can play classical guitar. When I meet difficulties in studies, I will take my guitar and play the song Green Sleeves. It makes me feel better and gives me the confidence.
	Ground truth	we should develop at least one personal hobby, not to show off, but express our emotion when we feel depressed or pressured
	BART-unsupervised	but not least, I love music
	BART-supervised	playing musical instrument is very important to me
(c) Insufficient	Argument	In addition to this, <MASK>. For instance, further enforcement banned smoking in capital in Sri Lanka has reduced this consumption related diseases and deaths, as per the ministry of health. As this shows, smoking restrictions has successfully daunted public from this bad puffing that put less strain on country's healthcare systems.
	Ground truth	introducing smoking ban in public places would greatly discourage people from engaging tobacco puffing
	BART-unsupervised	Sri Lankan government has taken several measures to curb smoking
	BART-supervised	smoking restrictions in Sri Lanka has brought a lot of benefits to the country

Table 3: Conclusions generated by the BART models for four arguments (with masked conclusion) compared to the *ground truth* conclusion: (a) BART-supervised almost reconstructs the ground truth. (b) Here, the two models increase sufficiency. (c) Sometimes, the generated conclusions remain rather vague and pick the wrong target.

Error Analysis & Examples To better understand the differences between the two BART models and the ground truth, we analyzed the 100 examples from our annotation study manually. Table 3 compares the conclusions for three arguments.

For the sufficient argument in Table 3(a), BART-supervised nearly perfectly reconstructs the ground truth, whereas BART-unsupervised generates a reasonable but less specific alternative. In Table 3(b), the approaches appear to make the argument more sufficient, particularly BART-supervised. Both examples speak for the truth of our hypothesis that the conclusion of sufficient arguments can be generated from the premises. This tendency is further backed by our analysis in which we found that for BART-supervised 20% (10/50) of the sufficient arguments have perfect matching conclusions (Table 3(a)) 60% (30/50) either are less abstract or have a different conclusion target but are of equal quality, and 20% (10/50) have a conclusion that is of lower quality, compared to the ground truth. In contrast, only 10% (5/50) of the insufficient arguments are perfect matches, 60% (30/50) either are less abstract or have a different conclusion target of equal quality, and 30% (15/50) have lower quality generated conclusions (Table 3(b)).

Further analysis reveals that for 58% (29/50) of the insufficient arguments, BART-supervised generated a sufficient conclusion with a different target (16/29) or a different level of abstraction, either more specific (11/29) or more abstract (2/29) than the ground truth. In Table 3(c), the BART models seem tricked by the anecdotal evidence given in the premises, mistakenly picking Sri Lanka as the conclusion's target.

Regarding the difference of our models, we found that BART-supervised more often generated conclusions with targets that are equally likely to the target of the human ground truth (68/100 vs. 42/100).

6 Evaluation of Sufficiency Assessment

Using our conclusion generation model, BART-supervised, we finally study our hypothesis on sufficiency assessment by experimenting with different input variations and testing on the corpus of Stab and Gurevych (2017b). The first setting is by just using the RoBERTa model (*direct sufficiency as-*

Assessment	Approach	Accuracy	Macro Pre.	Macro Rec.	Macro F1
Direct	Human upper bound	.911 ± .022	.873 ± .042	.903 ± .020	.883 ± .029
	CNN (Stab and Gurevych, 2017a)	.846 ± .022	.830 ± .021	.832 ± .028	.831 ± .023
	RoBERTa	**.889** ± .026	**.882** ± .057	**.880** ± .078	**.876** ± .031†
Indirect	RoBERTa-premises-only	.887 ± .031	.876 ± .051	.881 ± .071	.875 ± .037
	RoBERTa-conlusion-only	.641 ± .036	.582 ± .048	.567 ± .144	.553 ± .063
	RoBERTa-generated-only	.632 ± .025	.560 ± .038	.544 ± .106	.532 ± .043
	RoBERTa-premises+conclusion	**.896** ± .025	**.888** ± .061	.887 ± .048	**.885** ± .029†‡
	RoBERTa-premises+generated	.889 ± .028	.879 ± .052	.883 ± .064	.878 ± .030
	RoBERTa-conclusion+generated	.659 ± .026	.762 ± .030	.396 ± .092	.571 ± .036
	RoBERTa-all	**.896** ± .024	.886 ± .045	**.889** ± .054	**.885** ± .025†‡

Table 4: Results of argument sufficiency assessment: Accuracy as well as macro precision, recall, and F_1-score of all evaluated approaches, averaged over twenty 5-fold cross-validations. Significant gains over Stab and Gurevych (2017a) and the RoBERTa approach without structural enrichment are marked with † and ‡, respectively (computed using Wilcoxon signed-rank test, p-value .05). The human upper bound is obtained on a subset of 432 arguments.

sessment) and the second by introducing structural knowledge and our generated conclusions (*indirect* sufficiency assessment).

6.1 Direct Sufficiency Assessment

First, we compare the "base version" of our approach, RoBERTa without additional structure annotations, to the *human upper bound* and the state of the art *CNN* of Stab and Gurevych (2017b).[2]

Results The upper part of Table 4 shows the direct assessment results. Our RoBERTa model significantly outperforms the CNN both on accuracy (.889 vs. .846) and on macro F_1 score (.876 vs. .831), the latter being an improvement of whole 4.5 points. Our model also performs almost on par with the human upper bound, meaning it is approximately at the level of human performance. This underlines the potential of pre-trained transformer models in argument quality assessment.

6.2 Indirect Sufficiency Assessment

As our conclusion generation model starts from structural annotations of a given argument, we systematically study the benefit of knowing the premises and the original conclusion, as well of having the generated conclusion. We consider the following eight input variants for the assessment:

- *RoBERTa-premises-only.* Use the full argument as input, but replace the ground-truth conclusion with an <\unk> token.
- *RoBERTa-conclusion-only.* Use only the ground-truth conclusion as input.
- *RoBERTa-generated-only.* Use only the generated conclusion as input.
- *RoBERTa-premises+conclusion.* Use the full argument as input and highlight the ground-truth conclusion using <\s> tokens.
- *RoBERTa-premises+generated.* Use the full argument as input, but replace the ground-truth conclusion with its generated counterpart. Highlight the latter using <\s> tokens.
- *RoBERTa-conclusion+generated.* Use only the ground-truth and the generated conclusion as input, separated with a <\s> token
- *RoBERTa-all.* Use the full argument as input, insert the highlight the generated conclusion after the ground-truth conclusion and highlight both together using <\s> tokens.

Results The lower part of Table 4 shows that both *RoBERTa-premises+conclusion* and *RoBERTa-all* yield the best results overall, significantly outperforming our vanilla *RoBERTa* model by almost 1 point in terms of both accuracy (.896 vs. .889) and macro F_1-score (.885 vs. .876). The results suggest that using a generated conclusion for the argument does not really help, but also not hurts the model performance. This is also supported by *RoBERTa-premises-only*, which also matches the performance of *RoBERTa-premises+generated.* In general, however, bringing structural knowledge to the model gives a slight but significant improvement in sufficiency assessment.

[2]Note that the human upper bound of Stab and Gurevych (2017b) was computed on a subset of 433 arguments annotated by three annotators only. Thus, it is only an approximation of the actual human performance. The human scores are based on pairwise comparisons of the three annotators.

Looking at the weak performance of *RoBERTa-conclusion+generated* (macro F_1-score .571), we see that an opposition of the two conclusions alone is not enough four sufficiency assessment. Even though adding the generated one improves over having the ground-truth conclusion only, all variants that include the premises perform much better.

To better understand the role of premises and conclusions in sufficiency assessment, we trained the three *RoBERTa-<xy>-only* variants. The high performance of *RoBERTa-premises-only* (macro F_1-score .875) clearly reveals that the conclusion is of almost no importance on the data of Stab and Gurevych (2017b), being not significantly worse than vanilla RoBERTa. The low scores of *RoBERTa-conclusion-only* further support this hypothesis, suggesting that the knowledge obtained from the conclusion can be inferred from the argument without its conclusion alone. This result is very insightful in that it displays that the currently available data barely enables a study of sufficiency assessment in terms of its actual definition. Instead, we suppose that models mainly learn a correlation between the nature and the quality of a given set of premises and the possible sufficiency evolving from this. In particular, students who provide "good" premises for an argument in their essays can also deliver an inferrable conclusion.

7 Discussion

Our results suggest that large-scale pre-trained transformer models can help assess the quality of arguments, here their sufficiency. They even nearly matched human performance. However, an accurate understanding of the argument sufficiency task in terms of the actual definition of sufficiency seems barely possible on the available data.

Employing knowledge about argumentative structure can benefit sufficiency assessment, in line with findings on predicting essay-level argument quality (Wachsmuth et al., 2016). Our results suggest that there is at least some additional knowledge in an argument's conclusion that our model could not learn itself. However, we did not actually *mine* argumentative structure here, but we resorted to the human-annotated ground truth, which is usually not available in a real-world setting. Thus, the improvements obtained by the structure could vanish as soon as we resort to computational methods. We note, though, that we obtained state-of-the-art results also using RoBERTa on the plain text only.

Regarding the central hypothesis of this work, we study an example of a more task-aligned approach. However, our results show that answering the question of conclusion inferability by generating conclusions for an argument is difficult, as generated conclusions may be perceived as sufficient, likely, and novel, but may still not be unique. That is, for many premises, it may be possible to generated multiple sufficient conclusions, which naturally limits the impact of *quality assessment through generation*.

Consequently, although the task of sufficiency assessment appears to be solved on the given data, we argue for the need for more sophisticated corpora that better reflect the actual definition of the task, to ultimately allow studying whether approaches such as ours are needed in real-world applications.

8 Conclusion

In this work we have studied the task of argument sufficiency assessment based on auto-generated argument conclusions. According to our findings, traditional approaches can be improved by using large-scale pre-trained transformer models and by incorporating knowledge about argumentative structure. The effect of our proposed idea to leverage generation for the assessment turned out low though. However, this may likely be caused by the available data, wehere sufficiency seems to barely depend on the arguments' conclusions, thus preventing our and previous approaches from actually tackling the task as intended by its definition.

In general, the insights of this paper lay the foundation for more task-oriented approaches towards the assessment of argument quality dimensions, that are tailored towards the properties in scope (here the relation between premises and conclusion). To adequately evaluate such approaches, also refined corpora may be needed.

Acknowledgments

We thank Katharina Brennig, Simon Seidl, Abdullah Burak, Frederike Gurcke and Dr. Maurice Gurcke for their feedback. We gratefully acknowledge the computing time provided the described experiments by the Paderborn Center for Parallel Computing (PC^2). This project has been partially funded by the German Research Foundation (DFG) within the project OASiS, project number 455913891, as part of the Priority Program "Robust Argumentation Machines (RATIO)" (SPP-1999).

References

Milad Alshomary, Shahbaz Syed, Martin Potthast, and Henning Wachsmuth. 2020. Target inference in argument conclusion generation. In *Proceedings of the 58th Annual Meeting of the Association for Computational Linguistics*, pages 4334–4345, Online. Association for Computational Linguistics.

Jacob Devlin, Ming-Wei Chang, Kenton Lee, and Kristina Toutanova. 2019. BERT: Pre-training of deep bidirectional transformers for language understanding. In *Proceedings of the 2019 Conference of the North American Chapter of the Association for Computational Linguistics: Human Language Technologies, Volume 1 (Long and Short Papers)*, pages 4171–4186, Minneapolis, Minnesota. Association for Computational Linguistics.

Elad Eban, Mariano Schain, Alan Mackey, Ariel Gordon, Ryan Rifkin, and Gal Elidan. 2017. Scalable learning of non-decomposable objectives. In *Artificial intelligence and statistics*, pages 832–840. PMLR.

Roxanne El Baff, Henning Wachsmuth, Khalid Al Khatib, and Benno Stein. 2020. Analyzing the persuasive effect of style in news editorial argumentation. In *Proceedings of the 58th Annual Meeting of the Association for Computational Linguistics*, pages 3154–3160, Online. Association for Computational Linguistics.

Shai Gretz, Roni Friedman, Edo Cohen-Karlik, Assaf Toledo, Dan Lahav, Ranit Aharonov, and Noam Slonim. 2020. A large-scale dataset for argument quality ranking: Construction and analysis. In *Proceedings of the AAAI Conference on Artificial Intelligence*, volume 34, pages 7805–7813.

Ralph Henry Johnson and J Anthony Blair. 2006. *Logical self-defense*. Idea.

Anne Lauscher, Lily Ng, Courtney Napoles, and Joel Tetreault. 2020. Rhetoric, logic, and dialectic: Advancing theory-based argument quality assessment in natural language processing. In *Proceedings of the 28th International Conference on Computational Linguistics*, pages 4563–4574, Barcelona, Spain (Online). International Committee on Computational Linguistics.

Mike Lewis, Yinhan Liu, Naman Goyal, Marjan Ghazvininejad, Abdelrahman Mohamed, Omer Levy, Veselin Stoyanov, and Luke Zettlemoyer. 2020. BART: Denoising sequence-to-sequence pre-training for natural language generation, translation, and comprehension. In *Proceedings of the 58th Annual Meeting of the Association for Computational Linguistics*, pages 7871–7880, Online. Association for Computational Linguistics.

Yinhan Liu, Myle Ott, Naman Goyal, Jingfei Du, Mandar Joshi, Danqi Chen, Omer Levy, M. Lewis, Luke Zettlemoyer, and Veselin Stoyanov. 2019. Roberta: A robustly optimized bert pretraining approach. *ArXiv*, abs/1907.11692.

Shameem Puthiya Parambath, Nicolas Usunier, and Yves Grandvalet. 2014. Optimizing f-measures by cost-sensitive classification. *Advances in Neural Information Processing Systems*, 27:2123–2131.

Gabriella Skitalinskaya, Jonas Klaff, and Henning Wachsmuth. 2021. Learning from revisions: Quality assessment of claims in argumentation at scale. In *Proceedings of the 16th Conference of the European Chapter of the Association for Computational Linguistics: Main Volume*, pages 1718–1729, Online. Association for Computational Linguistics.

Noam Slonim, Yonatan Bilu, Carlos Alzate, Roy Bar-Haim, Ben Bogin, Francesca Bonin, Leshem Choshen, Edo Cohen-Karlik, Lena Dankin, Lilach Edelstein, et al. 2021. An autonomous debating system. *Nature*, 591(7850):379–384.

Christian Stab and Iryna Gurevych. 2017a. Parsing argumentation structures in persuasive essays. *Computational Linguistics*, 43(3):619–659.

Christian Matthias Edwin Stab. 2017. *Argumentative writing support by means of natural language processing*. Ph.D. thesis, Technische Universität Darmstadt.

Christian Matthias Edwin Stab and Iryna Gurevych. 2017b. Recognizing insufficiently supported arguments in argumentative essays. In *Proceedings of the 15th Conference of the European Chapter of the Association for Computational Linguistics: Volume 1, Long Papers*, pages 980–990.

Shahbaz Syed, Khalid Al Khatib, Milad Alshomary, Henning Wachsmuth, and Martin Potthast. 2021. Generating informative conclusions for argumentative texts. In *Findings of the Association for Computational Linguistics: ACL-IJCNLP 2021*, pages 3482–3493, Online. Association for Computational Linguistics.

Assaf Toledo, Shai Gretz, Edo Cohen-Karlik, Roni Friedman, Elad Venezian, Dan Lahav, Michal Jacovi, Ranit Aharonov, and Noam Slonim. 2019. Automatic argument quality assessment - new datasets and methods. In *Proceedings of the 2019 Conference on Empirical Methods in Natural Language Processing and the 9th International Joint Conference on Natural Language Processing (EMNLP-IJCNLP)*, pages 5625–5635, Hong Kong, China. Association for Computational Linguistics.

Henning Wachsmuth, Khalid Al Khatib, and Benno Stein. 2016. Using argument mining to assess the argumentation quality of essays. In *Proceedings of COLING 2016, the 26th International Conference on Computational Linguistics: Technical Papers*, pages 1680–1691.

Henning Wachsmuth, Nona Naderi, Yufang Hou, Yonatan Bilu, Vinodkumar Prabhakaran, Tim Alberdingk Thijm, Graeme Hirst, and Benno Stein. 2017a. Computational argumentation quality assessment in natural language. In *Proceedings of the 15th Conference of the European Chapter of the Association for Computational Linguistics: Volume 1, Long Papers*, pages 176–187.

Henning Wachsmuth, Martin Potthast, Khalid Al Khatib, Yamen Ajjour, Jana Puschmann, Jiani Qu, Jonas Dorsch, Viorel Morari, Janek Bevendorff, and Benno Stein. 2017b. Building an argument search engine for the web. In *Proceedings of the 4th Workshop on Argument Mining*, pages 49–59.

Henning Wachsmuth and Till Werner. 2020. Intrinsic quality assessment of arguments. In *Proceedings of the 28th International Conference on Computational Linguistics*, pages 6739–6745, Barcelona, Spain (Online). International Committee on Computational Linguistics.

Tianyi Zhang*, Varsha Kishore*, Felix Wu*, Kilian Q. Weinberger, and Yoav Artzi. 2020. Bertscore: Evaluating text generation with bert. In *International Conference on Learning Representations*.

M-Arg: Multimodal Argument Mining Dataset for Political Debates with Audio and Transcripts

Rafael Mestre[1,2,†], Razvan Milicin[2], Stuart E. Middleton[2,†], Matt Ryan[1,†], Jiatong Zhu[2] and Timothy J. Norman[2]

[1] School of Economic, Social and Political Science, University of Southampton
[2] School of Electronics and Computer Science, University of Southampton
†Corresponding authors: {R.Mestre, sem03, M.Ryan}@soton.ac.uk

Abstract

Argumentation mining aims at extracting, analysing and modelling people's arguments, but large, high-quality annotated datasets are limited, and no multimodal datasets exist for this task. In this paper, we present M-Arg, a multimodal argument mining dataset with a corpus of US 2020 presidential debates, annotated through crowd-sourced annotations. This dataset allows models to be trained to extract arguments from natural dialogue such as debates using information like the intonation and rhythm of the speaker. Our dataset contains 7 hours of annotated US presidential debates, 6527 utterances and 4104 relation labels, and we report results from different baseline models, namely a text-only model, an audio-only model and multimodal models that extract features from both text and audio. With accuracy reaching 0.86 in multimodal models, we find that audio features provide added value with respect to text-only models.

1 Introduction

Understanding and modelling argumentation is a recent and key challenge in Natural Language Processing (NLP). Most work addressing this task has focused on extracting arguments from argumentative essays (Stab and Gurevych, 2017), social networks like Twitter (Bosc et al., 2016) or online reviews (Cocarascu and Toni, 2018) and discussions (Habernal and Gurevych, 2017), and not much attention has been paid to mining arguments in natural dialogue. The two most common research questions consider how argumentative relations between units (e.g. support or attack) are annotated or how claims and/or premises are identified (Lawrence and Reed, 2019). We offer, to the best of our knowledge, the first multimodal argumentation mining dataset (M-Arg) of political debates annotated for such argumentative relations of support and attack, using crowd-sourcing techniques. Our contributions are: i) to provide a high quality annotated dataset of political debates with audio and time-stamped transcripts for multimodal argumentation mining; ii) to offer benchmark model results for the research community; and iii) a comparative analysis of the value that multi-modal models bring compared to text-only and audio-only models (Section 5).

The dataset is derived from a collection of US 2020 presidential debates. Five debates were used with the principal speakers being Donald Trump, Joe Biden, Mike Pence and Kamala Harris, and a moderator (Table 1). In three of the debates the candidates spoke only with each other and the moderator, while in the remaining two they interacted with the audience in so-called Town Hall events. The lengths of the audio files ranged from approximately 1 hour to 1 hour 35 minutes. The debates were tokenised by sentences or utterances, with 6527 in total. The relationship between pairs of sentences were then classified by crowd-workers as support, attack or neither using the annotation scheme proposed by Carstens and Toni (2015) (Section 3). The crowd-workers were presented with the sentence pair along with a small extract from the debate to provide context. The resulting dataset consists of 4104 pairs of sentences with the argumentative relationship between them classified, along with features such as the trustworthiness of the crowd-workers, the level of agreement between crowd-workers, and their self-confidence scores (Section 4). Prior to giving details of our methodology, the dataset and comparative analysis, we provide a brief review of related research.

2 Related work

Much of the research in argumentation mining has been dedicated to the identification of argumentative discourse units (ADUs) like claims, major claims and premises. For instance, in a first iteration, Stab and Gurevych (2014) annotated 90

Proceedings of The 8th Workshop on Argument Mining, pages 78–88
Punta Cana, Dominican Republic, November 10–11, 2021.

#	Duration	Split	Speakers	Moderator	# sentences	# labels
1	1:35:06	2	Donald Trump Joe Biden	Chris Wallace	1889	1214
2	1:34:15	2	Donald Trump Joe Biden	Kristen Weller	1648	1018
3	1:31:42	7	Joe Biden Audience	George Steph.	838	519
4	1:00:10	4	Donald Trump Audience	Savannah Guthrie	1132	707
5	1:29:37	2	Mike Pence Kamala Harris	Susan Page	1020	646
					6527	4104

Table 1: Description of the five debates used in the dataset. The column "Split" indicates the number of sub-files in which the audio was split.

persuasive essays with 1673 sentences and 1552 argumentative units. Then, they extended their dataset to 402 essays, achieving a total of 7116 sentences and 6089 argumentative components (Stab and Gurevych, 2017). Carstens and Toni (2015) advocate a relation-based approach towards argumentation mining. Instead of separating the issue of identifying argumentative units and their relation, they reconstitute the task as one of classifying the relationship between sentence pairs as support, attack or neither. They argue that this relation depends upon the context of the discussion. We take the same approach. There are, however, few datasets for relation-based argumentation mining (Paul et al., 2020). Carstens and Toni (2015), for example, annotate 854 pairs of sentences for support/attack without identifying the arguments first. Likewise, the DART dataset (Bosc et al., 2016) consists of 4000 tweets, 446 support relations and 112 attack relations, and Stab and Gurevych (2017) annotate 3616 supports and 219 attack relations in their second version of their essay dataset.

While certain tasks in argument mining have been applied in other disciplines, interdisciplinary approaches are important for the impact of these methods to be fully realised. Some research in political science has started to bridge the gap in tasks like identifying emotion rhetoric (Osnabrüge et al., 2021), gender and emotional expression in politics (Boussalis et al., 2021), emotional mining in political campaigns (Greco and Polli, 2020), lexicometrics of Euromanifestos (Jadot and Kelbel, 2017), and, from the AI perspective, *ethos* mining (Duthie and Budzynska, 2018) using Hansard as a dataset. Argument mining in political debate is, however, still largely to be explored, although Visser et al. (2021) provide an annotation of 2016 US presidential debates with argument types. Benoit et al. (2016) have advocated for the use of crowd-sourced text analysis for political science, finding high levels of agreement and reproducibility between crowd-workers and experts. However, in subjective tasks like identifying support/attack relations, lower levels of agreement are expected. For instance, Faulkner (2014) used Amazon Mechanical Turk (AMT) to annotate 8176 sentences with "for", "against" or "neutral", achieving about 66% of neutral cases and a Cohen's κ of 0.70. Al-Khatib et al. (2020) also used AMT to obtain 16429 labels of different types, including 1736 "relation" labels, defined in their case as "positive", "negative" or "no-argument", with $\kappa = 0.51$.

These datasets focus exclusively on text, and, as far as we can tell, there is not much argument mining research using multiple modalities such as both text and audio, particularly focusing on identifying support or attack relations between ADUs. There are, however, some datasets that could be used by the community for this task. For instance, Mirkin et al. (2019) and Orbach et al. (2020b) provide datasets of debate speeches with transcriptions that could help in the extraction of arguments. Likewise, Mirkin et al. (2020) and Orbach et al. (2020a) come closer to argumentation mining research offering datasets of argumentative content and general-purpose rebuttal in speeches. Also, Kopev et al. (2019) use audio and transcripts of political debates to detect deception. Other research explores emotion recognition or sentiment analysis using the IEMOCAP dataset, which contains text, audio and video with emotion annotations (Busso et al., 2008; Cai et al., 2019). Classic NLP models for relation classification have relied on bag of words (BoW) approaches with common classifiers like random forests, support vector machines or naïve Bayes (Carstens and Toni, 2017), although more recently LSTMs and Bi-LSTMs have been used with good results (Cocarascu and Toni, 2018). Some efforts are being devoted to the use of background knowledge or context. For instance, Paul et al. (2020) proposed Bi-LSTM encoders with self-attention, together with commonsense knowledge extraction. The use of both textual and audio features for the identification of argumentative relations, with approaches similar to those used in multimodal emotion recognition, seems to be mostly unexplored.

Argument mining of political debates can be seen as a long conversation text classification problem where context matters. Unlike the well studied

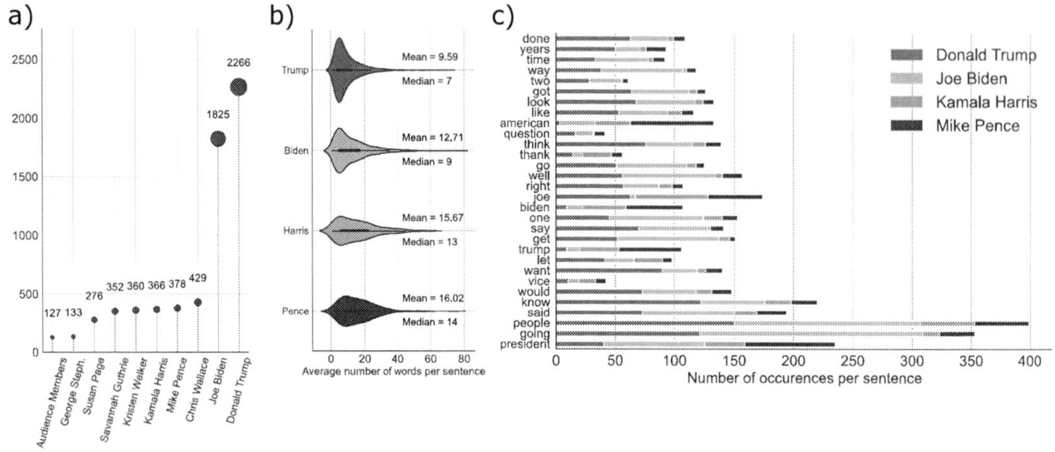

Figure 1: Descriptive visualisation of the original dataset. a) Number of utterances (after sentence tokenisation) by each person across all the debates. Audience members were all aggregated in the label "Audience Members". b) Average number of words per sentence of the four main participants of the debate, showing their density distribution. c) Number of sentences in which the most common used words appeared in by their speaker.

problem area of single and short utterance classification (e.g. 2–3 utterances), dialogue modelling and classification of longer conversations has received little attention to date (Xu et al., 2021). Recent approaches to handle long sequence classification include augmented transformer models with information retrieval (IR) or summarisation models (Xu et al. 2021; Tigunova et al. 2020). We constrain ourselves in this paper to providing results for a set of short conversation classification baseline models as we want to focus on showing the value of using multimodal data. However, we expect recent advances in long conversation classification models to yield good results with our dataset in the future.

3 Methodology

The original source of the M-Arg dataset was available as audio tracks with transcripts from a Kaggle competition.[1] This public-domain dataset was originally constructed by downloading audio from YouTube and transcripts from Rev,[2] as explained in the source metadata. The M-Arg dataset with annotations, full transcripts and audio files, source code and model checkpoints for reproducibility is available online in our GitHub repository.[3]

3.1 Data overview

The original data was presented as audio in .mp3 files and transcriptions in both .txt and .csv files. The .csv files contained three columns: *speaker*, *minute*, and *text*. Since the timestamps did not align perfectly to the audio clips, we performed our own tokenisation and text-audio alignment. The M-Arg dataset associates each sentence with a matched timestamp in the corresponding debate audio file. To do this, each text was split into utterances, defined as single sentences[4]. Visual inspection revealed the transcriptions to be grammatically correct, with no apparent typos and proper use of punctuation, and so automatic sentence-level tokenization performed well. The utterances were then force-aligned to the audio using the web application of the *aeneas* tool[5], obtaining new timestamps. The source audio files were split into different files to comply with the file size limit for the force alignment and to avoid segments where the debate was starting, finishing or going to a break, applause, music, etc. Table 1 summarises the datasets.

Across the five debates, Donald Trump and Joe Biden spoke the most, as can be seen in Figure 1(a). This is expected, as they were both present in three of the five debates. Mike Pence and Kamala Harris, who only participated in one of the debates

[1]The source materials can be found in `https://www.kaggle.com/headsortails/us-election-2020-presidential-debates` as of August 9th, 2021. The version used was v. 7.

[2]`https://www.rev.com`

[3]`https://github.com/rafamestre/m-arg_multimodal-argumentation-dataset`

[4]Using the sentence tokenizer *PunktSentenceTokenizer* from `www.nltk.org`.

[5]The website of the web application is `https://aeneasweb.org/help` and their GitHub `https://github.com/readbeyond/aeneas/`

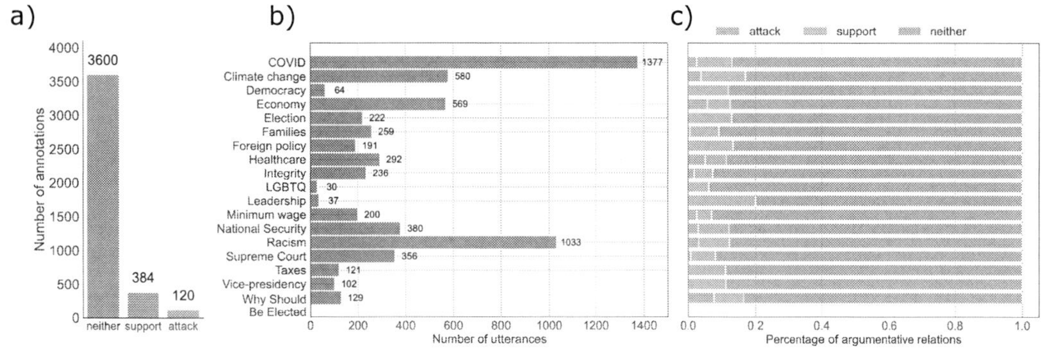

Figure 2: Descriptive visualisation of the annotated dataset, M-Arg. a) Number of pairs annotated for support, attack or neither. b) Total number of sentences in the original dataset labeled as one of the topics in the y-axis. c) Percentage of argumentative relations of pairs of sentences belonging to each one of the topics.

together, spoke a roughly similar number of utterances. Figure 1(b), however, indicates that the main participants in the debate did not speak in a similar manner. The violin plots show the probability density of the average number of words per sentence, and we can observe that Trump spoke sentences of a smaller average length than the rest of the participants. Finally, 1(c) shows the most common words (after removing stop-words) in a stacked barplot according to the speaker (removing moderators and audience members), with certain differences in the usage of words. These results indicate potentially important differences in communication strategies and styles.

3.2 Pairs creation

The M-Arg dataset consists of 4104 labelled pairs of sentences selected from the debates. Sections of the debates were manually labelled by the authors for their "topic", following the explanations of the moderator introducing each section, obtaining high level classifications like "foreign policy". Excerpts of 15 sentences were randomly selected (the "context") and a pair of sentences within the context were chosen to classify their relation (with their distance weighted by a Gaussian distribution to ensure they were close enough). Approximately 1500 sentences were forced to be from different speakers, to balance the dataset by increasing the possibility of finding attack relations. More details on the pair generation strategy and codes can be found in the repository alongside the dataset[6].

3.3 Annotation scheme

The annotation scheme was based on the relation-based argumentation scheme from Carstens and Toni (2015). They argue that an argumentative relation of support or attack is highly dependent on the context. Carstens and Toni (2015) suggest starting from a root claim to construct pairs or match sentences containing the same entities, but we chose to divide them into topics and weight them by distance as explained in Section 3.2. We presented the crowd-workers with a pair of sentences along with the labelled topic of discussion (e.g. "families" or "climate change"), as well as a short 15-sentence extract of the dialogue surrounding these sentences as context. The crowd-workers are asked to use this context, as well as any personal knowledge, to classify the argumentative relation as support, attack or neither, to the best of their ability. By not relying only on the surface meaning of the sentences, we open the way for the use of this dataset in more complex scenarios. For instance, it could be applied together with long- or short-text summarisation to take into account the context in a dialogue (Xu et al., 2021) or knowledge-based models linked to databases or fact-checking websites (Paul et al., 2020). Consider the following pair:

- **Joe Biden:** It's criminal.
- **Donald Trump:** They are so well taken care of.

At a first glance, it is not possible to know what Biden and Trump are talking about. We might assume that the relationship is attack, but this would be a big assumption only based on the fact that they are opposing candidates. Reading the context, we

[6]GitHub: `https://github.com/rafamestre/m-arg_multimodal-argumentation-dataset`

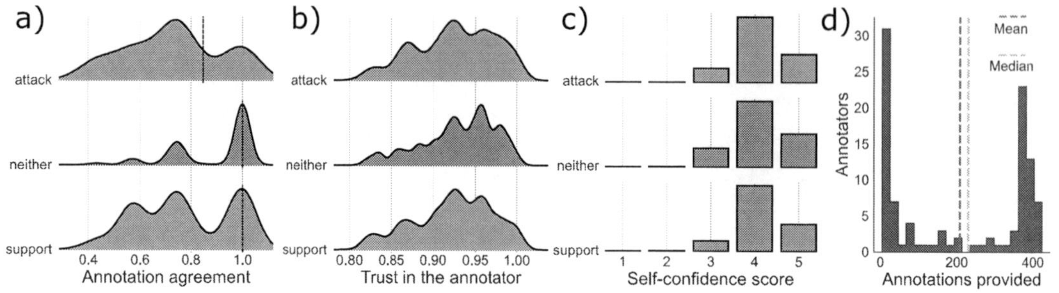

Figure 3: Relationship between annotations and confidence parameters. a) Distribution of annotations according to the annotation agreement; b) to the trust in the annotator; and c) to the self-confidence score given by the annotator. d) Distribution of the annotators with respect to the number of annotations they provided.

might find out that they are actually talking about the infamous controversy of the U.S. Immigration and Customs Enforcement's (ICE) camps, where children were put in cages and separated from their parents. Joe Biden claims that what the Trump administration has done is criminal. Trump answers by saying that they (the children) are "so well taken care of" because reporters went there and saw that the facilities were very clean. The argumentative relation between these two sentences is clearly an attack. Indeed, out of the 81 annotators who classified this test question, 84% of them agreed that this was an attack relation. Work on context summarisation or knowledge extraction could help train models to understand why this was an attack.

In our dataset, ADUs consist of sentences fully delimited by periods, but in many cases they will not (Lawrence and Reed, 2019). They might span several sentences or even be one of the clauses within a sentence. Likewise, during a heated debate, the structure of the argument might not be easily identifiable:

- **Joe Biden:** We learned that this president paid 50 times the tax in China as a secret bank account with China, does business in China, and in fact, is talking about me taking money?
- **Joe Biden:** What are you hiding?

This pair might be interpreted together as a legitimate question being raised to attack the *ethos* of Donald Trump. However, in and of itself, the second sentence can be taken as a rhetorical way of claiming that Trump is hiding something. In this context, the first sentence is supporting this claim. Annotators did well in this task, with 83% of judgements of this test question correctly labelling it as support.

3.4 Crowd-worker annotation

For the annotation task, the platform Appen was used.[7] Crowd-workers were presented with a pair of sentences, topic and context. They were asked to classify the argumentative relation and report their confidence on a Likert scale, ranging from 1: "not confident at all", to 5: "very confident". Each worker was then paid per "page" of work completed, with each page containing between 4 and 6 tasks. To ensure accuracy in the annotations, the contributors were quizzed at the beginning and during the annotations (once per page) with test (or gold) questions. The trust in the annotator was thus defined as the percentage of test questions that they answered correctly, and we set an accuracy threshold of 81%. Other quality settings were enabled, such as: minimum time spent per page to 90 seconds and no more than 60% of supports and 35% of attacks classified. If the annotators did not meet any of these standards, their judgements were not used. Dynamic judgements, that could range from 3 to 7 annotations if the agreement in the annotation was below 70%, were also enabled to improve the agreement of each annotation. A total of 101 test questions were used in this annotation and 104 reliable workers participated, out of 287 that attempted it. Overall, considering the quality settings (e.g. dynamic judgements, tainted answers), 21646 reliable annotations were collected (5746 belonging to gold questions and 15900 to random pairs), and a separate 1663 annotations were rejected.[8]

[7] `https://appen.com/`.

[8] Extensive details of the annotation scheme and quality settings can be found in the GitHub of the project: `https://github.com/rafamestre/m-arg_multimodal-argumentation-dataset`.

4 Dataset

4.1 Description and relevant examples

The M-Arg dataset consists of a total of 4104 pairs of sentences (including golden ones), of which 384 are support relations, 120 are attack relations and 3600 are neither support nor attack, as shown in Figure 2(a). Despite efforts to increase the number of support/attack relations, as explained in Section 3.2, the dataset is imbalanced towards the neither side. This is nevertheless expected, as most of the utterances during a debate are not argumentative in nature. Eighteen different topics were identified in the debates, with the most common ones being "COVID", "Racism", "Climate change" and "Economy". Figure 2b shows the total number of utterances from each topic throughout the whole dataset.[9] Some topics, such as "LGBTQ" or "Leadership" had very few instances, since they were only discussed briefly in one of the debates. Many of these topics, however, could be combined, such as "Taxes" and "Economy", as desired. For each topic we can see in Figure 2(c) the distribution of argumentative relations that were annotated. Topics such as "Foreign Policy" or "Taxes" did not contain attack relations, most likely due to the fact that those sections were small.

Whether an argument is supporting or attacking a claim is a subjective matter. Philosophy of argumentation has attempted to establish more or less general argumentation frameworks with different categorisations. However, it is almost certain that thresholds for what quality of information supports or attacks an argument, or judgements on whether such argument is sufficiently valid or not vary by person and context. Our annotated dataset, thus, provides a collective representation of how people reason and understand arguments, and a large number of disagreements are expected. Indeed, the prevalence of fake news or fallacies, or even reasonable disagreements over interpretation of values and inferences in everyday political discourse, has shown us that the same premises can be deemed supports or attacks in different contexts. As we cannot expect that everyone thinks of arguments or fallacies in the same way, the annotation task needs to be accessible and understandable but still closely guided and validated by the theoretical frameworks to reflect informed but real interpretations of support and attack in open dialogue in political domains. In the instructions for the annotation task, the contributors were asked to focus on whether a sentence provided a reason that supported or attacked its counterpart, in order to avoid confusing an attack *towards something/someone* with an attack *towards a claim*. Consider the following example in which Biden is not providing any reason to support his claim, although it was meant to attack Trump. Many people would interpret this as attack (as many annotators did):

- **Donald Trump:** There's abuse, tremendous abuse.
- **Joe Biden:** Simply not true.

This case was correctly labeled as neither, but only with an agreement score of 56%. In other cases, support was simply confused with repetition:

- **Joe Biden** And what's happening is too many transgender women of color are being murdered.
- **Joe Biden:** They're being murdered.

This was annotated as support by three crowd-workers, but this is simply coherence between the sentences or a simple reiteration of a claim. This subjectivity is summarised in Figure 3(a)-(c), which shows the agreement score, the trust in the annotator and the self-confidence score for each label. In general, crowd-workers labeled relations independently of their trust score and their self-confidence score. However, attack relations were more controversial with 25% of annotations above 0.87, whereas for support and neither at least 25% of annotations had an agreement of 1. Overall, the average agreement was 0.87 and the median agreement 1.

5 Evaluation

5.1 Crowd-worker agreement

The presence of subjectivity leads us to evaluate the agreement among crowd-workers (also known as intern-annotator agreement) using Krippendorf's α (Krippendorff, 1980). This agreement score allows for a variable number of annotations in each instance, with an unspecified number of crowd-workers that do not necessarily need to annotate every single instance, making it suitable for our case. Considering all the annotations, we obtained

[9] Due to the constraints in random pair generation, the topic distribution in the annotated dataset differs slightly, but the distribution closely resembles that of the original dataset.

	All annotations					Self-confidence = 5				
Trust	α	**Workers**	**# Annots.**	**Supports**	**Attacks**	α	**Workers**	**# Annots.**	**Supports**	**Attacks**
≥ 0.80	**0.43**	104	21646	4370	2036	0.57	93	5941	1133	530
≥ 0.85	0.44	96	20342	4056	1919	0.59	88	5666	1069	514
≥ 0.90	0.46	76	16747	3251	1508	0.63	69	4615	792	407
≥ 0.95	0.53	53	9066	1562	776	0.72	46	2393	346	175
$= 1$	0.44	27	746	248	117	0.79	25	227	74	31

Table 2: Krippendorff's α values for different filterings of the data. Notice the value in bold corresponds to the overall α from the whole dataset, since our trust threshold was ≥ 0.81. With decreasing number of annotations, high fluctuations in α are to be expected, hence the smaller value of 0.44 for the highest trust.

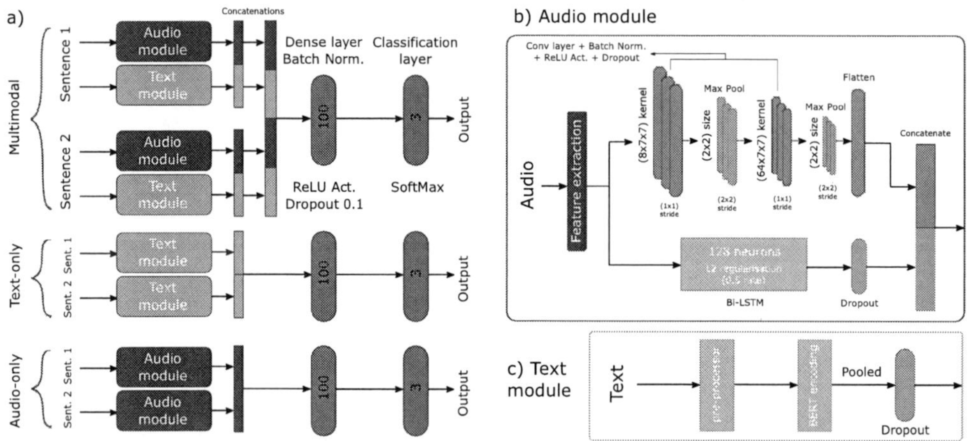

Figure 4: Schematic of the relation classification models. a) In the multimodal model each sentences is passed in parallel through an audio module and a text module. b) The text module consists only on a BERT encoding layer with dropout. c) The audio module is based on parallel CNN and Bi-LSTM.

$\alpha = 0.43$. Considering that the distribution of annotations show that some contributors annotated many sentences, while others very few (Figure 3(d)), we filtered by the most diligent workers but found no significant change in α.[10] However, given that annotators are assigned a trust score and they annotated with different self-confidence, we calculated different α's by filtering by these values. Table 2 shows the α scores when we filter by crowd-worker trust rating for all annotations (left) and only for those that were annotated with the maximum confidence (right). We can see that the crowd-worker agreement increases up to 0.53 when we filter annotators with higher trust (although it drops again for the maximum trust), however at the cost of decreasing the number of workers and annotations in the dataset. Likewise, if we only consider those annotations that were provided with high certainty, we see an overall large value of 0.57, going up to 0.79 if we also filter for high trust workers. Other reports in the literature classifying argumentative relations have yielded Cohen's $\kappa = 0.70$ (Faulkner, 2014), $\kappa = 0.51$ (Al-Khatib et al., 2020), $\alpha = 0.67$ (Bosc et al., 2016), $\alpha = 0.81$ (Stab and Gurevych, 2014).

It might seem surprising to obtain a low crowd-worker agreement, given that the average agreement in the annotation was 85%, as mentioned above. These numbers, however, need to be considered with care. Krippendorff's α measures disagreement beyond that expected by chance, but our data is not balanced, so our labels are not equally probable. It has been observed that Krippendorff's α can be heavily attenuated in imbalanced datasets (Jeni. et al., 2013). Indeed, if we sub-sample our dataset for 100 attack, support and neither relations, we find $\alpha = 0.540 \pm 0.015$ (standard deviation after 10 trials). If we sub-sample it unbalanced, with 10 attack, 10 support and 1000 neither, we find $\alpha = 0.170 \pm 0.047$ (standard deviation after 10 trials). This is a big difference in values, even though

[10] Krippendorff's α was calculated with the *nltk.metrics.agreement* module (v. 3.6). Results were double-checked with the *krippendorff* module, `https://github.com/pln-fing-udelar/fast-krippendorff`, which yielded almost identical results.

Model	Text dropout	Audio dropout	Acc.	M-F_1	w-F_1	Attack m-F_1	Neither m-F_1	Support m-F_1
Audio only		0.2	0.84	0.41	0.81	0.18	0.91	0.14
Text only	0.1		**0.86**	0.37	0.82	0.06	**0.92**	0.14
Multimodal	0.1	0.1	**0.86**	0.41	**0.83**	0.16	**0.92**	0.14
		0.2	0.85	**0.45**	**0.83**	**0.24**	**0.92**	**0.21**
Multimodal $\geq$0.85 agreement	0.1	0.2	**0.91**	0.40	**0.90**	0.12	**0.95**	0.10

Table 3: Models' performance. M-F_1 stands for macro-averaged F_1, w-F_1 for weighted-F_1, and m-F_1 for micro-averaged F_1.

the source data is the same. In any case, given the subjectivity of the task, we do not believe a small α to be necessarily a bad result, since many judgements might not lend an obvious collective answer and, most importantly, people might believe one instance is a supportive argument, while others believe it is not an argument at all. We believe there is significant value in these unclear annotations, as they give insight into how people understand the arguments put forward in political debate.

5.2 Argumentative relation classification

To measure the quality of our corpus and study the potential added value of audio features in argumentation mining, we evaluated the performance of different classification models based on a multimodal model, as well as text-only and audio-only models (Figure 4(a)). First, the input pair of sentences were split into audio and text. In the multimodal model, each sentence pair was passed through an audio and text module and their outputs concatenated, passed through a 100-unit middle layer and a 3-output classification layer. In the text-only and audio-only models, the sentences were only passed through the text or audio module, respectively, and the middle and classification layers were the same. The audio module shown in Figure 4(b) was based on a previous model by Cai et al. (2019) for multimodal emotion recognition and consisted of a feature extraction module followed by a CNN in parallel with a Bi-LSTM, chosen to maximise the extraction of local and global features. The text-only module Figure 4(c) consisted of a BERT preprocessor and a BERT encoding of L=12 hidden layers (i.e., Transformer blocks), a hidden size of H=768, and A=12 attention heads. The missing dropout rates can be found in Table 3.

Audio feature extraction was performed using the Python module "librosa" (McFee et al., 2015). The features were: Mel-frequency cepstral coefficients (MFCCs), which are widely used features for characterising and detecting voice signals (Klapuri and Davy, 2006); several spectral features like spectral centroids (Klapuri and Davy, 2006), spectral bandwidth (Klapuri and Davy, 2006), spectral roll-off (McFee et al., 2015) and spectral contrast (Jiang et al., 2002); and a 12-bit chroma vector (McFee et al., 2015). For each sentence, we used the timestamp to clip the audio file with a buffer of $\pm$2 s to ensure the full audio of the utterance was captured.

To train the three models, we used the Adam optimiser with a learning rate of 0.00005, a batch size of 16 and 50 epochs. A time-based learning rate schedule function was used with a decay rate of 0.0000002 and the loss function was categorical cross-entropy. Table 3 shows the evaluation metrics of these models. The values in "text dropout" and "audio dropout" are the rates of all the dropout layers of the respective models (Figure 4). All three models perform well identifying neither labels, but they do not perform so well identifying attacks or supports, with the highest F_1 values being 0.24 and 0.21, respectively. The text-only model fails to identify attack relations to the same level of the audio-only and multimodal models, most likely due to the imbalance of the data. A multimodal model with a dropout rate of 0.2, however, increases the F_1 for attacks from 0.06 in the text-only model to 0.24, and for supports from 0.14 to 0.21. Surprisingly, the audio-only model performs better than the text-only model in identifying attacks and neither, and closely matches the multimodal model. As proof of concept, we filtered the annotations by their agreement ($\geq$0.85) and we assessed the best performing multimodal model. We obtained an even higher accuracy value of 0.91, especially for neither labels, with m-F1 of 0.95, although identification of support and attack relations was worse, most likely due to a decrease of useful labels. Overall, we believe that audio provides relevant features for the identification of argumentative relations and its added value with respect to text helps recapitulate the complexity of this type of data in heavily unbalanced datasets.

6 Conclusions and future work

In this paper, we have presented a multimodal argumentation mining dataset (M-Arg) for political debates based on a corpus of the US 2020 presidential debates with audio and transcripts. The dataset was annotated using crowd-sourcing techniques and we present descriptive statistics of the dataset itself, as well as of the annotations, with discussion of some interesting examples. As a baseline for future research, we evaluated the classification performance of audio-only, text-only and multimodal models. We found that the audio-only and multimodal models could perform with high levels of accuracy and F_1, although they encountered problems classifying support and attack relations very efficiently. The text-only model performed similarly, but its accuracy in attack classifications was low due to the imbalance of the data. Adding the audio to the text, however, in a multimodal model, helped increase the metrics of both support and attacks, although they still remained quite low. We believe these to be encouraging results, as improvements like reinforcement learning to tackle data imbalance, optimised extraction of audio features, addition of (cross-)attention layers, summarisation of the surrounding context or use of background knowledge databases, could greatly improve these performance metrics. Moreover, the data can be filtered according to annotation agreement, the annotator's trust and self-confidence in the annotation, potentially training models with higher precision and/or recall, although with less data.

One limitation of our dataset is that ADUs are defined in a very simple manner (by a period with tokeniser). ADUs might be full sentences on certain occasions, but they might encompass several sentences or simply a clause within one. Further work to improve this dataset would include the identification of ADUs (without necessarily labelling them as claim or premise). Likewise, even if a sentence contains a full ADU, in natural dialogue it might not present as a clearly stated claim or premise, but might contain irony or rhetorical questions.

As already discussed, whether a pair of sentences are showing support or attack is a somewhat subjective matter, and for that reason we obtain Krippendorff's $\alpha = 0.43$. One cannot expect crowd-workers to identify, or even easily understand, all types of arguments or what constitutes a fallacy; philosophers continue to disagree. Yet with some instruction and information these annotations can better reflect real-world judgements about support and attack arguments. For certain applications, especially where including marginalised voices, AI systems will need to understand and detect how people argue, even if they do not follow the dictates of argumentation theory (Young, 2000). We believe our dataset will be of interest for understanding what people think a proper argument is.

Acknowledgements

This work has been funded by the Web Science Institute of the University of Southampton. The authors would also like to acknowledge the support of UK Research and Innovation (UKRI) funding (grant ref MR/S032711/1).

Ethical considerations

Ethics approval for this research was received from the University of Southampton's Faculty of Social Science Ethics and Research Governance committee, Ref: 66226, Date 22/07/2021. The original dataset in which we build the M-Arg dataset was available under license CC0: Public Domain. Fair treatment of the workers involved in the annotation of the dataset was ensured by Appen's code of ethics (`https://appen.com/crowd-wellness/`). We aimed at providing a fair wage for the work provided and, according to the platform statistics, the workers received an hourly compensation with median \$7.69 and interquartile mean \$7.57. Before sharing our annotated dataset, we have stripped all information that could be potentially sensitive, such as IP's or locations, and we have re-anonymised the anonymous worker ID's that were provided.

References

K. Al-Khatib, Y. Hou, H. Wachsmuth, C. Jochim, F. Bonin, and B. Stein. 2020. End-to-end argumentation knowledge graph construction. *Proc. AAAI Conference on Artificial Intelligence*, pages 7367–7374.

K. Benoit, D. Conway, B. E. Lauderdale, M. Laver, and S. Mikhaylov. 2016. Crowd-sourced text analysis: Reproducible and agile production of political data. *American Political Science Review*, 110(2):278–295.

T. Bosc, E. Cabrio, and S. Villata. 2016. DART: A dataset of arguments and their relations on twitter. *Proc. 10th Int. Conf. on Language Resources and Evaluation*, pages 1258–1263.

C. Boussalis, T. G. Coan, M. R. Holman, and S. Müller. 2021. Gender, candidate emotional expression, and voter reactions during televised debates. *American Political Science Review*, pages 1–16.

C. Busso, M. Bulut, C. C. Lee, A. Kazemzadeh, E. Mower, S. Kim, J. N. Chang, S. Lee, and S. S. Narayanan. 2008. IEMOCAP: Interactive emotional dyadic motion capture database. *Language Resources and Evaluation*, 42(4):335–359.

L. Cai, Y. Hu, J. Dong, and S. Zhou. 2019. Audio-textual emotion recognition based on improved neural networks. *Mathematical Problems in Engineering*, 2019.

L. Carstens and F. Toni. 2015. Towards relation based argumentation mining. In *Proc. 2nd Workshop on Argumentation Mining*, pages 29–34.

L. Carstens and F. Toni. 2017. Using argumentation to improve classification in natural language problems. *ACM Trans. on Internet Technology*, 17(3):1–23.

O. Cocarascu and F. Toni. 2018. Combining deep learning and argumentative reasoning for the analysis of social media textual content using small data sets. *Computational Linguistics*, 44(4):833–858.

R. Duthie and K. Budzynska. 2018. A deep modular RNN approach for ethos mining. *Proc. Int. Joint Conf. on Artificial Intelligence*, pages 4041–4047.

A. R. Faulkner. 2014. *Automated Classification of Argument Stance in Student Essays: A Linguistically Motivated Approach with an Application for Supporting Argument Summarization*. Ph.D. thesis, CUNY.

F. Greco and A. Polli. 2020. The political debate on immigration in the election campaigns in Europe. In *Springer Proceedings in Complexity*, pages 111–123. Springer, Cham.

I. Habernal and I. Gurevych. 2017. Argumentation mining in user-generated Web discourse. *Cmputational Linguistics*, 43(1):125–179.

C. Jadot and C. Kelbel. 2017. 'Same, same, but different.' Assessing the politicisation of the European debate using a lexicometric study of the 2014 Euromanifestos. *Politique Europeenne*, 55(1):60–85.

L. A. Jeni., J. F. Cohn, and F. De La Torre. 2013. Facing imbalanced data - Recommendations for the use of performance metrics. *Proceedings - 2013 Humaine Association Conference on Affective Computing and Intelligent Interaction, ACII 2013*, pages 245–251.

D. N. Jiang, L. Lu, H. J. Zhang, J. H. Tao, and L. H. Cai. 2002. Music type classification by spectral contrast feature. *Proc. IEEE Int. Conf. on Multimedia and Expo*, pages 113–116.

A. Klapuri and M. Davy. 2006. Signal processing methods for music transcription. In *Signal Processing Methods for Music Transcription*, chapter 5. Springer Science & Business Media.

D. Kopev, A. Ali, I. Koychev, and P. Nakov. 2019. Detecting deception in political debates using acoustic and textual features. In *Proc. IEEE Automatic Speech Recognition and Understanding Workshop*, pages 652–659.

K. Krippendorff. 1980. *Content Analysis: An Introduction to its Methodology.* SAGE Publications, Inc, Thousand Oaks, CA.

J. Lawrence and C. Reed. 2019. Argument mining: A survey. *Computational Linguistics*, 45(4):765–818.

B. McFee, C. Raffel, D. Liang, D. Ellis, M. McVicar, E. Battenberg, and O. Nieto. 2015. librosa: Audio and music signal analysis in Python. *Proc. 14th Python in Science Conference*, pages 18–24.

S. Mirkin, M. Jacovi, T. Lavee, H. K. Kuo, S. Thomas, L. Sager, L. Kotlerman, E. Venezian, and N. Slonim. 2019. A recorded debating dataset. In *LREC 2018 - 11th International Conference on Language Resources and Evaluation*, pages 250–254.

S. Mirkin, G. Moshkowich, M. Orbach, L. Kotlerman, Y. Kantor, T. Lavee, M. Jacovi, Y. Bilu, R. Aharonov, and N. Slonim. 2020. Listening comprehension over argumentative content. In *Proceedings of the 2018 Conference on Empirical Methods in Natural Language Processing, EMNLP 2018*, pages 719–724.

M. Orbach, Y. Bilu, A. Gera, Y. Kantor, L. Dankin, T. Lavee, L. Kotlerman, S. Mirkin, M. Jacovi, R. Aharonov, and N. Slonim. 2020a. A dataset of general-purpose rebuttal. In *EMNLP-IJCNLP 2019 - 2019 Conference on Empirical Methods in Natural Language Processing and 9th International Joint Conference on Natural Language Processing, Proceedings of the Conference*, pages 5591–5601. Association for Computational Linguistics.

M. Orbach, Y. Bilu, A. Toledo, D. Lahav, M. Jacovi, R. Aharonov, and N. Slonim. 2020b. Out of the Echo Chamber: Detecting Countering Debate Speeches. In *Proceedings of the 58th Annual Meeting of the Association for Computational Linguistics*, pages 7073–7086.

M. Osnabrüge, S. B. Hobolt, and T. Rodon. 2021. Playing to the gallery: Emotive rhetoric in parliaments. *American Political Science Review*, pages 1–15.

D. Paul, J. Opitz, M. Becker, J. Kobbe, G. Hirst, and A. Frank. 2020. Argumentative relation classification with background knowledge. *Frontiers in Artificial Intelligence and Applications*, 326:319–330.

C. Stab and I. Gurevych. 2014. Annotating argument components and relations in persuasive essays. In *Proc. 25th Int. Conf. on Computational Linguistics*, pages 1501–1510.

C. Stab and I. Gurevych. 2017. Parsing argumentation structures in persuasive essays. *Computational Linguistics*, 43(3):619–659.

A. Tigunova, A. Yates, P. Mirza, and G. Weikum. 2020. CHARM: Inferring personal attributes from conversations. In *Proc. 2020 Conference on Empirical Methods in Natural Language Processing*, pages 5391–5404.

J. Visser, J. Lawrence, C. Reed, J. Wagemans, and D. Walton. 2021. Annotating argument schemes. *Argumentation*, 35(1):101–139.

J. Xu, A. Szlam, and J. Weston. 2021. Beyond goldfish memory: Long-term open-domain conversation. arXiv:2107.07567.

I. M. Young. 2000. *Inclusion and Democracy*. Oxford University Press.

Citizen Involvement in Urban Planning - How Can Municipalities Be Supported in Evaluating Public Participation Processes for Mobility Transitions?

Julia Romberg
Institute of Social Sciences
Heinrich Heine University Düsseldorf
julia.romberg@hhu.de

Stefan Conrad
Institute of Computer Science
Heinrich Heine University Düsseldorf
stefan.conrad@hhu.de

Abstract

Public participation processes allow citizens to engage in municipal decision-making processes by expressing their opinions on specific issues. Municipalities often only have limited resources to analyze a possibly large amount of textual contributions that need to be evaluated in a timely and detailed manner. Automated support for the evaluation is therefore essential, e.g. to analyze arguments. In this paper, we address (A) the identification of *argumentative* discourse units and (B) their classification as *major position* or *premise* in German public participation processes. The objective of our work is to make argument mining viable for use in municipalities. We compare different argument mining approaches and develop a generic model that can successfully detect argument structures in different datasets of mobility-related urban planning. We introduce a new data corpus comprising five public participation processes. In our evaluation, we achieve high macro F_1 scores (0.76 - 0.80 for the identification of argumentative units; 0.86 - 0.93 for their classification) on all datasets. Additionally, we improve previous results for the classification of argumentative units on a similar German online participation dataset.

1 Introduction

In many democratic countries, political decisions are increasingly developed through the participation of citizens. *Public participation processes* allow citizens to voice their suggestions and concerns on specific issues, for example in urban planning, and thus influence decision-making processes. Participation can take place in formats that vary from on-site events such as citizen workshops, to written submissions via letter or e-mail, and to online platforms where citizens can discuss proposals digitally. Building on Scharpf (1999), we can distinguish two main goals of public participation processes. On the one hand, the additional input provided by citizens can influence the decision-making process and, potentially, lead to more effective policies. On the other hand, citizens are assumed to develop a higher acceptance of the output when given an opportunity to participate and, ultimately, the resulting decisions have a higher legitimacy.

In order to be able to include citizen comments in the further decision-making process, those comments first have to be evaluated. However, both offline and online participation formats have the potential to generate a high number of responses (Shulman, 2003; Schlosberg et al., 2008), e.g., thousands of contributions. Along with stringent schedules in decision-making processes, this often poses major challenges for municipalities. Still, participation contributions are commonly evaluated manually with considerable effort. Therefore, if municipalities do not have enough resources (human or monetary) to shoulder this effort, the detailed evaluation will have to be cut back. As a result, opinions might be completely omitted or not been taken into account equally. This in turn can have a negative influence on the goals of public participation processes. Filtering out individual or mass opinions risks loosing important clues for effective policies. It can also endanger citizens' confidence in the opportunity to participate in decision-making and weaken civic engagement (Mendelson, 2012). Besides, decision acceptance is influenced by perceived fairness (Esaiasson, 2010).

Automating the evaluation of public participation processes can help overcome these problems (OECD, 2004) and has been addressed by research initiatives such as the *Cornell eRulemaking Initiative* (CeRI)[1] and, more recently, the *Citizen participation and machine learning for a better democracy project*[2]. Over the years, several tasks that arise in the evaluation process have been high-

[1] https://scholarship.law.cornell.edu/ceri/
[2] https://www.turing.ac.uk/research/research-projects/citizen-participation-and-machine-learning-better-democracy

Proceedings of The 8th Workshop on Argument Mining, pages 89–99
Punta Cana, Dominican Republic, November 10–11, 2021. ©2021 Association for Computational Linguistics

lighted. These include thematic classification and clustering of citizen contributions (e.g. Kwon et al., 2007; Purpura et al., 2008; Arana-Catania et al., 2021; Teufl et al., 2009), summarization of similar content (e.g Arana-Catania et al., 2021), detection of duplicates (e.g. Yang et al., 2006), and analysis of arguments and opinions (e.g. Kwon et al., 2007; Park and Cardie, 2014; Lawrence et al., 2017).

In this paper, we focus on arguments in public participation processes that address sustainable mobility and land use in Germany. German cities have involved their citizens in hundreds of decision-making processes on these issues in recent years.[3] We look at five of them in detail, four of which are processes for concrete improvements to cycling infrastructure and one of which is a strategic process for creating a general mobility concept for a city. At the same time, we consider two very different participation formats, namely online platforms and questionnaires.

This paper's first objective is to analyze the strengths and weaknesses of previously published argument mining approaches for public participation processes when they are applied to different German datasets. Our attention is focused on the classification of text segments as *argumentative* or *non-argumentative*, as well as on the downstream classification of *argumentation components*. In addition to our datasets, we include the only other German public participation dataset (to the best of our knowledge) for argument mining (Liebeck et al., 2016) in the evaluation.

Our second objective is to improve the results obtained on the datasets under consideration by the previous approaches for both classification tasks. For this we apply BERT (Devlin et al., 2019) which is known to perform very well on many tasks including argument mining.

In practice, the use of argument mining to evaluate public participation processes only adds value when the benefits outweigh the effort. Manual coding of data and the training or fine-tuning of machine learning models are costly. In addition, machine learning requires expert knowledge and usually cannot be performed directly by the municipalities. An optimal solution would be a universally valid model that can be applied flexibly to new datasets. Our third objective is hence to investigate the extent to which trained models can recognize argument structures in other public participation processes that were not part of the training process.

Our contributions are: (1) We present a new data corpus of five mobility-related public participation processes that vary in content and format. The German corpus comprises $17,306$ sentences coded with an argument scheme tailored to informal public participation processes. (2) We perform a broad comparison of previously published best approaches for argument mining in public participation processes, which so far have been evaluated mostly on distinct datasets. We compare the algorithms directly on our data corpus and compare the performances. (3) We show that BERT surpasses previously published argument mining approaches for public participation processes on German data for both tasks. Especially when classifying argument components, macro F_1 results improve by between 0.05 and 0.12 depending on the dataset. (4) In a cross-dataset evaluation, we show that BERT models trained on one dataset can recognize argument structures in other public participation datasets (which were not part of the training) with comparable goodness of fit. This finding is an important step towards practical application in municipalities.

2 Related Work

Mining arguments in the domain of citizen participation has been the subject of several studies. Much of this work centers on U.S. e-rulemaking initiatives, where citizens are given the opportunity for feedback on rule proposals. An early attempt to identify, classify, and relate arguments in e-rulemaking was made by Kwon et al. (2006); Kwon and Hovy (2007). Arguments were built as trees of claims and subclaims or main-support with support relations. Eidelman and Grom (2019) extended the detection of generic argument components (support and opposition) with corpus-specific argument types. Niculae et al. (2017), Galassi et al. (2018) and Cocarascu et al. (2020) differentiate between five proposition types (fact, testimony, value, policy, and reference) and evidence or reason relations. In addition, other research examined specific properties of argumentation and discourse in public participation processes. Park and Cardie (2014) identified the lack of appropriate justifications as a common problem in the analysis of citizen contributions and tried to predict whether and by what means a proposal is verifiable. Subsequent work

[3]The research project *Citizen Involvement in Mobility Transitions* (CIMT) has identified more than 350 processes directly related to mobility since 2015.

was presented by Park et al. (2015) and Guggilla et al. (2016). Furthermore, Lawrence et al. (2017) and Konat et al. (2016) investigated discourse analysis in more detail and measured controversy and divisiveness in argument graphs.

Besides e-rulemaking initiatives, informal public participation processes were considered. Our work shares most similarity to Liebeck et al. (2016) who focused on a German-language process about the restructuring of a former airport area. The authors developed an argumentation scheme specifically adapted to discursive online public participation processes. With regard to languages other than German, Fierro et al. (2017) and in a follow-up work Giannakopoulos et al. (2019) studied a corpus consisting of over 200, 000 political arguments in Chilean Spanish dialect, derived from a participatory process to form a new constitution for Chile. The arguments were classified thematically according to constitutional concepts and also as either *policies*, *facts* or *values*. Further work (Morio and Fujita, 2018a,b) paid attention to the complex structure of arguments in public online participation. Relying on a Japanese dataset, the authors presented an annotation scheme for discussion threads taking care of inner-post relations and inter-post interactions.

Although the work to date has produced encouraging results, most approaches are not yet mature for practical use (e.g. with German public participation processes). Only few previous research addressed the development of general models (see Cocarascu et al. (2020), who perform a cross-dataset comparison of baselines for relation prediction). Therefore, this paper investigates the cross-data transferability of trained models for the identification and classification of argument components in public participation processes, an investigation that is highly relevant for practical use.

3 Data Corpus

3.1 Datasets

Our five datasets originate from urban planning and are concerned with mobility. Four of them represent very specific processes for improving cycling as a mode of transportation, the fourth dataset stems from a more general strategic process for developing a mobility concept. These five datasets comprise different participation types, i.e., online platforms and questionnaires.

Cycling dialogues The *cycling dialogues* were a pilot project for improving the cycle traffic infrastucture in three German cities, namely Bonn, Cologne and Moers. During a five-week period in 2017, citizens were able to participate (make propositions, discuss and rate propositions or comments) in a map-based online consultation[4]. While in Bonn and Moers suggestions for improvement could be made city-wide, the focus in Cologne was on a specific city district. As a result, three datasets of similar online public participation processes from different local contexts emerged. In the following, these datasets will be referred to as *CD_B*, *CD_C* and *CD_M*. We focus on the initial text contributions in which citizens make new proposals. CD_B is the largest dataset comprising 12, 103 sentences from 2, 364 contributions, whereas CD_C and CD_M are considerably smaller, with 366 and 459 contributions consisting of 1, 704 and 2, 193 sentences, respectively. On average, the contributions consist of 4.83, 4.66 and 4.78 sentences ($\sigma = 2.63$, $\sigma = 3.00$ and $\sigma = 2.61$) with 15.94, 15.16 and 15.43 tokens ($\sigma = 10.92$, $\sigma = 10.45$ and $\sigma = 10.81$).

Mobility concept Since 2019, the German city of Krefeld has been planning how the city's mobility should look like in the future. In addition to various on-site events, multiple public participation processes were carried out online. The here presented dataset *MC_K* includes the 2, 008 sentences of the 337 initial contributions from two interrelated online processes. In the first process, citizens were informed about the drafts of seven citywide action plans. The fields of action were *urban development and regional cooperation*, *flowing motor vehicle traffic*, *commercial transport*, *stationary traffic*, *public transport*, *bicycle traffic*, and *foot traffic*. As part of the planning process, citizens were asked to comment on the planned actions. The second process gave citizens the opportunity to submit concrete propositions for actions in specified city districts. Citizens wrote an average of 5.96 sentences ($\sigma = 5.63$), slightly more than in the processes described above. The average 15.25 words per sentence ($\sigma = 10.80$) resemble the cycling dialogues.

Citizen questionnaire on cycling Accompanying the cycling dialogues, a postal survey was con-

[4]In urban planning, propositions usually refer to specific places. Maps are often used to provide assistance.

	CD_B		CD_C		CD_M		MC_K		CQ_B	
non-arg	1,153	(11.3%)	197	(11.9%)	382	(17.8%)	431	(22.2%)	172	(12.4%)
mpos	2,589	(25.4%)	556	(33.6%)	359	(16.7%)	892	(46.0%)	960	(69.5%)
prem	6,438	(63.2%)	904	(54.6%)	1,407	(65.5%)	616	(31.8%)	250	(18.1%)
total	10,180		1,657		2,148		1,939		1,382	

Table 1: Distribution of sentences among the different coding categories per dataset (absolute and percentage).

ducted in a randomized sample of each city's population. The citizens were asked to submit suggestions for improvements to cycling in free-text fields. Respondents could fill out the questionnaire either by hand or online. In this paper, we focus on the 1,386 citizen contributions from the city of Bonn (*CQ_B*) which consist of 1,505 sentences. By comparing the length of the survey contributions (1.09 sentences on average ($\sigma = 0.37$), 7.75 tokens per sentence ($\sigma = 6.30$)) with the online platform contributions, we can clearly see that citizens write more succinct in surveys of this type.

3.2 Argumentation Model

A key aspect of public participation is that citizens can submit their own ideas on a given topic, such as the cycling infrastructure of a city or the development of a mobility concept. One contribution from CD_B, translated into English, e.g. states: "A new pavement is urgently needed here to be able to cycle along. The current pavement has grooves & cracks in the surface, so that cycling between Ringstraße & Kreuzherrenstraße is very risky, especially in wet conditions." The writer proposes to renew the pavement and substantiates this with the current poor and dangerous condition of the pavement. In urban planning processes, causes for suggested improvements are mostly descriptions of infrastructure problems or (perceived) planning deficits, while the propositions are measures to overcome these issues. Several interviews we conducted in 2020 with local authorities and urban planning practitioners emphasized the value in automatically recognizing the problems that citizens describe and the solutions they propose in text contributions (Romberg and Escher, 2020).

We follow the terminology of Liebeck et al. (2016), who developed an argumentation model for informal online public participation processes based on three argument components: *major positions* provide "options for actions or decisions that occur in the discussion". In simpler terms, these are the propositions that citizens make. *Premises* are "reasons that attack or support a major position, a claim or another premise". *Claims* are defined as "pro or contra stance towards a major position". In this work, we rely on the concepts of major positions and premises, as our focus is on the detection of propositions and underlying reasons. We leave for future work the detection of pro or contra stances expressed by fellow citizens in the feedback comments on initial proposals (in the case of dialogical processes).

3.3 Annotation Process

Coding guidelines were developed on 201 contributions from the cycling dialogues Bonn, which were excluded from the subsequent annotation process, reducing the sentences to be coded in CD_B to 10,442. Each sentence was labeled as *non-argumentative* (non-arg), *major position* (mpos) or *premise* (prem). In case a sentence contained multiple argumentation components, multi-labeling was allowed. Since contribution titles often contained parts of the argument, they were included as additional sentences.

We measured the inter-coder agreement on 10% of the contributions of each dataset, which were respectively annotated by three trained coders. In a subsequent curation step, disagreements were resolved by two supervisors to obtain unambiguous coding of the contributions used to measure the inter-coder agreement. High Fleiss' κ values prove the reliability of the codings: 0.76 (CD_B), 0.80 (CD_C), 0.77 (CD_M), 0.73 (MC_K), and 0.76 (CQ_B). During curation, certain edge cases became obvious. We believe that this subjectivity is also reflected in a human evaluation, which is why a small deviation in coding seems acceptable, also with regard to the training of the classification algorithms. The remaining 90% of the contributions were divided equally among the coders (each 30%) and annotated independently. These sentences were not curated; however, due to the high agreement on the over 1,700 sentences that were coded by all three annotators, we assume similar reliability on the sentences labeled by one person only.

Since the approaches we compare in this paper are tailored to single-label classifications, we omit sentences containing both major position and premise to be addressed in future work. This affects 548 sentences (262 in CD_B, 49 in CD_C, 45 in CD_M, 69 in MC_K, and 123 in CQ_B).

Table 1 shows the distribution of classes included in the evaluation across the five datasets. The majority of sentences in all datasets are argumentative, accounting for between 77.8% and 88.6%. Major positions and premises are distributed very differently throughout the datasets. While premises are made more frequently in the cycling dialogues, major positions are favored in MC_K and especially in CQ_B. The datasets are available under a Creative Commons License at https://github.com/juliaromberg/cimt-argument-mining-dataset/.

4 Methodology

Argument Mining can be divided into three subtasks: *segmentation*, *segment classification*, and *relation identification* (Peldszus and Stede, 2013). First, argumentative text is split into argument discourse units (ADUs). Second, ADUs are classified according to their function in the argument. Third, relations between ADUs are identified. Peldszus and Stede (2013) assume here that it is known which texts are argumentative or relevant for the argumentation. Lawrence and Reed (2019) widen the first task and include the *distinction between argumentative and non-argumentative units*.

In this work, we focus on (A) the classification of discourse units as argumentative (ADU) and non argumentative (non-ADU) and (B) the classification of ADUs according to contextual clausal properties for informal public participation processes. In the following, these two tasks will be referred to as *Task A* and *Task B*. We define each sentence as discourse unit, so that both tasks are sentence-level classification tasks.

4.1 Previously Applied Argument Mining Approaches for Public Participation

Our first objective is to compare the previously used approaches for solving Task A and Task B in public participation processes on our datasets. In the following, we provide an overview of these algorithms and describe in detail the setups we chose for our experiments (e.g. input features, hyperparameter selection). The results of our experiments are described and discussed in Section 5. For every dataset in consideration, we used a 5-fold cross-validation, dividing the datasets into 80% training and 20% test data each time. We tuned algorithm hyperparameters using a grid search with cross-validation (5 folds) for each split of the (outer) cross-validation.

4.1.1 Task A

All of the works considering the distinction between ADUs and non-ADUS have predefined sentences as elementary discourse units, as we do.

SVM Kwon et al. (2006), Liebeck et al. (2016) and Morio and Fujita (2018a) used support vector machines (Cortes and Vapnik, 1995) to detect ADUs with F_1 scores between 0.52 and 0.70.

For our experiments, we adopted the best setup of Liebeck et al. (2016) since their dataset is most similar to ours. Sentences were represented as a combination of unigrams and grammatical features, more precisely a L_2-normalized POS-Tag distribution[5] and a L_2-normalized distribution of dependencies[6]. We used the radial basis function kernel, and considered $C \in \{1, 10, 100\}$ and $\gamma \in \{0.001, 0.01, 0.1\}$ in the grid search. We further weighted the training samples inversely proportional to the class frequencies to take care of the strong class imbalance of our datasets.

fastText Eidelman and Grom (2019) suggested the use of fastText (Joulin et al., 2017) and proposed balancing the training data for highly imbalanced datasets. By downsampling the majority class in the corresponding dataset, they improved the macro F_1 outcome from 0.80 to 0.90.

In our experiments, we trained two fastText models per dataset: One on the original, imbalanced dataset and one on a balanced version of the dataset where the majority class was undersampled by randomly picking samples. We used pretrained fastText embeddings for German with 50 dimensions, and included learning rates of $1e-1$, $5e-1$ and $9e-1$, and 5 or 10 epochs of training in the grid search.

4.1.2 Task B

More attention has been paid to the classification of ADUs in previous work.

SVM Kwon et al. (2006), Park and Cardie (2014), Liebeck et al. (2016) and Morio and Fujita

[5] STTS tagset (Thielen and Schiller, 2011)

[6] TIGER scheme (Albert et al., 2003)

(2018a) classified argument components in public participation processes with SVMs. Depending on the dataset and argumentation scheme, they yielded macro F_1 values in the range of 0.56 to 0.77.

For our experiments, we again relied on the closely related work of Liebeck et al. (2016) and used the same setup as described in Section 4.1.1.

fastText In Fierro et al. (2017) and Eidelman and Grom (2019), fastText provided the best results (0.65 and 0.78). Of particular interest is that, on the Spanish dataset (Fierro et al., 2017), fastText surpassed the SVM. We were curious to see if this behavior applies to our datasets as well.

In our experiments, we replicated the implementation of Fierro et al. (2017) using pretrained fastText embeddings (we chose 50 dimensions) and word bigrams in the classification. Grid search considered learning rates of $1e-1$, $5e-1$ and $9e-1$, and 5 or 10 epochs of training. Similar to Task A, classes were imbalanced in our datasets, and we thus trained models with and without undersampling.

ECGA Further deep learning architectures have been considered by Guggilla et al. (2016) and Giannakopoulos et al. (2019). While Guggilla et al. (2016) showed that the use of convolutional neuronal networks (CNN) (LeCun et al., 1998) can marginally improve the results of an SVM, the advantages of deep learning become more obvious in the work of Giannakopoulos et al. (2019). Using an ensemble method called ECGA, a combination of multiple learners, they improved the results of Fierro et al. (2017) by 0.07. Each learner is composed of a CNN followed by bidirectional gated recurrent units (BiGRU) (Cho et al., 2014), connected to an attention layer (Bahdanau et al., 2015). The class predictions of the multiple learners are averaged to obtain final predictions. FastText embeddings build the input matrix. For argument classification, Giannakopoulos et al. (2019) proposed the use of two learners with kernel sizes of 2 and 3 as well as 512 filters in the convolution and 256 GRU units.

Since the proposed architecture failed to produce reasonable results on our datasets, we reduced the number of GRU units in our experiments to 64 and the number of convolution filters in to 128. We took our cue from the authors' best model for solving a different task, textual churn detection, with a smaller corresponding dataset. Despite the reduced model architecture, ECGA still tended to neglect the minority class in our datasets. To counteract this, we additionally evaluated ECGA with undersampling. We tried batch sizes of 2, 4, and 8, as well as 1 and 2 kernels or 2 and 3 kernels for the two learners. The training ran for 200 epochs with the option of early stopping if the loss did not improve within 10 epochs.

4.2 Bidirectional Encoder Representations from Transformers for Argument Mining in Public Participation Processes

Our second objective is to improve the results obtained by the previous approaches on our datasets for both classification tasks. To this end, we use BERT (Devlin et al., 2019) which has already provided promising results for Task A and Task B in other text domains, such as on persuasive online forums (Chakrabarty et al., 2019) and on heterogeneous sources of argumentative content (Reimers et al., 2019). With public participation processes, BERT has so far only been used to identify relations between ADUs (Cocarascu et al., 2020).

We expected BERT to also perform well for Task A and Task B on public participation datasets and to outperform the other algorithms in the evaluation. We used case-sensitive German BERT[7] with an additional linear layer for sequence classification. For fine-tuning, we relied on the suggestions of Devlin et al. (2019) and included batch sizes of 16 and 32, learning rates of $5e-5$, $3e-5$ and $2e-5$, and 1 to 4 epochs of training in the grid search.

4.3 Model Generalizability

This work's third objective is to investigate model generalizability in a cross-dataset evaluation. The previous two evaluation objectives were to determine which approach generates the best results for each dataset. To this end, both the training and the test data stem from the same dataset. In a practical application, this would mean that a sufficiently large amount of citizen contributions would have to be coded manually by local authorities. However, a more feasible and cost-effective solution would be to provide a pretrained classification model that can reliably recognize argument structures in new participation processes without the need for further training. Our goal is to provide such a model for public participation processes of mobility-related urban planning. The diversity in subjects and for-

[7] https://www.deepset.ai/german-bert

mats in our data corpus is well suited for testing the transferability to a range of processes.

For the cross-dataset evaluation, we used the evaluation setup described in Section 4.1 (5-fold cross validation, hyperparameter tuning) and trained on CD_B in our experiments. We intentionally chose the largest dataset for training to provide reliable models. For every approach, we then applied the five resulting models to the remaining datasets and averaged the results for each dataset to obtain an average macro F_1 score. Algorithms were implemented as described in Sections 4.1 and 4.2.

For Task A, we evaluated SVM, fastText without undersampling (as will be shown in Section 5.1.1, undersampling of CD_B provided no advantage), and BERT. For Task B, we chose to evaluate models trained on undersampled data and models trained on the original data alongside. Our decision was due to the very different distribution of ADU-types in our datasets: while premises prevail in the cycling dialogues (62%-80% prem), major positions are more present in MC_K (59% mpos) and in CQ_B (80% mpos). We thus wanted to investigate whether models trained on balanced data could provide more stable results across the different datasets. To sum up, we compared the behavior of eight approaches in the cross-dataset evaluation for Task B: SVM, fastText, ECGA, and BERT trained on the original CD_B dataset, and trained on an undersampled CD_B dataset.

5 Results and Discussion

5.1 Comparison of the Approaches

In the following, we evaluate for both classification tasks the approaches from previous work (see Section 4.1) and BERT (see Section 4.2) on our corpus from Section 3. For completeness, we also have a look at the only other German public participation dataset for argument mining, *THF Airport ArgMining Corpus* (Liebeck et al., 2016). *THF* provides 2,078 argumentative and 355 non-argumentative sentences for Task A, and 509 major positions, 1,170 premises, and 311 claims for Task B.[8]

5.1.1 Task A

Results for the classification of ADUs and non-ADUs are given in Table 2. For each dataset, only the results of the superior fastText model are listed.

		SVM	*fastText*	*BERT*
CD_B	arg	0.93 (0.00)	0.94 (0.00)	**0.95** (0.00)
	non-arg	0.52 (0.04)	0.41 (0.04)	**0.57** (0.04)
	macro	0.73 (0.02)	0.68 (0.02)	**0.76** (0.02)
CD_C	arg	0.93 (0.01)	0.87 (0.02)*	**0.95** (0.01)
	non-arg	0.53 (0.10)	0.42 (0.06)*	**0.58** (0.12)
	macro	0.73 (0.06)	0.64 (0.04)*	**0.77** (0.07)
CD_M	arg	0.90 (0.01)	0.92 (0.01)	**0.94** (0.01)
	non-arg	0.59 (0.05)	0.51 (0.05)	**0.67** (0.04)
	macro	0.75 (0.03)	0.71 (0.03)	**0.80** (0.03)
MC_K	arg	0.86 (0.01)	0.89 (0.01)	**0.91** (0.01)
	non-arg	0.53 (0.03)	0.45 (0.02)	**0.62** (0.06)
	macro	0.69 (0.02)	0.67 (0.01)	**0.77** (0.04)
CQ_B	arg	0.94 (0.02)	0.85 (0.02)*	**0.96** (0.01)
	non-arg	0.53 (0.07)	0.42 (0.04)*	**0.56** (0.16)
	macro	0.73 (0.05)	0.63 (0.03)*	**0.76** (0.09)
THF	arg	0.91 (0.01)	0.79 (0.03)*	**0.92** (0.01)
	non-arg	**0.48** (0.03)	0.37 (0.03)*	0.46 (0.05)
	macro	**0.70** (0.02)	0.58 (0.03)*	0.69 (0.03)

Table 2: Results for Task A on the individual datasets. Scores are mean F_1 values of the five test sets, standard deviation is given in parentheses.

Undersampling models are marked with an asterisk. Overall, BERT performed best with macro F_1 values up to 0.80, improving most SVM scores by at least 0.03.[9] However, on THF the SVM yielded slightly better results. FastText struggled with the minority class. The problem was particularly evident in the three datasets with the fewest non-argumentative samples, where undersampling could improve the results at least to some degree.

5.1.2 Task B

Table 3 shows the findings for argument component classification. For fastText and ECGA, two model variants were evaluated (with and without undersampling), of which the better one is listed. Undersampling models are marked with an asterisk. While undersampling slightly increased the macro performance of ECGA on all datasets, there was no enhancement with fastText. Contrary to our expectations, ECGA performed worse than fastText and could only keep up with the other approaches for datasets that have sufficient samples in the minority class. BERT showed outstanding results and could significantly advance the classification, especially for the minority classes: Compared to the also good SVM, the prediction of major positions

[8]We evaluate the dataset according to our methodology instead of the suggested train-test split by Liebeck et al. (2016).

[9]BERT models show a high standard deviation in the minority classes of CD_C and CQ_B. Variance is due to the small number of non-arg sentences in the cross-validation for hyperparameter tuning. Fixed hyperparameters yield comparable F_1 values and much lower standard deviation.

		SVM	*fastText*	*ECGA*	*BERT*
CD_B	mpos	0.82 (0.01)	0.79 (0.01)	0.78 (0.03)	**0.90** (0.01)
	prem	0.93 (0.01)	0.93 (0.00)	0.92 (0.01)	**0.96** (0.00)
	macro	0.88 (0.01)	0.86 (0.01)	0.85 (0.02)	**0.93** (0.01)
CD_C	mpos	0.77 (0.02)	0.74 (0.02)	0.76 (0.03)*	**0.89** (0.02)
	prem	0.85 (0.01)	0.86 (0.01)	0.84 (0.01)*	**0.93** (0.01)
	macro	0.81 (0.02)	0.80 (0.02)	0.80 (0.02)*	**0.91** (0.02)
CD_M	mpos	0.67 (0.03)	0.58 (0.03)	0.52 (0.08)*	**0.84** (0.06)
	prem	0.92 (0.01)	0.92 (0.00)	0.86 (0.05)*	**0.91** (0.04)
	macro	0.80 (0.03)	0.75 (0.02)	0.69 (0.06)*	**0.90** (0.03)
MC_K	mpos	0.83 (0.03)	0.83 (0.03)	0.84 (0.03)*	**0.88** (0.02)
	prem	0.75 (0.03)	0.74 (0.04)	0.74 (0.05)*	**0.84** (0.03)
	macro	0.79 (0.03)	0.78 (0.04)	0.79 (0.05)*	**0.86** (0.03)
CQ_B	mpos	0.93 (0.02)	0.92 (0.01)	0.89 (0.03)*	**0.97** (0.01)
	prem	0.70 (0.08)	0.58 (0.06)	0.55 (0.10)*	**0.88** (0.03)
	macro	0.81 (0.05)	0.75 (0.04)	0.72 (0.06)*	**0.93** (0.02)
THF	mpos	0.53 (0.05)	0.46 (0.03)	0.46 (0.04)*	**0.68** (0.03)
	prem	0.78 (0.01)	0.79 (0.01)	0.60 (0.06)*	**0.84** (0.03)
	claim	0.60 (0.03)	0.59 (0.06)	0.51 (0.06)*	**0.63** (0.06)
	macro	0.64 (0.02)	0.61 (0.03)	0.52 (0.04)*	**0.72** (0.04)

Table 3: Results for Task B on the individual datasets. Scores are mean F_1 values of the five test sets, standard deviation is given in parentheses.

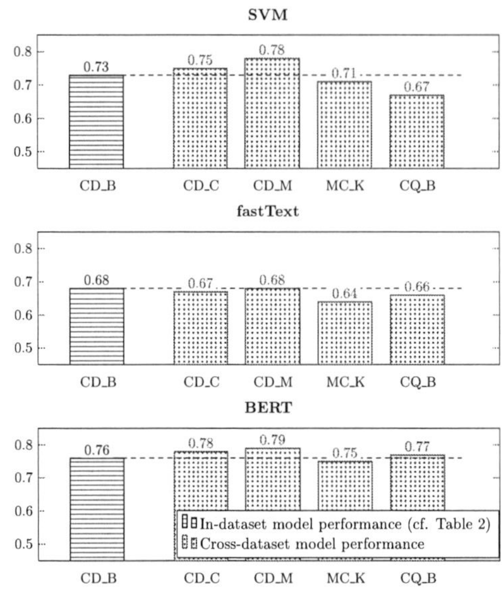

Figure 1: Cross-dataset evaluation for Task A. Results are averaged macro F_1 values of the five models trained on CD_B.

(CD_B, CD_C, CD_M, THF) improved by at least 0.08 up to 0.17. Premises were predicted with an improvement of 0.09 and 0.18 (MC_K, CQ_B).

5.2 Cross-Dataset Evaluation

Next, we look at the generalization performance of the learned models for both classification tasks.

5.2.1 Task A

Figure 1 shows the cross-dataset results of the CD_B models on the other datasets. BERT could consistently achieve good macro F_1 values (between 0.75 and 0.79) for all datasets, close to the score of 0.76 that BERT achieved on the refence dataset CD_B ($\sigma = 0.02$). The obtained values are also comparable to the results of dataset-internal results from Section 5.1. Equally stable was fastText ($\sigma = 0.02$), but results were on average 0.10 points lower. SVM predictions varied more ($\sigma = 0.04$), especially when transferring to CQ_B and MC_K.

5.2.2 Task B

Results for the cross-dataset classification of argument components are presented in Figure 2. Both BERT model variants generalized very well and achieved an average macro F_1 score of 0.90 across the different datasets. With $\sigma = 0.01$, the undersampling model predicted remarkably stable on our datasets ($\sigma = 0.02$ for the non-undersampling model). SVM, ECGA and fastText strongly benefited from balanced training data. With undersampling, the latter two approaches could surpass the in-dataset results from Section 5.1 and thus achieved best values for all datasets. SVM struggled with generalization on MC_K and CQ_B ($\sigma = 0.03$). Likewise fastText showed some weaknesses in generalization ($\sigma = 0.03$), which were particularly noticeable in the performance drop on CQ_B (0.76) compared to the reference value (0.84). ECGA achieved more uniform results with an average macro F_1 value of 0.83 ($\sigma = 0.02$), which, however, do not come close to the high values of BERT.

It turned out that the models generalize surprisingly well across the different processes. In both tasks, BERT showed superior results, but other methods were also able to provide stable predictions across the different test datasets. This suggests that universally valid patterns of argument structures could be learned, generalizing to a very different data type (from deliberative online platforms to questionnaire data), as well as to a process with a more general topic (from specific cycling to a comprehensive mobility concept).

6 Conclusion and Future Work

We investigated (A) the distinction of ADUs and non-ADUs and (B) the classification of major posi-

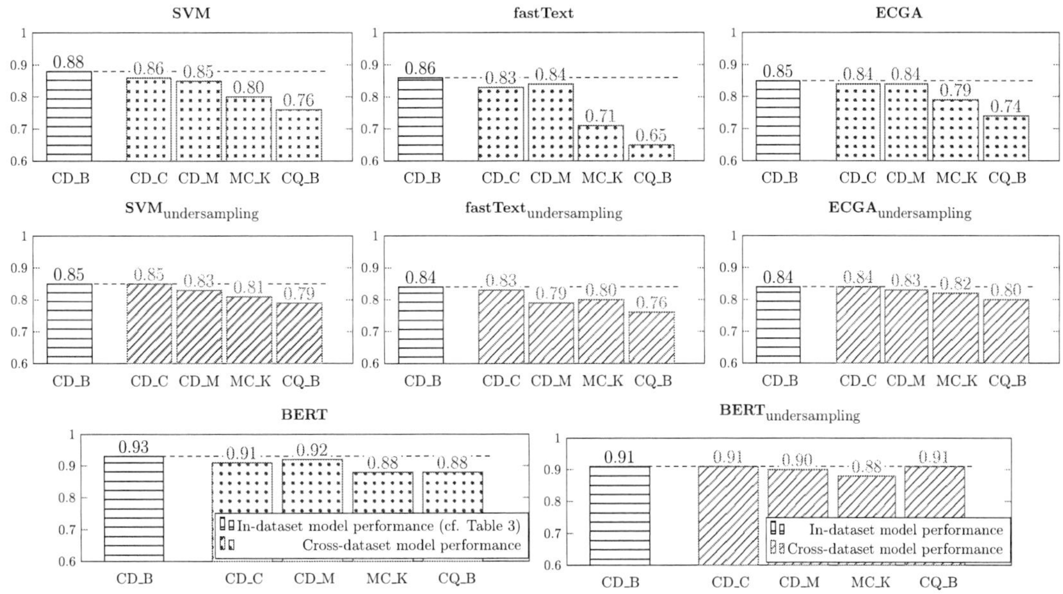

Figure 2: Cross-dataset evaluation for Task B. Results are averaged macro F_1 values of the five models trained on CD_B. (Note that in-dataset performance of CD_B with undersampling has not been reported in Table 3),

tions and premises for German public participation processes from urban planning. For this purpose, we introduced a new data corpus comprising five diverse mobility-related processes. Our first objective was to identify previously published approaches to solving the two classification tasks on public participation processes and test their performance on our datasets. Among these works, SVM achieved the best results in both tasks. Our second objective was to improve the previous results. We proposed the use of BERT and successfully demonstrated that the results of both tasks improved. On our datasets, BERT yielded highly promising macro F_1 scores, between 0.76 and 0.80 for Task A and between 0.86 and 0.93 for Task B. We additionally showed, that our approach outperforms previous results for Task B on a similar German online participation dataset. We further argued, that the use of pretrained models is one way to make argument mining applicable in municipalities. Our third objective was to prove the feasibility for processes from urban planning that differ in topic or format. We showed that BERT models outperform the other approaches, achieving average macro F_1 values of 0.77 ($\sigma = 0.02$) for Task A and 0.90 ($\sigma = 0.01$) for Task B in the cross-dataset evaluation. Our results are very positive and show that practical support for municipalities in evaluating mobility-related public participation processes is within reach by providing pretrained models.

In future work, we plan to investigate whether our best model can generalize to non-mobility public participation processes in urban planning to cover a broader range of topics. To further improve our models, we will concentrate on improving the detection of argumentative discourse units. Although we were able to achieve promising results, it has become apparent that distinguishing ADUs from non-ADUs is a particular challenge. Additionally, we will extend the classification for sentences that include multiple argument components (major position and premise) and address stance detection.

Acknowledgements

We are especially grateful to Tobias Escher, who provided significant support for this work through funding acquisition, the provision of data resources and comments to the manuscript. We thank him, Katharina Huseljić, Matthias Liebeck and Laura Mark for valuable discussions and feedback on earlier forms of this work. We thank the anonymous reviewers for their helpful comments. This publication is based on research in the project CIMT/Partizipationsnutzen, which is funded by the Federal Ministry of Education and Research as part of its Social-Ecological Research funding priority, funding no. 01UU1904. Responsibility for the content of this publication lies with the author.

References

Stefanie Albert, Jan Anderssen, Regine Bader, Stephanie Becker, Tobias Bracht, Sabine Brants, Thorsten Brants, Vera Demberg, Stefanie Dipper, Peter Eisenberg, Silvia Hansen, Hagen Hirschmann, Juliane Janitzek, Carolin Kirstein, Robert Langner, Lukas Michelbacher, Oliver Plaehn, Cordula Preis, Marcus Pussel, Marco Rower, Bettina Schrader, Anne Schwartz, Smith George, and Hans Uszkoreit. 2003. TIGER Annotationsschema. Technical report, Universität des Saarlandes, Universität Stuttgart, Universität Potsdam.

Miguel Arana-Catania, Felix-Anselm Van Lier, Rob Procter, Nataliya Tkachenko, Yulan He, Arkaitz Zubiaga, and Maria Liakata. 2021. Citizen participation and machine learning for a better democracy. *Digit. Gov.: Res. Pract.*, 2(3).

Dzmitry Bahdanau, Kyung Hyun Cho, and Yoshua Bengio. 2015. Neural Machine Translation by Jointly Learning to Align and Translate. In *3rd International Conference on Learning Representations*.

Tuhin Chakrabarty, Christopher Hidey, Smaranda Muresan, Kathy McKeown, and Alyssa Hwang. 2019. AMPERSAND: Argument Mining for PERSuAsive oNline Discussions. In *Proceedings of the 2019 Conference on Empirical Methods in Natural Language Processing and the 9th International Joint Conference on Natural Language Processing (EMNLP-IJCNLP)*, pages 2933–2943.

Kyunghyun Cho, Bart van Merriënboer, Caglar Gulcehre, Dzmitry Bahdanau, Fethi Bougares, Holger Schwenk, and Yoshua Bengio. 2014. Learning Phrase Representations using RNN Encoder–Decoder for Statistical Machine Translation. In *Proceedings of the 2014 Conference on Empirical Methods in Natural Language Processing (EMNLP)*, pages 1724–1734.

Oana Cocarascu, Elena Cabrio, Serena Villata, and Francesca Toni. 2020. Dataset independent baselines for relation prediction in argument mining. In *Computational Models of Argument - Proceedings of COMMA 2020*, pages 45–52.

Corinna Cortes and Vladimir Vapnik. 1995. Support-Vector Networks. *Machine Learning*, 20:273–297.

Jacob Devlin, Ming-Wei Chang, Kenton Lee, and Kristina Toutanova. 2019. BERT: Pre-training of Deep Bidirectional Transformers for Language Understanding. In *Proceedings of the 2019 Conference of the North American Chapter of the Association for Computational Linguistics: Human Language Technologies, Volume 1 (Long and Short Papers)*, pages 4171–4186.

Vlad Eidelman and Brian Grom. 2019. Argument Identification in Public Comments from eRulemaking. In *Proceedings of the Seventeenth International Conference on Artificial Intelligence and Law*, pages 199–203.

Peter Esaiasson. 2010. Will citizens take no for an answer? What government officials can do to enhance decision acceptance. *European Political Science Review*, 2(3):351–371.

Constanza Fierro, Claudio Fuentes, Jorge Pérez, and Mauricio Quezada. 2017. 200K+ Crowdsourced Political Arguments for a New Chilean Constitution. In *Proceedings of the 4th Workshop on Argument Mining*, pages 1–10.

Andrea Galassi, Marco Lippi, and Paolo Torroni. 2018. Argumentative Link Prediction using Residual Networks and Multi-Objective Learning. In *Proceedings of the 5th Workshop on Argument Mining*, pages 1–10.

Athanasios Giannakopoulos, Maxime Coriou, Andreea Hossmann, Michael Baeriswyl, and Claudiu Musat. 2019. Resilient Combination of Complementary CNN and RNN Features for Text Classification through Attention and Ensembling. In *6th Swiss Conference on Data Science (SDS)*, pages 57–62.

Chinnappa Guggilla, Tristan Miller, and Iryna Gurevych. 2016. CNN-and LSTM-based Claim Classification in Online User Comments. In *Proceedings of COLING 2016, the 26th International Conference on Computational Linguistics: Technical Papers*, pages 2740–2751.

Armand Joulin, Edouard Grave, Piotr Bojanowski, and Tomas Mikolov. 2017. Bag of Tricks for Efficient Text Classification. In *Proceedings of the 15th Conference of the European Chapter of the Association for Computational Linguistics: Volume 2, Short Papers*, pages 427–431.

Barbara Konat, John Lawrence, Joonsuk Park, Katarzyna Budzynska, and Chris Reed. 2016. A Corpus of Argument Networks: Using Graph Properties to Analyse Divisive Issues. In *Proceedings of the Tenth International Conference on Language Resources and Evaluation (LREC 2016)*, pages 3899–3906.

Namhee Kwon and Eduard Hovy. 2007. Information Acquisition using Multiple Classifications. In *Proceedings of the 4th International Conference on Knowledge Capture*, pages 111–118.

Namhee Kwon, Stuart W. Shulman, and Eduard Hovy. 2006. Multidimensional Text Analysis for eRulemaking. In *Proceedings of the 2006 International Conference on Digital Government Research*, pages 157–166.

Namhee Kwon, Liang Zhou, Eduard Hovy, and Stuart W. Shulman. 2007. Identifying and Classifying Subjective Claims. In *Proceedings of the 8th Annual International Conference on Digital Government Research: Bridging Disciplines & Domains*, pages 76–81.

John Lawrence, Joonsuk Park, Katarzyna Budzynska, Claire Cardie, Barbara Konat, and Chris Reed. 2017. Using Argumentative Structure to Interpret Debates in Online Deliberative Democracy and eRulemaking. *ACM Transactions on Internet Technology*, 17(3):1–22.

John Lawrence and Chris Reed. 2019. Argument Mining: A Survey. *Computational Linguistics*, 45(4):765–818.

Yann LeCun, Léon Bottou, Yoshua Bengio, and Patrick Haffner. 1998. Gradient-Based Learning Applied to Document Recognition. *Proceedings of the IEEE*, 86(11):2278–2324.

Matthias Liebeck, Katharina Esau, and Stefan Conrad. 2016. What to Do with an Airport? Mining Arguments in the German Online Participation Project Tempelhofer Feld. In *Proceedings of the 3rd Workshop on Argument Mining*, pages 144–153.

Nina A. Mendelson. 2012. Should Mass Comments Count? *Mich. J. Envtl. & Admin. L.* 2, 2:173–183.

Gaku Morio and Katsuhide Fujita. 2018a. Annotating Online Civic Discussion Threads for Argument Mining. In *2018 IEEE/WIC/ACM International Conference on Web Intelligence (WI)*, pages 546–553.

Gaku Morio and Katsuhide Fujita. 2018b. End-to-End Argument Mining for Discussion Threads Based on Parallel Constrained Pointer Architecture. In *Proceedings of the 5th Workshop on Argument Mining*, pages 11–21.

Vlad Niculae, Joonsuk Park, and Claire Cardie. 2017. Argument Mining with Structured SVMs and RNNs. In *Proceedings of the 55th Annual Meeting of the Association for Computational Linguistics (Volume 1: Long Papers)*, pages 985–995.

OECD. 2004. *Promise and Problems of E-Democracy*. OECD Publishing.

Joonsuk Park and Claire Cardie. 2014. Identifying Appropriate Support for Propositions in Online User Comments. In *Proceedings of the First Workshop on Argumentation Mining*, pages 29–38.

Joonsuk Park, Arzoo Katiyar, and Bishan Yang. 2015. Conditional Random Fields for Identifying Appropriate Types of Support for Propositions in Online User Comments. In *Proceedings of the 2nd Workshop on Argumentation Mining*, pages 39–44.

Andreas Peldszus and Manfred Stede. 2013. From Argument Diagrams to Argumentation Mining in Texts: A Survey. *International Journal of Cognitive Informatics and Natural Intelligence (IJCINI)*, 7(1):1–31.

Stephen Purpura, Claire Cardie, and Jesse Simons. 2008. Active Learning for e-Rulemaking: Public Comment Categorization. In *Proceedings of the 2008 International Conference on Digital Government Research*, pages 234–243.

Nils Reimers, Benjamin Schiller, Tilman Beck, Johannes Daxenberger, Christian Stab, and Iryna Gurevych. 2019. Classification and Clustering of Arguments with Contextualized Word Embeddings. In *Proceedings of the 57th Annual Meeting of the Association for Computational Linguistics*, pages 567–578.

Julia Romberg and Tobias Escher. 2020. Analyse der Anforderungen an eine Software zur (teil-)automatisierten Unterstützung bei der Auswertung von Beteiligungsverfahren. Working Paper 1, CIMT Research Group, Institute for Social Sciences, Heinrich Heine University Düsseldorf.

Fritz W. Scharpf. 1999. *Governing in Europe: Effective and Democratic?* Oxford: Oxford University Press.

David Schlosberg, Stephen Zavestoski, and Stuart W. Shulman. 2008. Democracy and E-Rulemaking: Web-Based Technologies, Participation, and the Potential for Deliberation. *Journal of Information Technology & Politics*, 4(1):37–55.

Stuart W. Shulman. 2003. An experiment in digital government at the United States National Organic Program. *Agriculture and Human Values*, 20:253–265.

Peter Teufl, Udo Payer, and Peter Parycek. 2009. Automated Analysis of e-Participation Data by Utilizing Associative Networks, Spreading Activation and Unsupervised Learning. In *International Conference on Electronic Participation*, pages 139–150.

Christine Thielen and Anne Schiller. 2011. Ein kleines und erweitertes Tagset fürs Deutsche. In *Lexikon und Text: Wiederverwendbare Methoden und Ressourcen zur linguistischen Erschließung des Deutschen*, pages 193–204. Max Niemeyer Verlag.

Hui Yang, Jamie Callan, and Stuart Shulman. 2006. Next Steps in Near-Duplicate Detection for eRulemaking. In *Proceedings of the 2006 International Conference on Digital Government Research*, pages 239–248.

Argumentation Mining in Scientific Literature for Sustainable Development

Aris Fergadis[1,2(✉)], **Dimitris Pappas**[2], **Antonia Karamolegkou**[2], and **Haris Papageorgiou**[2]
[1]School of Electrical and Computer Engineering, National Technical University of Athens
[2]Athena Research and Innovation Center
aris.fergadis@athenarc.gr

Abstract

Science, technology and innovation (STI) policies have evolved in the past decade. We are now progressing towards policies that are more aligned with sustainable development through integrating social, economic and environmental dimensions. In this new policy environment, the need to keep track of innovation from its conception in Science and Research has emerged. Argumentation mining, an interdisciplinary NLP field, gives rise to the required technologies. In this study, we present the first STI-driven multidisciplinary corpus of scientific abstracts annotated for argumentative units (AUs) on the sustainable development goals (SDGs) set by the United Nations (UN). AUs are the sentences conveying the Claim(s) reported in the author's original research and the Evidence provided for support. We also present a set of strong, BERT-based neural baselines achieving an f1-score of 70.0 for Claim and 62.4 for Evidence identification evaluated with 10-fold cross-validation. To demonstrate the effectiveness of our models, we experiment with different test sets showing comparable performance across various SDG policy domains. Our dataset and models are publicly available for research purposes[1].

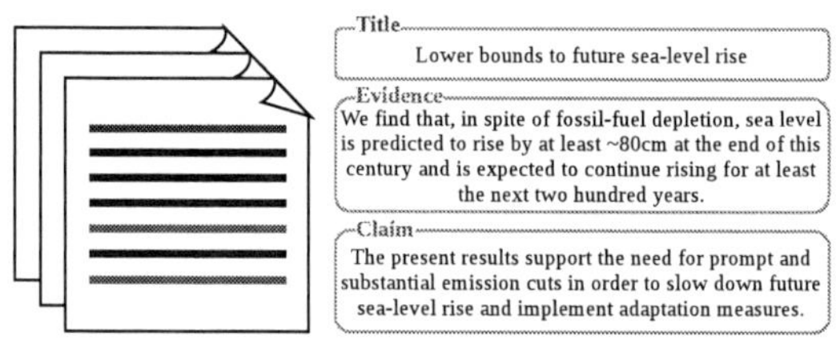

Figure 1: Example of an annotated paper. The authors (Zecca and Chiari, 2012) claim that a substantial emission cut is needed to slow down sea-level rise. The evidence they provide is the result of their method that predicts a continued rising for at least the next two hundred years.

1 Introduction

Arguments are the fundamental building blocks (i.e., groups of statements) in the reasoning path from assumptions to conclusions. Argumentation mining (AM[2]) is becoming increasingly a popular topic that addresses the issue of converting unstructured text into structured argument data (Green et al., 2014; Cardie et al., 2015; Reed, 2016; Habernal et al., 2017; Slonim and Aharonov, 2018; Stein and Wachsmuth, 2019).

AM datasets have been developed in various domains such as legal collections (Mochales and Ieven, 2009; Savelka and Ashley, 2016; Yamada et al., 2017), political debate fora (Walker et al., 2012; Abbott et al., 2016), persuasive essays (Stab and Gurevych, 2014; Carlile et al., 2018), biomedical publications (Wilbur et al., 2006; Blake, 2010; Achakulvisut et al., 2019; Mayer et al., 2020), newspapers, blogs, and the social web (Goudas et al., 2015; Kiesel et al., 2015; Habernal and Gurevych, 2017).

These datasets facilitate practical applications of argumentation mining such as supporting sense-making (Schneider, 2014), practical reasoning (Walton, 2015), argument retrieval (Rastegar-Mojarad et al., 2016), sentiment analysis (Liu et al., 2017), and claim verification (Thorne et al., 2018; Wadden et al., 2020). We present a novel AM framework streamlining evidence-informed policy making.

The *Resolution adopted by the UN General Assembly on 25th of September 2015*[3] set 17 interlinked SDGs and 169 targets to "...stimulate action over the next 15 years in areas of critical importance for humanity and the planet". In this context, policy makers and public administrators seek evidence-based scientific claims assisting the formulation of optimal STI policy for achieving

[1]https://github.com/afergadis/SciARK

[2]Both argument and argumentation mining terms are used in the literature.

[3]https://undocs.org/A/RES/70/1

Proceedings of The 8th Workshop on Argument Mining, pages 100–111
Punta Cana, Dominican Republic, November 10–11, 2021.

the sustainable path of development. To this end, we construct SciARK, a novel multidisciplinary dataset with abstracts of scientific publications related to six Sustainable Development Goals (SDGs) of the United Nations (UN). SciARK abstracts are annotated for their *Argument Units*, i.e., sentences in which the authors state their *Claims* and the *Evidence* to support them. We present such an example in Figure 1.

The term *Claim* in SciARK refers to the main findings reported in the authors' original research and usually coincides with the conclusions. In addition, we use the term *Evidence* for the sentences that refer to particular kinds of arguments, such as those based on observations, factual findings, statistics, experimental tests or other scientific findings. Implicitly, all the relations are *Supporting*, and we justify our decision in Section 3.1. We develop end-to-end neural baselines on SciARK, showing that all baselines can benefit from training on a diverse set of SDG policy domains[4]. The major contributions of this paper can be summarised as follows:

1. We introduce a novel STI-driven multidisciplinary dataset with argumentation annotation. The dataset covers six of the 17 Sustainable Development Goals of United Nations covering a wide range of sustainability aspects, from Climate to Clean Energy to Health and well-being to Gender equality and responsible consumption and production.

2. We formalise and develop an annotation protocol assuring quality by accounting for different groups of annotators curating publications in different domains.

3. We interpret the magnitude of inter-annotator agreement following the Cumulative Probability approach (Gwet, 2014), instead of a simple scale matching.

4. We provide three strong modern deep learning baselines addressing the claim/evidence extraction as a classification task, showing their effectiveness in a diverse set of sustainability domains.

5. We demonstrate the capacity of our models and dataset in tackling unseen SDG domains. Compared to previous domain-specific approaches, our best model can handle snippets of claims and evidence in a broad spectrum of SDG domains.

[4]We also use the term "SDG domain" or "SDG" for short.

2 Related Work

A large number of annotated datasets has been released for argumentation mining in various domains (Lawrence and Reed, 2019). Many researchers approach the claim annotation task under the prism of functional roles (Blake, 2010; Alamri and Stevenson, 2016) or ownership (Lauscher et al., 2018; Mayer et al., 2020). Evidence annotation has analogous categorisation, ranging from its strength (Wilbur et al., 2006; Shatkay et al., 2008) to reproduction and generalisation (Mayer et al., 2018). However, it is not always possible to apply these fine-grained differentiations to other domains.

Recently, researchers employed argumentative schemes that incorporate both argumentative units and their relationships. The most common argumentative relationships employed are the "support" and "attack" ones (Peldszus and Stede, 2013; Mayer et al., 2020). Researchers also adapt additional relation types from Rhetorical Structure Theory (Mann and Thompson, 1988) such as "semantically same" (Lauscher et al., 2018), "detail", "sequence" (Kirschner et al., 2015), and "additional" (Accuosto and Saggion, 2019). Although those fine-grained relation types are of great value, their presence in the context of a scientific abstract is limited.

The most recent methods for the AU classification task leverage neural networks architectures. A common architecture is the one comprising a BiLSTM layer followed by a CRF layer for sequence tagging (Achakulvisut et al., 2019; Accuosto and Saggion, 2019). Mayer et al. (2020) evaluate many different neural network models and shows that those based on Transformers have better performance on the AU extraction and the relation classification tasks. The before mentioned models classify sequences of words within a AU ignoring the context before and after the AU. We experiment with Transformers and BiLSTM layers taking advantage of the context of AUs.

Most of the datasets based on scientific literature are domain specific with strong emphasis on the biomedical domain (Blake, 2010; Alamri and Stevenson, 2016; Achakulvisut et al., 2019; Mayer et al., 2020). Other domains are education (Kirschner et al., 2015), computer graphics (Lauscher et al., 2018), and computational linguistics (Accuosto and Saggion, 2019). SciARK, as a multidisciplinary dataset, includes abstract from biomedical, social, environmental and other domains.

3 Corpus

3.1 Annotation Schema

A popular schema in argumentation mining application is Toulmin's model (Lytos et al., 2019). Toulmin (1958) defines the functional roles of *datum, claim, warrant, backing, qualifiers,* and *rebuttal*. We use a subset of functional roles, comprising datum and claim, as a scheme for annotating our corpus (Lauscher et al., 2018; Stede and Schneider, 2019).

Arguments due to their pragmatic nature can be expressed by a variety of forms and linguistic cues. This is why there have been efforts to classify the two basic argument components, claim and evidence, into further categories. Blake (2010) introduced a Claim Framework distinguishing five claim categories, but they found that the majority of the claims in a corpus of scientific publications were explicit claims. Similarly, Mayer et al. (2018) suggest fine-grained evidence categories, but they do not use those in their extended dataset (Mayer et al., 2020). Regarding argument relations, there have been also attempts to distinguish them into supporting and attacking. However, Accuosto and Saggion (2019) did not found any attack relation in 60 abstracts of the SciDTB corpus (Yang and Li, 2018). Also, Lauscher et al. (2018) and Mayer et al. (2020) found that the number of attacking relations in full papers and abstracts is relatively low.

Based on the reported studies and the context of our corpus, we choose to keep our annotation schema simple. We focus on the kernel of an argument that is the *Evidence* and the *Claim* without further categorisation. Our argumentative units are sentences, a decision following Kirschner et al. (2015), and supported by Accuosto and Saggion (2019) that report 93% of argumentative units in their corpus coincide with the boundaries of the sentences. Implicitly, a supportive relation holds between Evidence and Claim.

In SciARK, we define Argument, Claim and Evidence, in the context of scientific abstract, as follows:

Argument: a set of statements with two different categories: Claim and Evidence.

Claim: an argumentative statement that reports the study findings and derives from the author's original work.

Evidence: statement that reports observations, statistical findings, and experimental results used to support a claim.

SDG	Annotators	Abstracts
3	6	300
5	5	255
7	3[a]	61
10	3[a]	70
12	3[a]	52
13	6	262
Total	20	1000

[a] The same annotators in SDGs 7, 10 and 12.

Table 1: Number of annotators and annotated abstracts grouped by SDG policy domain.

3.2 Data Collection

Our dataset is the first one that connects *Policy Targets* and *Scientific Literature*. In SDGs, we find specific targets defined by policymakers to deliver a more sustainable, prosperous and peaceful global future. We collect (a small part of) the scientific literature that provides scientific arguments related to real policy targets. To formulate the policy targets, we leverage the definition of the SDG targets and their indicators as keyterms (Duran-Silva et al., 2019) for searching in publisher's portals and scientific literature search engines (e.g., PubMed, Semantic Scholar etc.). The keyterms we use are from the SDGs 3 (good health and well-being), 5 (gender equality), 7 (affordable and clean energy), 10 (reduce inequalities), 12 (responsible consumption and production), and 13 (climate action). Examples of such keywords are: (Neonatal OR Maternal) Mortality, Female Genital Mutilation, Clean (Fuels OR Fossil-Fuel Technology), (Climate OR Natural Disaster) Resilience, etc.

We use the term *domain* to group abstracts under policy targets as described in SDGs targets. So, all the abstracts we gather using keyterms from the SDG5 targets, form the SDG5 policy domain, and so on. In Table 1, we present the number of abstracts collected per policy domain.

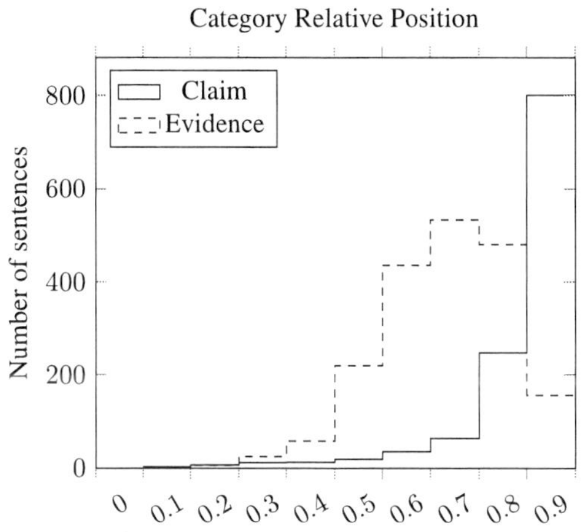

Figure 2: Histogram with the relative positions of Claim and Evidence categories within an abstract.

3.3 Exploratory Data Analysis

SciARK consists of 1,000 abstracts with 12,374 sentences, 1,202 sentences annotated as Claim and 1,915 annotated as Evidence. On average, per abstract, 1.2 sentences are annotated as Claim and 1.92 sentences as Evidence.

To investigate the position of the Claim and Evidence categories within the abstracts, we calculate the relative position for each sentence. The first sentence is in relative position 0 and the last in position 1. Figure 2 depicts the positions of the categories displaying the histograms of the two argumentative units. A Claim is located mainly in the last sentences. Specifically, about 40% of the total claims are in the last sentence and about 80% in the $[0.9 - 1]$ range. That is expected for scientific abstracts because usually, the claim coincides with the conclusions, which are the last sentences of an abstract.

The Evidence category lies in the middle to the end of the abstracts. We find the Evidence category in the range $[0.8 - 1]$ with a percentage of about 33% and about 62% in the range $[0.5 - 0.8)$ where, usually, we find the results and their analysis. These findings serve as a baseline for SciARK evaluation in Section 5.2.

Figure 2 shows that the most common pattern of the argument structure is the one that Claim follows the Evidence. Table 2 shows the trend on each domain. The main reason that this pattern is almost a rule on SDG3 and SDG5 is that many abstracts are from the biomedical domain. Most of those abstracts follow the IMRAD (Sollaci and Pereira, 2004) or the CONSORT format (Hopewell et al., 2008) that instruct the discussion/conclusions to be at the end of the abstract.

SDG	3	5	7	10	12	13
Structure						
Evidence / Claim (%)	99.67	95.29	88.52	90.00	86.54	88.17
Claim / Evidence (%)	00.34	04.71	11.48	10.00	13.46	11.83

Table 2: The argument structure on the corpus, i.e., Evidence followed by Claim or Claim followed by Evidence.

SDG	3	5	7	10	12	13
κ_{a_1}	.671	.595	.596	.665	.628	.557
κ_{a_2}	.621	.610	.641	.657	.653	.518
κ_{a_3}	.721	.740	.567	.577	.503	.525
κ_{a_4}	.599	.725				.542
κ_{a_5}	.622	.748				.582
κ_{a_6}	.705					.553

Table 3: Annotator assessment coefficients (κ_{α_i}). Each cell represents an annotator and the allocation represents the annotator distribution to each SDG.

4 Assessing Agreement

4.1 Annotators

The task of annotating such abstract constructs as the argumentative units is quite challenging (Lippi and Torroni, 2016). Also, our multidisciplinary corpus requires experts from a variety of scientific domains, which was beyond our scope. Twenty postgraduate students with background in engineering, economics, and applied sciences, provided annotations (Table 1) in a distributed fashion. The annotators selected the SDGs that were more familiar with and felt more comfortable to work on. Each annotator worked independently on an average of 150 abstracts, and three annotators annotated each abstract. Annotators should categorise all the sentences in an abstract into one of the mutually exclusive categories: *Claim*, *Evidence*, or *Neither*. We used MACE (Hovy et al., 2013) and majority vote between all annotator triplets to get category predictions. The predictions of MACE and the majority vote output were identical.

4.2 Annotator Assessment

In tasks which incorporate a large number of annotators or use crowd-sourcing, one needs to have methods to filter out biased annotators. To assess

Strength of Agreement	Substantial [0.6 - 0.8)	Moderate [0.4 - 0.6)
Corpus ($\kappa = .669$)	88%	100%
Claim ($\kappa_C = .730$)	100%	
Evidence ($\kappa_E = .637$)	13%	100%
Neither ($\kappa_N = .664$)	82%	100%

Table 4: Estimated agreement coefficient interpretation using the cumulative probability approach (Gwet, 2014) on the Landis-Koch scale (Landis and Koch, 1977). Using the simple match to the benchmark, all kappa values are interpreted as *Substantial.*

the reliability of the annotators we use the *Annotator* κ (Toledo et al., 2019) as an annotator quality control coefficient. This metric is calculated as the average of all pairwise agreement for each annotator. Toledo et al. (2019) use Equation 1 to calculate the Annotator κ of an annotator i

$$\kappa_{\alpha_i} = \frac{\sum_{j=1,j\neq i}^{n} F(i,j)}{N_i} \quad (1)$$

where n is the total number of annotators, $F(i,j)$ is the pairwise Fleiss' κ between annotators i, j, and N_i the number of annotator pairs that the annotator i is a member.

The rationale of this metric is that an annotator who systematically disagrees will have all pairwise scores low and consequently a low κ_α value. The opposite holds for a reliable annotator.

Table 3 shows the values we calculate on our corpus. Each row $\kappa_{\alpha_i}, i \in [1,6]$ corresponds to an annotator who worked on an SDG. Annotator κ_{α_1} in SDG3, is a different person than annotator κ_{α_1} in SDG5. Some rows have empty values because there were fewer than 6 annotators. The table follows the allocation we present in Table 1.

We expect to capture biased annotators as outliers in the columns of Table 3. Toledo et al. (2019) use the value .35 as a threshold to discard annotators with lower Annotator κ values. In our case, all annotators achieve a satisfactory average pair-wise agreement, despite the difficulty of the task and the lack of expertise in every domain.

4.3 Inter-Annotator Agreement

Fleiss' κ (Fleiss, 1971) was run to estimate the magnitude of agreement between annotators resulting[5] in κ_F=.669 (95% Confidence Interval (CI), .658 to .681), Standard Error (SE) .006, p < .001.

To further investigate the difficulties of the annotation task, we calculate the level of agreement on each of the three categories computing the individual kappa values. The individual kappas are simply Fleiss' κ calculated for each of the categories separately against all other categories combined. The Claim category has an estimated level of agreement equal to κ_C=.730 (95% CI, .713 to .746), SE .009, p < .001. Agreement for the Evidence category is equal to κ_E=.637 (95% CI, .622 to .652), SE .008, p < .001, and for the Neither category κ_N=.664 (95% CI, .652 to .676), SE .006, p < .001. The results are statistically significant and show an agreement above the agreement expected by chance.

Many benchmark scales (Landis and Koch, 1977; Cicchetti and Sparrow, 1981; Altman, 1990; Regier et al., 2013) aim to interpret the magnitude of agreement using the inter-annotator agreement coefficients. Usually, this is done by simple matching the calculated coefficient value within a benchmark range and report the corresponding interpretation.

However, Gwet (2014) demonstrated that this approach is highly optimistic for the characterisation of the agreement. Thus, Gwet recommends the *"Cumulative Probability"* approach, a probabilistic process that takes into account the standard error to calculate the likelihood that a coefficient falls into the benchmark range of values. Using the Landis-Koch scale (Landis and Koch, 1977) and the Cumulative Probability approach (Gwet, 2014), we report[6] our interpretation in Table 4. The results indicate that the likelihood of our corpus to fall into the substantial range of values is 88%. Also, the results show that the agreement can be characterised as moderate with a likelihood of 100%. Claim agreement is substantial with a likelihood of 100%, while the Evidence category is harder for the annotators as we have a moderate agreement (only 13% likelihood of substantial agreement).

The Claim category is usually found in the concluding sentences of the abstract. Also, we find strong discourse markers introducing the claim, such as "overall, this study reveals that", "in conclusion, these findings confirm", "the data suggest that" etc. The above observations mainly explain the substantial agreement on the Claim category. A source of disagreement is found in sentences in

[5]For the calculations we use the library irrCAC v1.0 for R (https://cran.r-project.org/web/packages/irrCAC/)

[6]One can easily confirm the results using the beforementioned library, the coefficient values with their corresponding standard error values reported in this section.

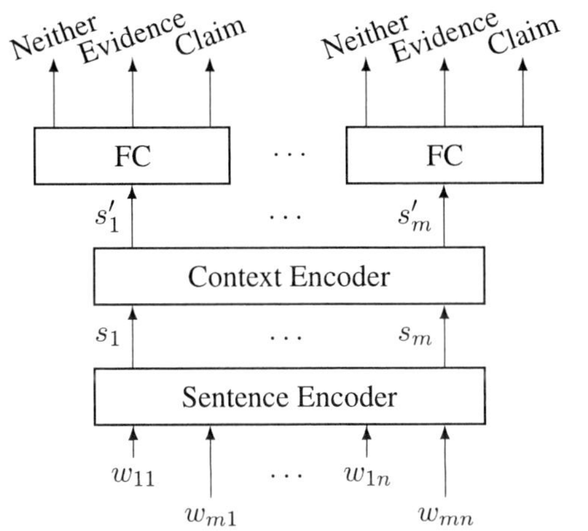

Figure 3: Diagram of our neural network architecture for the Sentence Sequence Tagging task. The *Sentence Encoder* layer outputs m sentence vectors for the m sentences of an abstract with n words each, and the *Context Encoder* updates the sentence vectors utilising their context. A *Fully Connected* layer gives a label for each sentence.

which the authors express possibility (may) or opinion ("we propose/suggest/believe"). Our annotation protocol is to avoid annotating such sentences as Claim *unless* there are no other declarative sentences baring the claim *and* there are sentences that provide evidence to support the claim.

Sentences annotated as Evidence do not have such strong discourse markers as those found for the Claim. For the Evidence category, annotators had to choose mostly between sentences that report experimental results or observations. The instructions to the annotators were to select the minimum number of sentences that provide enough support to the Claim. We pose this restriction to avoid the case to categorise as Evidence every sentence reporting results. The increased number of candidate sentences and the restriction mentioned are the main reasons that explain the level of agreement for the Evidence category.

Finally, the agreement on the Neither category is affected by the Evidence category and is characterised as moderate but with a likelihood of 82% to be substantial. Overall, we show that the strength of agreement in our corpus is moderate above chance and with a very high probability can be characterised as substantial.

5 Argumentation Units Classification

5.1 Setup

We formulate the argumentation units classification as a Sentence Sequence Tagging task within the context of the abstract. In Figure 3, our SciARK architecture is depicted encompassing three layers: a) the *Sentence Encoder*, b) *Context Encoder*, and c) a *Fully Connected* layer.

The input of the Sentence Encoder is a matrix $\mathcal{A} \in \mathbb{R}^{m \times n}$ that represents an abstract $\mathcal{A}$ with m sentences of n words each. We set $m = 20$ and $n = 40$, values representing 90% of the corpus in the number of sentences and number of words in a sentence, respectively. In cases where the sentences of an abstract exceed the limit, we truncate the sentences in the beginning. The truncated sentences get the Neither label.

The output is a sentence vector $\boldsymbol{s} \in \mathbb{R}^d$, where d is the output dimensionality of the layer. A Context Encoder layer updates each sentence vector $\boldsymbol{s}$ utilising the *context*, before and after, each sentence to a new vector $\boldsymbol{s}' \in \mathbb{R}^{d'}$. Finally, a Fully Connected layer classifies each sentence as *Evidence*, *Claim*, or *Neither*.

We implement the architecture in Figure 3 as a SciBERT - BiLSTM model. The uncased version of the SciBERT (Beltagy et al., 2019) model serves as a Sentence Encoder. We use the `[CLS]` token of each sentence from the SciBERT, a sentence vector $\boldsymbol{s} \in \mathbb{R}^{728}$, as input to the Context Encoder. To implement the Context Encoder layer, we use a bidirectional LSTM. We set the LSTM layer size to 64 with 0.3 forward and backward dropout. The values were selected by testing all the combinations of the following hyper-parameters: LSTM units 32, 64 and 128, forward and backward dropout 0.1, 0.3 and 0.5. Thus, the output of the Context Encoder is a vector $\boldsymbol{s}' \in \mathbb{R}^{128}$. Also, we experiment by replacing the SciBERT with an uncased BERT-base model (Devlin et al., 2018) keeping the same hyper-parameters.

As a last variation in our architecture, we replace SciBERT with a BiLSTM. The Sentence Encoder BiLSTM layer encodes the word embeddings of a sentence to a sentence vector using attention. As word embeddings, we use 200-dimensional pre-trained Glove embeddings[7] (Pennington et al., 2014) with Gaussian noise sampled from a zero-mean distribution with $\sigma = 0.1$. The LSTM layer

[7] https://nlp.stanford.edu/data/glove.6B.zip

	Claim			Evidence		
	P	R	F	P	R	F
Baseline	42.2	**72.8**	53.3	38.5	**77.5**	51.4
Mayer et al. (2020)	65.2	56.8	60.5	56.7	56.7	56.7
SciBERT	69.7	47.8	55.9	55.9	57.0	56.0
BiLSTM - BiLSTM	62.6	56.2	58.3	57.0	51.5	53.8
BERT - BiLSTM	69.6	65.8	67.3	**62.6**	57.5	59.2
SciBERT - BiLSTM	**73.5**	67.3	**70.0**	62.4	62.8	**62.4**

Table 5: The baseline and the performance of neural network models on SciARK calculated with 10-fold cross-validation.

size is 64 with 0.3 forward and backward dropout. Follows a dropout layer with 0.4 and an attention layer which outputs a 128 dimensional sentence vector, $s \in \mathbb{R}^{128}$. We also tested all combinations with 200 and 300-dimensional vectors, $\sigma \in [0.1, 0.2]$ and dropout 0.2, 0.3, 0.4 and 0.5.

To validate the contribution of the Context Encoder layer of our architecture, we present results of a) an intuitive baseline, b) a SciBERT model as Sentence Encoder only, and c) the SciBERT-GRU-CRF model of Mayer et al. (2020).

The baseline utilises the observations presented in Section 3.3. For the baseline all sentences that have a relative position within an abstract in the range $[0.5 - 0.8)$ are categorised as Evidence, those in the range $[0.8 - 1]$ as Claim and the rest as Neither. Finally, the SciBERT-GRU-CRF model of Mayer et al. (2020) gave the best results in the multi-class sequence tagging task on their dataset (AbstRCT). Since the model classifies spans of text using the BIO format, instead of sentence, we do the following modifications. If a sentence has a Claim or Evidence category, the first token of the sentence gets the B-Claim/Evidence label and all the rest the I-Clam/Evidence label. All other sentences get an O label on every token. To get a category for a sentence, we take the most common label of all tokens of the sentence.

5.2 Results

We present the results of the models described in Table 5. All results, expect the ones of the Baseline, are calculated using 10-fold cross-validation on our dataset using 20% of the training set for validation.

The Baseline has the best recall in both categories which is expected since for each abstract 30% of the sentences are categorised as Evidence and 20% as Claim. On the other hand, this method has the lowest precision.

	Prediction		
	Claim	Evidence	Neither
Claim	807 (67.1%)	84 (7%)	311 (25.9%)
Evidence	58 (3%)	1203 (62.8%)	654 (34.2%)
Neither	238 (3%)	647 (7%)	8372 (90%)

Table 6: Confusion matrix of the predictions by the SciBERT - BiLSTM model.

From the neural network models, the SciBERT - BiLSTM model has the most balanced performance with the highest f1-score in both categories and the best precision on the Claim category. Also, the results highlight the contribution of the Context Encoder comparing to the plain Sentence Encoder (SciBERT). The model of Mayer et al. (2020) does not seem to benefit from the CRF layer because the classification spans are sentences and their model does not utilise the context before and after the classified sentence.

In Table 6 we present the confusion matrix with the predictions of the SciBERT - BiLSTM model. The results show that the model has a good discrimination between the two argumentative categories. Most misclassified Claim and Evidence sentences get the Neither category. The results overall are very promising taking into account the conceptual difficulty of the task and the variety of the policy domains in the dataset.

5.3 Generalising to New Policy Domains

We utilise the multidisciplinary characteristic of our dataset to experiment on a cross-domain task, holding successively one SDG policy domain exclusively as a test set, similarly to Stab et al. (2018). With this experiment, we expect to get results showing that models benefit from the diversity of the dataset and generalise to new policy domains, comparing with a fixed one. We use AbstRCT (Mayer et al., 2020), a corpus of randomised control trials, as a fixed dataset that is comparable to the size of our dataset, is on scientific abstracts and has Claim and Evidence annotations.

The experiment has two phases. On the first one, the SciBERT-BiLSTM model is trained on the five of the SDG domains and is tested on the sixth. On the second one, the model is trained on AbstRCT and successively tested on each SDG domain.

In Figure 4 we present our results on the Claim and Evidence identification. The results clearly show that the model has better scores with the

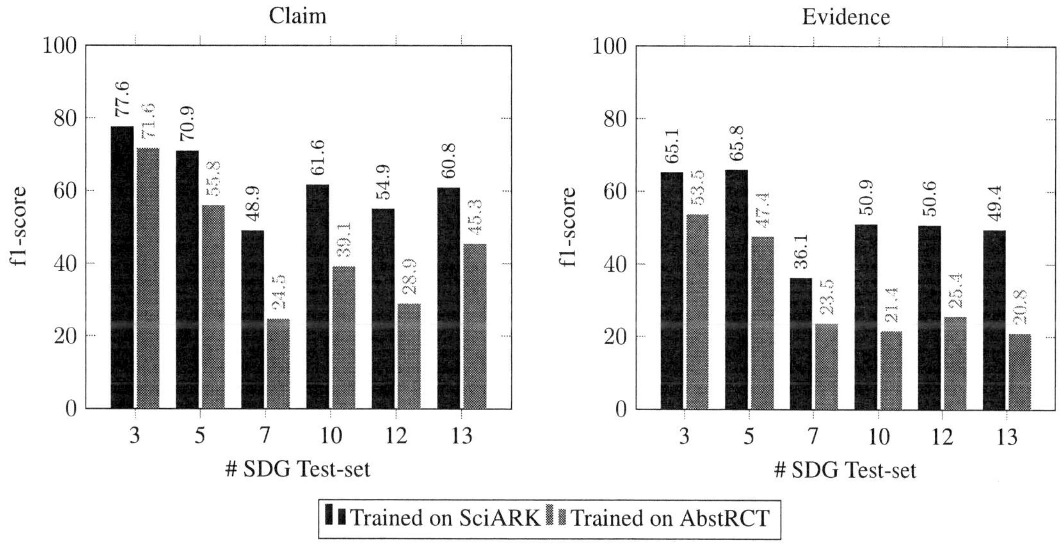

Figure 4: F1-scores for the Claim and Evidence using as a test set the SDG policy domains 3, 5, 7, 10, 12, and 13 successively. The results are from the SciBERT-BiLSTM model once trained on the remaining domains of SciARK dataset and once trained on AbstRCT dataset.

SciARK dataset. The imbalance of the dataset (Table 1), the different argument structure (Table 2), and the domains distinct characteristics are the main reasons that explain the variability of the results.

6 Discussion

In this section, we discuss some of the erroneous predictions of our model. All possible misclassifications are: Neither to Claim/Evidence, Claim to Evidence/Neither, and Evidence to Claim/Neither. In Table 7 we present at least one misclassification, from each combination, in their context in order to better understand the type of errors.

A common source of errors, for both argumentation categories, are the discourse markers discussed in Section 4.3. The example sentences 2, 6 and 10 have common claim discourse markers but in the context of those abstracts, other sentences bare the author's claim. Another source of errors are when the authors express possibility (may) or opinion ("we propose/suggest/beleive"). Annotators should categorise those sentences as Claim if there is no other declarative one that has a claim. Two examples of such sentences that the model predicted as Claim, are 12 and 15.

The model selects sentences for the Evidence category mainly from those that report results. However, as we mentioned in Section 4.3, the instruction to the annotators was to select the minimum sentences that support the claim. Following the instruction, annotators find that sentences 1, 4 and 8 are surplus. However, the model predicted those as Evidence because of their position on the abstract and the fact that they report results.

Finally, to highlight the difficulty of the task we discuss abstract #3. Sentence 11 has a claim that "under-five mortality rate is a serious problem". Although from the general knowledge of our world we recognise the statement as a claim, in the abstract there is no sentence to support it. On the other hand, the claim that "the hazard of under-five mortality has a decreasing pattern in years" is supported by sentence 10.

7 Conclusions

Argumentation mining is a young and gradually maturing research area within computational linguistics. To develop practical applications of importance, we need reliable datasets. In this paper, we describe SciARK, a novel STI-driven multidisciplinary dataset with argumentation annotation on six of the 17 SDGs of the United Nations. Our annotation protocol resulted in a reliable dataset with a significant inter-annotation agreement. We evaluated the dataset on the claim/evidence extraction task using modern deep learning models getting promising results. We also demonstrate the need for multidisciplinary datasets since they could enable models to generalise better on unseen data

	Annotators	Prediction	Sentence
#1			*Climate-driven polar motion: 2003-2015* (Adhikari and Ivins, 2016)
1	Neither	Evidence	The changes in terrestrial water storage (TWS) and global cryosphere together explain nearly the entire amplitude ...
2	Evidence	Claim	We also find that the TWS variability fully explains the decadal-like changes in polar motion observed during the ...
3	Claim	Neither	This newly discovered link between polar motion and global-scale TWS variability has broad implications for the study of ...
#2			*The impact of large scale biomass production on ozone air pollution in Europe* (Beltman et al., 2013)
4	Neither	Evidence	Although this scenario is rather conservative, our simulations project that isoprene emissions are substantially increased ...
5	Evidence	Evidence	As a consequence, ozone peak values are expected to increase by up to 6%, and ozone indicators for damage to human health ...
6	Evidence	Claim	Finally, we show that after the change in land use NOx emission reductions of 15-20 % in Europe would be required to ...
7	Claim	Claim	Because biomass production is expected to increase throughout Europe in the coming decades, we conclude that...
#3			*Comparison of under-five mortality for 2000, 2005 and 2011 surveys in Ethiopia* (Ayele and Zewotir, 2016)
8	Neither	Evidence	The effect of respondent's current age, age at first birth and educational level on the under-five mortality rate ...
9	Evidence	Neither	Regarding total children ever born, child death is more for the year 2000 followed by 2005 and 2011.
10	Neither	Claim	Conclusion: Based on the study, our findings confirmed that under-five mortality is a serious problem in the country.
11	Claim	Claim	The analysis displayed that the hazard of under-five mortality has a decreasing pattern in years.
12	Neither	Claim	Our study suggests that the impact of demographic characteristics and socio-economic factors on child mortality should ...
#4			*Renewable energy consumption-economic growth nexus in emerging countries* (Ozcan and Ozturk, 2019)
13	Evidence	Evidence	The results indicated that the neutrality hypothesis does hold for all of the markets studied except for Poland, ...
14	Claim	Evidence	As such, because of the nonexistence of causality running from renewable energy demand to economic growth, energy saving ...
15	Neither	Claim	For Poland; however, energy conservation policies may have detrimental effects on the country's economic performance level.

Table 7: Excerpts from abstracts with the categories by the annotators and the model prediction. All other sentences have the Neither category.

and outperform systems trained on domain-specific data.

SciARK facilitates the development of "Policy Intelligence" by streamlining a big data, STI-driven policy modelling approach, improving human judgement for evidence-informed policy making. Our SciARK framework will be further exploited in adapting policies in the continuously evolving STI landscape, addressing sustainable development.

Acknowledgement

We thank all the annotators who have contributed to the annotations of our training data. This research work has received funding from the European Union's Horizon 2020 Research and Innovation Programme under grant agreement No 101004870 (the IntelComp Project).

References

Rob Abbott, Brian Ecker, Pranav Anand, and Marilyn A. Walker. 2016. Internet argument corpus 2.0: An SQL schema for dialogic social media and the corpora to go with it. In *Proceedings of the Tenth International Conference on Language Resources and Evaluation LREC 2016, Portorož, Slovenia, May 23-28, 2016*. European Language Resources Association (ELRA).

Pablo Accuosto and Horacio Saggion. 2019. Discourse-driven argument mining in scientific abstracts. In *Natural Language Processing and Information Systems - 24th International Conference on Applications of Natural Language to Information Systems, NLDB 2019, Salford, UK, June 26-28, 2019, Proceedings*, volume 11608 of *Lecture Notes in Computer Science*, pages 182–194. Springer.

Titipat Achakulvisut, Chandra Bhagavatula, Daniel E. Acuña, and Konrad P. Körding. 2019. Claim extraction in biomedical publications using deep discourse model and transfer learning. *CoRR*, abs/1907.00962.

S. Adhikari and E. Ivins. 2016. Climate-driven polar motion: 2003–2015. *Science Advances*, 2.

Abdulaziz Alamri and Mark Stevenson. 2016. A corpus of potentially contradictory research claims from cardiovascular research abstracts. *J. Biomed. Semant.*, 7:36.

D. Altman. 1990. *Practical statistics for medical research*. Chapman and Hall/CRC.

D. Ayele and T. Zewotir. 2016. Comparison of under-five mortality for 2000, 2005 and 2011 surveys in ethiopia. *BMC Public Health*, 16.

Iz Beltagy, Kyle Lo, and Arman Cohan. 2019. Scibert: A pretrained language model for scientific text. In *Proceedings of the 2019 Conference on Empirical Methods in Natural Language Processing and the 9th International Joint Conference on Natural Language Processing, EMNLP-IJCNLP 2019, Hong Kong, China, November 3-7, 2019*, pages 3613–3618. Association for Computational Linguistics.

J. Beltman, C. Hendriks, M. Tum, and M. Schaap. 2013. The impact of large scale biomass production on ozone air pollution in europe. *Atmospheric Environment*, 71:352–363.

Catherine Blake. 2010. Beyond genes, proteins, and abstracts: Identifying scientific claims from full-text biomedical articles. *J. Biomed. Informatics*, 43(2):173–189.

Claire Cardie, Nancy Green, Iryna Gurevych, Graeme Hirst, Diane Litman, Smaranda Muresan, Georgios Petasis, Manfred Stede, Marilyn Walker, and Janyce Wiebe, editors. 2015. *Proceedings of the 2nd Workshop on Argumentation Mining, ArgMining@HLT-NAACL 2015, June 4, 2015, Denver, Colorado, USA*. The Association for Computational Linguistics.

Winston Carlile, Nishant Gurrapadi, Zixuan Ke, and Vincent Ng. 2018. Give me more feedback: Annotating argument persuasiveness and related attributes in student essays. In *Proceedings of the 56th Annual Meeting of the Association for Computational Linguistics, ACL 2018, Melbourne, Australia, July 15-20, 2018, Volume 1: Long Papers*, pages 621–631. Association for Computational Linguistics.

Domenic V Cicchetti and Sara A Sparrow. 1981. Developing criteria for establishing interrater reliability of specific items: applications to assessment of adaptive behavior. *American journal of mental deficiency*.

Jacob Devlin, Ming-Wei Chang, Kenton Lee, and Kristina Toutanova. 2018. BERT: pre-training of deep bidirectional transformers for language understanding. *CoRR*, abs/1810.04805.

Nicolau Duran-Silva, Enric Fuster, Francesco Alessandro Massucci, and Arnau Quinquillà. 2019. A controlled vocabulary defining the semantic perimeter of sustainable development goals.

Joseph L Fleiss. 1971. Measuring nominal scale agreement among many raters. *Psychological bulletin*, 76(5):378.

Theodosios Goudas, Christos Louizos, Georgios Petasis, and Vangelis Karkaletsis. 2015. Argument extraction from news, blogs, and the social web. *Int. J. Artif. Intell. Tools*, 24(5):1540024:1–1540024:22.

Nancy Green, Kevin Ashley, Diane Litman, Chris Reed, and Vern Walker, editors. 2014. *Proceedings of the First Workshop on Argumentation Mining*. Association for Computational Linguistics, Baltimore, Maryland.

Kilem L Gwet. 2014. *Handbook of inter-rater reliability: The definitive guide to measuring the extent of agreement among raters*. Advanced Analytics, LLC.

Ivan Habernal and Iryna Gurevych. 2017. Argumentation mining in user-generated web discourse. *Comput. Linguistics*, 43(1):125–179.

Ivan Habernal, Iryna Gurevych, Kevin D. Ashley, Claire Cardie, Nancy Green, Diane J. Litman, Georgios Petasis, Chris Reed, Noam Slonim, and Vern R. Walker, editors. 2017. *Proceedings of the 4th Workshop on Argument Mining, ArgMining@EMNLP 2017, Copenhagen, Denmark, September 8, 2017*. Association for Computational Linguistics.

S. Hopewell, M. Clarke, D. Moher, E. Wager, P. Middleton, D. Altman, and K. Schulz. 2008. Consort for reporting randomized controlled trials in journal and conference abstracts: Explanation and elaboration. *PLoS Medicine*, 5.

Dirk Hovy, Taylor Berg-Kirkpatrick, Ashish Vaswani, and Eduard H. Hovy. 2013. Learning whom to trust with MACE. In *Human Language Technologies: Conference of the North American Chapter of the Association of Computational Linguistics, Proceedings, June 9-14, 2013, Westin Peachtree Plaza Hotel, Atlanta, Georgia, USA*, pages 1120–1130. The Association for Computational Linguistics.

Johannes Kiesel, Khalid Al Khatib, Matthias Hagen, and Benno Stein. 2015. A shared task on argumentation mining in newspaper editorials. In *Proceedings of the 2nd Workshop on Argumentation Mining, ArgMining@HLT-NAACL 2015, June 4, 2015, Denver, Colorado, USA*, pages 35–38. The Association for Computational Linguistics.

Christian Kirschner, Judith Eckle-Kohler, and Iryna Gurevych. 2015. Linking the thoughts: Analysis of argumentation structures in scientific publications. In *Proceedings of the 2nd Workshop on Argumentation Mining, ArgMining@HLT-NAACL 2015, June 4, 2015, Denver, Colorado, USA*, pages 1–11. The Association for Computational Linguistics.

J Richard Landis and Gary G Koch. 1977. The measurement of observer agreement for categorical data. *biometrics*, pages 159–174.

Anne Lauscher, Goran Glavas, and Simone Paolo Ponzetto. 2018. An argument-annotated corpus of scientific publications. In *Proceedings of the 5th Workshop on Argument Mining, ArgMining@EMNLP 2018, Brussels, Belgium, November 1, 2018*, pages 40–46. Association for Computational Linguistics.

John Lawrence and Chris Reed. 2019. Argument mining: A survey. *Computational Linguistics*, 45(4):765–818.

Marco Lippi and Paolo Torroni. 2016. Argumentation mining: State of the art and emerging trends. *ACM Trans. Internet Technol.*, 16(2).

Haijing Liu, Yang Gao, Pin Lv, Mengxue Li, Shiqiang Geng, Minglan Li, and Hao Wang. 2017. Using argument-based features to predict and analyse review helpfulness. In *Proceedings of the 2017 Conference on Empirical Methods in Natural Language Processing, EMNLP 2017, Copenhagen, Denmark, September 9-11, 2017*, pages 1358–1363. Association for Computational Linguistics.

Anastasios Lytos, Thomas Lagkas, Panagiotis G. Sarigiannidis, and Kalina Bontcheva. 2019. The evolution of argumentation mining: From models to social media and emerging tools. *CoRR*, abs/1907.02258.

William C. Mann and Sandra A. Thompson. 1988. Rhetorical structure theory: Toward a functional theory of text organization. *Text - Interdisciplinary Journal for the Study of Discourse*, 8(3):243–281.

Tobias Mayer, Elena Cabrio, and Serena Villata. 2018. Evidence type classification in randomized controlled trials. In *Proceedings of the 5th Workshop on Argument Mining, ArgMining@EMNLP 2018, Brussels, Belgium, November 1, 2018*, pages 29–34. Association for Computational Linguistics.

Tobias Mayer, Elena Cabrio, and Serena Villata. 2020. Transformer-based argument mining for healthcare applications. In *ECAI 2020 - 24th European Conference on Artificial Intelligence, 29 August-8 September 2020, Santiago de Compostela, Spain, August 29 - September 8, 2020 - Including 10th Conference on Prestigious Applications of Artificial Intelligence (PAIS 2020)*, volume 325 of *Frontiers in Artificial Intelligence and Applications*, pages 2108–2115. IOS Press.

Raquel Mochales and Aagje Ieven. 2009. Creating an argumentation corpus: do theories apply to real arguments?: a case study on the legal argumentation of the ECHR. In *The 12th International Conference on Artificial Intelligence and Law, Proceedings of the Conference, June 8-12, 2009, Barcelona, Spain*, pages 21–30. ACM.

B. Ozcan and I. Ozturk. 2019. Renewable energy consumption-economic growth nexus in emerging countries: A bootstrap panel causality test. *Renewable & Sustainable Energy Reviews*, 104:30–37.

Andreas Peldszus and Manfred Stede. 2013. From argument diagrams to argumentation mining in texts: A survey. *Int. J. Cogn. Informatics Nat. Intell.*, 7(1):1–31.

Jeffrey Pennington, Richard Socher, and Christopher Manning. 2014. GloVe: Global vectors for word representation. In *Proceedings of the 2014 Conference on Empirical Methods in Natural Language Processing (EMNLP)*, pages 1532–1543, Doha, Qatar. Association for Computational Linguistics.

Majid Rastegar-Mojarad, Ravikumar Komandur Elayavilli, and Hongfang Liu. 2016. Beltracker: evidence sentence retrieval for BEL statements. *Database J. Biol. Databases Curation*, 2016.

Chris Reed, editor. 2016. *Proceedings of the Third Workshop on Argument Mining, hosted by the 54th Annual Meeting of the Association for Computational Linguistics, ArgMining@ACL 2016, August 12, Berlin, Germany*. The Association for Computer Linguistics.

Darrel A Regier, William E Narrow, Diana E Clarke, Helena C Kraemer, S Janet Kuramoto, Emily A Kuhl, and David J Kupfer. 2013. Dsm-5 field trials in the united states and canada, part ii: test-retest reliability of selected categorical diagnoses. *American journal of psychiatry*, 170(1):59–70.

Jaromír Savelka and Kevin D. Ashley. 2016. Extracting case law sentences for argumentation about the meaning of statutory terms. In *Proceedings of the Third Workshop on Argument Mining, hosted by the 54th Annual Meeting of the Association for Computational Linguistics, ArgMining@ACL 2016, August 12, Berlin, Germany*. The Association for Computer Linguistics.

Jodi Schneider. 2014. Automated argumentation mining to the rescue? envisioning argumentation and decision-making support for debates in open online collaboration communities. In *Proceedings of the First Workshop on Argument Mining, hosted by the 52nd Annual Meeting of the Association for Computational Linguistics, ArgMining@ACL 2014, June 26, 2014, Baltimore, Maryland, USA*, pages 59–63. The Association for Computer Linguistics.

Hagit Shatkay, Fengxia Pan, Andrey Rzhetsky, and W. John Wilbur. 2008. Multi-dimensional classification of biomedical text: Toward automated, practical provision of high-utility text to diverse users. *Bioinform.*, 24(18):2086–2093.

Noam Slonim and Ranit Aharonov, editors. 2018. *Proceedings of the 5th Workshop on Argument Mining, ArgMining@EMNLP 2018, Brussels, Belgium, November 1, 2018*. Association for Computational Linguistics.

Luciana B Sollaci and M. G. Pereira. 2004. The introduction, methods, results, and discussion (imrad) structure: a fifty-year survey. *Journal of the Medical Library Association : JMLA*, 92 3:364–367.

Christian Stab and Iryna Gurevych. 2014. Annotating argument components and relations in persuasive essays. In *COLING 2014, 25th International Conference on Computational Linguistics, Proceedings of the Conference: Technical Papers, August 23-29, 2014, Dublin, Ireland*, pages 1501–1510. ACL.

Christian Stab, Tristan Miller, Benjamin Schiller, Pranav Rai, and Iryna Gurevych. 2018. Cross-topic argument mining from heterogeneous sources. In *Proceedings of the 2018 Conference on Empirical Methods in Natural Language Processing*, pages 3664–3674, Brussels, Belgium. Association for Computational Linguistics.

Manfred Stede and Jodi Schneider. 2019. *Argumentation mining*. Morgan & Claypool Publishers.

Benno Stein and Henning Wachsmuth, editors. 2019. *Proceedings of the 6th Workshop on Argument Mining, ArgMining@ACL 2019, Florence, Italy, August 1, 2019*. Association for Computational Linguistics.

James Thorne, Andreas Vlachos, Christos Christodoulopoulos, and Arpit Mittal. 2018. FEVER: a large-scale dataset for fact extraction and verification. In *Proceedings of the 2018 Conference of the North American Chapter of the Association for Computational Linguistics: Human*

Language Technologies, NAACL-HLT 2018, New Orleans, Louisiana, USA, June 1-6, 2018, Volume 1 (Long Papers), pages 809–819. Association for Computational Linguistics.

Assaf Toledo, Shai Gretz, Edo Cohen-Karlik, Roni Friedman, Elad Venezian, Dan Lahav, Michal Jacovi, Ranit Aharonov, and Noam Slonim. 2019. Automatic argument quality assessment - new datasets and methods. In *Proceedings of the 2019 Conference on Empirical Methods in Natural Language Processing and the 9th International Joint Conference on Natural Language Processing, EMNLP-IJCNLP 2019, Hong Kong, China, November 3-7, 2019*, pages 5624–5634. Association for Computational Linguistics.

Stephen E Toulmin. 1958. *The uses of argument*. Cambridge university press.

David Wadden, Shanchuan Lin, Kyle Lo, Lucy Lu Wang, Madeleine van Zuylen, Arman Cohan, and Hannaneh Hajishirzi. 2020. Fact or fiction: Verifying scientific claims. In *Proceedings of the 2020 Conference on Empirical Methods in Natural Language Processing, EMNLP 2020, Online, November 16-20, 2020*, pages 7534–7550. Association for Computational Linguistics.

Marilyn A. Walker, Jean E. Fox Tree, Pranav Anand, Rob Abbott, and Joseph King. 2012. A corpus for research on deliberation and debate. In *Proceedings of the Eighth International Conference on Language Resources and Evaluation, LREC 2012, Istanbul, Turkey, May 23-25, 2012*, pages 812–817. European Language Resources Association (ELRA).

Douglas Walton. 2015. *Goal-based Reasoning for Argumentation*. Cambridge University Press.

W. John Wilbur, Andrey Rzhetsky, and Hagit Shatkay. 2006. New directions in biomedical text annotation: definitions, guidelines and corpus construction. *BMC Bioinform.*, 7:356.

Hiroaki Yamada, Simone Teufel, and Takenobu Tokunaga. 2017. Annotation of argument structure in japanese legal documents. In *Proceedings of the 4th Workshop on Argument Mining, ArgMining@EMNLP 2017, Copenhagen, Denmark, September 8, 2017*, pages 22–31. Association for Computational Linguistics.

An Yang and Sujian Li. 2018. Scidtb: Discourse dependency treebank for scientific abstracts. In *Proceedings of the 56th Annual Meeting of the Association for Computational Linguistics, ACL 2018, Melbourne, Australia, July 15-20, 2018, Volume 2: Short Papers*, pages 444–449. Association for Computational Linguistics.

Antonio Zecca and Luca Chiari. 2012. Lower bounds to future sea-level rise. *Global and Planetary Change*, 98-99:1–5.

Bayesian Argumentation-Scheme Networks: A Probabilistic Model of Argument Validity Facilitated by Argumentation Schemes

Takahiro Kondo[1], Koki Washio[1], Katsuhiko Hayashi[2] and Yusuke Miyao[1]

[1]The University of Tokyo
[2]Gunma University
{takahiro_kondo, kwashio, yusuke}@is.s.u-tokyo.ac.jp
khayashi0201@gmail.com

Abstract

We propose a methodology for representing the reasoning structure of arguments using Bayesian networks and predicate logic facilitated by argumentation schemes. We express the meaning of text segments using predicate logic and map the boolean values of predicate logic expressions to nodes in a Bayesian network. The reasoning structure among text segments is described with a directed acyclic graph. While our formalism is highly expressive and capable of describing the informal logic of human arguments, it is too open-ended to actually build a network for an argument. It is not at all obvious which segment of argumentative text should be considered as a node in a Bayesian network, and how to decide the dependencies among nodes. To alleviate the difficulty, we provide abstract network fragments, called idioms, which represent typical argument justification patterns derived from argumentation schemes. The network construction process is decomposed into idiom selection, idiom instantiation, and idiom combination. We define 17 idioms in total by referring to argumentation schemes as well as analyzing actual arguments and fitting idioms to them. We also create a dataset consisting of pairs of an argumentative text and a corresponding Bayesian network. Our dataset contains about 2,400 pairs, which is large in the research area of argumentation schemes.

1 Introduction

We propose to formalize the reasoning structure of an argument towards quantitative validity assessment. To assess the validity, we need to understand what kind of reasoning is applied. The following example is a discussion on whether the death penalty deters crime.

> **P**: We should introduce the death penalty to deter crime.
> **Q**: Criminologists do not believe that it deters crime.

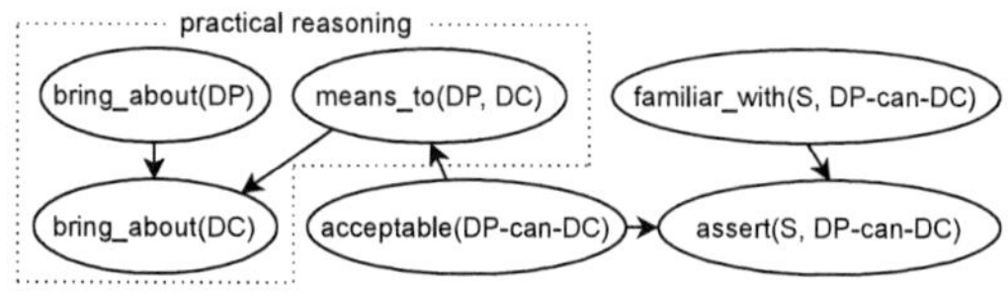

Figure 1: A bayesian network on whether the death penalty deters crime. **DP**: introducing the death penalty, **DC**: deterring crime, **S**: criminologists.

P justifies the introduction of the death penalty as a means to deter crime. Q's objection is justified based on expert opinion. By understanding how the argument is justified, we can identify more specific issues that need to be validated. For example, we can ask whether the goal of deterring crime is worth achieving, or whether the criminologist's area of expertise is really relevant to the assertion.

We use Bayesian networks and predicate logic to represent the reasoning structure of an argument as shown in Fig. 1. We express the meaning of text segments using predicate logic. For example, 'the death penalty is a means to deter crime' is expressed as *means_to(the death penalty, dettering crime)*. Then, we represent the dependencies between text segments using a Bayesian network. For example, whether or not a crime can be deterred depends on whether or not the death penalty has a deterrent effect on crime and whether or not the death penalty is actually introduced. This formalism is expressive and flexible to represent a variety of human justifications as it just models conditional dependencies. However, due to its flexibility, it is too open-ended to build a network for an argument. Why do we use the predicate *means_to* for a node in the example network? How can we decide the dependencies among nodes?

To facilitate a network construction, we prepare abstract network fragments, called *idioms*, which represent typical argument justification patterns derived from argumentation schemes (Walton et al.,

Proceedings of The 8th Workshop on Argument Mining, pages 112–124
Punta Cana, Dominican Republic, November 10–11, 2021. ©2021 Association for Computational Linguistics

2008). For example, one of the argumentation schemes, *practical reasoning*, is defined as follows.

> **Major Premise**: I have a goal G.
> **Minor Premise**: Carrying out this action A is a means to realize G.
> **Conclusion**: Therefore, I ought (practically speaking) to carry out this action A.

We define an idiom for the justification of means to an end referring to practical reasoning. The dotted line in Fig. 1 uses this idiom. By preparing idioms, the network construction process is decomposed into **idiom selection**, **idiom instantiation**, and **idiom combination**. We define 17 idioms in total by referring to argumentation schemes as well as analyzing actual arguments and fitting idioms to them.

We also create a dataset consisting of pairs of an argumentative text and a corresponding Bayesian network. The problem is that annotating argumentation schemes in argumentative texts is too expensive. In addition to identifying justification patterns, we need to represent the reasoning structure with Bayesian networks, which is almost impossible. We solve the problem by adopting a procedure to generate a text from a built network inspired by OVERNIGHT, the data building method in semantic parsing (Wang et al., 2015). As a result, we can make about 2,400 argument-network pairs, which is large in the research area of argumentation schemes. Our dataset is publicly available at `https://github.com/mynlp/basn`.

In summary, our contribution is twofold.

- We propose a methodology for representing the reasoning structure of arguments using Bayesian networks and predicate logic facilitated by argumentation schemes. (Sec. 3)
- We create a dataset consisting of pairs of an argumentative text and a corresponding Bayesian network while reducing an annotation effort. (Sec. 4)

2 Related Work

2.1 Argument Validity Assessment

Wachsmuth et al. (2017) divided argumentation quality into three main dimensions, *Cogency*, *Effectiveness*, and *Reasonableness*, through comprehensive survey. Our method mainly focuses on cogency which relates to the acceptability of premises and the relevance of a premise to a conclusion. Reasonableness is about acceptability in the dialectical context. Our method can serve in the dialectical context because we can model the validity of an argument and its counterargument together in the same Bayesian network. On the other hand, we do not focus on effectiveness which relates to an emotional appeal and the style of an argument.

The previous models for quantitatively assessing the quality of an argument, no matter which dimension of quality is being addressed, predict a score with either feature-based machine learning (Persing et al., 2010; Persing and Ng, 2013, 2015; Ghosh et al., 2016; Wachsmuth et al., 2016; Wachsmuth and Stein, 2017; Ke et al., 2019; Wachsmuth and Werner, 2020) or neural networks (Ke et al., 2018; Lauscher et al., 2020). In contrast, our method uses a probabilistic model to calculate the validity.

In argumentation theory, the probabilistic model for argument assessment is not mature. Baroni et al. (2018) provide a comprehensive survey of formal argumentation. In chapter 2 of the book, Prakken states 'systematic studies of the combination of argumentation with probability were sparse.' Our method is based on Bayesian networks. The use of Bayesian networks in argumentation has been studied through practice rather than theory, as in the case of the legal field discussed next.

2.2 Bayesian Networks with Argumentation Schemes

Argumentation schemes describe typical justification patterns in an argument. Walton et al. (2008) lists 60 representative argumentation schemes from various literature, and many studies refer to their list. In the list, argumentation schemes are defined by premises and a conclusion as shown in Sec. 1 and express the claim that a conclusion is plausible if all premises are true.

In the legal domain, argumentation schemes help to construct a Bayesian network though network construction is manual. In the analysis of court cases, it has been attempted to calculate the validity of hypotheses based on evidence or testimony using Bayesian networks (Fenton et al., 2013; Vlek et al., 2014). Since the arbitrariness of the network construction procedure is an issue, Timmer (2017) transforms an argumentation scheme that can be used in court cases into a fragment of a Bayesian network which provides a typical network structure. While the research shows that Bayesian networks and argumentation schemes are compatible, argumentation schemes are used for assisting manual network construction by humans. It does not aim to automatically construct a network from the argumentative text. We combine Bayesian networks with predicate logic towards automatic network construction using natural language processing. In addition, we also prepare fragments for the argumentation schemes that are not covered in the legal domain, such as practical reasoning.

2.3 Datasets

A few datasets annotate argument structures in argument texts for the purpose of argument evaluation. Stab and Gurevych (2014) annotate argument components (major claim, claim, and premises) and relations (support and attack) in persuasive essays. Ghosh et al. (2016) apply the same annotation as Stab and Gurevych (2014) to TOEFL essays associated with holistic scores (high/medium/low). Our dataset consists of pairs of a short argumentative text and its corresponding Bayesian network for modeling the validity of arguments.

The major challenge in dataset creation is the difficulty of annotating argumentation schemes. Among existing datasets, the AraucariaDB corpus (Reed et al., 2008) is the largest as far as we know and includes approximately 660 manually annotated arguments (Feng and Hirst, 2011). Lawrence et al. (2019) state that annotated corpora of argumentation schemes are scarce, small, and unrepresentative. They provide an annotation tool to address the issue. We adopt a different approach inspired by Wang et al. (2015), in which they create training data for a semantic parser by generating canonical utterances from logical forms and paraphrasing them using crowdsourcing to reduce annotation effort. We employ a procedure to generate an argument text from a pre-built Bayesian network.

3 Bayesian Argumentation-Scheme Networks

Our goal is to represent the reasoning structure of arguments with Bayesian networks towards an argument validity assessment. Fig. 2 shows the overall process of network construction. First, we prepare abstract Bayesian network fragments which represent typical argument justification patterns derived from argumentation schemes. We call the abstract fragments *network idioms*. Then, through the analysis of an argument, appropriate idioms are selected and embodied by assigning logical variables. We call the embodied fragments *network instances*. Finally, by combining the network instances, we can construct a Bayesian network for the entire argument.

In the following, we first describe a formalism of an argument network. Second, we explain how network idioms are defined and introduce three representative idioms. Third, we provide network combination rules to construct an entire argument network. Finally, we explain the advantages of our methodology.

3.1 Argument Reasoning Structure with Bayesian Networks and Prediate Logic

We formalize the reasoning structure of arguments with Bayesian networks and typed predicate logic. We represent a network node using a boolean random variable of a predicate logical expression. Logical variables (i.e. predicate arguments) are typed. A type is formally equivalent to using a specific (pre-defined) predicate to impose constraints on a logical variable. Edges represent conditional dependencies among boolean random variables.

3.2 Network Idioms

Idioms are abstract Bayesian network fragments that represent typical argument justification patterns. Argumentation schemes help us to identify justification patterns. We can determine the network structure of an idiom according to the characteristic of justification. For example, practical reasoning deals with the causal relationship between means and ends. We connect an edge from means to ends along the direction of causality. In addition, argumentation schemes can also be used as a reference to decide predicates of idioms. For example, one of the premises in practical reasoning, 'Carrying out this action A is a means to realize G', can be expressed as *means_to*(G, A) in predicate logic. Thus, we regard *means_to* as a candidate of predicates.

In defining idioms, we refer to Walton et al. (2008)'s list of argumentation schemes as well as analyze actual arguments and fit idioms to them. In this work, we analyze arguments in ProCon.org[1], which presents sourced pros and cons of debatable issues. As a result, we define a total of 17 idioms using a finite set of predicates and variable types. Currently, we define idioms for the justification

[1] `https://www.procon.org/`

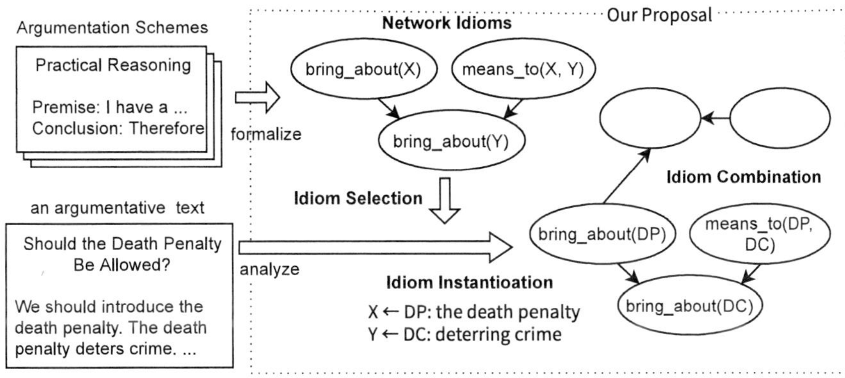

Figure 2: Overall Process of Our Methodology

patterns that appear in the actual argument we analyze. Our idiom covers 25 out of 60 argumentation schemes in the Walton et al. (2008)'s list.

Regarding the design of idioms, unlike annotation schemes of argument mining datasets (Stab and Gurevych, 2017, 2014; Peldszus and Stede, 2015), the direction of an edge is not necessarily from a premise to a conclusion. The reason is that an idiom is designed to express the reasoning structure behind the justification of an argument. Although the justifications described by argumentation schemes often involve logical leaps, we can sometimes find a deductive relationship among premises and a conclusion. For example, practical reasoning concludes 'I ought to carry out this action A' from the two premises, 'I have a goal G' and 'carrying out this action A is a means to realize G.' That justification is fallacious from a formal logic perspective. Instead, if the two propositions, 'I carry out this action A' and 'carrying out this action A is a means to realize G', are true, then 'G is realized' is deductively true. By expressing such a relationship among premises and a conclusion in argumentation schemes, we model what reasoning is behind them.

In this section, we introduce three representative idioms. All idioms and the definition of variable types are shown in Appendix A, Appendix B respectively. In the following explanations, the types of logical variables are omitted. In the figures shown below, a node symbol p corresponds to a premise and a symbol c to a conclusion.

Idiom 1: Means for Goal

This idiom expresses the justification of means to an end. Fig. 3 shows the network structure. A conclusion node is c: *bring_about*(X).

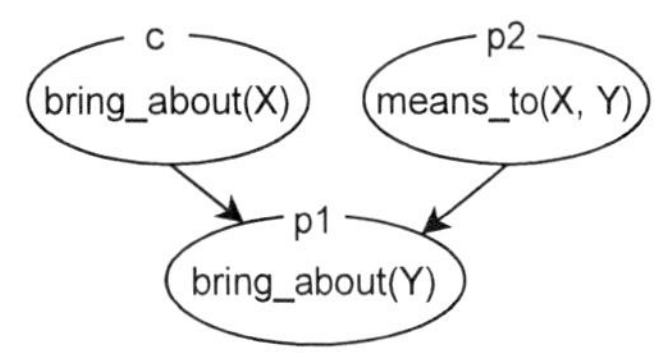

Figure 3: Means for Goal Idiom

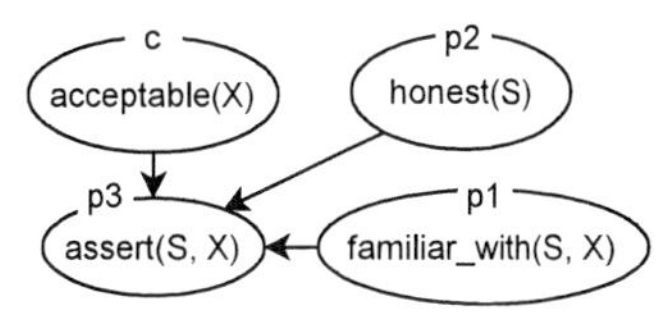

Figure 4: From Source Knowledge Idiom

Two premise nodes are p_1: *brign_about*(Y) and p_2: *means_to*(X, Y). The edges are from c to p_1 and from p_2 to p_1. It expresses the relationship that X causes Y.

The description in the argumentation-scheme-like format is as follows.

> **Premise1**: Bringing about Y is desirable.
> **Premise2**: Bringing about X is a means to realize Y.
> **Conclusion**: We should bring about X.

In the list of Walton et al. (2008), *practical reasoning* corresponds to this idiom. Moreover, *argument from need for help* and *argument from distress* also correspond by interpreting them as a justification of an action aimed at solving the problem.

Idiom 2: From Source Knowledge

This idiom is about justification based on the knowledge of a source. Fig. 4 shows the network structure. This idiom has four essential nodes. A con-

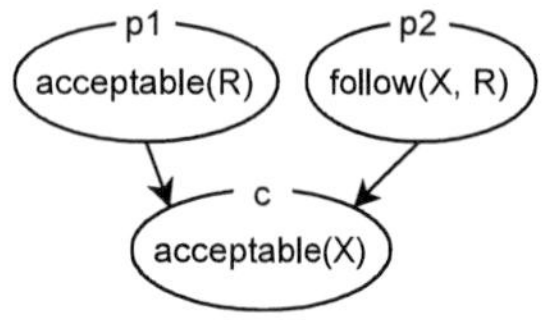

Figure 5: Rule or Principle Idiom

clusion node is c: *acceptable*(X). Three premise nodes are p_1: *familiar_with*(S, X), p_2: *honest*(S), and p_3: *assert*(S, X). The edges are from c to p_3, from p_1 to p_3, and from p_2 to p_3. It expresses the relationship between a hypothesis and evidence. A source's assertion is the evidence that a hypothesis is true. This idiom has optional premise nodes o_1: *position_to_know*(S, X) and o_2: *expert_in*(S, X). Both nodes back up the source's knowledge by linking them to p_1.

The description in the argumentation-scheme-like format is as follows.

> **Premise1**: S is familiar with X.
> **Premise3**: S is honest.
> **Premise3**: S asserts X.
> **Conclusion**: X is acceptable.

In the list of Walton et al. (2008), *argument from position to know*, *argument from expert opinion*, and *argument from witness testimony* correspond to this idiom.

Idiom 3: Rule or Principle

This idiom is about justification based on whether a claim is in accordance with rules or norms. Fig. 5 shows the network structure. A conclusion node is c: *acceptable*(X). Two premise nodes are p_1: *acceptable*(R) and p_2: *follow*(X, R). The edges are from p_1 to c and from p_2 to c. It expresses the relationship between a general rule and a specific case. If the case is subject to the rule, the acceptability of the case follows the acceptability of the rule.

The description in the argumentation-scheme-like format is as follows.

> **Premise1**: R is acceptable.
> **Premise2**: X follows R.
> **Conclusion**: X is acceptable.

There is a negation variant for this idiom.

> **Premise1**: R must be obeyed.
> **Premise2**: X does not follow R.
> **Conclusion**: X is not acceptable.

In the list of Walton et al. (2008), no argumentation scheme corresponds to this idiom. One of the argumentation schemes, *argument from rule* assumes that a rule describes specific actions to follow. However, in the actual arguments we analyze, the main point at issue is whether individual cases fall under the rules like the Constitution.

3.3 Combination Rules

A Bayesian network for an entire argument often contains multiple network instances because multiple justifications may be combined, or a counterargument may be listed together. To construct an entire network, we need to combine network instances. We define the following four rules and *default inference* to merge or link nodes.

Rule 1: merge the nodes with the same logical expressions

Merge nodes if the logical expression of nodes is equivalent.

Rule 2: link a node to its negational form

Link a node to the node with the negational form. For example, link *acceptable*(X) to $\neg$*acceptable*(X). The edge can be either direction. A boolean value is inverted through the edge.

Rule 3: link a propositional expression to its predicate expression

The same content can be expressed in two ways, predicates or propositions. For example, *means_to*(X, Y) has the same meaning as *acceptable*(P) if P is a propotition that X is a means to Y. In such case, we link a propositional expression like *acceptable*(P) to a predicate expression like *means_to*(X, Y). A boolean value remains unchanged through the edge.

Rule 4: link nodes whose variables are synonymous

Link nodes if the predicates of two nodes are the same and logical variables are of synonymous meaning. For example, link *bring_about*(X) to *bring_about*(X') if the meaning of X is synonymous to that of X'. A boolean value remains unchanged through the edge.

Default Inference

Besides the formal rules, we may need to link nodes according to the reasoning that does not fit into any of the justification patterns of prepared network idioms. When Visser et al. (2018) annotated argumentation schemes, they also define default inference as not fitting any of the 60 argumentation schemes.

3.4 Advantages of Our Method

The advantages of our method are threefold.

Incorporating Argumentation Schemes into NLP Models for Argument Evaluation

Argumentation schemes are useful for validating arguments as they help to teach critical thinking skills in pedagogy (Reed and Walton, 2001). However, few NLP models apply argumentation schemes to argument validity assessment. One reason for this could be that the mathematical formalism of argumentation schemes had not been established. We hope that our proposal will encourage more research on incorporating argumentation schemes into NLP models.

Extending Existing Techniques of Formal Semantic Representation to Discourse Analysis

NLP techniques for transforming the meaning of a text into a formal representation are mainly based on sentences as the unit of analysis. Empirical research for applying discourse-level formal representation to real-world examples has not progressed. Although our proposal is limited to the analysis of arguments, we extend existing techniques to discourse analysis.

Flexibility to Describe Human's Informal Logic and Applicability to Actual Arguments

Human reasoning to justify arguments differs from formal logic. In general, a conclusion is not a logical consequence of premises. Humans make a variety of justifications expanding on deductive, inductive, and hypothetical reasoning. It is difficult to explain them in a unified manner. Our formalism is flexible enough to describe human reasoning because it just expresses the relationship between premises and conclusions with conditional probabilities. Though due to its flexibility, there is a large degree of freedom to express argument structure, the network can be patterned according to justification patterns provided by argumentation schemes.

4 Dataset Creation

We create a dataset consisting of pairs of relatively short English argument texts and their corresponding Bayesian networks. Our dataset not only helps us to train a machine learning model but also empirically shows that our approach can model the reasoning structure of actual arguments.

As described in Sec. 2.3, annotating argumentation schemes is very costly. In addition, our proposed method requires annotating a network structure. Therefore, it is difficult to prepare a large amount of high-quality data by the procedure of giving an argument text and annotating a network. In this work, we adopt the procedure of generating an argument text from a pre-built network.

4.1 Dataset Creation Procedure

Dataset creation is done in the following steps.

Create a Bayesian network from a wide range of discussions on a particular topic.

ProCon.org is a website that collects a wide range of opinions for and against controversial issues, mainly in the United States. We select six topics (the death penalty, gun control, minimum wage, legal abortion, school uniforms, and nuclear power) that are also selected in the existing argument mining dataset (Stab et al., 2018). We divide each topic into several subtopics. For each subtopic, we summarize the main points of discussion on the site and create a Bayesian network by applying network idioms. For example, for the subtopic on the death penalty, 'Does the death penalty deter crime?', we create a network like Fig. 1. We also create a text corresponding to the network we have created. This procedure is carried out by the author.

Decompose the built network into network fragments.

We decompose the built Bayesian network, which represents the entire argument of each subtopic, into network fragments so that one fragment contains only one network instance as much as possible. For example, from the network of Fig. 1, only the part surrounded by the dotted line is cut out.

Convert a network fragment into premises and a conclusion.

The predicate logical expression of each node in the network instance is converted into natural language and divided into premises and a conclusion as the description of argumentation schemes. For example, the predicate expression $means\_to(\text{the death penalty}, \text{deterring crime})$ is converted to 'The death penalty is a means to deter crime' and classified as a premise. This pro-

Table 1: The number of premises-conclusion patterns. Patterns are counted by topic and by idiom.

Idiom \ Topic	death-pena	gun-ctrl	min-wage	abortion	sc-uniform	nuclear	all
Means for Goal	4	7	2	5	0	2	20
Goal from Means	0	0	0	0	0	5	5
From Consequence	14	11	19	10	19	5	78
Source Knowledge	4	0	0	0	2	0	6
Source Authority	0	1	0	3	2	0	6
Rule or Principle	8	4	3	4	0	0	19
Others	5	3	0	0	1	4	13
Total	35	26	24	22	24	16	147

cedure is almost done by a simple templating generation like 'argument1 predicate argument2.' The author adjusts it so that it is grammatically natural. As an example, the following premises and conclusion are generated.

> **Premise1**: The death penalty is a means to deter crime.
> **Premise2**: Deterring crime is desirable.
> **Conclusion**: The death penalty is necessary.

Generate an argument text from premises and a conclusion by crowdsourcing.

We present premises and a conclusion to crowdworkers and ask them to convert given contents into a natural language text while preserving the original meaning. In addition, the following two instructions are given to the crowdworkers.

> You can omit phrases considered to be common sense like 'Saving lives is desirable.'
>
> Do not use the following phrases in your writing.
>
> - follow, above, desirable, acceptable, necessary, true, questionable
> - be means to/for, lead to, some may argue, either A or B
> - X is evidence/example that Y, X is enough to achieve the goal
> - respect to, obey, assert, credible, familiar, popular

The latter prohibits using idiom-derived keyphrases in the presented premises or conclusions.

Table 2: Subtopics of the death penalty in our dataset.

The death penalty
- Is the Death Penalty Immoral?
- Is the Death Penalty Unconstitutional?
- Has DNA Testing Led to Significant Improvements in the Criminal Justice System?
- Does the Death Penalty Deter Crime?
- Should the Death Penalty Be Used for Retribution?
- Does a Person's Race Affect the Likelihood of Receiving the Death Penalty?
- Should the Death Penalty Be Abolished or Paused Because of the Alleged - - Possibility of an Innocent Person Being Executed?
- Is Life in Prison without Parole a Better Option Than the Death Penalty?

4.2 Results

We created networks for a total of 53 subtopics of 6 topics and extracted 147 network fragments from them. The subtopics of the death penalty are shown in Table 2. We use Amazon Mechanical Turk and ask 20 crowd workers to generate an argument text per premises-conclusion pair made from the network fragments. Workers were paid 0.15$ per response. The number of subtopics per topic and the number of premises-conclusion patterns presented to the workers are shown in Table 1.

As a result of the crowdsourcing, 2,370 valid responses were obtained. 1,359 responses that did not follow the instructions were excluded as invalid responses. The vocabulary size and average sentence length (word counting) of the responses are shown in Table 3. The following metrics are measured in order to verify the diversity and bias of the created data since the procedure of present-

Table 3: Summary of crowdsourcing responses.

Topic	death-pena	gun-ctrl	min-wage	abortion	sc-uniform	nuclear	all
#responses	535	417	446	289	411	272	2,370
vocab size	1,052	776	549	692	735	609	2,493
sentence len	23.7	23.0	18.2	19.8	19.2	23.8	21.3

Table 4: Metrics of the diversity of our dataset.

Metric	death-pena	gun-ctrl	min-wage	abortion	sc-uniform	nuclear	all
SIM-INOUT	0.69	0.66	0.69	0.62	0.65	0.68	0.67
SIM-RES	0.57	0.54	0.59	0.48	0.54	0.55	0.55
BECAUSE	6.4	5.8	10.3	1.7	5.1	7.4	6.3

ing premises-conclusion pairs to the crowdworkers would result in a large bias. The results are shown in Table 4.

SIM-INOUT: Cosine Similarity between Inputs and Responses in Crowdsourcing

We measure the cosine similarity of the Bag of Words (BoW) representation between a premises-conclusion pair presented to crowdworkers and their response.

SIM-RES: Cosine Similarity among Responses in Crowdsourcing

We measure the BoW cosine similarity among the responses to the same premises-conclusion pair and average the values.

BECAUSE: Percentage of 'Conclusion because Premises' Response Pattern

A cloud worker may simply answer by combining premises with a conclusion using 'because.' We investigate the ratio of such responses. We divide responses into the first half and the second half separated by 'because.' Then, we calculate the BoW cosine similarity between the first half and a conclusion, and between the second half and premises. We compute the percentage of responses where both similarity values are more than 0.7.

4.3 Characteristics of Our Dataset

The data size is large in the research area of argumentation schemes. We create 2,370 pairs of argumentative text and a corresponding Bayesian network in total. The number of arguments is larger than the largest existing dataset (Reed et al., 2008) annotated with argumentation schemes though the vocabulary size is smaller.

As for the diversity of the dataset, the bias is suppressed. Table 4 shows the values of metrics. The following example is the case where a SIM-INOUT (the BOW cosine similarity between a premises-conclusion pair and a response) is 0.67.

> **Premises**: Gun ownership causes an accidental gun death. Accidental gun death is not desirable.
> **Conclusion**: Gun ownership is not necessary.
> **Worker's Response**: Lots of accidental gun death results from gun ownership which is completely avoidable.

Since this is an average example in terms of the metric, we can infer that the responses are not biased toward uniformity. We also come to the same conclusion based on our observations of all the responses. Furthermore, the BECAUSE metric is 6.3, which indicates few workers used the response pattern of 'Conclusion because Premises.'

4.4 A Baseline Model of Idiom Selection

We set up a task to select idioms for argumentative texts to investigate how well the existing NLP model would work. We use idiom names listed in Table 1 as labels. Infrequent idioms are labeled as 'others.' We separate a dataset according to topics. The data for the death penalty is used as a test set and the rest as a training set.

We apply BERT for sequence classification (Devlin et al., 2019; Wolf et al., 2020) as a baseline. The pre-trained model is BERT-Base Uncased and is not finetuned. Since learning without no sampling leads to always predicting the most frequent idiom in training data, we employ

Table 5: The results of a baseline idiom classifier for a test set. Some idioms do not apper in the test set.

Idiom	Prec	Recall	F1
Means for Goal	0.283	0.374	0.287
Goal from Means	-	-	-
From Consequence	0.636	0.169	0.230
Source Knowledge	0	0	NA
Source Authority	-	-	-
Rule or Principle	0.321	0.735	0.430
Others	0.137	0.061	0.077

both oversampling and undersampling[2]. Parameters are optimized using AdamW (Loshchilov and Hutter, 2019). We perform 5fold cross-validation on the training set and determine hyperparameters. The learning rate is 10^{-5} chosen from $\{10^{-4}, 10^{-5}, 10^{-6}\}$ and the weight decay is 10^{-3} chosen from $\{10^{-2}, 10^{-3}, 10^{-4}\}$. The max epoch is 400 and the batch size is 64. We repeat the experiment ten times. The averages of precision, recall, and f1 for each idiom are shown in Table 5. The average of overall accuracies for the test set is 27.5%. It indicates just selecting a suitable idiom is not an easy task.

5 Conclusion and Future Work

We propose a methodology for representing the reasoning structure of arguments using Bayesian networks and predicate logic. We define 17 network idioms derived from argumentation schemes to facilitate the network construction by giving typical network patterns. We also create a large dataset consisting of 2,370 pairs of argument text and a corresponding Bayesian network. In future work, we train a model for automatic network construction.

Acknowledgements

We thank Naoya Inoue for providing information about literature on argumentation schemes and web resources for argumentative texts.

References

Pietro Baroni, Dov M Gabbay, Massimiliano Giacomin, and Leendert van der Torre. 2018. *Handbook of formal argumentation*. College Publications.

Jacob Devlin, Ming-Wei Chang, Kenton Lee, and Kristina Toutanova. 2019. BERT: Pre-training of deep bidirectional transformers for language understanding. In *Proceedings of the 2019 Conference of the North American Chapter of the Association for Computational Linguistics: Human Language Technologies, Volume 1 (Long and Short Papers)*, pages 4171–4186, Minneapolis, Minnesota. Association for Computational Linguistics.

Vanessa Wei Feng and Graeme Hirst. 2011. Classifying arguments by scheme. In *Proceedings of the 49th Annual Meeting of the Association for Computational Linguistics: Human Language Technologies*, pages 987–996, Portland, Oregon, USA. Association for Computational Linguistics.

Norman Fenton, Martin Neil, and David A. Lagnado. 2013. A general structure for legal arguments about evidence using bayesian networks. *Cognitive Science*, 37(1):61–102.

Debanjan Ghosh, Aquila Khanam, Yubo Han, and Smaranda Muresan. 2016. Coarse-grained argumentation features for scoring persuasive essays. In *Proceedings of the 54th Annual Meeting of the Association for Computational Linguistics (Volume 2: Short Papers)*, pages 549–554, Berlin, Germany. Association for Computational Linguistics.

Zixuan Ke, W. Carlile, Nishant Gurrapadi, and Vincent Ng. 2018. Learning to give feedback: Modeling attributes affecting argument persuasiveness in student essays. In *IJCAI*.

Zixuan Ke, Hrishikesh Inamdar, Hui Lin, and Vincent Ng. 2019. Give me more feedback II: Annotating thesis strength and related attributes in student essays. In *Proceedings of the 57th Annual Meeting of the Association for Computational Linguistics*, pages 3994–4004, Florence, Italy. Association for Computational Linguistics.

Anne Lauscher, Lily Ng, Courtney Napoles, and Joel Tetreault. 2020. Rhetoric, logic, and dialectic: Advancing theory-based argument quality assessment in natural language processing. In *Proceedings of the 28th International Conference on Computational Linguistics*, pages 4563–4574, Barcelona, Spain (Online). International Committee on Computational Linguistics.

John Lawrence, Jacky Visser, and Chris Reed. 2019. An online annotation assistant for argument schemes. In *Proceedings of the 13th Linguistic Annotation Workshop*, pages 100–107, Florence, Italy. Association for Computational Linguistics.

I. Loshchilov and F. Hutter. 2019. Decoupled weight decay regularization. In *ICLR*.

Andreas Peldszus and Manfred Stede. 2015. An annotated corpus of argumentative microtexts. In *Proceedings of the First European Conference on Argumentation: Argumentation and Reasoned Action*, Lisbon, Portugal.

[2]`https://github.com/ufoym/imbalanced-dataset-sampler`

Isaac Persing, Alan Davis, and Vincent Ng. 2010. Modeling organization in student essays. In *Proceedings of the 2010 Conference on Empirical Methods in Natural Language Processing*, pages 229–239, Cambridge, MA. Association for Computational Linguistics.

Isaac Persing and Vincent Ng. 2013. Modeling thesis clarity in student essays. In *Proceedings of the 51st Annual Meeting of the Association for Computational Linguistics (Volume 1: Long Papers)*, pages 260–269, Sofia, Bulgaria. Association for Computational Linguistics.

Isaac Persing and Vincent Ng. 2015. Modeling argument strength in student essays. In *Proceedings of the 53rd Annual Meeting of the Association for Computational Linguistics and the 7th International Joint Conference on Natural Language Processing (Volume 1: Long Papers)*, pages 543–552, Beijing, China. Association for Computational Linguistics.

C. Reed and D. Walton. 2001. Applications of argumentation schemes. In *Proceedings of the 4th Conference of the Ontario Society for the Study of Argument (OSSA2001)*.

Chris Reed, Raquel Mochales Palau, Glenn Rowe, and Marie-Francine Moens. 2008. Language resources for studying argument. In *Proceedings of the Sixth International Conference on Language Resources and Evaluation (LREC'08)*, Marrakech, Morocco. European Language Resources Association (ELRA).

Christian Stab and Iryna Gurevych. 2014. Annotating argument components and relations in persuasive essays. In *Proceedings of COLING 2014, the 25th International Conference on Computational Linguistics: Technical Papers*, pages 1501–1510, Dublin, Ireland. Dublin City University and Association for Computational Linguistics.

Christian Stab and Iryna Gurevych. 2017. Parsing argumentation structures in persuasive essays. *Computational Linguistics*, 43(3):619–659.

Christian Stab, Tristan Miller, Benjamin Schiller, Pranav Rai, and Iryna Gurevych. 2018. Cross-topic argument mining from heterogeneous sources. In *Proceedings of the 2018 Conference on Empirical Methods in Natural Language Processing*, pages 3664–3674, Brussels, Belgium. Association for Computational Linguistics.

Sjoerd T. Timmer. 2017. *Designing and Understanding Forensic Bayesian Networks using Argumentation*. Ph.D. thesis, Utrecht University.

J. Visser, John Lawrence, Jean H. M. Wagemans, and C. Reed. 2018. Revisiting computational models of argument schemes: Classification, annotation, comparison. In *COMMA*.

Charlotte Vlek, Henry Prakken, Silja Renooij, and Bart Verheij. 2014. Building bayesian networks for legal evidence with narratives: a case study evaluation. *Artificial Intelligence and Law*, 22.

Henning Wachsmuth, Khalid Al-Khatib, and Benno Stein. 2016. Using argument mining to assess the argumentation quality of essays. In *Proceedings of COLING 2016, the 26th International Conference on Computational Linguistics: Technical Papers*, pages 1680–1691, Osaka, Japan. The COLING 2016 Organizing Committee.

Henning Wachsmuth, Nona Naderi, Yufang Hou, Yonatan Bilu, Vinodkumar Prabhakaran, Tim Alberdingk Thijm, Graeme Hirst, and Benno Stein. 2017. Computational argumentation quality assessment in natural language. In *Proceedings of the 15th Conference of the European Chapter of the Association for Computational Linguistics: Volume 1, Long Papers*, pages 176–187, Valencia, Spain. Association for Computational Linguistics.

Henning Wachsmuth and Benno Stein. 2017. A universal model for discourse-level argumentation analysis. *ACM Transactions on Internet Technology (TOIT)*, 17:1 – 24.

Henning Wachsmuth and Till Werner. 2020. Intrinsic quality assessment of arguments. In *Proceedings of the 28th International Conference on Computational Linguistics*, pages 6739–6745, Barcelona, Spain (Online). International Committee on Computational Linguistics.

Douglas Walton, Christopher Reed, and Fabrizio Macagno. 2008. *Argumentation Schemes*. Cambridge University Press.

Yushi Wang, Jonathan Berant, and Percy Liang. 2015. Building a semantic parser overnight. In *Proceedings of the 53rd Annual Meeting of the Association for Computational Linguistics and the 7th International Joint Conference on Natural Language Processing (Volume 1: Long Papers)*, pages 1332–1342, Beijing, China. Association for Computational Linguistics.

Thomas Wolf, Lysandre Debut, Victor Sanh, Julien Chaumond, Clement Delangue, Anthony Moi, Pierric Cistac, Tim Rault, Remi Louf, Morgan Funtowicz, Joe Davison, Sam Shleifer, Patrick von Platen, Clara Ma, Yacine Jernite, Julien Plu, Canwen Xu, Teven Le Scao, Sylvain Gugger, Mariama Drame, Quentin Lhoest, and Alexander Rush. 2020. Transformers: State-of-the-art natural language processing. In *Proceedings of the 2020 Conference on Empirical Methods in Natural Language Processing: System Demonstrations*, pages 38–45, Online. Association for Computational Linguistics.

A All Idioms

A.1 Cause to Effect

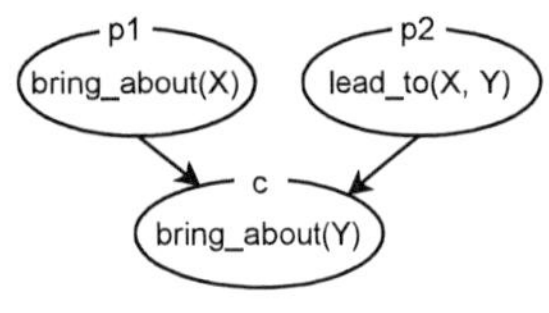

Figure 6: Cause to Effect Idiom

Variable type: X is Action or Case. Y is Case.

Referenced argumentation schemes: argument from cause to effect.

A.2 From Consequence

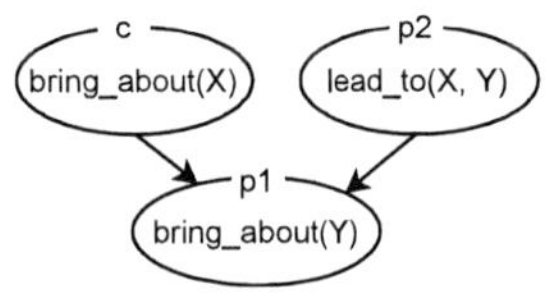

Figure 7: From Consequence Idiom

Variable type: X is Action or Case. Y is Case.

Referenced argumentation schemes: argument from consequence, pragatic argument from alternatives, argument from threat, argument from fear appeal, argument from danger appeal.

A.3 Goal from Means

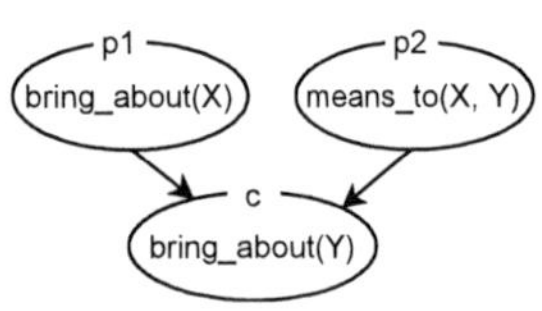

Figure 8: Goal from Means Idiom

Variable type: X is Action or Case. Y is Case.

A.4 Means for Goal

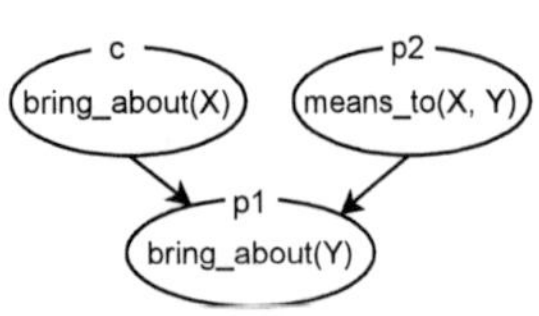

Figure 9: Means for Goal Idiom

Variable type: X is Action or Case. Y is Case.

Referenced argumentation schemes: practical reasoning, argument fron need for help, argument from distress.

A.5 From Source Knowledge

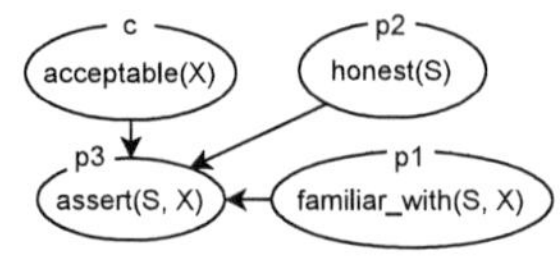

Figure 10: From Source Knowledge Idiom

Variable type: X is Proposition. S is Person(s) or Thing(s).

Referenced argumentation schemes: argument from position to know, argument from expert opinion, argument from witness testimony, argument from popular practice.

A.6 From Source Authority

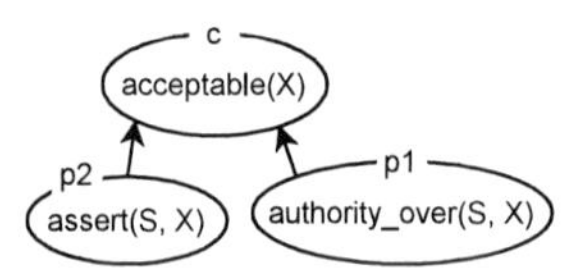

Figure 11: From Source Authority Idiom

Variable type: X is Proposition. S is Person(s) or Thing(s).

Referenced argumentation schemes: argument from popular opinion, argument from rules.

A.7 Rule or Principle

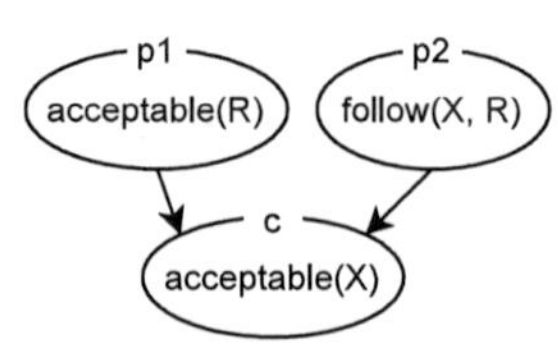

Figure 12: Rule or Principle Idiom

Variable type: R is Proposition. X is Action or Case.

A.8 Interpretation

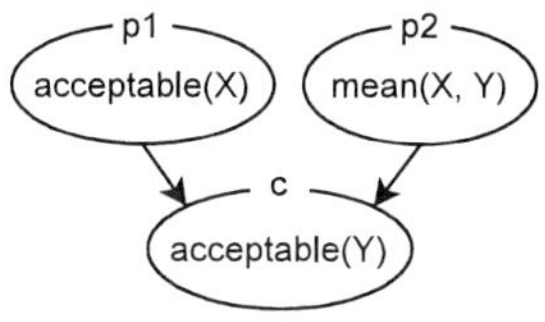

Figure 13: Interpretation Idiom

Variable type: Both X and Y are Proposition.

A.9 From Evidence

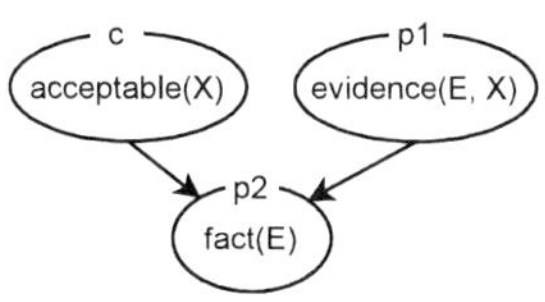

Figure 14: From Evidence Idiom

Variable type: X is Proposition. E is Case.
Referenced argumentation schemes: argument from sign, argument from evidence to a hypothesis.

A.10 From Example

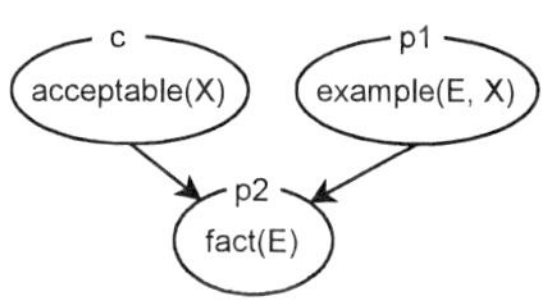

Figure 15: From Example Idiom

Variable type: X is Proposition. E is Case.
Referenced argumentation schemes: argument from example.

A.11 Constraint Idioms

The newtork structure of an idiom in this group is either Fig. 16 or Fig. 17. The predicate *CONSTRAINT* is defined for each idiom.

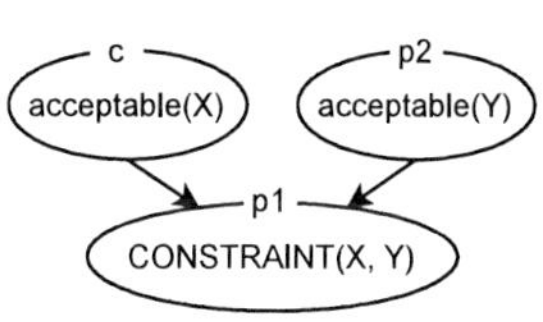

Figure 16: Constraint Idiom1

Variable type: Both X and Y are Action or Case.

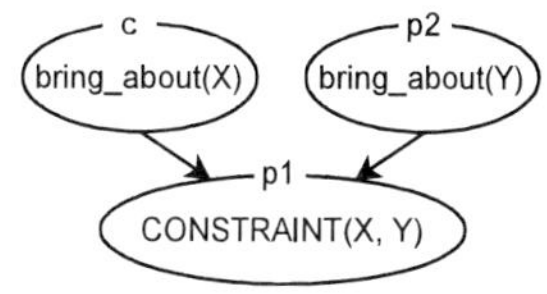

Figure 17: Constraint Idiom2

Variable type: Both X and Y are Action or Case.

A.11.1 Either Constraint

Use *either* as CONSTRAINT.
Referenced argumentation schemes: argument from alternatives.

A.11.2 Contradict Constraint

Use *contradict* as CONSTRAINT.
Referenced argumentation schemes: argument from oppositions.

A.11.3 Consistent Constraint

Use *consistent* as CONSTRAINT.
Referenced argumentation schemes: pragmatic inconsistency, argument fron inconsistent commitment.

A.11.4 Comparative Constraint

Use *better_than* as CONSTRAINT.

A.12 Verbal Classification

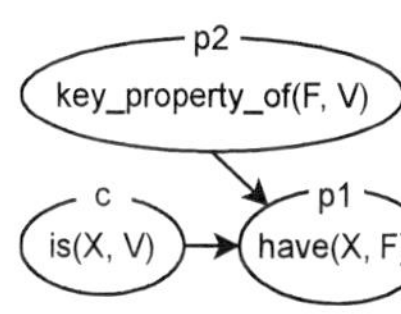

Figure 18: Verbal Classification Idiom

Variable type: X is Thins(s). V is Concept. F is Property.
Referenced argumentation schemes: argument from verbal classification, argument from definition to verbal classification.

A.13 Verbal Evaluation

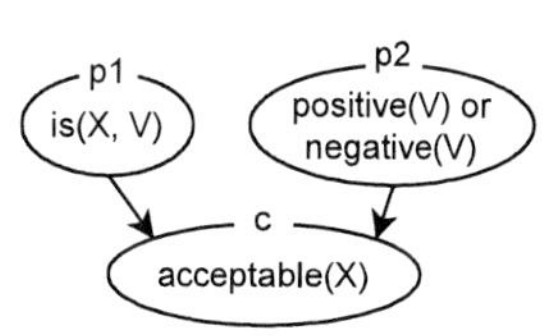

Figure 19: Verbal Evaluation Idiom

Variable type: X is Thins(s). V is Concept.

A.14 Correlation to Cause

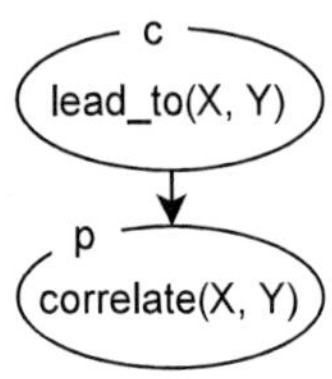

Figure 20: Correlation to Cause Idiom

Variable type: X is Action or Case. Y is Case. Referenced argumentation schemes: argument from correlation to cause.

B Variable Types

Table 6: Variable Types

Type	Description and Examples
Person(s)	A person or persons. e.g. Criminologists.
Thing(s)	A thing or things. e.g. The death penalty.
Action	An action. e.g. Introduce the death penalty.
Case	A situation or state of affairs. e.g. The death penalty has been introduced.
Proposition	A rule, an assertion, a fact, etc. e.g. The death penalty deters crime.
Concept	A concept or a term. e.g. Retribution.
Property	A characteristic of something. e.g. Punishment in proportion to serious crime.

Multilingual Counter Narrative Type Classification

Yi-Ling Chung[◇,♣], **Marco Guerini**[♣], **and Rodrigo Agerri**[♠]

[◇]University of Trento
[♣]Fondazione Bruno Kessler
[♠]HiTZ Center - Ixa, University of the Basque Country UPV/EHU

ychung@fbk.eu, guerini@fbk.eu, rodrigo.agerri@ehu.eus

Abstract

The growing interest in employing counter narratives for hatred intervention brings with it a focus on dataset creation and automation strategies. In this scenario, learning to recognize counter narrative types from natural text is expected to be useful for applications such as hate speech countering, where operators from non-governmental organizations are supposed to answer to hate with several and diverse arguments that can be mined from online sources. This paper presents the first multilingual work on counter narrative type classification, evaluating SoTA pre-trained language models in monolingual, multilingual and cross-lingual settings. When considering a fine-grained annotation of counter narrative classes, we report strong baseline classification results for the majority of the counter narrative types, especially if we translate every language to English before cross-lingual prediction. This suggests that knowledge about counter narratives can be successfully transferred across languages.

1 Introduction

The pervasive problem of online hate speech (HS) has motivated the research community to investigate methods for mitigating hatred, such as hate speech detection (Schmidt and Wiegand, 2017; Fortuna and Nunes, 2018) and, more recently, hate moderation through counter narratives (CNs). CNs are non-negative responses to hateful messages providing fact-bound arguments or alternative viewpoints. Distinct from standard approaches to hate intervention by content moderation, counter narratives are preferable as they preserve the right to freedom of speech and encourage peaceful conversations (Benesch, 2014; Schieb and Preuss, 2016).

In particular, the NLP community has started exploring CN generation (Qian et al., 2019; Tekiroğlu et al., 2020; Chung et al., 2021; Fanton et al., 2021; Zhu and Bhat, 2021), also in multilingual settings (Chung et al., 2020) with the aim of helping non-governmental organizations (NGOs) fight HS. However, automatic generation and detection of counter narratives still face three important challenges. First, counter narratives vary considerably in manner of expression and strategies (Benesch et al., 2016), see Table 1, posing difficulties to automatic CN evaluation and CN classification. Second, few corpora are available since domain experts are required to obtain high-quality data. Third, the only existing work on classifying counter narratives targeted just English (Mathew et al., 2019).

In our view, automated mechanisms to distinguish CN characteristics are crucial for developing hate countering applications that can address personalization or for tasks such as counter narrative mining from user-generated content. Classifying counter narratives would also help to establish which counter narratives are more effective to target hate speech. Finally, it may also be useful for NGO operators to answer hate speech with diverse counter narratives (not just the most common ones) which could be mined from online sources.

HS: *Muslims and non-British people are raping, enslaving and murdering our women! How disgusting!*
CN1 (Denouncing): *This is not acceptable. Hatred cannot be tolerated and must be stopped.*
CN2 (Facts): *Please notice that, regardless of religions, huge numbers of girls and children experience domestic sexual abuse by a partner or family member. We should encourage people to help victims and prevent sexual crimes.*

Table 1: An example hate speech with counter narratives (CN1 and CN2) using different strategies.

To the best of our knowledge, this work is the first to tackle counter narrative classification from a multilingual perspective, predicting the types/strategies employed in a counter narrative message given a hateful message. Other contributions include: (1) the first empirical analysis of counter narrative characteristics on expert-based hate countering data targeting Islamophobia (Chung et al., 2019); (2) strong baseline re-

Proceedings of The 8th Workshop on Argument Mining, pages 125–132
Punta Cana, Dominican Republic, November 10–11, 2021.

sults for multilingual and multi-class counter narrative classification by experimenting with the large pre-trained model XLM-R (Conneau et al., 2020); and (3) a set of cross-lingual zero-shot experiments showing that huge improvements can be obtained by translating the training data from other languages to English, which is coherent with previous work on the multilinguality of language models (Pires et al., 2019). This result also shows that common characteristics of some counter narrative types are carried across languages. Data splits and training scripts are available at `https://github.com/yilingchung/multilingualCN-classification`.

2 Counter Arguments v.s. Counter Narratives

While counter arguments and counter narratives have a similar purpose - to present an alternative stance to a statement - a counter argument is not necessarily a counter narrative, and vice versa. The main differences between the two are briefly discussed below, and point for the development of specific classification approaches for CNs.

Presence of an argument. A counter argument is typically defined as an argument (equivalent to a claim or standpoint) contradicting the initial statement with supporting evidence or reasoning (Khishfe, 2012; Schiappa and Nordin, 2013; Stab et al., 2018). The presence of supported evidence or reasoning is essential for counter-argumentation and argumentative information retrieval, regardless of it being implicit or explicit (e.g., Statement: *Nuclear energy should be used to replace fossil fuels.* v.s. Counter argument: *Renewable energy is a better option for replacing fossil fuels than unsustainable and expensive energy like nuclear power.*). In contrast, counter narratives can be formulated without using arguments. For example, a counter narrative can be without supporting evidence (e.g., Hate speech: *Islam is a plague.* v.s. Counter narrative: *How can you use such language to describe a religion of 1.6 billion people?*).

Non-negative arguments. Following guidelines[1] generally adopted by NGOs, an appropriate counter narrative should not contain hostile language, prejudice, and unlawful content. Using negative tones as responses may risk escalating the conversation and engaging in hateful sentiment. On the contrary, counter arguments are not bound by such constraints.

[1]As an example: https://getthetrollsout.org/stoppinghate

3 Counter Narrative Type Classification

Classifying counter narrative types is a new and challenging task. We hypothesize that underlying linguistic features in one language can facilitate the classification performance in other languages. Accordingly, we approach this task in a multilingual setting focusing on English, French and Italian. We experimented in the following learning settings: (1) **monolingual**, in which the train and test set are in the same language; (2) **multilingual**, in which we train in 3 languages and test on each of them; (3) **zero-shot cross-lingual**, where we train in one language and evaluate on the other two unseen languages; and, (4) **zero-shot translated**, similar to the multilingual experiment but translating the Italian and French training data into English.

3.1 Dataset

	Train			Test		
	EN	IT	FR	EN	IT	FR
Facts	957	1080	1329	237	270	333
Question	258	285	342	66	72	84
Denouncing	405	153	705	102	36	174
Humor	162	96	213	42	24	51
Hypocrisy	270	111	348	66	27	87
Total	2052	1725	2937	513	429	729

Table 2: Number of instances by types.

In our experiments we use CONAN (Chung et al., 2019), the only multilingual hate countering dataset currently available that has been niche-sourced to NGO operators. The dataset consists of 14k HS-CN pairs with counter narrative type annotation over English, French, and Italian. For each language, an original pair is augmented with two paraphrases of the original HS coupled with the original CN. In CONAN annotation, one CN could be assigned more than one CN type. As a first investigation into multilingual counter narrative classification, we select the pairs annotated with just one CN type for simplicity, discarding 25%, 17%, and 27% of samples for EN, FR and IT, respectively. Considering that the class balance is skewed, we narrow down the categories to majority classes over 3 languages: *facts* (35%), *denouncing* (13%), *question* (9%), *hypocrisy* (7%), and *humor* (5%). We then randomly sampled 80% and 20% of the dataset for the training and testing, ensuring that one HS and its two HS paraphrases paired with the same counter narrative are kept in the same split, so that the same CN does not appear by chance in both the training and testing sets. While the class imbalance poses a challenge, it reflects the practical scenario where certain types are less frequent.

Since CONAN contains only positive examples of CN, we further created 200 instances for the classes *support* and *unrelated*.[2] Support is a response that endorses the hate speech and *unrelated* is a text not connected to the hate speech in any sense. Clearly these two classes do not fall into the categories of CN and in fact they do not exist in CONAN. We include them to ensure that the models are exposed to varied non-CN text. Such setting can avoid model overfitting and increase the applicability of a system to the real world full of noisy content. The amount of these instances (200) is set to be close to the less populated class (*humor*). For the *unrelated* pairs, we randomly sampled data from Wikilingua[3] (Ladhak et al., 2020), featuring topics unrelated to islamophobia. The *support* pairs consist of HS paired with each of the two paraphrases. Table 2 reports the distribution of training and testing examples per class across the three languages.

3.2 Models

The XLM-R language model (Conneau et al., 2020), pre-trained on CommonCrawl for 100 languages, reports strong performance on several cross-lingual downstream tasks such as natural language inference or named entity recognition, and also on multilingual stance detection, close related to CN classification (Zotova et al., 2021). In this paper we leverage XLM-R to provide a strong baseline in the task of CN type classification in both monolingual and multilingual settings, using the Transformers library (Wolf et al., 2020). For every experiment, we fine-tuned the base version of XLM-R for 10 epochs with batch size 32 and 2e-5 learning rate.

4 Experimental Results

Similarly to stance detection and argument mining tasks (Mohammad et al., 2016; Stab et al., 2018), we report average macro F1 score over the CN types to avoid obtaining very high scores simply deriving from the dominant classes in the dataset. Furthermore, we also follow previous literature on stance detection (Mohammad et al., 2016) and report only the performance over the relevant classes.

Monolingual results. As shown by Table 3, monolingual models consistently yield the best performance in predicting the majority classes *facts* and *question*. As for *denouncing*, we obtain results above average for English, French and Italian (0.65, 0.58, and 0.51 respectively). Worst results are obtained for *humor* and *hypocrisy*. For Italian and French the model completely fails to identify *humor*, the most difficult and under-represented class; for English, the prediction is moderate (0.45). Lastly, the low results for the *hypocrisy* class seemed to be caused by the difficulty for the model in discriminating *hypocrisy* from *facts*. For example, 38% of the prediction errors for the *hypocrisy* class in English are caused by wrongly classifying *hypocrisy* instances as *facts* (more details are provided in the Appendix, Figure 1).

In a post-hoc manual analysis, annotators expressed difficulties in differentiating these two classes, difficulties illustrated by the examples provided in Table 4. This issue seems to be further confirmed by annotation statistics obtained from CONAN: among all the instances that contains the *hypocrisy* label, 45% were annotated with *hypocrisy* alone, 27% with *hypocrisy* and *facts*, while other multi-label cases were much lower. We hypothesize that *hypocrisy* could be a subclass of *facts*. After all, pointing out the contradiction in a hate statement may imply correcting misstatements via facts. Future work can try to merge two classes together to improve classification performance.

Multilingual results. As it is reported in Table 3, multilingual learning obtains better overall results than monolingual variants. In general the model trained on all languages improve the per-type performance although we observe decreases in *denouncing* and *hypocrisy* for Italian. Also, *humor* is still challenging for each language with more than 50% of miss-categorization.

Zero-shot cross-lingual results. For each target language, we provide the average F1 of zero-shot cross-lingual models trained on the other 2 source languages in Table 3. Although the results are lower than in the monolingual setting, results show that cross-lingual transfer can be a feasible strategy for classifying counter narratives for languages for

[2]This allows, for instance, to address cases where we need to identify counter narratives in a conversation containing both abusive and non-abusive language.

[3]Wikilingua is a multilingual dataset for summarization covering how-to guides on various topics written by human from WikiHow.

	Monolingual			Multilingual			Zero-shot			Zero-shot transl$_{en}$		
Target language	EN	IT	FR	EN	IT	FR	EN	IT	FR	EN	IT	FR
Average	0.60	0.59	0.49	**0.65**	0.56	0.49	0.45	0.46	0.40	**0.65**	**0.69**	**0.72**
Facts	0.84	0.91	0.71	0.82	0.94	0.74	0.71	0.86	0.67	**0.85**	**0.95**	**0.83**
Question	0.73	0.91	0.68	**0.81**	0.91	0.69	0.65	0.85	0.52	0.75	**0.93**	**0.87**
Denouncing	0.65	0.51	0.58	0.68	0.46	0.61	0.28	0.36	0.39	**0.70**	**0.69**	**0.75**
Humor	0.45	0.08	0.15	0.44	0.00	0.05	0.34	0.00	0.20	**0.56**	**0.42**	**0.51**
Hypocrisy	0.35	0.52	0.36	**0.49**	**0.48**	0.35	0.30	0.25	0.23	0.40	0.46	**0.62**

Table 3: Macro-F1 results under various configurations. For each target language in zero-shot setting, the scores are averaged over the models trained on the other two source languages.

HS	CN (Gold CN Type)	Prediction
Not all Muslims are terrorists, but all terrorists are Muslims.	*Only because when a non-muslim commits a terrorist act it is not called terrorism. Instead they're a 'lone wolf' with a 'traumatic past'.* (Hypocrisy)	Facts
Women of our culture that decide to become Islamic are so selfish. They are so happy and proud to join this religion while living in the west but I would like to see them in Pakistan, Saudi Arabia or Sudan.	*Maybe that 'sisterhood of tolerance and understanding' is challenging sexism everywhere including those men who feel they can tell women what they should believe in and how to live their lives.* (Facts)	Hypocrisy

Table 4: Examples of misclassified counter narratives.

which no training data is readily available, especially for the majority classes. Best results in this scenario are obtained when English is the source language, obtaining lower but close results with respect to the monolingual results in Italian and French (for more details about the results per language pair see Table 5 in the Appendix).

Zero-shot translated results. Data augmentation through translation has been widely employed to improve classification performance (Toledo-Ronen et al., 2020), also in cross-lingual settings (Zotova et al., 2021). At the same time, the cross-lingual capabilities of Transformer models such as XLM-R and mBERT are being actively investigated (Muller et al., 2021; Pires et al., 2019; Wu and Dredze, 2019). Thus, we conduct an additional experiment adding, to the English training set, the manually translated Italian and French training data before testing on the target languages (Italian and French). The aim is to investigate if XLM-R benefits from fine-tuning on a high resource language (English) instead of combining English with other languages, such as Italian and French, which are not so well represented in pre-trained multilingual models (Martin et al., 2020; Agerri et al., 2020; Espinosa et al., 2020). By doing so, in this 'zero-shot transl$_{en}$' setting we aim to expose the model with semantic knowledge from some target languages without actually seeing those languages (Italian and French). Table 3 shows that we obtain a huge performance jump with respect to the multilingual results, with 13 points improvement in macro-F1 score for Italian and 23 points for French. Interestingly, the improvement is more impressive for the *humor* class, the most challenging of them all.

5 Related Work

Broadly speaking, counter narrative type classification is related to stance detection (Toledo-Ronen et al., 2020; Schiller et al., 2021), which is crucial for argument search (Stab et al., 2018). In contrast to stance detection, that concentrates on binary or relatively simple classification – e.g., determine if an argument supports or contests a given topic (Sridhar et al., 2015; Rosenthal and McKeown, 2015; Stab et al., 2018) – we present a multi-class approach to counter narrative classification.

Counter narratives have been adopted as a direct and effective response to online hatred in several campaigns and on social media platforms including Twitter (Munger, 2017; Wright et al., 2017), Facebook (Schieb and Preuss, 2016), and Youtube (Ernst et al., 2017; Mathew et al., 2019). Although it has been argued that hate speech detection can benefit from CN classification, there are very few studies on this regard, with only one previous work on classifying counter narrative types (Mathew et al., 2019). However, unlike our present work, they consider hostile language as one of the main types of counter narratives, which is explicitly discouraged by NGOs working on hatred intervention. Furthermore, we investigate multilingual and cross-lingual CN classification leveraging a SoTA pre-trained multilingual language model.

6 Conclusion

We present the first work on multilingual CN type classification. Our results show that: (i) the performance is promising for the majority classes (*facts*, *question*, *denouncing*); (ii) classifying *humor* and *hypocrisy* CNs is still challenging; (iii) combining training data from the three source languages improves performance over the monolingual evaluation; and (iv), the best overall results are obtained in the 'zero-shot $transl_{en}$' approach where the training data for Italian and French is translated to English. This shows that some knowledge about CNs is transferred across languages. While this is coherent with previous literature about multilingual language models, the exact source of such successful transfer across languages remains an open topic.

Acknowledgements

Rodrigo Agerri is funded by the RYC-2017–23647 fellowship and by the DeepReading (RTI2018-096846-B-C21, MCIU/AEI/FEDER, UE, Spanish Ministry of Science, Innovation and Universities) and DeepText (KK-2020/00088, Basque Government) projects.

References

Rodrigo Agerri, Iñaki San Vicente, Jon Ander Campos, Ander Barrena, Xabier Saralegi, Aitor Soroa, and Eneko Agirre. 2020. Give your text representation models some love: the case for Basque. In *Proceedings of the 12th Language Resources and Evaluation Conference*, pages 4781–4788, Marseille, France. European Language Resources Association.

Susan Benesch. 2014. Countering dangerous speech: New ideas for genocide prevention. *Washington, DC: United States Holocaust Memorial Museum.*

Susan Benesch, Derek Ruths, Kelly P Dillon, Haji Mohammad Saleem, and Lucas Wright. 2016. Counterspeech on twitter: A field study. *Dangerous Speech Project.*

Yi-Ling Chung, Elizaveta Kuzmenko, Serra Sinem Tekiroglu, and Marco Guerini. 2019. CONAN - COunter NArratives through nichesourcing: a multilingual dataset of responses to fight online hate speech. In *Proceedings of the 57th Annual Meeting of the Association for Computational Linguistics*, pages 2819–2829, Florence, Italy. Association for Computational Linguistics.

Yi-Ling Chung, Serra Sinem Tekiroglu, and Marco Guerini. 2020. Italian counter narrative generation to fight online hate speech. In *Proceedings of the Seventh Italian Conference on Computational Linguistics*, Bologna, Italy.

Yi-Ling Chung, Serra Sinem Tekiroğlu, and Marco Guerini. 2021. Towards knowledge-grounded counter narrative generation for hate speech. In *Findings of the Association for Computational Linguistics: ACL-IJCNLP 2021*, pages 899–914, Online. Association for Computational Linguistics.

Alexis Conneau, Kartikay Khandelwal, Naman Goyal, Vishrav Chaudhary, Guillaume Wenzek, Francisco Guzmán, Edouard Grave, Myle Ott, Luke Zettlemoyer, and Veselin Stoyanov. 2020. Unsupervised cross-lingual representation learning at scale. In *Proceedings of the 58th Annual Meeting of the Association for Computational Linguistics*, pages 8440–8451, Online. Association for Computational Linguistics.

Julian Ernst, Josephine B Schmitt, Diana Rieger, Ann Kristin Beier, Peter Vorderer, Gary Bente, and Hans-Joachim Roth. 2017. Hate beneath the counter speech? a qualitative content analysis of user comments on youtube related to counter speech videos. *Journal for Deradicalization*, 10:1–49.

María S. Espinosa, Rodrigo Agerri, Álvaro Rodrigo, and Roberto Centeno. 2020. Deepreading @ sardistance 2020: Combining textual, social and emotional features. In *EVALITA*.

Margherita Fanton, Helena Bonaldi, Serra Sinem Tekiroğlu, and Marco Guerini. 2021. Human-in-the-loop for data collection: a multi-target counter narrative dataset to fight online hate speech. In *Proceedings of the 59th Annual Meeting of the Association for Computational Linguistics and the 11th International Joint Conference on Natural Language Processing (Volume 1: Long Papers)*, pages 3226–3240, Online. Association for Computational Linguistics.

Paula Fortuna and Sérgio Nunes. 2018. A survey on automatic detection of hate speech in text. *ACM Computing Surveys (CSUR)*, 51(4):85.

Rola Khishfe. 2012. Relationship between nature of science understandings and argumentation skills: A role for counterargument and contextual factors. *Journal of Research in Science Teaching*, 49(4):489–514.

Faisal Ladhak, Esin Durmus, Claire Cardie, and Kathleen McKeown. 2020. WikiLingua: A new benchmark dataset for cross-lingual abstractive summarization. In *Findings of the Association for Computational Linguistics: EMNLP 2020*, pages 4034–4048, Online. Association for Computational Linguistics.

Louis Martin, Benjamin Muller, Pedro Javier Ortiz Suárez, Yoann Dupont, Laurent Romary, Éric de la Clergerie, Djamé Seddah, and Benoît Sagot. 2020. CamemBERT: a tasty French language model. In *Proceedings of the 58th Annual Meeting of the Association for Computational Linguistics*, pages 7203–7219, Online. Association for Computational Linguistics.

Binny Mathew, Punyajoy Saha, Hardik Tharad, Subham Rajgaria, Prajwal Singhania, Suman Kalyan Maity, Pawan Goyal, and Animesh Mukherjee. 2019. Thou shalt not hate: Countering online hate speech. In *Proceedings of the International AAAI Conference on Web and Social Media*, volume 13, pages 369–380.

Saif Mohammad, Svetlana Kiritchenko, Parinaz Sobhani, Xiaodan Zhu, and Colin Cherry. 2016. SemEval-2016 task 6: Detecting stance in tweets. In *Proceedings of the 10th International Workshop on Semantic Evaluation (SemEval-2016)*, pages 31–41, San Diego, California. Association for Computational Linguistics.

Benjamin Muller, Yanai Elazar, Benoît Sagot, and Djamé Seddah. 2021. First align, then predict: Understanding the cross-lingual ability of multilingual BERT. In *Proceedings of the 16th Conference of the European Chapter of the Association for Computational Linguistics: Main Volume*, pages 2214–2231, Online. Association for Computational Linguistics.

Kevin Munger. 2017. Tweetment effects on the tweeted: Experimentally reducing racist harassment. *Political Behavior*, 39(3):629–649.

Telmo Pires, Eva Schlinger, and Dan Garrette. 2019. How multilingual is multilingual BERT? In *Proceedings of the 57th Annual Meeting of the Association for Computational Linguistics*, pages 4996–5001, Florence, Italy. Association for Computational Linguistics.

Jing Qian, Anna Bethke, Yinyin Liu, Elizabeth Belding, and William Yang Wang. 2019. A benchmark dataset for learning to intervene in online hate speech. In *Proceedings of the 2019 Conference on Empirical Methods in Natural Language Processing and the 9th International Joint Conference on Natural Language Processing*, pages 4755–4764, Hong Kong, China. Association for Computational Linguistics.

Sara Rosenthal and Kathy McKeown. 2015. I couldn't agree more: The role of conversational structure in agreement and disagreement detection in online discussions. In *Proceedings of the 16th Annual Meeting of the Special Interest Group on Discourse and Dialogue*, pages 168–177, Prague, Czech Republic. Association for Computational Linguistics.

Edward Schiappa and John P. Nordin. 2013. *Argumentation: Keeping Faith with ReasonKeeping Faith With Reason*. Pearson UK.

Carla Schieb and Mike Preuss. 2016. Governing hate speech by means of counterspeech on facebook. In *66th ICA Annual Conference*, pages 1–23, Fukuoka, Japan.

Benjamin Schiller, Johannes Daxenberger, and Iryna Gurevych. 2021. Stance detection benchmark: How robust is your stance detection? *KI-Künstliche Intelligenz*, pages 1–13.

Anna Schmidt and Michael Wiegand. 2017. A survey on hate speech detection using natural language processing. In *Proceedings of the Fifth International Workshop on Natural Language Processing for Social Media*, pages 1–10.

Dhanya Sridhar, James Foulds, Bert Huang, Lise Getoor, and Marilyn Walker. 2015. Joint models of disagreement and stance in online debate. In *Proceedings of the 53rd Annual Meeting of the Association for Computational Linguistics and the 7th International Joint Conference on Natural Language Processing (Volume 1: Long Papers)*, pages 116–125, Beijing, China. Association for Computational Linguistics.

Christian Stab, Tristan Miller, Benjamin Schiller, Pranav Rai, and Iryna Gurevych. 2018. Cross-topic argument mining from heterogeneous sources. In *Proceedings of the 2018 Conference on Empirical Methods in Natural Language Processing*, pages 3664–3674, Brussels, Belgium. Association for Computational Linguistics.

Serra Sinem Tekiroğlu, Yi-Ling Chung, and Marco Guerini. 2020. Generating counter narratives against online hate speech: Data and strategies. In *Proceedings of the 58th Annual Meeting of the Association for Computational Linguistics*, pages 1177–1190, Online. Association for Computational Linguistics.

Orith Toledo-Ronen, Matan Orbach, Yonatan Bilu, Artem Spector, and Noam Slonim. 2020. Multilingual argument mining: Datasets and analysis. In *Findings of the Association for Computational Linguistics: EMNLP 2020*, pages 303–317, Online. Association for Computational Linguistics.

Thomas Wolf, Lysandre Debut, Victor Sanh, Julien Chaumond, Clement Delangue, Anthony Moi, Pierric Cistac, Tim Rault, Remi Louf, Morgan Funtowicz, Joe Davison, Sam Shleifer, Patrick von Platen, Clara Ma, Yacine Jernite, Julien Plu, Canwen Xu, Teven Le Scao, Sylvain Gugger, Mariama Drame, Quentin Lhoest, and Alexander Rush. 2020. Transformers: State-of-the-art natural language processing. In *Proceedings of the 2020 Conference on Empirical Methods in Natural Language Processing: System Demonstrations*, pages 38–45, Online. Association for Computational Linguistics.

Lucas Wright, Derek Ruths, Kelly P Dillon, Haji Mohammad Saleem, and Susan Benesch. 2017. Vectors for counterspeech on Twitter. In *Proceedings of the First Workshop on Abusive Language Online*, pages 57–62, Vancouver, BC, Canada. Association for Computational Linguistics.

Shijie Wu and Mark Dredze. 2019. Beto, bentz, becas: The surprising cross-lingual effectiveness of BERT. In *Proceedings of the 2019 Conference on Empirical Methods in Natural Language Processing and the 9th International Joint Conference on Natural Language Processing (EMNLP-IJCNLP)*, pages

833–844, Hong Kong, China. Association for Computational Linguistics.

Wanzheng Zhu and Suma Bhat. 2021. Generate, prune, select: A pipeline for counterspeech generation against online hate speech. In *Findings of the Association for Computational Linguistics: ACL-IJCNLP 2021*, pages 134–149, Online. Association for Computational Linguistics.

Elena Zotova, Rodrigo Agerri, and German Rigau. 2021. Semi-automatic generation of multilingual datasets for stance detection in twitter. *Expert Syst. Appl.*, 170:114547.

A Appendices

	IT -> EN	FR -> EN	EN -> IT	FR -> IT	EN -> FR	IT -> FR
Average	0.41	0.50	0.48	0.45	0.43	0.37
Facts	0.71	0.71	0.88	0.84	0.73	0.60
Question	0.56	0.74	0.84	0.87	0.48	0.55
Denouncing	0.30	0.25	0.46	0.26	0.44	0.33
Humor	0.24	0.43	0.00	0.00	0.22	0.18
Hypocrisy	0.22	0.38	0.24	0.27	0.28	0.17

Table 5: Zero-shot cross-lingual results in terms of macro-F1 per type.

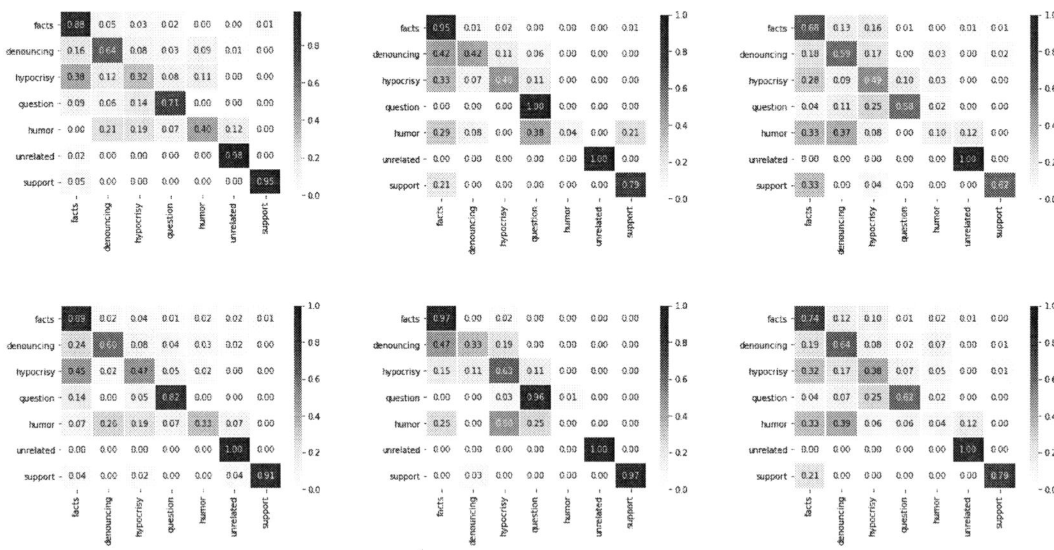

Figure 1: Confusion matrix on monolingual training for EN, IT, and FR from left to right (upper part); multilingual model tested on EN, IT, and FR from left to right (down part). The predictions are represented by columns and gold class is represented in rows.

Predicting Moderation of Deliberative Arguments: Is Argument Quality the Key?

Neele Falk*, **Iman Jundi***, **Eva Maria Vecchi, Gabriella Lapesa**
Institute for Natural Language Processing
University of Stuttgart (Germany)
first[-middle].last@ims.uni-stuttgart.de

Abstract

Human moderation is commonly employed in deliberative contexts (argumentation and discussion targeting a shared decision on an issue relevant to a group, e.g., citizens arguing on how to employ a shared budget). As the scale of discussion enlarges in online settings, the overall discussion quality risks to drop and moderation becomes more important to assist participants in having a cooperative and productive interaction. The scale also makes it more important to employ NLP methods for (semi-)automatic moderation, e.g. to prioritize when moderation is most needed.

In this work, we make the first steps towards (semi-)automatic moderation by using state-of-the-art classification models to predict which posts require moderation, showing that while the task is undoubtedly difficult, performance is significantly above baseline. We further investigate whether argument quality is a key indicator of the need for moderation, showing that surprisingly, high quality arguments also trigger moderation. We make our code and data publicly available.[1]

1 Introduction

Digital innovations reshaped direct democracy, allowing a large group of citizens to be involved in public decisions. However, as pointed out by Lampe et al. (2014), "Participation in discussions about the public interest can be enhanced by technology, but can also create an environment in which participants are overwhelmed by the quantity, quality, and diversity of information and arguments.". Poor quality discussions risk to lead to poor decisions. That is why research on Deliberative Theory does not focus on the output of democratic decision-making, but on the discourse exchange that precedes it (Bächtiger and Parkinson, 2019; Steenbergen et al., 2003; Steiner et al., 2005).

Moderation plays a crucial role in deliberation, in presence or online. Moderators assist participants in having a cooperative and productive discussion: indeed, in the deliberation terminology, moderation is referred to as *facilitation* (Kaner et al., 2007; Trénel, 2009), highlighting the positive nature of the moderation outcome more than the negative assessment of its input. A closer look at moderation in deliberative settings reveals a quite heterogeneous set of actions: stimulate discussion, solve conflicts, help participants to formulate clear and understandable comments while keeping them on topic and focus on solutions, make participants feel valued (e.g., addressing them personally).

The need for trained moderators is a clear bottleneck when scaling to large audiences. NLP can provide a crucial contribution, by making moderation automatic or (more realistically) semi-automatic – providing support to human moderators in some of the many moderator tasks. An important task here could be defined as identifying when a moderation intervention is needed. Our work makes the first steps towards NLP moderation and this task, by modeling and analysing the moderation signal in an e-deliberation forum *RegulationRoom* (Park and Cardie, 2018), addressing two research questions: (Q1) Can we predict automatically whether a forum post (comment) will trigger a moderation intervention? (Q2) What is the relation between Argument Quality (Wachsmuth et al., 2017a,b) and moderation and is AQ a key signal for moderation?

Regarding (Q1) we show that state of the art classification models can predict moderation reasonably well, but the task is quite difficult and even taking into account a broader context (i.e., preceding post) does not significantly improve performance. The moderation signal might be too heterogeneous, suggesting that the different moderation functions

* denotes equal contribution

[1] Code and annotated sample available here: https://github.com/imanjundi/arguments-moderation

Proceedings of The 8th Workshop on Argument Mining, pages 133–141
Punta Cana, Dominican Republic, November 10–11, 2021.

might be better targeted individually. We thus focus on a subset of the *RegulationRoom* dataset annotated with moderator functions, and concentrate on those explicitly annotated as an attempt to improve comment quality. To address (Q2) we employ an off-the-shelf Argument Quality classifier (Lauscher et al., 2020) and conduct a manual annotation experiment to analyse the relation between moderation and AQ. This can help us better understand if low-quality comments are mainly the ones that trigger moderation; the results are interesting and surprising: contrary to intuitive expectations, high AQ also triggers moderation. In high AQ cases, it seems that moderators "pick up" on interesting, well made points and ask the users to elaborate further.

The contribution of this work is thus twofold: first, we address the task of moderation prediction for the first time and with encouraging results; second, we uncover unexpected dynamics of the modulation of AQ with respect to moderation, thereby contributing to the empirical characterization of the moderation signal in deliberative settings.

2 Data

We investigate our research questions on data taken from the deliberation platform, *RegulationRoom*[2] which allows ordinary citizens to take part in the decision process about regulations proposed by federal agencies. The agencies provide detailed information about the rules under discussion such that participants can comment and share their opinions about them. To promote a fruitful discussion, human moderators monitor the discussion and intervene to help and support the participants. Besides general supervision functions (policing, helping with technical difficulties) the moderators can intervene to help users improving the content of their posts or to activate other participants to join the discussion. The moderators were trained and equipped with a 'moderator protocol' (eRulemaking Initiative et al., 2017), which describes the possible reasons for an intervention. Figure 1 illustrates an example of a moderator intervention in *RegulationRoom*.

The full *RegulationRoom* dataset (used in the experiments in section 3.1) contains 3k comments spanning various topics (refer to Table 3 in the Appendix for the distribution of the different topics) with 717 (23.63%) moderated comments vs. 2317

[2]http://regulationroom.org/

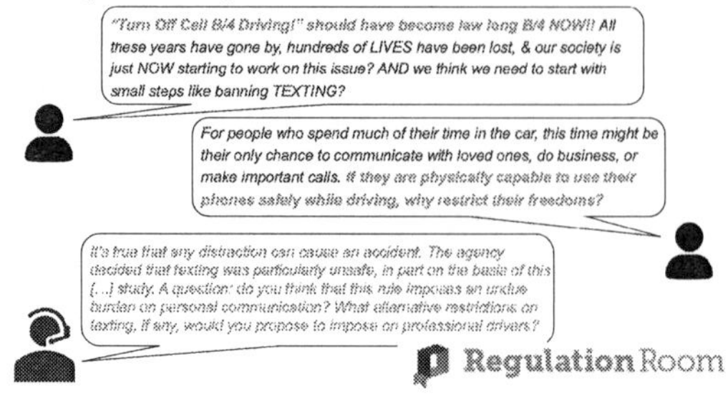

Figure 1: Moderation in RegulationRoom

(76.36%) not-moderated.

A subset of moderator interventions from this data (303 comments, topics marked with an asterisk in Table 3) has been annotated in Park et al. (2012) with the reasons for an intervention (moderator functions). The annotation schema for the moderator functions was inspired by the original moderator training protocol but due to the large variety of different possible reasons for a moderator intervention, the functions where merged into more general categories. The authors use the annotated subset to predict what type of moderator action would be required, focusing on the two most frequent types of intervention, *broadening the discussion* and *improving argument quality* (refer to Table 5 in the Appendix for a full list of annotated categories and their distribution). Unlike Park et al. (2012), we focus on predicting and analyzing when a moderation intervention is needed which was still not tackled before, although this is where the bottleneck in online moderation usually lies.

3 Experiments

We conduct classification experiments on two tasks: predicting if there was a moderator intervention for a comment *Any Moderation Intervention* then narrowing the scope to predicting if there was a moderator intervention to improve quality for a comment *Quality Moderation Intervention.* We fine-tune a Pretrained Language Model, RoBERTa-base (Liu et al., 2019), with a classification head using the Huggingface Transformers library (Wolf et al., 2020) for each task.

The dataset for each experiment is split into 60%, 20%, 20% train, dev and test respectively. Given the small size of the dataset, we evaluate on a 5-fold split of the whole dataset and report the average and standard deviation to get a more robust result that is less sensitive to the variance caused by the random dataset split. We compare the trained mod-

context	BAC	F1 macro	F1 positive
(random)	51.08 ± 2.2	47.70 ± 2.5	33.37 ± 3.0
parent=0	$64.77 \pm 2.1*$	$62.51 \pm 2.2*$	$46.32 \pm 2.6*$
parent=1	65.30 ± 1.1	63.63 ± 1.4	47.07 ± 1.4
parent=2	66.03 ± 1.7	64.95 ± 1.6	47.99 ± 2.5

Table 1: Results of *Any Moderation Intervention*
The difference is statistically significant ($p < 0.05$)

context	BAC	F1 macro	F1 positive
(random)	50.14 ± 1.3	45.40 ± 2.1	28.99 ± 1.5
parent=0	$58.52 \pm 3.5*$	$56.98 \pm 2.6*$	$34.27 \pm 5.0*$
parent=1	58.14 ± 6.3	56.64 ± 6.9	34.92 ± 8.1
parent=2	55.38 ± 4.3	55.41 ± 4.1	27.44 ± 7.1

Table 2: Results of *Quality Moderation Intervention*
The difference is statistically significant ($p < 0.05$)

els to a random prediction baseline and report the balanced accuracy (BAC), F1 macro and F1 for the positive class. The statistical significance is calculated using McNemar's Test.

To represent the context of the comment we consider the previous $parent \in \{0, 1, 2\}$ comments where $parent = 0$ is considering the comment itself alone with no previous context. We concatenate the comments to form the full context while adding a separation token </s> in-between.

We train for 10 epochs and choose the best performing model on the dev split, finally reporting the results on the test split. We do hyperparameter optimization on the dev split using grid search over $parent \in \{0, 1, 2\}$ and learning rate $lr \in [3e^{-6}, 3e^{-5}]$. We also try sequence length 256 and 512 to deal with the increased length due to the longer context with more parent comments. We further do a search for the optimal threshold (threshold moving) to better deal with data imbalance.

3.1 Any Moderation Intervention

In our first experiment we train a model to predict any moderator intervention. This has practical application in automatically assisting moderators and predicting where their effort is most needed. This is particularly crucial with moderation on a large-scale where it's not feasible for the moderator to check every comment.

The full dataset (Table 3) is used here where the moderator intervention is used as a noisy label: a user comment followed by a moderator comment is labeled as moderated, 23.63% of the comments, while the rest is labeled as not-moderated. The model performs better than chance as seen in in Table 1, but it is also clear that the task is still difficult. This can be due to the noisy labels, the ambiguity inherent in the task, and the small size of the training data.

Including more context leads to better performance although the increase is not statistically significant, but that might be also due to the small size of the dataset. Consider, however, that the majority of the comments (~60%) is not nested i.e. it is only for ~40% that we can exploit a larger context to support classification prediction (see Table 4 in the Appendix for more details).

3.2 Quality Moderation Intervention

In our second experiment we narrow the task to predicting a moderator intervention for improving a comments quality. This type of moderation is one of the most important functions in a deliberative setting, as good quality contributions help to ensure that the different perspectives are understood by others. While it is questionable whether a function like *broadening discussion* can be predicted from the content of the discussion post itself, it is expected that its quality can at least be approximated from certain linguistic and structural particularities in the comment itself. If this is the case, this type of moderation is also suitable to be supported by automated methods. By dropping comments that were moderated for other reasons, the positive instances may form a more homogeneous group and may therefore be easier to model.

For this experiment we rely on the annotated subset (Park et al., 2012) described in section 2, considering only comments whose moderator intervention was annotated with *improve comment quality* as positive instances. We use all other comments from the same topics as negative instances. This subset (further referred to as *RegroomForQual*) contains 876 negative and 222 positive instances (~ 75%/ ~ 25%). Again, the model performs better than the baseline (cf. Table 2), but has a lower performance than in the first experiment. Adding context does not improve the results but rather hurts the performance (the distribution of available context in *RegroomForQual*, displayed in Table 6 in the Appendix is comparable to that of the larger dataset).

4 Analysis

Given that the task of predicting *Quality Moderation Intervention* is still challenging to model, this raises the question of how exactly *comment quality* was defined by the moderators/annotators of the underlying dataset and to what extent an explicit prediction of, for example argument quality, would help to improve the results on this task. To gain a more comprehensive understanding of the argument quality in this dataset, we collected quality scores using a manual and an automatic annotation to examine them in the context of a moderation intervention.

4.1 AQ Annotation

In both research areas, argument mining and deliberative theory, theoretical and empirical definitions of argument quality exist. They range from assessing more specific aspects of argument quality (e.g. persuasion in Liane Longpre and Cardie, 2019) to measuring argument quality as a relative assessment (given two arguments, which is more convincing (Habernal and Gurevych, 2016). In deliberative theory the focus lies on aspects important for a fruitful discussion related to a decision process (e.g. respectful tone, constructiveness) and aggregating the single scores to measure the quality of the overall discourse.

Manual Annotation Although there is a large variance in different definitions of quality and methods to assess it, it was shown that a common perception of overall argument quality exists and that there are correlations between different measurement methods (Wachsmuth et al., 2017a). We therefor simplify our annotation for this phenomenon and quantify argument quality in one aggregated score. This allows us to check whether the annotators' intuitive understanding of Argument Quality is consistent with the moderator interventions. We still provide the annotators with detailed information on sub-dimensions of argument and deliberative quality to consider when annotating[3].

We collected a set of AQ annotations on comments sampled from the *RegroomForQual* dataset. Four annotators were asked to estimate the argument quality of 112 comments, providing a score ranging from 0 (very low quality) to 5 (very high quality). Note that the annotators did not know whether a comment triggered a moderator intervention or not.

The items were sampled balancing two criteria: moderated vs. not moderated; high quality vs. low quality according to the off-the-shelf AQ model by Lauscher et al. (2020).[4] The average pairwise inter-annotator agreement (weighted Cohen's kappa) was 0.40, and the average pairwise correlation between annotators was 0.62 (pairwise details in Table 7).

Automatic Annotation We use a classifier by Lauscher et al. (2020) to automatically score the comments on the three core argument quality dimensions *Cogency, Effectiveness, Reasonableness* (Wachsmuth et al., 2017b) and an aggregated score (*overall quality*). The classifier was trained on the *GAQCorpus* (Ng et al., 2020) that contains data from different online forums annotated with scores between 1 and 5. As a sanity check, we first compared the human AQ on our annotated set to the automatically predicted ones: AQ scores predicted by the system correlate with human ones ($\tau = 0.72, p < 0.01$ with *overall quality*, $\tau = 0.70, p < 0.01$ with all three subdimensions). The scores for the subdimensions highly correlate with *overall quality* ($\tau > 0.98, p < 0.01$), so we focus on this score for further investigations.

4.2 Relation between Moderation and AQ

To get a first impression about the relationship between moderation and argument quality we look at the distributions of the quality scores for the comments that triggered moderation vs. the comments that did not trigger an intervention. The intuitive expectation is that comments with low quality scores would be more likely to trigger moderation to improve their quality. The visualization of the actual distributions in Figure 2 does not confirm this hypothesis. For the manually annotated data, we find a peak in the middle range of scores (2 to 4), but both lower and higher quality comments were moderated (see Fig. 2a). Likewise, there were also low quality comments that were not moderated. The distributions for the automatic scores initially show that they have less variance (few comments were annotated with extreme scores), with a tendency to mid-high scores (most data points have scores between 3 and 4, maximum score would be 5). There is no significant difference between the distributions of moderated and non-moderated data, which again disproves the hypothesis that low-quality comments are more likely to be moderated (cf. Fig. 2b).

Similarly we analyse the model that was trained

[3]The Annotation Guidelines are provided in the Appendix.

[4]We provide all details on the sampling criteria for HQ vs. LQ in the Appendix, section A.4.1.

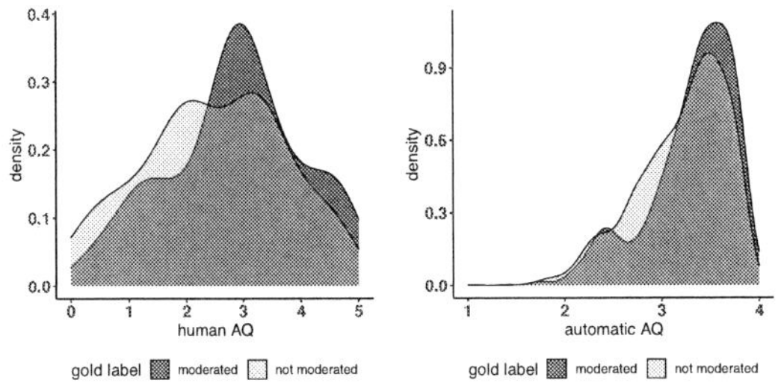

(a) Annotation with human AQ (b) *RegroomForQual* with automatic AQ

Figure 2: Density plots for AQ: Comparing distribution for moderated and not moderated comments

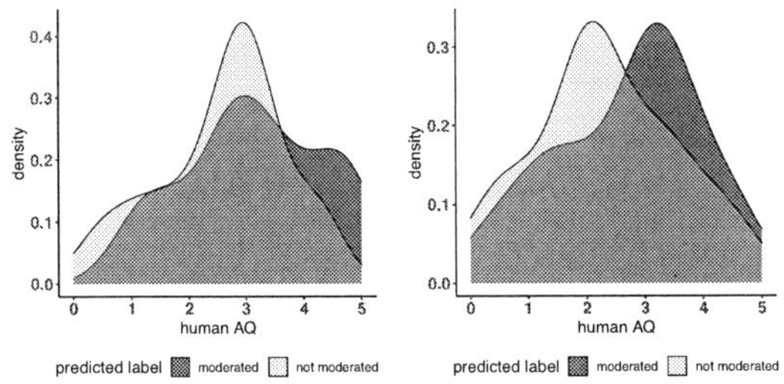

(a) True positives vs. false negatives (b) True negatives vs. false positives.

Figure 3: Density plots for AQ: Comparing distribution for model predictions, using the best model trained on *Quality Moderation Intervention*.

on *quality moderation intervention* to check if it picks up on Argument Quality as a signal for an intervention. We plot the distribution of the human annotated quality scores for the moderated instances (gold label = 1) and compare the true positives and false negatives (Figure 3a): The model is able to capture the majority of the high-quality comments and struggles to correctly classify comments with medium quality scores (2-3). For the instances that were not moderated (gold label = 0, Figure 3b), the model produces a high amount of false positives for arguments with high AQ, so we can see that for both types of comments, moderated and not moderated, the model is more likely to predict a moderator intervention for higher quality arguments (cf. Figure 3).

We notice a similar pattern on the *RegroomForQual* data: moderation is triggered by both low and high AQ. The probabilities of the model for a moderator intervention correlate positively with the automatic quality scores ($\tau = 0.33, p < 0.01$).

This trend shows that a simplified definition of AQ is not the key to moderation. Neither the automatically produced AQ scores, nor the annotators' intuition of high and low AQ do correlate with moderators' interventions. While agreement is most often encouraging, the disagreement among annotators (e.g. annot3 and annot4 in Table 7) suggests that AQ may be a hard notion to pinpoint.

In fact, there are various cases which are quite hard to annotate based on a general notion of argument quality. In some cases, an argument is well-written, clearly presented, and properly supported with examples or data, however the argument itself is not good and should be considered for moderation. Examples include arguments based on personal accounts (hearsay/antidote) and conspiracy theories (false or intentionally contrived support), see Appendix A.5 for specific examples. In these cases AQ is not only hard to assess, even if measured based on a more fine-grained definition of AQ (e.g. several scores on different aspects of quality), but also these types of arguments might score high on the majority of dimensions and still be moderated in a deliberative setting. Furthermore moderating high-quality arguments can be beneficial if they present a new opinion to help other participants understand that perspective. Moderation is thus a multidimensional, complex problem for which a sole focus on argument quality seems to not be sufficient.

5 Conclusion

Our experiments target the prediction of the need for a moderator intervention in a deliberative setup: our models perform better than chance, but the task is very challenging due to the ambiguity inherent in the task and to the small data available usually in such domains. We further explore the interplay of moderation and AQ (automatically predicted and manually annotated): contrary to the expectation of moderation exclusively "correcting" low quality, high quality is very often moderated, as well.

Acknowledgments

We would like to thank Anne Lauscher for providing us with the code and models for the AQ classifier. We acknowledge funding by the Bundesministeriumfur Bildung und Forschung (BMBF) through the project E-DELIB (*Powering up E-deliberation: towards AI-supported moderation*).

References

Andre Bächtiger and John Parkinson. 2019. *Towards a New Deliberative Quality*. Oxford University Press, Cambridge, MA, USA.

Ivan Habernal and Iryna Gurevych. 2016. Which argument is more convincing? analyzing and predicting convincingness of web arguments using bidirectional LSTM. In *Proceedings of the 54th Annual Meeting of the Association for Computational Linguistics (Volume 1: Long Papers)*, pages 1589–1599, Berlin, Germany. Association for Computational Linguistics.

Cornell eRulemaking Initiative et al. 2017. Ceri (cornell e-rulemaking) moderator protocol.

Sam Kaner, Lenny Lind, Catherine Tolid, Sarah Fisk, and Duane Berger. 2007. *Facilitator's guide to participatory decision-making*. John Wiley & Sons/Jossey-Bass, San Francisco.

Cliff Lampe, Paul Zube, Jusil Lee, Chul Hyun Park, and Erik Johnston. 2014. Crowdsourcing civility: A natural experiment examining the effects of distributed moderation in online forums. *Government Information Quarterly*, 31(2):317 – 326.

Anne Lauscher, Lily Ng, Courtney Napoles, and Joel Tetreault. 2020. Rhetoric, logic, and dialectic: Advancing theory-based argument quality assessment in natural language processing. In *Proceedings of the 28th International Conference on Computational Linguistics*, pages 4563–4574, Barcelona, Spain (Online). International Committee on Computational Linguistics.

Esin Durmus Liane Longpre and Claire Cardie. 2019. Persuasion of the undecided: Language vs. the listener. In *Proceedings of the 6th workshop on Argument Mining*, pages 167–176.

Yinhan Liu, Myle Ott, Naman Goyal, Jingfei Du, Mandar Joshi, Danqi Chen, Omer Levy, M. Lewis, Luke Zettlemoyer, and Veselin Stoyanov. 2019. Roberta: A robustly optimized bert pretraining approach. *ArXiv*, abs/1907.11692.

Lily Ng, Anne Lauscher, Joel Tetreault, and Courtney Napoles. 2020. Creating a domain-diverse corpus for theory-based argument quality assessment. In *Proceedings of the 7th Workshop on Argument Mining*, pages 117–126, Online. Association for Computational Linguistics.

Joonsuk Park and Claire Cardie. 2018. A corpus of eRulemaking user comments for measuring evaluability of arguments. In *Proceedings of the Eleventh International Conference on Language Resources and Evaluation (LREC 2018)*, Miyazaki, Japan. European Language Resources Association (ELRA).

Joonsuk Park, Sally Klingel, Claire Cardie, Mary J. Newhart, Cynthia Farina, and J. Vallbé. 2012. Facilitative moderation for online participation in erulemaking. In *dg.o '12*.

M. Steenbergen, Andre Baechtiger, Markus Spörndli, and J. Steiner. 2003. Measuring political deliberation: A discourse quality index. *Comparative European Politics*, 1:21–48.

Jürg Steiner, André Bächtiger, Markus Spörndli, and Marco R. Steenbergen. 2005. *Deliberative Politics in Action: Analyzing Parliamentary Discourse*. Theories of Institutional Design. Cambridge University Press.

Matthias Trénel. 2009. Facilitation and inclusive deliberation. *Online deliberation: Design, research, and practice*, pages 253–257.

Henning Wachsmuth, Nona Naderi, Ivan Habernal, Yufang Hou, Graeme Hirst, Iryna Gurevych, and Benno Stein. 2017a. Argumentation quality assessment: Theory vs. practice. In *Proceedings of the 55th Annual Meeting of the Association for Computational Linguistics (Volume 2: Short Papers)*, pages 250–255, Vancouver, Canada. Association for Computational Linguistics.

Henning Wachsmuth, Nona Naderi, Yufang Hou, Yonatan Bilu, Vinodkumar Prabhakaran, Tim Alberdingk Thijm, Graeme Hirst, and Benno Stein. 2017b. Computational argumentation quality assessment in natural language. In *Proceedings of the 15th Conference of the European Chapter of the Association for Computational Linguistics: Volume 1, Long Papers*, pages 176–187, Valencia, Spain. Association for Computational Linguistics.

Thomas Wolf, Lysandre Debut, Victor Sanh, Julien Chaumond, Clement Delangue, Anthony Moi, Pierric Cistac, Tim Rault, Remi Louf, Morgan Funtowicz, Joe Davison, Sam Shleifer, Patrick von Platen, Clara Ma, Yacine Jernite, Julien Plu, Canwen Xu, Teven Le Scao, Sylvain Gugger, Mariama Drame, Quentin Lhoest, and Alexander Rush. 2020. Transformers: State-of-the-art natural language processing. In *Proceedings of the 2020 Conference on Empirical Methods in Natural Language Processing: System Demonstrations*, pages 38–45, Online. Association for Computational Linguistics.

A Appendix

A.1 *RegulationRoom* full dataset: statistics

Topic	count	percentage
Consumer Debt Collection	971	32.00%
Airline Passenger Rights (*)	931	30.68%
Home Mortgage	235	7.74%
NYC Congestion	207	6.82%
Health IT	174	5.73%
Electronic On-Board Recorders (*)	167	5.50%
Proposed Move NY Fair Plan	163	5.37%
Air Travel Accessibility	128	4.21%
Distracted Driving & Texting	30	0.98%
Social Media in Rulemaking	28	0.92%
Total	3034	

Table 3: Moderation dataset: statistics. Full dataset is used in *Any Moderation Intervention* experiments. The (annotated) subtopics marked with * are used in the *Quality Moderation Intervention* experiments

context	count	percentage
parent=0	1850	60.96%
parent=1	604	19.90%
parent=2	485	15.98%
parent>2	95	3.16%

Table 4: *RegulationRoom* Moderation Dataset: Available Context

A.2 *RegulationRoom* subset by (Park et al., 2012): moderator functions

moderator intervention type	frequency
social functions	227
resolving site use issues	18
organizin discussion	19
policing	1
keeping discussion on target	19
improving comment quality	238
broadening discussion	84

Table 5: Moderator intervention types in the *RegulationRoom* subset by (Park et al., 2012)

A.3 *RegRoomForQual* subset of (Park et al., 2012)

context	count	percentage
parent=0	620	56.47%
parent=1	211	19.21%
parent=2	177	16.12%
parent>2	90	8.20%

Table 6: *RegRoomForQual* subset: Available Context

A.4 Annotation study: details

A.4.1 Sampling criteria for HQ vs. LQ

To sample the HQ vs. LQ items for our annotation, we proceeded as follows:

1. We annotated the comments in *RegRoomForQual* with the AQ classifier by Lauscher et al. (2020). This model is trained on a mixed-domain corpus (Ng et al., 2020) including online forum posts and is based on a more coarse-grained version of the taxonomy for AQ by (Wachsmuth et al., 2017a).

2. The distribution of the automatic AQ annotations is as follows: minimum value: 1.7; 1st quartile: 2.9; median: 3.3; mean: 3.2; 3rd quartile: 3.6; maximum value: 3.9. Note that while the range of the classifier is potentially between 1 and 5, we only cover a subportion of that range.

3. We exclude the 10 percent of the shortest and the 10 percent of the longest comments from the sampling. The comments have a length between 29 and 319 tokens, with a mean of 129.

4. We sampled 56 posts (25 moderated, 25 not moderated) from the highest quartile (HQ) and 56 (25 moderated, 25 not moderated) from the lowest quartile (LQ)

A.4.2 Annotators and Agreement

Out of the four annotators, three are MA students in Computational Linguistics who had completed an Argument Mining course. One of them is a native speaker of English, the other two have an excellent command of it. The fourth annotator is one of the authors of the paper, and a native speaker of English.

Table 7 displays the pairwise weighted κ and Pearson correlation for the four annotators, along with their average values.

	κ_w	r
annot 1 / annot 2	0.55	0.76
annot 1 / annot 3	0.26	0.52
annot 1 / annot 4	0.56	0.75
annot 2 / annot 3	0.32	0.53
annot 2 / annot 4	0.46	0.68
annot 3 / annot 4	0.23	0.47
average	0.40	0.62

Table 7: Agreement btw. annotator pairs and average: weighted Cohens κ and Pearson correlation.

A.5 Annotation Examples: difficult cases

Below are a set of examples of comments that follow either a "conspiracy theory" approach or are personal accounts, which in the end are difficult to annotate based entirely on argument quality.

- Example 1 This is merely another phase of Big Brother. For all we know, they could have listening devices installed within. One thing about it: If the door is opened even merely enough for someone to get their foot inside, they always tend to take more and more. That is exactly how this government has grown so out of control. Now they are financing their purses with more money which could have been better spent in maintenance of our vehicles or the payment of taxes we already owe. If you just think about it: why did they just go through hiring so many new law enforcement officers? Law Enforcement needs to focus more on those who PURSUE making money illegally, and let a person earn a fair income honorably.

  human annot.: 2 ; 0 ; 2 ; 2 ; (mean = 1.5)
  moderated: no
  automatic AQ: 3.5

- Example 2 Airlines should require a gate agent to give hourly status or tell passengers when to return to the gate for status. I endured an all-day wait without being advised of status. We were scheduled for an 8am departure. Gate personnel advised us of mechanical problems and said to check back at 10am. At 9am, a gate agent advised maybe a 11am boarding (people who did not arrive till 10am per prior instruction never heard that announcement). After that NO ONE gave us status. It was 6pm before we found out the flight was canceled by calling the airlines. The notice on the departure boards and at the gate said "delayed"... a gate agent never gave us status after 9am! A fellow passenger happened to work at this airline, so he made some calls and was able to get status from the maintenance crew... the maintenance chief said his estimated time of fix was 5PM - maybe. If some "official" from the airline had done the same thing, the passengers could have done something else for those many hours rather than hang around the airport, checking the departures board for status. Also no compensation given...but that's another discussion. No, it would not have changed the delay/cancellation situation, but if an agent had said check back in x number of hours, then actually come to the gate at that time, people could have done something else. I've worked in customer service before. Customers want to know what's happening if only to be told "this is the problem, we're still working on it..."

  human annot.: 3; 3; 5; 2; (mean = 3.25)
  moderated: no
  automatic AQ: 3.7

- Example 3 I do not think there should be a compensation cap. If a passenger is bumped from a flight and misses an important business meeting, high school graduation or wedding, there is no price that can compensate for that. Certainly not $1300. In addition, even if the entire flight fare is refunded (easily over $1300 on some long overseas flights), there are other costs that the bumped passenger could face such as non-refundable/prepaid hotel reservations or other travel and travel related expenses. If a passenger can prove that he or she has additional expense above and beyond what the airline offers and the government requires he or she should be awarded more compensation.

  human annot.: 5; 5; 5; 4; (mean = 4.75)
  moderated: yes
  automatic AQ: 3.7

  Moderator response: Note that the proposed regulation states that for delays longer then 2hrs, a passenger can receive compensation amounting to double the price of their ticket or up to $1300. I understand that you think that the cap is too low, but does this doubling of the price of the ticket address your concern that non-refundable expenses should be paid for as well? Or would you propose something like double the ticket price and expenses on top of that? At what point, if any, do you think it becomes unfair for the airline to have to pay these expenses?

A.6 Annotation guidelines

The Annotation Guidelines are depicted in Figure 4.

1 Introduction

In this annotation study you should estimate the argument quality of comments taken from an online discussion forum, called *RegulationRoom*. For each comment you have to give a score from 0 (very low quality) to 5 (very high quality).

Before you start annotating, have a look at the additional information where you find an explanation about the type of data you are looking at and the topics the people have discussed there. Also have a look at the website of the discussion forum. *(link)*.

2 Annotation: General Guidelines

Read the comment and rate the quality with a score between 0 and 5 (0 equals to very low quality, 5 to very high quality). You can consider the following points when annotating the quality of the argument: Example

hints for bad quality	hints for good quality
language / grammar issues	well formed, grammatically correct
unclear / hard to follow / vague	unambiguous, avoids unnecessary complexity
weak /wrong reasoning	makes you think, well thought through, persuasive
off-topic / irrelevant	on-topic / relevant / interesting
no facts or examples as evidence	provides examples, facts as evidence
offensive / attacking / abusive	respectful tone, values / considers other opinions
inappropriate language or use of emotions	emotionally effective, makes you more open towards the perspective

1 and example 2 show two comments from RegulationRoom. The first one (1) is written in clear language and respectful tone. The user criticizes the rule, but without attacking the institution personally. The user refutes a potential counterargument with an official source and the argument is well structured so that it is understandable and easy to follow. This should be annotated with a high quality score. In the second example (2), the user becomes offensive towards the company. The users' opinion is clear, but it is not substantiated with comprehensible reasons. At the end, another personal attack is added that actually has nothing to do with the topic of discussion. This example should be annotated with a low quality score.

(1) Driver fatigue is not a real problem according to an FMCSA webinar, that was publicly was communicated on September 30, 2010, hosted by the FMCSA titled: 2009 " " Historic Truck Crash Declines. The number is 1.4% fatigue related accidents in trucking. No, I do not believe the EOBR will be effective of reducing truck crashes - mainly because it will be on the wrong vehicles. My primary concern is FMCSA falsifying its own information to make it seem that new regulations and such are needed. Plus, adding yet another COST to the trucking company or owner operator - without a firm reasoning

(2) The EOBR is a get rich in a hurry gift to the primary company that is making the unit is making a lot of money and on top of that we are forced to pay 40. dollars a month to stay compliant if that is not another way off letting government reach in your pocket to give it to there friends. And the FMCSA wonders why very few owner operators trust them.

1

Figure 4: Excerpt of annotation guidelines

Self-trained Pretrained Language Models for Evidence Detection

Mohamed Elaraby
University of Pittsburgh
mse30@pitt.edu

Diane Litman
University of Pittsburgh
dlitman@pitt.edu

Abstract

Argument role labeling is a fundamental task in Argument Mining research. However, such research often suffers from a lack of large-scale datasets labeled for argument roles such as evidence, which is crucial for neural model training. While large pretrained language models have somewhat alleviated the need for massive manually labeled datasets, how much these models can further benefit from self-training techniques hasn't been widely explored in the literature in general and in Argument Mining specifically. In this work, we focus on self-trained language models (particularly BERT) for evidence detection. We provide a thorough investigation on how to utilize pseudo labels effectively in the self-training scheme. We also assess whether adding pseudo labels from an out-of-domain source can be beneficial. Experiments on sentence level evidence detection show that self-training can complement pretrained language models to provide performance improvements.

1 Introduction

In the area of Argument Mining, obtaining high-quality manually labeled data is often a complicated and expensive task (Habernal et al., 2018). Therefore, utilizing unlabeled data can help to achieve further improvements over standard supervised models. Recently, pretrained language models have achieved significant improvements in a wide variety of downstream NLP tasks (Kenton and Toutanova, 2019; Liu et al., 2019; Yang et al., 2019). These models utilize large unlabeled datasets to learn meaningful representations that are transferable across several tasks. In this work, we extend the utilization of unlabelled data in Argument Mining by proposing to use *pretrained language models in a self-training manner*. We focus on evidence detection which is an essential component in building natural language systems that are capable of arguing and debating.

Self-training is a semi-supervised technique that employs unlabeled data by using a teacher model, trained on labeled data, to generate pseudo labels out of unlabeled examples (Yarowsky, 1995; Scudder, 1965). The pseudo labeled data are then blended with manually labeled data to train a student model of a similar or larger size of the teacher model. Another way to use pseudo labels is to blend them with labeled data and train a smaller student model. This method is referred to as knowledge distillation (Hinton et al., 2015).

In this paper, we seek to answer the following research questions:

Q1. Under which conditions can self-training improve finetuned pretrained language models? To answer this question, we experiment with three different techniques to utilize the automatically generated pseudo labels to assess whether large pretrained models can benefit from self-training or not. *(a) Bootstrapped self-training:* where we select automatically annotated instances of high confidence and add them to the training data during finetuning. *(b) Pretrain on pseudo labels:* where we use the selected samples in pretraining the model before finetuning on the manually labeled set. *(c) Masked language model pretraining:* where we use the selected samples to pretrain the model using a masked language model objective before finetuning the model on the manually labeled set.

Q2. Is there a constraint on the domain of unlabeled data? In our experiments, we employ both in-domain and out-of-domain unlabeled corpora.

Q3. Does increasing the similarity between labeled and unlabeled data improve self-training? We provide a retrieval step to filter unlabeled data by considering the most similar *N* samples to each example in the training data . Our aim is to increase the similarity between labeled and unlabeled data by filtration.

Our contributions are as follows. *(a)* We propose a thorough investigation of self-training meth-

Proceedings of The 8th Workshop on Argument Mining, pages 142–147
Punta Cana, Dominican Republic, November 10–11, 2021. ©2021 Association for Computational Linguistics

ods for *evidence detection* over large pretrained language models. *(b)* We empirically show that with proper adjustments, self-training can indeed achieve improvements over a pretrained baseline.

2 Related Work

Argument Mining spans various lines of research work. Stab and Gurevych (2014), Habernal and Gurevych (2017), and Persing and Ng (2015) focus on identifying and classifying argument roles in text. Another direction is to mine argument units that are relevant to specific claims or topics (Shnarch et al., 2018; Biran and Rambow, 2011; Levy et al., 2017). Our work directly extends the work in this area by Shnarch et al. (2018). *Evidence detection*, as viewed in this work, aims at classifying relevant sentences to a certain topic. Shnarch et al. (2018) benefits from large-scale weakly labeled data described in Levy et al. (2017) blended with manually annotated data to train a BiLSTM with GLoVe embeddings and integrate the topic with an attention mechanism. Our work also aims at making use of weakly labeled data. However, instead of using the retrieved data described in Levy et al. (2017) directly, we employ a teacher model trained on the manually annotated data to generate the pseudo labels for the unlabeled set.

Our work falls under the umbrella of semi-supervised learning. In natural language processing, the recent use of unlabeled data has focused on pretraining large language models (Kenton and Toutanova, 2019; Howard and Ruder, 2018; Radford et al., 2018), which has led to remarkable improvements across a wide variety of NLP downstream tasks. In Argument Mining, Chakrabarty et al. (2019) retrieved sentences with seeds as *In My Opinion (IMO)* and *In My Humble Opinion (IMHO)* and used them to finetune a language model before finetuning on a claims dataset. Reimers et al. (2019) used contextualized embeddings (*ELMo* and *BERT*) to classify and cluster argument components. In their work, they reported an 80% accuracy when finetuning BERT over the evidence data described in Shnarch et al. (2018) and 81% when concatenating the topic with the input evidence. Following the same line of work, we first finetune BERT over the same evidence dataset and use it as our baseline model. We then extend finetuned BERT by utilizing it as a teacher in a self-training manner, which hasn't been explored in the literature before.

Self-training has proven to be beneficial in a wide variety of tasks (Yalniz et al., 2019; Xie et al., 2020; Zoph et al., 2020; Kahn et al., 2020; Pino et al., 2020; Wang et al., 2021). In natural language processing, Ruder and Plank (2018) evaluated several semi-supervised baselines on sentiment analysis and part of speech tagging. They built their experiment over a BiLSTM baseline. While their work established solid baselines for semi-supervised learning in neural models, their methods focused on recurrent neural models. On the other hand, our experiments study self-training in the context of large pretrained language models.

Self-trained pretrained language models haven't been studied extensively in the literature. Du et al. (2021) studied self-training as another way of leveraging unlabeled data on top of large pretrained language models. They achieved 2.6% improvements in standard classification tasks. Khalifa et al. (2021) used simple bootstrapped self-training over *BERT* to improve zero-shot and few-shot classification of Arabic dialects. We instead use self-training on top of pretrained language models for sentence-level evidence classification. Our main incentive is to explore the utility of self-training techniques in *argument mining* where acquiring manually labeled data is usually hard to get in large quantities.

3 Datasets

3.1 Manually labeled dataset

We make use of the *IBM debater* evidence dataset[1] created by Shnarch et al. (2018), which is composed of 118 topics chosen from various debate portals. The dataset consists of 5785 topic-dependent sentences in total split into two sets: 4066 instances for training and 1719 instances for testing. For each topic, Shnarch et al. (2018) retrieved sentences from *Wikipedia* which are then manually annotated by 10 workers per topic. The crowd-annotators either select whether a sentence is *evidence* or *non-evidence* for a given topic. Table 1 shows examples from the *evidence* and *non-evidence* sentences in the *IBM debater* evidence dataset.

3.2 Unlabeled datasets

In our experiments, we rely on two sets of unlabeled (for evidence) data. The first one is an in-domain argumentative corpus from *Wikipedia*. The second one is a slightly out of domain (not

[1] https://www.research.ibm.com/artificial-intelligence/project-debater/

sentences	
Topic: "We should limit executive compensation"	
evidence	A February 2009 report, published by the Institute for Policy Studies notes the impact excessive executive compensation has on taxpayers: U.S. taxpayers subsidize excessive executive compensation - by more than $20 billion per year - via a variety of tax and accounting loopholes.
non-evidence	A say on pay - a non-binding vote of the general meeting to approve director pay packages, is practised in a growing number of countries.

Table 1: Labeled *Wikipedia* examples in the *IBM Debater* evidence dataset

Wikipedia) argumentative corpus called Webis-Debate-16, that is unlike Wikipedia, constructed from online debates.

Wikipedia unlabeled data. Following the method described in Levy et al. (2017), we use the data retrieved by querying *Wikipedia* with a query composed of *"that" + topic_concept*. The work done by (Shnarch et al., 2018) suggests that the previous query can yield argumentative sentences in general, not just claims . The resultant corpus is composed of $29k$ candidate sentences. Table 2 shows an example unlabeled retrieved sentence out of *Wikipedia*.

sentences	
Topic: "Doping in sport"	
example	In October, the International Volleyball Federation closed the doping charges after concluding that "there is no evidence of an anti-doping rule violation" [REF].

Table 2: Unlabeled example retrieved from *Wikipedia*

Webis-Debate-16 dataset. In order to assess whether out of domain unlabeled data can improve performance, we experiment with the Webis-Debate-16 corpus[2] (created from debates extracted from *idebate.org*) as an unlabeled argumentative source for evidence detection. The dataset is labeled on the sentence level with argumentative versus non-argumentative labels. The dataset contains 10846 argumentative phrases and 5556 non-argumentative phrases, therefore, we utilize it as an unlabeled (for evidence) argumentative source. Table 3 shows examples of non-argumentative and argumentative sentences from the Webis-Debate-16 corpus.

[2]https://webis.de/data/webis-debate-16.html

sentences	
Debate Topic: "Economy"	
non-argumentative	the price tag was set as being £32.7billion.
argumentative	"high speed two will help to solve this inequality by increasing connections between north and south ."

Table 3: (Non-)Argumentative examples (unlabeled for evidence) in the Webis-Debate-16 dataset

4 Approach

Our primary goal is to investigate different methods of self-training on top of large pretrained language models for evidence extraction.

4.1 Finetune-BERT baseline

We start with finetune-BERT as our baseline, which achieved the best results on *IBM Debater* evidence dataset in Reimers et al. (2019). In our experiments, we refer to this baseline as *evidenceBERT*.

4.2 Bootstrapped self-training

Our first self-training setting is bootstrapped self-training, where we employ *evidenceBERT* to annotate unlabeled data. Every epoch, we make predictions over unlabeled data U. For each instance x in U, we extract the probability assigned to the most likely class $p(x) = argmaxM(x)$ where $x \epsilon U$ and M is our *evidenceBERT*. The examples are then ranked based on the probabilities and the *top N* examples selected. In our experiments, we determine N by choosing the percentile of the top examples. Due to limited computational resources, we vary the percentiles from 10% to maximum 50%.

4.3 Pretrain on pseudo labels

Weakly labeled data has been used in pre-training neural models in information retrieval (Dehghani et al., 2017) and sentiment analysis (Severyn and Moschitti, 2015). We employ the generated pseudo labels from *evidenceBERT* to initially finetune BERT before finetuning over the manually labeled set.

4.4 Masked language model pretraining

In these experiments, we use the *top N* examples from the automatically labeled data to train on a masked language model objective. We finetune the masked language model using Wolf et al. (2019).

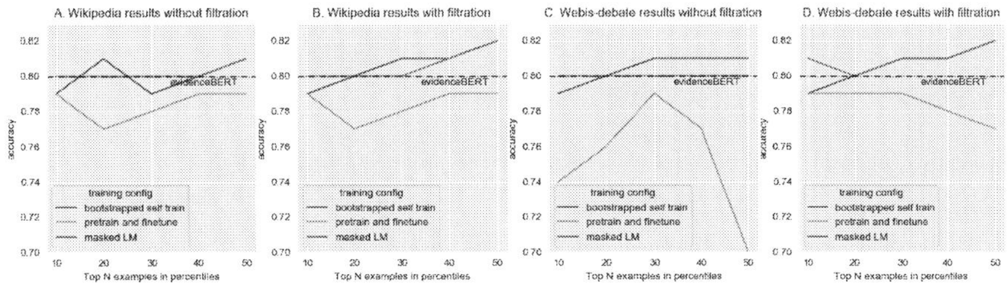

Figure 1: Self-training techniques results

4.5 K-nearest neighbors based filtration

Following the selection from unlabeled data method in Du et al. (2021), we encode manually labeled and unlabeled datasets using *XMLR RoBERTa* (Conneau et al., 2020) which achieves state-of-the-art results on the Semantic Textual Similarity benchmark (Cer et al., 2017). Then, for each instance in the manually labeled set, we select the top 5 nearest neighbors from the unlabeled set. We hypothesize that this process will yield more evidence like data from the whole argumentative set. We employ the new retrieved set in the three configurations of self-training we experiment with.

5 Results

After presenting the baseline pretrained finetuned language model results, we discuss how adding the different self-training approaches sheds light on the three research questions introduced in Section 1.

evidenceBERT. We start by replicating the results in Reimers et al. (2019), using the *BERT* implementation from Wolf et al. (2019). For training hyperparameters, we finetune *BERT* for 6 epochs of training. We employ *Adam* (Kingma and Ba, 2014) optimizer for training and an initial learning rate of $4e-5$. We chose our training parameters based on a manual search optimized on 5% of the training data. We achieve an accuracy of 80% on the test set, which is almost the same result reported in Reimers et al. (2019).

***Q1.* Under which conditions can self-training improve finetuned pretrained language models?** Results suggest that by adding appropriate N pseudo examples, bootstrapped self-training and masked language model pretraining can improve accuracy over *evidenceBERT*. Figure 1 shows that both bootstrapped self-training and masked language model pretraining can improve accuracy by 1% to 2% over finetuned BERT at optimal N.[3] While both masked language model pretraining and bootstrapped self-training can improve performance, the masked language model pretraining is more robust to the selected N pseudo examples (e.g., masked language modeling never degrades baseline performance). On the other hand, Figure 1 implies that utilizing pseudo examples in regular pretraining always performs poorly when compared to the *evidenceBERT* baseline.

***Q2.* Is there a constraint on the domain of unlabeled data?** Comparing Figure 1 C and D to Figure 1 A and B, respectively, suggests that using an unlabeled corpus from a different distribution like *Webis-Debate-16* largely can achieve similar improvements as using unlabeled *Wikipedia*. This is true for masked language model pretraining and bootstrapped self-training, both when comparing results to *evidenceBERT* at optimal N pseudo examples (except for masked language modeling in C versus A) and with respect to robustness over N.

Q3. Does increasing the similarity between labeled and unlabeled data improve self-training? Comparing Figure 1 B and D to Figure 1 A and C, respectively, shows that increasing the similarity between labeled and unlabeled data yields improvements in terms of accuracy at optimal N, particularly when using out of domain unlabeled data as both masked language modeling and bootstrapped self-training improve. Robustness also improves.

6 Conclusion and Future Work

We explored a variety of self-training configurations for evidence detection on top of BERT. Results show that 1) self-training with bootstrapped self-training and masked language model pretraining (but not with pretrain on pseudo labels) can improve finetuned large pretrained language models such as BERT; 2) unlabeled data can be utilized from both in-domain (*Wikipedia*) or out-of-domain

[3] A similar level of improvement was found by Du et al. (2021) in classification tasks outside of argument mining.

(*Webis-Debate-16*) sources; and 3) filtration of unlabeled data via selecting nearest neighbors with semantic similarity improves results. Future plans include covering more Argument Mining tasks and domains, optimizing selection of nearest neighbors instead of using fixed k, and using various blending techniques of pseudo labeled data during training.

7 Acknowledgment

The authors would like to thank Ahmed Magooda, Nhat Tran, and Mahmoud Azab for their fruitful comments and corrections.

References

Or Biran and Owen Rambow. 2011. Identifying justifications in written dialogs. In *2011 IEEE Fifth International Conference on Semantic Computing*, pages 162–168. IEEE.

Daniel Cer, Mona Diab, Eneko Agirre, Iñigo Lopez-Gazpio, and Lucia Specia. 2017. Semeval-2017 task 1: Semantic textual similarity multilingual and crosslingual focused evaluation. In *Proceedings of the 11th International Workshop on Semantic Evaluation (SemEval-2017)*, pages 1–14.

Tuhin Chakrabarty, Christopher Hidey, and Kathleen McKeown. 2019. Imho fine-tuning improves claim detection. In *Proceedings of the 2019 Conference of the North American Chapter of the Association for Computational Linguistics: Human Language Technologies, Volume 1 (Long and Short Papers)*, pages 558–563.

Alexis Conneau, Kartikay Khandelwal, Naman Goyal, Vishrav Chaudhary, Guillaume Wenzek, Francisco Guzmán, Édouard Grave, Myle Ott, Luke Zettlemoyer, and Veselin Stoyanov. 2020. Unsupervised cross-lingual representation learning at scale. In *Proceedings of the 58th Annual Meeting of the Association for Computational Linguistics*, pages 8440–8451.

Mostafa Dehghani, Hamed Zamani, Aliaksei Severyn, Jaap Kamps, and W Bruce Croft. 2017. Neural ranking models with weak supervision. In *Proceedings of the 40th International ACM SIGIR Conference on Research and Development in Information Retrieval*, pages 65–74.

Jingfei Du, Édouard Grave, Beliz Gunel, Vishrav Chaudhary, Onur Celebi, Michael Auli, Veselin Stoyanov, and Alexis Conneau. 2021. Self-training improves pre-training for natural language understanding. In *Proceedings of the 2021 Conference of the North American Chapter of the Association for Computational Linguistics: Human Language Technologies*, pages 5408–5418.

Ivan Habernal and Iryna Gurevych. 2017. Argumentation mining in user-generated web discourse. *Computational Linguistics*, 43(1):125–179.

Ivan Habernal, Henning Wachsmuth, Iryna Gurevych, and Benno Stein. 2018. The argument reasoning comprehension task: Identification and reconstruction of implicit warrants. In *Proceedings of the 2018 Conference of the North American Chapter of the Association for Computational Linguistics: Human Language Technologies, Volume 1 (Long Papers)*, pages 1930–1940.

Geoffrey Hinton, Oriol Vinyals, and Jeff Dean. 2015. Distilling the knowledge in a neural network. *arXiv preprint arXiv:1503.02531*.

Jeremy Howard and Sebastian Ruder. 2018. Universal language model fine-tuning for text classification. In *Proceedings of the 56th Annual Meeting of the Association for Computational Linguistics (Volume 1: Long Papers)*, pages 328–339.

Jacob Kahn, Ann Lee, and Awni Hannun. 2020. Self-training for end-to-end speech recognition. In *ICASSP 2020-2020 IEEE International Conference on Acoustics, Speech and Signal Processing (ICASSP)*, pages 7084–7088. IEEE.

Jacob Devlin Ming-Wei Chang Kenton and Lee Kristina Toutanova. 2019. Bert: Pre-training of deep bidirectional transformers for language understanding. In *Proceedings of NAACL-HLT*, pages 4171–4186.

Muhammad Khalifa, Muhammad Abdul-Mageed, and Khaled Shaalan. 2021. Self-training pre-trained language models for zero-and few-shot multi-dialectal arabic sequence labeling. In *Proceedings of the 16th Conference of the European Chapter of the Association for Computational Linguistics: Main Volume*, pages 769–782.

Diederik P Kingma and Jimmy Ba. 2014. Adam: A method for stochastic optimization. *arXiv preprint arXiv:1412.6980*.

Ran Levy, Shai Gretz, Benjamin Sznajder, Shay Hummel, Ranit Aharonov, and Noam Slonim. 2017. Unsupervised corpus–wide claim detection. In *Proceedings of the 4th Workshop on Argument Mining*, pages 79–84.

Yinhan Liu, Myle Ott, Naman Goyal, Jingfei Du, Mandar Joshi, Danqi Chen, Omer Levy, Mike Lewis, Luke Zettlemoyer, and Veselin Stoyanov. 2019. Roberta: A robustly optimized bert pretraining approach. *arXiv preprint arXiv:1907.11692*.

Isaac Persing and Vincent Ng. 2015. Modeling argument strength in student essays. In *Proceedings of the 53rd Annual Meeting of the Association for Computational Linguistics and the 7th International Joint Conference on Natural Language Processing (Volume 1: Long Papers)*, pages 543–552.

Juan Pino, Qiantong Xu, Xutai Ma, Mohammad Javad Dousti, and Yun Tang. 2020. Self-training for end-to-end speech translation.

Alec Radford, Karthik Narasimhan, Tim Salimans, and Ilya Sutskever. 2018. Improving language understanding by generative pre-training.

Nils Reimers, Benjamin Schiller, Tilman Beck, Johannes Daxenberger, Christian Stab, and Iryna Gurevych. 2019. Classification and clustering of arguments with contextualized word embeddings. In *Proceedings of the 57th Annual Meeting of the Association for Computational Linguistics*, pages 567–578.

Sebastian Ruder and Barbara Plank. 2018. Strong baselines for neural semi-supervised learning under domain shift. In *Proceedings of the 56th Annual Meeting of the Association for Computational Linguistics (Volume 1: Long Papers)*, pages 1044–1054.

Henry Scudder. 1965. Probability of error of some adaptive pattern-recognition machines. *IEEE Transactions on Information Theory*, 11(3):363–371.

Aliaksei Severyn and Alessandro Moschitti. 2015. Unitn: Training deep convolutional neural network for twitter sentiment classification. In *Proceedings of the 9th international workshop on semantic evaluation (SemEval 2015)*, pages 464–469.

Eyal Shnarch, Carlos Alzate, Lena Dankin, Martin Gleize, Yufang Hou, Leshem Choshen, Ranit Aharonov, and Noam Slonim. 2018. Will it blend? blending weak and strong labeled data in a neural network for argumentation mining. In *Proceedings of the 56th Annual Meeting of the Association for Computational Linguistics (Volume 2: Short Papers)*, pages 599–605.

Christian Stab and Iryna Gurevych. 2014. Identifying argumentative discourse structures in persuasive essays. In *Proceedings of the 2014 Conference on Empirical Methods in Natural Language Processing (EMNLP)*, pages 46–56.

Zhepei Wang, Ritwik Giri, Umut Isik, Jean-Marc Valin, and Arvindh Krishnaswamy. 2021. Semi-supervised singing voice separation with noisy self-training. In *ICASSP 2021-2021 IEEE International Conference on Acoustics, Speech and Signal Processing (ICASSP)*, pages 31–35. IEEE.

Thomas Wolf, Lysandre Debut, Victor Sanh, Julien Chaumond, Clement Delangue, Anthony Moi, Pierric Cistac, Tim Rault, Rémi Louf, Morgan Funtowicz, et al. 2019. Huggingface's transformers: State-of-the-art natural language processing. *arXiv preprint arXiv:1910.03771*.

Qizhe Xie, Minh-Thang Luong, Eduard Hovy, and Quoc V Le. 2020. Self-training with noisy student improves imagenet classification. In *Proceedings of the IEEE/CVF Conference on Computer Vision and Pattern Recognition*, pages 10687–10698.

I Zeki Yalniz, Hervé Jégou, Kan Chen, Manohar Paluri, and Dhruv Mahajan. 2019. Billion-scale semi-supervised learning for image classification. *arXiv preprint arXiv:1905.00546*.

Zhilin Yang, Zihang Dai, Yiming Yang, Jaime Carbonell, Russ R Salakhutdinov, and Quoc V Le. 2019. Xlnet: Generalized autoregressive pretraining for language understanding. *Advances in neural information processing systems*, 32.

David Yarowsky. 1995. Unsupervised word sense disambiguation rivaling supervised methods. In *33rd annual meeting of the association for computational linguistics*, pages 189–196.

Barret Zoph, Golnaz Ghiasi, Tsung-Yi Lin, Yin Cui, Hanxiao Liu, Ekin Dogus Cubuk, and Quoc Le. 2020. Rethinking pre-training and self-training. *Advances in Neural Information Processing Systems*, 33.

Multi-task Learning in Argument Mining for Persuasive Online Discussions

Nhat Tran
University of Pittsburgh
nlt26@pitt.edu

Diane Litman
University of Pittsburgh
dlitman@pitt.edu

Abstract

We utilize multi-task learning to improve argument mining in persuasive online discussions, in which both micro-level and macro-level argumentation must be taken into consideration. Our models learn to identify argument components and the relations between them at the same time. We also tackle the low-precision which arises from imbalanced relation data by experimenting with SMOTE and XGBoost. Our approaches improve over baselines that use the same pre-trained language model but process the argument component task and two relation tasks separately. Furthermore, our results suggest that the tasks to be incorporated into multi-task learning should be taken into consideration as using all relevant tasks does not always lead to the best performance.

1 Introduction

Argument mining (AM) focuses on automatically identifying argumentative structures in text, and utilizing these structures in applications. AM tasks include identifying argument components (e.g., "claim") and relations between them (e.g., "support"). However, most AM studies have focused on monologues or micro-level models of arguments (Peldszus and Stede, 2015; Persing and Ng, 2016; Stab and Gurevych, 2017). AM in dialogues and macro-level models have received less attention (Bentahar et al., 2010; Chakrabarty et al., 2019b).

In this study, we extend the work of Chakrabarty et al. (2019b) in AM for persuasive online discussions. Particularly, we take advantage of a multi-task learning (MTL) approach to automatically identify the argument structures in persuasive dialogues that contain both micro-level and macro-level argumentation. We identify argument components (claim, components, non-argumentative) and two types of relations: intra-turn relations within one post and inter-turn relations across posts. Our results demonstrate that using MTL improves the performance of both argument component and intra-turn/inter-turn relation classification. However, further analysis shows that the tasks in the MTL configuration should be chosen carefully depending on the focused task. We then try several techniques to increase the innate low precision of the relation classification tasks due to the highly imbalanced data, specifically SMOTE (Chawla et al., 2002) and XGBoost (Chen and Guestrin, 2016). Our results demonstrate that SMOTE is not very helpful but XGBoost, when used with the representations learnt from MTL, can increase the precision and F-scores of the relation identification tasks.

2 Related Work

Our work is closely related to Chakrabarty et al. (2019b). Their system, called AMPERSAND, tackles three AM tasks on a dataset created from the Change My View (CMV) subreddit[1] (Hidey et al., 2017) and focuses on transfer learning approaches with BERT (Devlin et al., 2019) that take advantage of discourse and dialogue context. Specifically, they define three separate tasks: argument component classification and intra/inter relation identification. For the first task, the requirement is to classify a given sentence into either Claim, Premise or Non-argumentative. For the intra-relation identification task, given a pair of argumentative sentences from the same post, we need to answer if an argumentative relation between these two sentences exists. The inter-relation identification task is similar, except that the two sentences are from different posts. However, they treated the tasks of argument component classification and relation prediction separately and had independent BERT models for the tasks. Our approach works on the assumption that the three tasks are related to each other.

Many studies have shown that jointly learning several tasks during training usually leads to better

[1] https://www.reddit.com/r/changemyview

Proceedings of The 8th Workshop on Argument Mining, pages 148–153
Punta Cana, Dominican Republic, November 10–11, 2021.

performance in NLP problems (Søgaard and Goldberg, 2016; Yang et al., 2016; Liu et al., 2019; Peng et al., 2020). Focusing on one single domain and dataset, Eger et al. (2017) treats AM as a sequence tagging problem and uses sub-tasks such as component identification and relation classification as auxiliaries in MTL to improve performances. Schulz et al. (2018) also formalizes argument component identification as a sequence tagging problem but utilizes multiple datasets from different domains in their MTL setup. They observe that the results on a small AM dataset can be improved when other AM datasets are leveraged as auxiliary tasks. These approaches, however, work on monologues where each data instance is from one person and therefore ignore the macro-structure of arguments. Our work tackles AM at dialogical level, specifically on online discussion forums. We hypothesize that MTL can help represent both micro and macro structure and use BERT with a MTL setup to classify argument components and relations at the same time.

3 Data

We use the same data from Chakrabarty et al. (2019b). They reuse the CMV corpus (Hidey et al., 2017), where each sentence in a thread of the CMV subreddit is annotated as claim, premise or non-argumentative. Additionally, they annotate the argument relation among these propositions (inter-turn/intra-turn) and expand the corpus by annotating additional argument components using the same guidelines.

The final dataset consists of 112 threads with 2756 sentences. The proportions of claims, premises and non-argumentative components are 34%, 43% and 23% respectively. Although several types of relations are annotated, the relation identification task only uses a binary label to represent if a relation exists between two components. The dataset is highly imbalanced in terms of relations, with only 4.6% of 27254 possible pairs having intra-turn and only 3.2% of 26695 having inter-turn relations, making low precision a major modeling challenge.

Below is an example of a discussion. User A makes a claim and supports it with a premise (intra-turn relation). User B, however, disagrees with the reasoning made by user A (inter-turn relation).

> A: [I think the biggest threat to global stability comes from the political fringes.]$_{0:\text{CLAIM}}$ [It has been like that in the past.]$_{1:\text{PREMISE:SUPPORT:0}}$
>
> B: [What happened in the past has nothing to do with the present]$_{2:\text{ATTACK:1}}$

Realizing that the data size is small, Chakrabarty et al. (2019b) utilizes distant-labeled data and uses transfer learning for fine-tuning BERT depending on the context. The IMHO+context dataset (Chakrabarty et al., 2019a) is used as micro-level context data. This is a corpus of opinionated claims in the form of sentences containing the internet acronyms IMO (in my opinion) or IMHO (in my humble opinion) from Reddit. The assumtion is that a relation exists between a sentence containing IMHO and the following one. For macro-level context data, they use the Reddit quote feature and construct the QR dataset containing quote-response pairs. In Reddit, when responding to a post, a user can quote another user's response and this feature is used to highlight what part of someone's argument a particular user is targeting in the CMV corpus. Specifically, the QR dataset treats the quoted text and the following sentence as a positive inter-turn relation example. For a fair comparison, we also fine-tune BERT using both distant datasets.

4 Methods

We use AMPERSAND's (Chakrabarty et al., 2019b) two relation classification constraints. For intra-turn relations, the source has to be a premise and the target can be a premise or a claim. For inter-turn relations, the source must be a claim.

4.1 Multi-task Learning on BERT

We follow the architecture of Liu et al. (2019) for MTL. It has lower BERT encoder layers shared across all tasks with task-specific classification layers on top of them. In this procedure, each task can be either single-sentence classification or sentence pair classification, which fits our tasks of component classification and relation identification. The latter task can be further divided into intra-turn and inter-turn relations, resulting in three tasks in total.

We have three MTL configurations, each one represents a different combination of tasks incorporated in the MTL process. First, all three tasks are used for MTL (**MTL_ALL**). Second, only argument component and intra-turn relation tasks are used (**MTL_intra**). Third, in **MTL_inter**, the intra-turn relation classification task is excluded.

Our reason is that intra-turn and inter-turn relations can be different in nature and including inter-turn prediction could possibly degrade intra-turn prediction, or vice versa. The argument component classification task is essential for both relation identification tasks since it helps filter out pairs of sentences that do not follow the constraints. Thus, it is kept in all MTL configurations.

4.2 Low Precision in Relation Prediction

Due to imbalanced data with less than 5% of pairs having relations, low precision is expected. AMPERSAND (Chakrabarty et al., 2019b) attempts to increase intra-turn relation precision with window clipping. Specifically, the best F-scores are reported when limiting the prediction of an intra-turn relation to be within a window of 1. Since this approach only works for intra-turn relations and is dependent on the data, we instead try two universal approaches which are corpus-independent to raise model precision.

SMOTE (Chawla et al., 2002) is an oversampling technique where synthetic samples are generated for the minority class. It focuses on the feature space to generate new instances by using interpolation between positive instances that lie together.

Gradient boosting is also useful when data is highly skewed (Brown and Mues, 2012; Teramoto, 2009). We experiment using XGBoost (Chen and Guestrin, 2016), a decision-tree-based boosting algorithm, as the classifier on top of the BERT representation instead of the normal softmax layer.

4.3 Implementation Details

In the **MTL_ALL** setup, we first fine-tune the BERT model on the IMHO+context and QR datasets using both the masked language modeling and next sentence prediction objectives. We then fine-tune BERT using MTL by learning the three tasks jointly. For the **MTL_intra** configurations, only the IMHO+context data is used for the first fine-tuning step and only the argument component classification and intra-turn identification tasks are used in the MTL procedures. The same settings are applied for **MTL_inter**, but the QR data is used for the first fine-tuning step instead.

Peng et al. (2020) observe that additional fine-tuning after the training process can increase performance. They remove the last layer, which is basically a linear and a softmax layer on top of the BERT representation to make the final classification, of the trained model and replace it with a new untrained one. Then they use a smaller learning rate to continue training all layers on each specific task. We call this step *refinement*.

AMPERSAND uses an additional RST classifier and ensembles its result with the prediction from the BERT classifier to predict the existence of a relation. Rhetorical Structure Theory (RST) provides an explanation for the coherence of text, in the form of a tree where leaves represent elementary discourse units and other nodes represent discourse relations. Specifically, they create a RST parse tree for the concatenated two argumentative components and take the predicted discourse relation at the root of the parse tree as a categorical feature in a binary classifier. They also use a candidate target selection procedure built from extractive summarization for inter-turn relation identification. Since these two are not involved in training and only work as additional filters, we keep them unchanged.

For XGBoost, since the 768-dimension vector from BERT is too large, we reduce the dimension to 128 using a two-layer neural network (512 and 128 neurons, respectively). We did an experiment and see that this reduction only affects performance with XGBoost, so we keep the 128 dimensions for all models to make the comparisons fair.

5 Results

Using the same train/test split from **Ampersand** (10% of the data for testing) (Chakrabarty et al., 2019b), we compare our results with AMPERSAND. In Tables 1, 2 and 3, *XG* stands for XGBoost, *SMO* for SMOTE, and *refine* for the refinement step from Sec. 4.3. Best results are in bold.

To make the comparisons more consistent with our models, we applied refinement and XGBoost on top of the final BERT representation of AMPERSAND. The reported numbers from the second row of the tables are from our own rerun of Ampersand and therefore they are slightly different from ones in the original paper. Although we used the AMPERSAND published code, the difference in Pytorch version could be the cause for this discrepancy. The best results of AMPERSAND from the original paper (Chakrabarty et al., 2019b) are reported in the first rows of the tables as Ampersand*.

5.1 Argumentative Component Classification

Table 1 shows that compared to Ampersand, in two MTL configurations MTL_ALL and MTL_intra,

Method	C	P	NA
Ampersand*	67.1	72.5	75.7
Ampersand	67.1	72.3	75.3
+ *refine*	67.3	72.9	76.1
MTL_ALL	67.8	75.2	77.8
+ *refine*	**70.0**	**76.6**	**78.1**
MTL_intra	68.3	74.8	76.5
+ *refine*	69.5	75.1	76.9
MTL_inter	66.2	72.1	73.9
+ *refine*	66.8	73.4	75.3

Table 1: F-scores for 3-way Classification: Claim (C), Premise (P), Non-Argument (NA). The best results from Chakrabarty et al. (2019b) are reported as Ampersand*

Method	Precision		Recall		F-score	
	G	P	G	P	G	P
Ampersand*	16.7	15.5	73.0	70.2	27.2	25.4
Ampersand	16.7	15.5	73.0	70.0	27.2	25.4
+ *refine*	16.7	15.7	73.0	70.0	27.2	25.6
/w XG	17.0	16.5	73.1	68.9	27.6	26.6
MTL_ALL	17.4	15.9	72.1	69.6	28.0	25.9
+ *refine*	18.1	16.3	72.2	68.4	28.9	26.3
/w SMO	17.7	16.2	**73.1**	71.0	28.5	26.4
/w XG	20.8	19.5	72.4	**73.0**	32.3	30.8
MTL_intra	19.3	17.3	71.1	69.5	30.4	27.7
+ *refine*	19.9	18.4	71.8	70.2	31.2	29.2
/w SMO	20.0	18.4	69.3	70.1	31.0	29.1
/w XG	**23.6**	**22.5**	**73.1**	69.8	**35.7**	**34.0**

Table 2: Results for Intra-turn Relation Prediction

Method	Precision		Recall		F-score	
	G	P	G	P	G	P
Ampersand*	18.9	17.5	**79.4**	**75.6**	30.5	28.3
Ampersand	18.7	17.1	**79.4**	**75.1**	30.3	27.9
+ *refine*	19.3	18.1	77.8	**75.1**	30.9	29.2
/w XG	17.0	16.5	73.1	68.9	27.6	26.6
MTL_ALL	20.3	18.2	79.1	74.5	32.3	29.3
+ *refine*	20.3	18.3	79.1	74.5	32.5	29.4
/w SMO	20.5	18.0	78.8	74.9	32.5	29.0
/w XG	21.2	**19.5**	75.7	65.2	33.1	**29.7**
MTL_inter	20.1	17.9	79.1	74.0	32.1	28.8
+ *refine*	20.2	18.3	79.0	74.2	32.2	29.4
/w SMO	20.0	18.2	**79.4**	74.9	32.0	29.3
/w XG	**21.5**	18.8	77.5	67.4	**33.7**	29.4

Table 3: Results for Inter-turn Relation Prediction

F-scores are improved for all three classes. The MTL_ALL model achieves 67.8, 75.2 and 77.8 for Claim, Premise and Non-argumentative respectively. When the inter-turn relation identification task is removed from the MTL configuration, MTL_intra model observes a slight drop in Premise (0.4%) and NA (1.3%) but a small increase in Claim (0.5%). On the other hand, taking out the intra-turn relation identification task (MTL_inter) degrades the F-scores in all categories. This implies that in our setting, intra-turn relation identification plays a crucial role in classifying components. Furthermore, including only inter-turn relation identification can hurt component classification as MTL_inter is inferior to AMPERSAND.

The additional fine-tuning step on each separate task also helps boost the F-scores. We witness slight increases in all of the three classes for all of the MTL configurations and the Ampersand model with this refinement step. Our best results are obtained with the MTL_ALL model with refinement.

5.2 Relation Prediction

For each metric in Tables 2 and 3, we report results with both gold-standard (G) and predicted (P) components from the argument component classifier.

5.2.1 Intra-turn Relations

The results from Table 2 demonstrate that MTL is still helpful in this task. Both MTL_ALL and MTL_intra have higher F-scores in comparison with the equivalent version of AMPERSAND.

MTL_intra models outperform the equivalent MTL_ALL models in terms of precision and F_1 scores. This suggests that we should eliminate the inter-turn relation task from MTL specifically for the intra-turn relation task. Our reasoning is that the inter-turn relations have some special characteristics and are harder to identify, which leads to the decrease in performance for the intra-turn task when it is included in the MTL configuration.

The refinement step generally helps improve the performance, but the gain is not very remarkable, especially in the case of MTL_ALL when the increases in F-score are less than 1 point for both gold and predicted components.

The XGBoost classifier raises the already low precision scores noticeably for MTL. For both MTL configurations, precision scores are increased by at least 2.7 points while recall scores are not decreased by more than 0.4 points. This leads to an improvement in F-scores based on predicted components of 4.5 points for MTL_ALL and 4.8 points for MTL_intra. Our best results are obtained by using XGBoost on the features of MTL_intra. In contrast, SMOTE does not help much.

5.2.2 Inter-turn Relations

For this task, the results from Table 3 demonstrate that MTL models still generally outperform the comparable baselines, but the gap is marginal compared to the previous two tasks.

In contrast to intra-turn relation prediction, removing the intra-turn task does not always improve the result of the inter-turn task. In other words, MTL_inter models do not always outperform the equivalent MTL_ALL model. Also, the gain with XGBoost is now smaller, with less than 2 points in F-scores for both MTL configurations, regardless of gold-standard or predicted components. The reason is due to a now large recall drop (e.g., 9.3% and 6.8% drop for MTL_ALL and MTL_inter respectively, with predicted components).

For predicted components, MTL_ALL with XGBoost achieves the best F-score, while for gold components, MTL_inter with XGBoost is best.

6 Qualitative Analysis of Intra-turn Degradation using MTL_ALL

One noticeable observation from Section 5.2.1 and Table 2 is that the incorporation of the inter-turn prediction task into the MTL process indeed hurts the performance of intra-turn. To further analyze this phenomenon, we retrieve examples which were predicted correctly by MTL_intra but incorrectly by MTL_ALL. In many of these examples, there is a wrong "inference" that if A has an **inter-turn** relation with C and B has an **inter-turn** relation with C, then A has an **intra-turn** relation with B.

Below is a concrete example of this error. C_0 and C_1 are two argumentative components from post P_1, while C_2 and C_3 are two consecutive argumentative components from another post P_2 replying to P_1. The MTL_ALL model predicts there exists an intra-turn relation between C_2 and C_3, which is incorrect. In this example, C_0 presents a claim that "There have been many dark animated movies that become famous" and premise C_1 supports this claim with two examples of "The Iron Giant" and "Land Before Time". Although both C_2 and C_3 challenge the connection from one of the two mentioned movies to the claim of C_0, there should not be an intra-turn relation between them. C_2 and C_3 may both support a claim attacking C_0, but they do not support or attack each other.

> P_1: [There have been a great many "dark" animated movies and shows that grew to become extremely famous.]$_{\mathbf{C_0:CLAIM}}$ [If we're using a level of "dark" of the level of Brave Little Toaster then why did things like **The Iron Giant** and **Land Before Time** get a ton of love associated with them.]$_{\mathbf{C_1:PREMISE:SUPPORT:0}}$
>
> P_2: [**Land before Time** has about 15 other movies in the franchise which make it popular, much like toy story,]$_{\mathbf{C_2:PREMISE:ATTACK:C_1}}$ and [**Iron Giant** doesn't really deal with much that's terribly dark or controversial.]$_{\mathbf{C_3:PREMISE:ATTACK:C_1}}$

This type of error raises the number of false positive cases in intra-turn relation identification. As a result, the precision scores of MTL_ALL are inferior to MTL_intra.

7 Conclusion

We show that using multi-task learning with micro and macro structures represented improves the performance of argumentative component classification and two relation prediction tasks, both with and without *refinement*. Also, we observe that combining all tasks may not always be beneficial since we can have conflicts between some of them. Further, our results demonstrate that using the XGBoost model as the final classifier on top of the representation from BERT, while not affecting the recall much, raises the precision scores for the intra-turn and inter-turn relation tasks. In sum, we achieve better results with MTL compared to the single-task training of Chakrabarty et al. (2019b), with and without our refinement and XGBoost enhancements. Future plans include leveraging contextual information to further improve performance and conducting further analyses on the incompatibility between intra-turn and inter-turn relation identification task in MTL.

Acknowledgements

We would like to thank Ahmed Magooda, Mingzhi Yu, Muhammad Salem and Ravneet Singh for their constructive feedback on the initial draft of the paper and the anonymous reviewers for their helpful comments.

References

Jamal Bentahar, Bernard Moulin, and Micheline Bélanger. 2010. A taxonomy of argumentation models used for knowledge representation. *Artificial Intelligence Review*, 33(3):211–259.

Iain Brown and Christophe Mues. 2012. An experimental comparison of classification algorithms for imbalanced credit scoring data sets. *Expert Systems with Applications*, 39(3):3446–3453.

Tuhin Chakrabarty, Christopher Hidey, and Kathy McKeown. 2019a. IMHO fine-tuning improves claim detection. In *Proceedings of the 2019 Conference of the North American Chapter of the Association for Computational Linguistics: Human Language Technologies, Volume 1 (Long and Short Papers)*, pages 558–563, Minneapolis, Minnesota. Association for Computational Linguistics.

Tuhin Chakrabarty, Christopher Hidey, Smaranda Muresan, Kathy McKeown, and Alyssa Hwang. 2019b. AMPERSAND: Argument mining for PERSuAsive oNline discussions. In *Proceedings of the 2019 Conference on Empirical Methods in Natural Language Processing and the 9th International Joint Conference on Natural Language Processing (EMNLP-IJCNLP)*, pages 2933–2943, Hong Kong, China. Association for Computational Linguistics.

Nitesh V Chawla, Kevin W Bowyer, Lawrence O Hall, and W Philip Kegelmeyer. 2002. SMOTE: synthetic minority over-sampling technique. *Journal of artificial intelligence research*, 16:321–357.

Tianqi Chen and Carlos Guestrin. 2016. Xgboost: A scalable tree boosting system. In *Proceedings of the 22nd ACM SIGKDD International Conference on Knowledge Discovery and Data Mining*, KDD '16, page 785–794, New York, NY, USA. Association for Computing Machinery.

Jacob Devlin, Ming-Wei Chang, Kenton Lee, and Kristina Toutanova. 2019. BERT: Pre-training of deep bidirectional transformers for language understanding. In *Proceedings of the 2019 Conference of the North American Chapter of the Association for Computational Linguistics: Human Language Technologies, Volume 1 (Long and Short Papers)*, pages 4171–4186, Minneapolis, Minnesota. Association for Computational Linguistics.

Steffen Eger, Johannes Daxenberger, and Iryna Gurevych. 2017. Neural end-to-end learning for computational argumentation mining. In *Proceedings of the 55th Annual Meeting of the Association for Computational Linguistics (Volume 1: Long Papers)*, pages 11–22, Vancouver, Canada. Association for Computational Linguistics.

Christopher Hidey, Elena Musi, Alyssa Hwang, Smaranda Muresan, and Kathy McKeown. 2017. Analyzing the semantic types of claims and premises in an online persuasive forum. In *Proceedings of the 4th Workshop on Argument Mining*, pages 11–21, Copenhagen, Denmark. Association for Computational Linguistics.

Xiaodong Liu, Pengcheng He, Weizhu Chen, and Jianfeng Gao. 2019. Multi-task deep neural networks for natural language understanding. In *Proceedings of the 57th Annual Meeting of the Association for Computational Linguistics*, pages 4487–4496, Florence, Italy. Association for Computational Linguistics.

Andreas Peldszus and Manfred Stede. 2015. Joint prediction in MST-style discourse parsing for argumentation mining. In *Proceedings of the 2015 Conference on Empirical Methods in Natural Language Processing*, pages 938–948, Lisbon, Portugal. Association for Computational Linguistics.

Yifan Peng, Qingyu Chen, and Zhiyong Lu. 2020. An empirical study of multi-task learning on BERT for biomedical text mining. In *Proceedings of the 19th SIGBioMed Workshop on Biomedical Language Processing*, pages 205–214, Online. Association for Computational Linguistics.

Isaac Persing and Vincent Ng. 2016. End-to-end argumentation mining in student essays. In *Proceedings of the 2016 Conference of the North American Chapter of the Association for Computational Linguistics: Human Language Technologies*, pages 1384–1394, San Diego, California. Association for Computational Linguistics.

Claudia Schulz, Steffen Eger, Johannes Daxenberger, Tobias Kahse, and Iryna Gurevych. 2018. Multi-task learning for argumentation mining in low-resource settings. In *Proceedings of the 2018 Conference of the North American Chapter of the Association for Computational Linguistics: Human Language Technologies, Volume 2 (Short Papers)*, pages 35–41, New Orleans, Louisiana. Association for Computational Linguistics.

Anders Søgaard and Yoav Goldberg. 2016. Deep multi-task learning with low level tasks supervised at lower layers. In *Proceedings of the 54th Annual Meeting of the Association for Computational Linguistics (Volume 2: Short Papers)*, pages 231–235, Berlin, Germany. Association for Computational Linguistics.

Christian Stab and Iryna Gurevych. 2017. Parsing argumentation structures in persuasive essays. *Computational Linguistics*, 43(3):619–659.

Reiji Teramoto. 2009. Balanced gradient boosting from imbalanced data for clinical outcome prediction. *Statistical applications in genetics and molecular biology*, 8(1).

Zhilin Yang, Ruslan Salakhutdinov, and William W. Cohen. 2016. Multi-task cross-lingual sequence tagging from scratch. *CoRR*, abs/1603.06270.

Overview of the 2021 Key Point Analysis Shared Task

Roni Friedman*, Lena Dankin*, Yufang Hou, Ranit Aharonov, Yoav Katz and Noam Slonim
IBM Research
{roni.friedman-melamed,lenad,ranit.aharonov2,katz,noams}@il.ibm.com
yhou@ie.ibm.com

Abstract

We describe the 2021 Key Point Analysis (KPA-2021) shared task on key point analysis that we organized as a part of the 8th Workshop on Argument Mining (ArgMining 2021) at EMNLP 2021. We outline various approaches and discuss the results of the shared task. We expect the task and the findings reported in this paper to be relevant for researchers working on text summarization and argument mining.

1 Introduction

Key Point Analysis (KPA) was introduced in Bar-Haim et al. (2020a,b) as a challenging NLP task with tight relations to Computational Argumentation, Opinion Analysis, and Summarization, and with many practical applications (Bar-Haim et al., 2021). Given a potentially large collection of relatively short, opinionated texts focused on a topic of interest, the goal of KPA is to produce a succinct list of the most prominent key-points (KPs) in the input corpus, along with their relative prevalence. Thus, the output of KPA is a bullet-like summary, with an important quantitative angle. Successful solutions to KPA can be used to gain better insights from public opinions as expressed in social media, surveys, and so forth, giving rise to a new form of a communication channel between decision makers and people that might be impacted by the decision.

Various requirements govern the value of the KPA output. KPs are expected to be succinct, non-redundant, capturing points that are central to the topic of interest, and reflecting a clear stance towards that topic. Ideally, they should be at the right granularity for summarising the input data – not too specific and yet still informative and not overly general. In addition, accurate mapping of input texts to KPs is obviously essential. First, to ensure a reliable estimate of the prevalence of each key point. And second, to enable the user to drill-down, to gain a deeper understanding of the issues underlying each key point, as expressed by the input texts mapped to that key point.

The goal of the KPA-2021 shared task was to further increase the attention of the NLP community to this emerging task, while enriching the space of existing KPA solutions. Since providing a complete KPA solution is challenging, we divided the task into two tracks, enabling teams to participate only in the first, relatively simpler track. Specifically, in the first track, referred to as *Matching Track*, KPs are given as part of the input, and the task is focused on mapping input text to these KPs. In contrast, in the second track, referred to as *Generation Track*, no KPs are provided and the task requires to further generate the KPs. The data being considered for evaluation on both tracks are crowd sourced arguments on three debatable topics.

The nature of the KPA task requires to consider various evaluation measures to estimate the quality of the results across different dimensions. In this paper we report and analyze the results of 22 models submitted by 17 teams to the KPA-2021 shared task across these different evaluation measures. We also discuss lessons learned from these multiple submissions, that can guide future development of new KPA algorithms and associated evaluation methods.

2 Related Work

Our shared task is based on Bar-Haim et al. (2020a,b), which introduced the problem of KPA and proposed an extractive approach to address the task. In particular, we focus on benchmarking two sub tasks: (1) Key point matching; and (2) Key point generation and matching.

For the matching task Bar-Haim et al. (2020b) uses RoBERTa (Liu et al., 2019) based classifier, trained on argument-KP pairs. For the generation task (Bar-Haim et al., 2020b) employs the follow-

*These authors equally contributed to this work.

Proceedings of The 8th Workshop on Argument Mining, pages 154–164
Punta Cana, Dominican Republic, November 10–11, 2021. ©2021 Association for Computational Linguistics

ing steps: First, compiling a list of high quality arguments that serve as KP candidates. Next, a match confidence score is calculated between all KP candidate-argument pairs, as well as between all the KP candidates to themselves. Finally, several filtering and ordering strategies are employed to maintain the most salient, yet non-overlapping KP candidates to serve as KPs.

Below we briefly review the work closely related to KPA in a few fields.

Multi-document summarization (MDS). Most prior work on MDS has been focused on the news, Wikipedia, and scientific literature domains (Dang, 2005; Baumel et al., 2016; Liu et al., 2018; Lu et al., 2020). MDS techniques are typically query-based and extractive, where models select a set of non-redundant sentences that are most relevant to the query to include in the summary (Xu and Lapata, 2020). A few studies (Liu et al., 2018; Shapira et al., 2021) have explored generating the most salient queries the users might be interested in. However, it is still unclear how these salient queries/points are represented in the source documents. KPA addresses this problem by reporting the prevalence of each KP in the input data.

Opinion and argument summarization. Recently there has been an increasing interest in summarizing opinions expressed in various reviews (Amplayo and Lapata, 2021; Elsahar et al., 2021) or argumentative text (Wang and Ling, 2016; Chen et al., 2019; Syed et al., 2020). KPA contributes to this line of work by adding a quantitative dimension which reflects the distribution of opinions in the examined data. For a detailed discussion of the relation between KPA and argument clustering and summarization see (Bar-Haim et al., 2020a,b).

3 Task Details

3.1 Task Description

Given a collection of arguments, with either pro or con stance towards a certain debatable topic, the goal of the KPA-2021 task is to generate a KP-based quantitative summary. The *Generation Track* requires models to perform the entire task – i.e., generate a list of KPs for each topic and stance, and then predict for each argument in this topic and stance the confidence by which it is matched to each KP. Since this is rather challenging we also established the *Matching Track*, in which a set of KPs, generated by an expert per topic and stance, is given as part of the input, requiring models to only predict a match confidence score for each argument in the input, towards each of the provided KPs. In both tracks, the confidence score expresses the model's confidence that the KP represents the essence of the argument, and can be associated with it for the purpose of a KP-based quantitative summary. Since in the ground truth data (defined in the next section), only 5% of the arguments map to multiple KPs, we take a simplifying approach in the evaluation, where we consider for each argument only the KP with the highest confidence score as true positive.

Since in the ground truth data, a significant portion of the arguments are not matched to any KP, it is not enough for a model to rank the KPs per argument. Rather, it should also provide a threshold on the confidence that determines whether the highest scoring KP is matched to the argument, or whether this argument has no matching KP. In this shared task, we opted for a simpler approach, in which the submitted models are not required to determine the threshold. Rather, we evaluate all models by considering only the top 50% of the argument-KP pairs, as ranked by the confidence scores of all pairs.

The full terms of the KPA-2021 task can be found online[1].

3.2 The ArgKP-2021 data set

For KPA-2021 we use a data set covering a set of debatable topics, where for each topic and stance, a set of triplets of the form <argument, KP, label> is provided. The data set is based on the ArgKP data set (Bar-Haim et al., 2020a), which contains arguments contributed by the crowd on 28 debatable topics, split by their stance towards the topic, and KPs written by an expert for those topics. As described in (Bar-Haim et al., 2020a), crowd annotations were collected to determine whether a KP represents an argument, i.e., is a match for an argument, and based on these annotations every argument-KP pair received a label that can take three values: (i) positive - 60% or more of the annotations determined there is a match; (ii) negative - 15% or less of the annotations determined there is a match; and (iii) undecided - neither positive nor negative. For example, in the pro stance towards the topic "Homeschooling should be banned", and

[1] https://github.com/ibm/KPA_2021_shared_task

for the KP "Mainstream schools are essential to develop social skills", the argument "children can not learn to interact with their peers when taught at home" was labeled as positive and the argument "homeschooling causes a decline in education" as negative. The arguments in ArgKP are a subset of the IBM-ArgQ-Rank-30kArgs data set (Gretz et al., 2020), which consists of 30K crowd-sourced arguments on 71 controversial topics, where each argument is labeled for its stance towards the topic as well as for its quality.

The ArgKP data set, which is publicly available, served as the training data for our task. The 28 topics in the data set were split to train (24 topics) and dev (4 topics) sets and were offered to the participants with a recommendation to use as such in the preparation of their models. For *Generation Track*, in addition to the ArgKP data set, the participants were encouraged to use the remaining arguments from the IBM-ArgQ-Rank-30kArgs data set.

For a test set, we extended ArgKP, adding three new debatable topics, that were also not part of IBM-ArgQ-Rank-30kArgs. The test set was collected specifically for KPA-2021, and was carefully designed to be similar in various aspects to the training data[2]. For each topic, crowd sourced arguments were collected, expert KPs generated, and match/no match annotations for argument/KP pairs obtained, resulting in a data set compatible with the ArgKP format. Arguments collection strictly adhered to the guidelines, quality measures, and post processing used for the collection of arguments in IBM-ArgQ-Rank-30kArgs (Gretz et al., 2020), while the generation of expert KPs, collection of match annotations, and final data set creation strictly adhered to the manner in which ArgKP was created (Bar-Haim et al., 2020a).

The full data set, i.e., ArgKP together with the test set, is termed ArgKP-2021 and is available online[3]. See Table 1 for data statistics.

3.3 Evaluation Metrics

3.3.1 *Matching Track*

For the submitted prediction files, we extract argument-KP pairs as follows. First, each argument is paired with the highest scoring KP assigned to it (randomly chosen in case of a tie)[4]. Second, the top 50% of the argument-KP pairs are extracted for each topic and stance as an ordered list, based on the confidence score. Finally, given the ground truth data, Average Precision (AP, Turpin and Scholer (2006)), is calculated per topic and stance. Note that a perfect score of 1 can only be achieved when all top 50% matches are correct. We chose AP as the evaluation metric, since it supports evaluating the correlation between a model's confidence and prediction success. We obtain the mean AP (mAP) by macro averaging over all topics and stances so that each topic and stance has the same effect over final score.

When evaluating the models, we need to address the issue of the undecided argument-KP pairs in the labeled data. Considering a prediction of undecided pairs as a false prediction is too strict, since $> 15\%$ of the annotators found this match correct, and hence it is not entirely wrong. Discarding predictions of undecided pairs from the set of a model's predictions, as was done in (Bar-Haim et al., 2020a), is not relevant for KPA-2021, as it would have rendered the evaluation process inconsistent across different models. We therefore relied on two measures for this track - **relaxed** and **strict** mAP. In the strict evaluation score, undecided pairs are considered as wrong predictions, while in the relaxed evaluation score they are considered as correct, i.e., true positives. The final rank of a model in this track is the average between the rank of the model in the strict score and its rank in the relaxed score.

3.3.2 *Generation Track*

Models submitted to this track were evaluated on two aspects: The first is how well the set of generated KPs serves as a summary of possible arguments for this topic and stance. The second is how well does the model match between the arguments and the generated KPs. We note that evaluating only how well the arguments match the generated KPs is insufficient since one may obtain relatively high mAP scores by generating redundant and/or very general and non-informative KPs. It is therefore crucial to establish the quality of the set of KPs as a standalone evaluation. Due to the nature of this track, no ground truth data is available, and we therefore perform the evaluation of the submit-

[2]Those aspects include, among others – number of arguments in each topic; the distribution of their quality and length; the amount and style of expert KPs produced for them; as well the coverage of those as obtained by crowd labeling.

[3]`https://www.research.ibm.com/haifa/dept/vst/debating_data.shtml`

[4]In such cases, each experiment was repeated 10 times with different random seeds, and we report the resulting average. Standard deviation for those rare cases is insignificant.

Split	#Args	#KPs	Positive	Negative	Undecided	Strict coverage	Relaxed coverage
train (24)	5583	207	0.17	0.67	0.16	0.72	0.94
dev (4)	932	36	0.18	0.65	0.18	0.72	0.95
test (3)	723	33	0.14	0.73	0.13	0.69	0.91

Table 1: The ArgKP-2021 data set. The number of topics in each split is given in brackets. Coverage represents the fraction of arguments that have at least one matching KP. The strict view considers only argument-KP pairs with a positive label, while the relaxed view considers all pairs with a positive or undecided label. See text for details.

ted results using crowd annotations via the Appen platform[5]. The annotations were generated by a selected group of annotators which performed well in previous tasks, and further obtained good results in sanity-test questions and demonstrated high agreement with other annotators (Gretz et al. (2020), Toledo et al. (2019)).

The first evaluation considers the model's ability to correctly match arguments to KPs. As in *Matching Track*, an argument is matched to a single KP, and only the top 50% matches are considered for evaluation. Unlike *Matching Track*, here the evaluation of the match must be retrospective, since the KPs are provided by the submitted models. Following Bar-Haim et al. (2020b), we presented each argument to the annotators with its top matching KP, and asked if the KP matches the argument. Possible answers are 'Yes'/'No'/'Faulty KP'. We consider 'Faulty KP' as no match. Since here we directly ask regarding the predicted match, rather than showing annotators all possible pairs (as was done when generating the ground truth data for the *Matching Track*), we generate a binary label from the annotations by the majority vote, and compute a single mAP score.

The second evaluation aspect concerns the quality of the set of KPs generated by the submitted model. Here we asked annotators to perform a pairwise comparison between two sets of KPs, each taken from a different model, on the same topic and stance. We perform such pairwise comparisons between all pairs of top models according to *Generation Track* mAP score. Each KP set is sorted, such that the more prevalent KPs according to this model's matching are higher in the list. KPs that match 1% or less of the arguments are not presented to the annotators.

The annotators are first asked to determine for each KP set what is the stance of the set towards the topic (All support the topic/All contest the topic/Most support the topic/Most contest the topic). This initial question is not positioned as a comparative question. However, annotators' answers are compared to the stance of the arguments of the KP set, and in case one model is correct and the other is not (either all or some KPs are judged not to be in the correct stance), this is counted as a win for the former. Two comparative questions follow: *Which of the two summaries is less redundant?* and *Which of the two summaries captures points that are more central to the topic?*, where the latter question aims for the relevance of the KP set. Possible answers for those questions are *Summary A/Summary B/Both are equal in this respect.* For each of the three questions, ranking is calculated using the Bradley-Terry model (Bradley and Terry, 1952), which predicts the probability of a given participant to win a paired comparison, based on previous paired comparison results of multiple participants, and thus allows ranking them. The final rank of a model in the KP set quality aspect is the average of the three ranks.

Finally, a model's rank in the *Generation Track* is the average of its rank in the mAP evaluation aspect and its rank in the evaluation of the KP set quality. In case of a tie between the two ranks, mAP score is given preference.

4 Submitted models

In total, 17 models were submitted to *Matching Track*, and 5 models to *Generation Track*. Note that some teams did not provide description for their model. Still, we show their results in the results section, but we cannot provide their descriptions.

4.1 *Matching Track*

As in other NLP related tasks, transformer based approaches are preferable among the participants, with a clear dominance of RoBERTa (Liu and Lapata, 2019). None of the participants found the undecided pairs as useful for training, thus training was focused only on positive and negative pairs. Most of the participants used the topic as an in-

[5]www.appen.com.

put to their models, and ignored the stance. We also note that some of the models (SMatchToPR, MatchTStm) utilized contrastive learning, taking advantage of the fact that arguments are provided with matched and unmatched KPs. **SiamBERT**, though not directly by contrastive learning, also shows two key points for one argument in training.

SMatchToPageRank (hereafter as **SMatchToPR**) (Alshomary et al., 2021) aims to learn an embedding space where matching argument-KP pairs are closer than non-matching pairs. This model has two inputs: (1) the argument; and (2) the concatenation of the KP and the topic. The tokens of each input are embedded using RoBERTa-large. Next, those inputs are passed to a siamese Sentence-BERT network that is trained with a contrastive loss.

Team **NLP@UIT** use ALBERT XXLarge (Lan et al., 2019) pre-trained model for sentence-pair classification for pairs of argument and KP. Five models are fine-tuned on different cross-validation splits, and for inference the average of all models is considered as the final score.

Modern Talking - RoBERTa-Base (hereafter as **ModrnTalk**) (Reimer et al., 2021) is a RoBERTa-Base model fine-tuned on the concatenation of arguments-kps pairs. At training, the model is warmed up on 6% of the data.

Enigma (Kapadnis et al., 2021) is based on a DeBERTa-Large (He et al., 2020) pre-trained model. The input to the model is the concatenation of KP, argument, and topic. The output of the DeBerta model is concatenated with the POS tags representation of the three text pieces, and then fed to two more dense layers.

Matching the statement (hereafter as **MatchTStm** (Phan et al., 2021) embeds each argument and KP separately along with their context that is represented by the topic and stance. RoBERTa is utilized to extract all text embeddings. Next, the statement pairs are passed to a fully connected network. Finally, a contrastive learning is employed by grouping matching and non matching arguments for the same KP in a single batch.

poledro (Cosenza, 2021) is a fine-tuned ALBERT-XXLarge model, similarly to NLP@UIT. The input to the model is a concatenated argument-KP pair.

XLNet is a vanilla XLNet-Large auto-regressive model (Yang et al., 2019) fine-tuned on argument-KP pairs.

RoBERTa-large-concat (hereafter as **RoBERTaLC**) is a fined tuned RoBERTa-large model. The input to the model is the concatenation of the topic, the KP, and the argument. Training data is balanced between positive and negative match examples by over sampling positive instances.

Siamese BERT classifier (hereafter as **SiamBERT**) is a siamese BERT (Devlin et al., 2019) based model trained on pairs of arguments and KPs. At each training step, the same argument with two different KPs, one that matches and one that doesn't, is passed to the model, and it learns to prefer the matching pair.

4.2 *Generation Track*

SMatchToPR applies an extractive approach. First, arguments with high quality scores (using (Toledo et al., 2019; Gretz et al., 2020)) are selected as KP candidates. Next, arguments with high matching score (using *Matching Track* models) are connected to form an undirected graph, where the nodes are the arguments. Finally, an importance score is calculated for each node, and most important nodes are selected as KPs. Note that KP candidates that have high confidence scores with other candidate are ignored, to ensure diversity.

Enigma approaches this task as an abstractive summarization task. First, Pegasus (Zhang et al., 2020) is fine-tuned with an input of concatenated arguments and topics. The set of corresponding KPs are provided as a ground truth summary. For each pair of arguments and the corresponding topic, several summaries were generated. Next, those summaries are ranked by the ROUGE-1 score with respect to the input pair, and the top 5 summaries are selected as KPs for each stance.

XLNet applies the XLNet model developed for *Matching Track* on all possible pairs of arguments, so that each argument is evaluated as a potential KP summarizing another argument. Arguments with the highest average confidence scores are selected as KPs.

5 Results

In addition to the submitted models, we evaluate the state of the art RoBERTa based model described in (Bar-Haim et al., 2020b) and in section 2, termed hereafter BarH.

5.1 *Matching Track*

Table 2 describes the evaluation results for the *Matching Track*. By definition, the relaxed mAP is higher than the strict mAP. Still, it is interesting to note that many models achieve a high relaxed mAP, while differences between models are more evident when considering the strict mAP. The top-ranked model in this track, SMatchToPR, is also ranked first when considering the average *value* of the mAP scores, as well as p@50%. However, the other models tend to swap positions when considering different measures, though there is a distinct group of high performing models. Figure 1(a) depicts strict mAP scores for each topic and stance, for the top performing models and for BarH. Evidently, some topic/stance pairs are easier than others for all models.

5.2 *Generation Track*

The results of the *Generation Track* are presented in Table 3 for both the matching aspect (mAP) as well as the quality of the generated KPs. The full results of the comparative annotation of the sets can be found in Table 6 in the appendix. In general, BarH clearly outperformed all submitted models, while SMatchToPR obtained the best results amongst the submitted models. Figure 1(b) shows the mAP scores for each topic and stance, for the top performing models and for BarH. We note that the inconsistent ranking of XLNet, namely first rank on relevance, while scoring much worse on other quality questions, stems from the fact that the model provided the set of KPs of the positive stance arguments for both the positive and negative stance. Although such a result can achieve high relevance, it fails when considering stance and redundancy, as indicated by the results.

It is interesting to note that BarH outperformed all submitted models by a significant margin, even though it had a relatively low rank in *Matching Track*. This could be due to its specific failure in matching to expert KPs in one of the topic/stance pairs (see Figure 1(a), second set of bars) coupled with the usage of macro-averaging.

When designing the task, we did not direct the participants regarding whether to use an extractive or abstractive approach for generating the KPs. Indeed, three models, BarH, SMatchToPR, and XLNet used an extractive approach, selecting specific arguments as KPs, while three models, Enigma, pa_vincent, and mozhiwen opted for an abstractive approach, generating KPs de novo. Evidently, the extractive approach prevailed. Out of the three models taking the abstractive approach, only Enigma generated comprehensible KPs. The other two, received near zero scores in the matching evaluation, and hence, according the to KPA-2021 terms, were not included in the KP set evaluation.

6 Additional Analysis

Accurate matching of arguments to KPs aims to properly reflect the prevalence of each KP in the data to facilitate more informed decision making. In this section we analyze how well different models were able to reproduce the presumably true distribution of KPs in the input data. To that end, we focus on the *Matching Track*, and consider the distribution of the expert KPs as the ground truth distribution. As can be seen in the top row of Figure 2(a), the five KPs provided by the expert for this topic and stance are not equally represented in the argument set. Nearly 40% of the arguments were matched by the annotators to "Social media regulation is required to deal with malicious users" (kp-1-9); around 30% were matched to "Social media regulation can help to deal with negative content" (kp-1-8); and so on. Correspondingly, for each model submitted in this track, we compare the distribution of KPs as predicted by its matching to the manually obtained ground truth distribution. To that end, we use the Jensen Shannon divergence (JSd). The smaller the divergence, the more accurate is the summary generated by a model (based on the 50% of the arguments that pass the threshold). We find that the average topic-stance JSd for the top 5 ranking models ranges from 0.152 to 0.238 (see Table 7 in the appendix for more details). Interestingly, the models which perform best in the *Matching Track* evaluation, i.e., have the highest mAP scores, are not those with the lowest JSd scores. This can also be seen in Figure 2(b). The rank of all models based on their JSd score is plotted vs. their rank in the matching task, for all topics and stances. Although it is evident that models which perform poorly on the matching task are also ranked low by JSd, the overall correlation is low. In other words, a model with sub-optimal matching capabilities may still perform relatively well in capturing the overall distribution of the KPs in the input data.

In the *Generation Track*, there is no single set of KPs, since each model generates its own set. It is

Model	Rank	Strict mAP (r)	Relaxed mAP (r)	Mean of mAP (r)	Strict p@50% (r)
SMatchToPR *	1	0.789 (1)	0.927 (4)	0.858 (1)	0.848 (1)
NLP@UIT *	2	0.746 (3)	0.93 (3)	0.838 (2)	0.827 (3)
ModrnTalk *	3	0.754 (2)	0.902 (6)	0.828 (4)	0.806 (5)
Enigma *	4	0.739 (5)	0.928 (4)	0.833 (3)	0.828 (2)
MatchTStm *	5	0.745 (4)	0.902 (6)	0.824 (5)	0.808 (4)
mozhiwen	5	0.681 (9)	0.948 (1)	0.814 (6)	0.784 (7)
fengdoudou	7	0.676 (10)	0.944 (2)	0.81 (7)	0.753 (13)
poledro *	8	0.717 (6)	0.901 (8)	0.809 (8)	0.799 (6)
Fibelkorn	9	0.706 (7)	0.872 (12)	0.789 (9)	0.779 (9)
XLNet *	10	0.684 (8)	0.869 (13)	0.777 (10)	0.765 (11)
RoBERTa-LC *	11	0.661 (13)	0.885 (10)	0.773 (11)	0.774 (10)
pa_vincent	12	0.596 (15)	0.893 (9)	0.744 (14)	0.689 (15)
BarH *	13	0.674 (11)	0.865 (14)	0.77 (12)	0.78 (8)
np-quadrat	13	0.601 (14)	0.877 (11)	0.739 (15)	0.729 (14)
niksss	15	0.672 (12)	0.857 (15)	0.764 (13)	0.759 (12)
SiamBERT *	16	0.555 (16)	0.729 (16)	0.642 (16)	0.678 (16)
yamenajjour	17	0.539 (17)	0.682 (17)	0.61 (17)	0.667 (17)
danielwaechtleruni	18	0.39 (18)	0.601 (18)	0.495 (18)	0.511 (18)

Table 2: *Matching Track* results. Ranks on each measure are in brackets. In addition to the official evaluation metrics, two more scores are provided: the average value of the strict and relaxed mAP values, and p@50% for the strict view. Submissions that provided a descriptions are marked with (*).

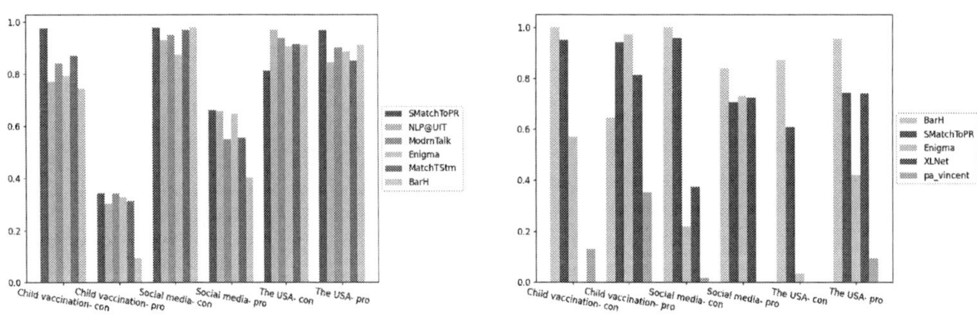

(a) (b)

Figure 1: AP per topic and stance for the top models and BarH. (a) *Matching Track*. (b) *Generation Track*. Missing bars mean a value of 0.

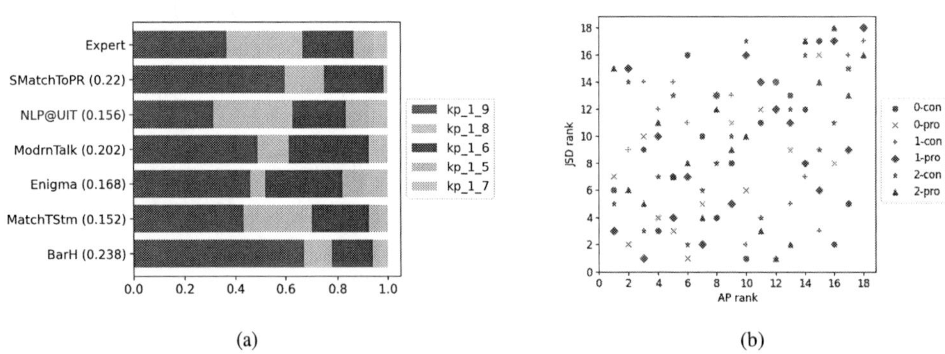

(a) (b)

Figure 2: (a): The distribution of KPs among the arguments, in the pro stance on the topic *Social media platforms should be regulated by the government*, for the expert ground truth (strict view) and selected models, normalized to the number of arguments that match to a KP. The JSd vs. the expert distribution is given in brackets. (b) JSd rank vs. AP rank for all models in the *Matching Track*, per topic and stance. The map between topic id, and topic text can be found at Table 4. Rank 1 means best performance.

Model	Rank	mAP (r)	KP set rank
BarH	1	0.885 (1)	1 / (1,1,2)
SMatchToPR	2	0.818 (2)	2 / (2,1,2)
Enigma	3	0.491 (3)	4 / (2,4,3)
XLNet	4	0.443 (4)	3 / (4,3,1)
pa_vincent	5	0.096 (5)	None
mozhiwen	6	0 (6)	None

Table 3: *Generation Track* results. KP set rank shows the overall rank and in brackets the rank on each of the three questions: stance, redundancy, relevance.

Topic id	Text
0	Routine child vaccinations should be mandatory
1	Social media platforms should be regulated by the government
2	The USA is a good country to live in

Table 4: Topics of the test set.

therefore not relevant to compare the distributions over KPs as done above. However, it is possible to perform a qualitative anecdotal analysis. Table 8 in the appendix lists the KPs generated for one topic and stance, by the expert and the different models. Importantly, the expert produced KPs *a priori*, without seeing the actual set of arguments; while the models generated KPs based on the input arguments. Inspection of the generated KPs suggests that correspondingly, some KPs were perhaps overlooked by the expert. For example, BarH generated a KP concerning keeping schools safe, and another one concerning prevention of pandemic outbreaks, both of which are not in the expert set, even though there are expert KPs that are related. In Table 5 we show an example of one expert KP, to which we manually matched generated KPs from the top 3 models, as an anecdotal distribution comparison. In this example, BarH and SMatchToPR extracted the exact same KP, yet in BarH it maps to 35% of the arguments, which is in line with the weight of this KP in the expert ground truth, while SMatchToPR maps it to a much larger fraction of the arguments.

7 Discussion

We presented KPA-2021, the first shared task focused on key point analysis. The shared task received 22 submissions from 17 teams, covering both the *Matching Track* and the *Generation Track*. We presented the submitted models, their performance on different evaluation measures, and further analyzed the results.

As expected by its simpler nature, *Matching Track* received more submissions. However, evidently, success in this intermediate matching task, does not guarantee success in the overall KPA task, which also requires generating the KPs. Future work should determine whether future KPA shared tasks should focus on the *Generation Track*, or perhaps modify the evaluation measures of the intermediate *Matching Track*, such that they better reflect the model performance in the full KPA task.

Given the inherent subjective nature of matching arguments to KPs, we opted for a ternary label, allowing argument-KP pairs to receive an "undecided" label, if the annotators votes were inconclusive. These undecided pairs are eventually considered either as positive or as negative matches, resulting with two gold standards, one potentially too strict, while the other perhaps too lenient. In future tasks, it may be valuable to consider a binary labeling scheme that will give rise to a single gold standard. Such labeling may be created conditionally, such that an undecided pair is marked as a positive match if and only if a minimum number of annotators marked it as positive and no other KP was labeled as matching to that argument.

A further point for future consideration, is the choice of a pre-defined threshold of 50%, that guided our evaluation. Although, this has the advantage of not requiring submissions to tune a confidence threshold, it has the limitation that it complicates the evaluation, since the ground truth coverage depends on the arguments, topic and stance. A possible alternative would be to require each model to set its own minimum confidence threshold to determine if an input argument should not be matched to any KP.

Finally, in this task, we used comparative evaluations to determine the quality of the sets of generated KPs. Obviously, this results with ranking-based evaluation. Establishing an absolute evaluation metric in this context merits further investigation.

We thank all participating teams for taking the time to participate in this challenging new shared task. We believe that these contributions, along with the data collected and shared in this report, will be valuable to further advance the research around KPA and related tasks.

Acknowledgments

We would like to thank Roy Bar-Haim for his helpful comments and suggestions.

Model	KP	Fraction
expert	Children should not suffer from preventable diseases	29.0
BarH	Vaccines help children grow up healthy and avoid dangerous diseases	35.0
SMatchToPR	Vaccines help children grow up healthy and avoid dangerous diseases	77.0
Enigma	Child vaccinations are necessary to protect against diseases in the child	50.0
	A mandatory vaccination is important to protect against diseases in the child	25.0

Table 5: KPs for *Routine child vaccinations should be mandatory* in the pro stance, related to the expert KP on the top row. Fraction is out of all arguments with a matched KP (for expert we use the strict view).

References

Milad Alshomary, Timon Gurcke, Shahbaz Syed, Philipp Heinisch, Maximilian Spliethöver, Philipp Cimiano, Martin Potthast, and Henning Wachsmuth. 2021. Key point analysis via contrastive learning and extractive argument summarization. In *Proceedings of the 8th Workshop on Argument Mining*, Online. Association for Computational Linguistics.

Reinald Kim Amplayo and Mirella Lapata. 2021. Informative and controllable opinion summarization. In *Proceedings of the 16th Conference of the European Chapter of the Association for Computational Linguistics: Main Volume*, pages 2662–2672, Online. Association for Computational Linguistics.

Roy Bar-Haim, Lilach Eden, Roni Friedman, Yoav Kantor, Dan Lahav, and Noam Slonim. 2020a. From arguments to key points: Towards automatic argument summarization. In *Proceedings of the 58th Annual Meeting of the Association for Computational Linguistics*, pages 4029–4039, Online. Association for Computational Linguistics.

Roy Bar-Haim, Lilach Eden, Yoav Kantor, Roni Friedman, and Noam Slonim. 2021. Every bite is an experience: Key Point Analysis of business reviews. In *Proceedings of the 59th Annual Meeting of the Association for Computational Linguistics and the 11th International Joint Conference on Natural Language Processing (Volume 1: Long Papers)*, pages 3376–3386, Online. Association for Computational Linguistics.

Roy Bar-Haim, Yoav Kantor, Lilach Eden, Roni Friedman, Dan Lahav, and Noam Slonim. 2020b. Quantitative argument summarization and beyond: Cross-domain key point analysis. In *Proceedings of the 2020 Conference on Empirical Methods in Natural Language Processing (EMNLP)*, pages 39–49, Online. Association for Computational Linguistics.

Tal Baumel, Raphael Cohen, and Michael Elhadad. 2016. Topic concentration in query focused summarization datasets. In *Proceedings of the Thirtieth AAAI Conference on Artificial Intelligence*, AAAI'16, page 2573–2579. AAAI Press.

Ralph Allan Bradley and Milton E. Terry. 1952. RANK ANALYSIS OF INCOMPLETE BLOCK DESIGNS: THE METHOD OF PAIRED COMPARISONS. *Biometrika*, 39(3-4):324–345.

Sihao Chen, Daniel Khashabi, Wenpeng Yin, Chris Callison-Burch, and Dan Roth. 2019. Seeing things from a different angle:discovering diverse perspectives about claims. In *Proceedings of the 2019 Conference of the North American Chapter of the Association for Computational Linguistics: Human Language Technologies, Volume 1 (Long and Short Papers)*, pages 542–557, Minneapolis, Minnesota. Association for Computational Linguistics.

Emanuele Cosenza. 2021. Key point matching with transformers. In *Proceedings of the 8th Workshop on Argument Mining*, Online. Association for Computational Linguistics.

H. Dang. 2005. Overview of duc 2005.

Jacob Devlin, Ming-Wei Chang, Kenton Lee, and Kristina Toutanova. 2019. BERT: Pre-training of deep bidirectional transformers for language understanding. In *Proceedings of the 2019 Conference of the North American Chapter of the Association for Computational Linguistics: Human Language Technologies, Volume 1 (Long and Short Papers)*, pages 4171–4186, Minneapolis, Minnesota. Association for Computational Linguistics.

Hady Elsahar, Maximin Coavoux, Jos Rozen, and Matthias Gallé. 2021. Self-supervised and controlled multi-document opinion summarization. In *Proceedings of the 16th Conference of the European Chapter of the Association for Computational Linguistics: Main Volume*, pages 1646–1662, Online. Association for Computational Linguistics.

Shai Gretz, Roni Friedman, Edo Cohen-Karlik, Assaf Toledo, Dan Lahav, Ranit Aharonov, and Noam Slonim. 2020. A large-scale dataset for argument quality ranking: Construction and analysis. *Proceedings of the AAAI Conference on Artificial Intelligence*, 34(05):7805–7813.

Pengcheng He, Xiaodong Liu, Jianfeng Gao, and Weizhu Chen. 2020. Deberta: Decoding-enhanced bert with disentangled attention.

Manav Nitin Kapadnis, Sohan Patnaik, Siba Smarak Panigrahi, Varun Madhavan, and Abhilash Nandy. 2021. Team enigma at argmining-emnlp 2021: Leveraging pre-trained language models for key point matching. In *Proceedings of the 8th Workshop on Argument Mining*, Online. Association for Computational Linguistics.

Zhenzhong Lan, Mingda Chen, Sebastian Goodman, Kevin Gimpel, Piyush Sharma, and Radu Soricut. 2019. ALBERT: A lite BERT for self-supervised learning of language representations. *CoRR*, abs/1909.11942.

Peter J. Liu, Mohammad Saleh, Etienne Pot, Ben Goodrich, Ryan Sepassi, Lukasz Kaiser, and Noam Shazeer. 2018. Generating wikipedia by summarizing long sequences. In *International Conference on Learning Representations*.

Yang Liu and Mirella Lapata. 2019. Text summarization with pretrained encoders. In *Proceedings of the 2019 Conference on Empirical Methods in Natural Language Processing and the 9th International Joint Conference on Natural Language Processing (EMNLP-IJCNLP)*, pages 3730–3740, Hong Kong, China. Association for Computational Linguistics.

Yinhan Liu, Myle Ott, Naman Goyal, Jingfei Du, Mandar Joshi, Danqi Chen, Omer Levy, M. Lewis, Luke Zettlemoyer, and Veselin Stoyanov. 2019. Roberta: A robustly optimized bert pretraining approach. *ArXiv*, abs/1907.11692.

Yao Lu, Yue Dong, and Laurent Charlin. 2020. Multi-XScience: A large-scale dataset for extreme multi-document summarization of scientific articles. In *Proceedings of the 2020 Conference on Empirical Methods in Natural Language Processing (EMNLP)*, pages 8068–8074, Online. Association for Computational Linguistics.

Hoang Viet Phan, Long Tien Nguyen, Long Duc Nguyen, and Khanh Doan. 2021. Matching the statements: A simple and accurate model for key point analysis. In *Proceedings of the 8th Workshop on Argument Mining*, Online. Association for Computational Linguistics.

Jan Heinrich Reimer, Thi Kim Hanh Luu, Max Henze, and Yamen Ajjour. 2021. Modern talking in key point analysis: Key point matching using pretrained encoders. In *Proceedings of the 8th Workshop on Argument Mining*, Online. Association for Computational Linguistics.

Ori Shapira, Ramakanth Pasunuru, Hadar Ronen, Mohit Bansal, Yael Amsterdamer, and Ido Dagan. 2021. Extending multi-document summarization evaluation to the interactive setting. In *Proceedings of the 2021 Conference of the North American Chapter of the Association for Computational Linguistics: Human Language Technologies*, pages 657–677, Online. Association for Computational Linguistics.

Shahbaz Syed, Roxanne El Baff, Johannes Kiesel, Khalid Al Khatib, Benno Stein, and Martin Potthast. 2020. News editorials: Towards summarizing long argumentative texts. In *Proceedings of the 28th International Conference on Computational Linguistics*, pages 5384–5396, Barcelona, Spain (Online). International Committee on Computational Linguistics.

Assaf Toledo, Shai Gretz, Edo Cohen-Karlik, Roni Friedman, Elad Venezian, Dan Lahav, Michal Jacovi, Ranit Aharonov, and Noam Slonim. 2019. Automatic argument quality assessment - new datasets and methods. In *Proceedings of the 2019 Conference on Empirical Methods in Natural Language Processing and the 9th International Joint Conference on Natural Language Processing (EMNLP-IJCNLP)*, pages 5625–5635, Hong Kong, China. Association for Computational Linguistics.

Andrew Turpin and Falk Scholer. 2006. User performance versus precision measures for simple search tasks. In *Proceedings of the 29th Annual International ACM SIGIR Conference on Research and Development in Information Retrieval*, SIGIR '06, page 11–18, New York, NY, USA. Association for Computing Machinery.

Lu Wang and Wang Ling. 2016. Neural network-based abstract generation for opinions and arguments. In *Proceedings of the 2016 Conference of the North American Chapter of the Association for Computational Linguistics: Human Language Technologies*, pages 47–57, San Diego, California. Association for Computational Linguistics.

Yumo Xu and Mirella Lapata. 2020. Coarse-to-fine query focused multi-document summarization. In *Proceedings of the 2020 Conference on Empirical Methods in Natural Language Processing (EMNLP)*, pages 3632–3645, Online. Association for Computational Linguistics.

Zhilin Yang, Zihang Dai, Yiming Yang, Jaime Carbonell, Russ R Salakhutdinov, and Quoc V Le. 2019. Xlnet: Generalized autoregressive pretraining for language understanding. In *Advances in Neural Information Processing Systems*, volume 32. Curran Associates, Inc.

Jingqing Zhang, Yao Zhao, Mohammad Saleh, and Peter Liu. 2020. PEGASUS: Pre-training with extracted gap-sentences for abstractive summarization. In *Proceedings of the 37th International Conference on Machine Learning*, volume 119 of *Proceedings of Machine Learning Research*, pages 11328–11339. PMLR.

A Appendix

Model	Stance	Redundancy	Relevance
BarH	95.46	42.73	28.63
SMatchToPR	2.91	42.92	28.62
Enigma	1.37	4.47	0.0
XLNet	0.27	9.89	42.76

Table 6: Bradley Terry scores for the comparative evaluation of the top models in *Generation Track*.

Model	Routine child vaccinations should be mandatory		Social media platforms should be regulated by the government		The USA is a good country to live in		Average
	pos	neg	pos	neg	pos	neg	
SMatchToPR	0.29	0.13	0.247	0.245	0.157	0.252	0.22
NLP@UIT	0.328	0.144	**0.0455**	0.205	**0.0585**	0.153	0.156
ModrnTalk	0.238	0.131	0.242	0.216	0.125	0.263	0.202
Enigma	0.223	0.131	0.232	**0.158**	0.146	**0.118**	0.168
MatchTStm	**0.181**	**0.105**	0.0797	0.245	0.107	0.196	0.152
BarH	0.431	0.172	0.236	0.205	0.121	0.261	0.238

Table 7: Jansen-Shannon divergence for top five models and the state of the art model. The divergence is reported for each motion, and is also averaged. Best score for each model is bolded.

model	key point	%
Expert	Routine child vaccinations should be mandatory to prevent virus/disease spreading	37
	Children should not suffer from preventable diseases	29
	Child vaccination saves lives	20
	Routine child vaccinations are necessary to protect others	8
	Routine child vaccinations are effective	6
BarH	to keep schools safe children must be vaccinated	35
	Vaccines help children grow up healthy and avoid dangerous diseases	35
	The use of child vaccines saves lives	11
	our children have the right to be vaccinated	6
	in this way, pandemic outbreaks are avoided	5
	After getting vaccinated, our immune system produces antibodies.	4
	Child vaccination should be mandatory to provide decent healthcare equally	2
SMatchToPR	Vaccines help children grow up healthy and avoid dangerous diseases	77
	child vaccinations should be mandatory to provide decent health care to all.	12
	child vaccinations should be mandatory so our children will be safe and protected.	9
Enigma	Child vaccinations are necessary to protect against diseases in the child	50
	A mandatory vaccination is important to protect against diseases in the child	25
	Children should be vaccinated against diseases	23
	Children should be vaccinated against diseases as soon as possible	2
XLNet	It is important to protect the health of the next generation so to do that means the routine child vaccinations have to be mandatory.	57
	vaccines must be compulsory for children because in this way we prevent later diseases in infants	11
	Making routine child vaccinations mandatory would prevent the unnecessary deaths and suffering that currently result from the diseases that the vaccines prevent.	8
	child vaccinations should be mandatory so our children will be safe and protected.	8
	Child vaccination has to be mandatory since it takes care of our children to be immune to any type of disease so I think it has to be mandatory	4
	childhood vaccines should be mandatory because a child at an early age needs to strengthen their immune system and the state should be in the power to provide such protection	4
	If routine infallible vaccinations are mandatory, that way we avoid the spread and make our children immune from any disease.	2
	The main reason is that many diseases have been prevented thanks to vaccines, thus millions of lives have been saved.	2
pa_vincent	vaccines have be able to protect diseases	46
	child are be used to prevent diseases	33
	parents vaccines should be safe for children	7
	vaccines harms risk of the child	6
	vaccines is important for protection	6

Table 8: Expert and generated key points for *Routine child vaccinations should be mandatory* pro stance. Fraction is out of all arguments with a matched KP (for expert we use the strict view).

Matching The Statements: A Simple and Accurate Model for Key Point Analysis

Viet Hoang Phan **Tien Long Nguyen** **Duc Long Nguyen** **Ngoc Khanh Doan**
School of Information and Communication Technology
Hanoi University of Science and Technology
`{hoang.pv180086, long.nt180129, long.nd183583, khanh.dn180110}@sis.hust.edu.vn`

Abstract

Key Point Analysis (KPA) is one of the most essential tasks in building an Opinion Summarization system, which is capable of generating key points for a collection of arguments toward a particular topic. Furthermore, KPA allows quantifying the coverage of each summary by counting its matched arguments. With the aim of creating high-quality summaries, it is necessary to have an in-depth understanding of each individual argument as well as its universal semantic in a specified context. In this paper, we introduce a promising model, named Matching the Statements (MTS) that incorporates the discussed topic information into arguments/key points comprehension to fully understand their meanings, thus accurately performing ranking and retrieving best-match key points for an input argument. Our approach[1] has achieved the 4th place in Track 1 of the Quantitative Summarization – Key Point Analysis Shared Task by IBM, yielding a competitive performance of 0.8956 (3rd) and 0.9632 (7th) strict and relaxed mean Average Precision, respectively.

1 Introduction

Prior work in Opinion Summarization often followed the extractive strategy, which identifies the most representative pieces of information from the source text and copies them verbatim to serve as summaries (Angelidis and Lapata, 2018; Brazinskas et al., 2019). Abstractive summarization is a less popular strategy compared to the previous one yet offers more coherent output texts. Approaches governed by this vein could generate new phrases, sentences or even paragraphs that may not appear in the input documents (Ganesan et al., 2010; Isonuma et al., 2021). Both extractive and abstractive methods are the straightforward applications of multi-document summarization (Liu et al., 2018; Fabbri et al., 2019), which has been an emerging research domain of natural language processing in recent years.

As is well known, in traditional multi-document summarization methods, the role of an individual or a subset of key points among the summaries is often neglected. To be more specific, Bar-Haim et al. (2020) posed a question regarding the summarized ability of a small group of key points, and to some extent answered that question on their own by developing baseline models that could produce a concise bullet-like summary for the crowd-contributed arguments. With a pre-defined list of summaries, this task is known as Key Point Matching (KPM). Figure 1 provides a simple illustration of the KPM problem, where the most relevant key points are retrieved for each given argument within a certain topic (i.e. context).

Inspired by the previous work that studied the problem of learning sentence representation (Cer et al., 2018; Reimers and Gurevych, 2019) and semantic similarity (Yan et al., 2021), we propose Matching The Statements (MTS), which further takes the topic information into account and effectively utilizes such proper features to learn a high performance unified model. Our approach has benefited from the recent developments of pre-trained language models such as BERT (Devlin et al., 2018), ALBERT (Lan et al., 2019) or RoBERTa (Liu et al., 2019).

Our contributions in this paper could be depicted as follows:

- Firstly, we design a simple yet efficient network architecture to fuse the context into sentence-level representations. Instead of letting the model infer the implicit reasoning structure, we provide our model with the information on whether an argument or key point (which are collectively referred to as statements in the remainder of this paper) supports its main topic or not.

[1]The code is available at: `https://github.com/VietHoang1512/KPA`

Proceedings of The 8th Workshop on Argument Mining, pages 165–174
Punta Cana, Dominican Republic, November 10–11, 2021. ©2021 Association for Computational Linguistics

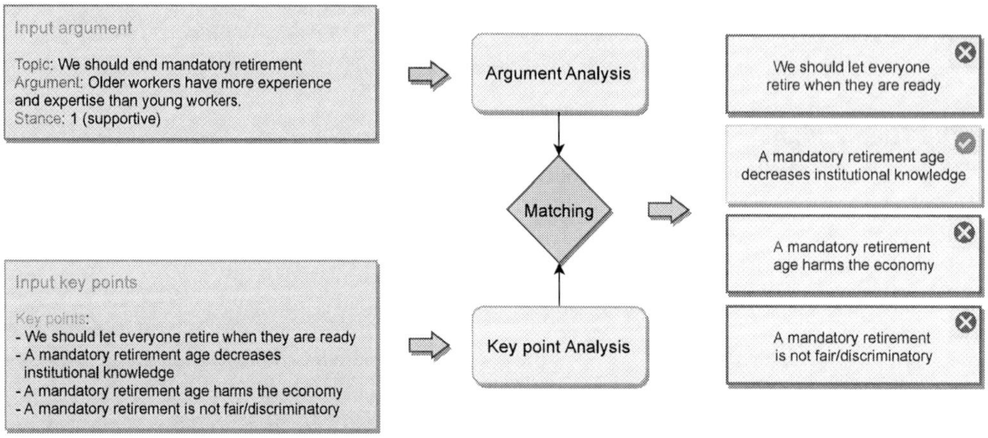

Figure 1: Overview of the Key Point Matching workflow in the Quantitative Summarization – Key Point Analysis Shared Task Track 1. From the information retrieval perspective, this task is to identify the most salient point that reinforces a given query.

- Secondly, our method adopts the pseudo-labels mechanism (Ge et al., 2020; Zhang et al., 2021), where we label arguments that belong to the same key point (and the key point itself) by the same index. The goal is to learn an embedding space in which the embedded vectors of mutual supportive statement pairs (i.e. having the same label) are pulled closer whereas unrelated ones are pushed apart.
- Finally, we validate the proposed MTS on the ArgKP-2021 (Bar-Haim et al., 2020) dataset in a variety of protocols. Extensive experiment results show that our proposed method strongly outperforms other baselines without using external data, thus becoming a potential method for the Key Point Matching problem.

The rest of this paper is organized in the following way: Section 2 briefly reviews the related work, while section 3 formulates the KPM problem. Next, we describe our methodology in section 4, followed by the experimental results in section 5. Finally, section 6 will conclude our work and discuss future directions for further improvements.

2 Related Work

A standard approach for key points and arguments analysis is properly extracting their meaningful semantics. Our model stems from recent literatures that are based on siamese neural networks (Reimers and Gurevych, 2019; Gao et al., 2021) to measure the semantic similarity between documents. Even though, MTS has its own unique characteristics to incorporate context information.

2.1 Sentence Embeddings

The representation of sentences in a fixed-dimensional vector space plays a crucial role in enhancing a model's performance on downstream tasks. Early methods relied on static word embeddings (Pennington et al., 2014; Bojanowski et al., 2017), which encoded a sentence by directly averaging its word vectors or employing recurrent neural network (RNN) encoders (Conneau et al., 2017) and taking the pooled output from the hidden units. Despite the fact that these methods can leverage both syntactic and semantic features, they often fail to retain the contextual information or suffer from slow training (due to the sequential nature of RNNs).

That is where BERT (Devlin et al., 2018) as well as its variants come in and dominate the modern NLP research. Training these architectures can exploit the parallel computational capacity of GPUs/TPUs hardware accelerators. In SBERT, Reimers and Gurevych (2019) proposed a sentence embedding method via fine-tuning BERT models on natural language inference (NLI) datasets. More recent studies in learning sentence representation followed the contrastive learning paradigm and achieved state-of-the-art performance on numerous of benchmark tasks (Liao, 2021; Yan et al., 2021).

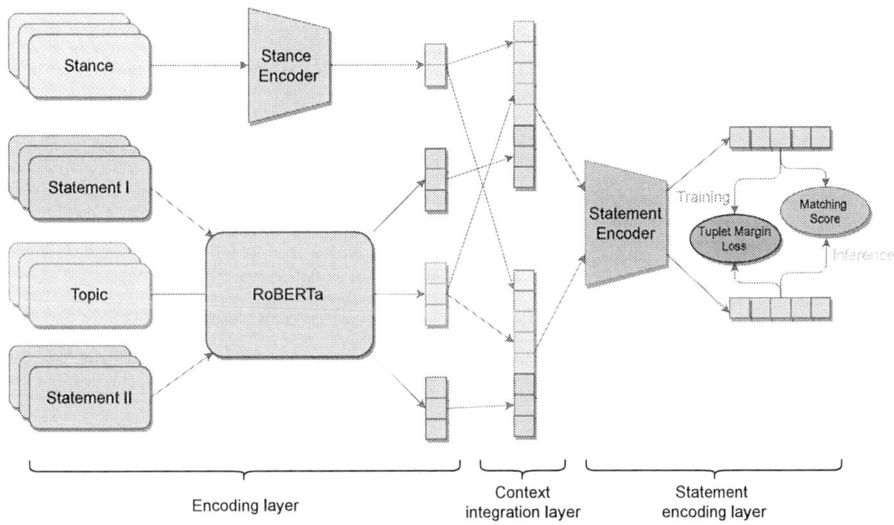

Figure 2: The overall design of our Matching The Statements architecture.

2.2 Semantic matching

Semantic matching is a long-standing problem and has a wide range of applications, such as: question-answering (Yang et al., 2015), text summarization (Zhong et al., 2020) and especially, information retrieval (Huang et al., 2013; Guo et al., 2016). Jiang et al. (2019) introduced a hierarchical recurrent neural network that could capture long-term dependency and synthesize information from different granularities (i.e. words, sentences or paragraphs). Similarly, Yang et al. (2020) replaced the RNN backbones with transformer-based models and modified self-attention architectures to adapt with long document inputs.

However, most of the existing work focuses only on assessing the similarity between pairs of sentences without paying attention to their context - which can help the reader to get an overview of the discussed topic. Recently, the ArgKP-2021 dataset has been published by Bar-Haim et al. (2020), which consists of annotations about whether two statements and their stances towards a specific topic match or not. The next sections will provide an overview of this dataset and how our model is applicable in the Quantitative Summarization – Key Point Analysis Shared Task [2].

3 Problem definition

In this shared task, we are provided with a dataset consisting of 28 different topics. Each topic contains a set of associated arguments and key points in the form of matching (with label 1) or non-matching (with label 0) pairs. The stances of these statements (whether a claim agrees or disagrees with its topic) are also exposed, we further evaluate the impact of this information in section 5.6.2.

In short, the Key Point Matching problem is formulated as follows: Given a controversial topic T with a list of m arguments and n key points $A_1, A_2, \ldots, A_m$; $K_1, K_2, \ldots, K_n$, along with their corresponding stances $S_1, S_2, \ldots, S_{m+n}$ ($S_i \in \{-1, 1\}$), which imply the attack or support relationships against the topic, our task is to rank key points that have the same stance with an input argument by the matching score. This priority is dependent on both the topic and the semantic of statements.

4 Methodology

The proposed MTS architecture is graphically shown in figure 2. It takes four separate inputs: (i) discussed topic, (ii) first statement, (iii) second statement, and (iv) their stance toward the topic. The final output is the similarity score of the fed in statements with respect to the main context. In the remainder of this section, we would like to describe three main components of MTS: encoding, context integration and statement encoding layers.

4.1 Data preparation

We observe that a small percentage of the arguments (4.71%) belong to two or more key points,

[2] https://2021.argmining.org/shared_task_ibm.html

while the rest are matched with at most one. For that reason, a straightforward idea is gathering arguments, which belong to the same key point, and label the clusters in order. In other words, each cluster is represented by a key point K_i, contains K_i and its matching arguments. Our clustering technique results in the fact that there are a small number of arguments that belong to multiple clusters. Arguments that do not match any of the key points are grouped into the NON-MATCH set.

Intuitively, if two different arguments support the same key point, they tend to convey similar meanings and should be considered as a matching pair of statements. Conversely, statements from different clusters are considered non-match in our approach. This pseudo-label method thus utilizes the similar semantic of within-cluster documents and enhances the model robustness. In the remainder of this paper, those arguments that come from the same cluster are referred to as positive pairs, otherwise, they are negative pairs.

During training, we use each key point and its matching/non-matching arguments (based on the annotation in the ArgKP-2021 dataset) in a mini-batch. Moreover, we also sample a small proportion of the NON-MATCH arguments and merge them into the mini-batch. Specifically, all the NON-MATCH arguments are considered to come from different and novel clusters. Because the definition of positive/negative statement pairs is well-defined, we can easily compute the loss in each mini-batch with a usual metric learning loss (Chopra et al., 2005; Yu and Tao, 2019).

4.2 Encoding layer

We first extract the contextualized representation for textual inputs using the RoBERTa (Liu et al., 2019) model. We adopt a canonical method (Sun et al., 2019) to achieve the final embedding of a given input, which is concatenating the last four hidden states of the [CLS] token. These embeddings are fed into the context integration layer as an aggregate representation for topics, arguments and key points. For example, a statement vector at this point is denoted as [3]:

$$\begin{aligned}\mathbf{h}^X &= [\, h_1^X, h_2^X, \ldots, h_{4\times 768}^X \,] \;\; (h_i^X \in \mathbb{R}) \\ &= [\, h_1^X, h_2^X, \ldots, h_{3072}^X \,]\end{aligned}$$

[3]For a consistent notation, statements and stances are denoted by uppercase letters: X and S

with 768 is the number of hidden layers produced by the RoBERTa-base model.

For the stance encoding, we employ a fully-connected network with no activation function to map the scalar input to a N-dimensional vector space. The representation of each topic, statement and stance are denoted as $\mathbf{h}^T, \mathbf{h}^X$ and $\mathbf{h}^S$, respectively.

4.3 Context integration layer

After using the RoBERTa backbone and a shallow neural network to extract the embeddings acquired from multiple inputs, we conduct a simple concatenation with the aim of incorporating the topic (i.e. context) and stance information into its argument/key point representations. After this step, the obtained vector for each statement is ($[;]$ notation indicates the concatenation operator):

$$\mathbf{v}^X = [\mathbf{h}^S; \mathbf{h}^T; \mathbf{h}^X]$$

where $\mathbf{v}^X \in \mathbb{R}^{N+2\times 3072}$

4.4 Statement encoding layer

The statement encoding component has another fully-connected network on top of the context integration layer to get the final D-dimensional embeddings for key points or arguments:

$$\mathbf{e}^X = \mathbf{v}^X\,\mathbf{W} + \mathbf{b}$$

where $\mathbf{W} \in \mathbb{R}^{(N+6144)\times D}$ and $\mathbf{b} \in \mathbb{R}^D$ are the weight and bias parameters.

Concretely, training our model is equivalent to learning a function $f(S, T, X)$ that maps the similar statements onto close points and dissimilar ones onto distant points in $\mathbb{R}^{(N+6144)\times D}$.

4.5 Training

In each iteration, we consider each input statement from the incoming mini-batch as an anchor document and sample positive/negative documents from within/inter clusters. For calculating the matching score between two statements, we compute the cosine distance of their embeddings:

$$\begin{aligned}\mathcal{D}_{\text{cosine}}(\mathbf{e}^{X_1}, \mathbf{e}^{X_2}) &= 1 - \cos(\mathbf{e}^{X_1}, \mathbf{e}^{X_2}) \quad (1) \\ &= 1 - \frac{\mathbf{e}^{X_1 T}\mathbf{e}^{X_2}}{||\mathbf{e}^{X_1}||_2\, ||\mathbf{e}^{X_2}||_2}\end{aligned}$$

Empirical results show that cosine distance yields the best performance compared to Manhattan distance ($||\mathbf{e}^{X_1} - \mathbf{e}^{X_2}||_1$) and Euclidean distance ($||\mathbf{e}^{X_1} - \mathbf{e}^{X_2}||_2$). Hence, we use cosine as the default distance metric throughout our experiments. We also revisit several loss functions, such as contrastive loss (Chopra et al., 2005), triplet loss (Dong and Shen, 2018) and tuplet margin loss (Yu and Tao, 2019). Unlike previous work, Yu and Tao (2019) use another distance metric, which will be described below.

Assume that a mini-batch consists of $k+1$ samples $\{X_a, X_p, X_{n_1}, X_{n_2}, \dots, X_{n_{k-1}}\}$, which satisfies the tuplet constraint: X_p is a positive statement whereas X_{n_i} are X_a's negative statements w.r.t X_a. Mathematically, the tuplet margin loss function is defined as:

$$\mathcal{L}_{\text{tuplet}} = \log(1 + \sum_{i=1}^{k-1} \mathrm{e}^{s(\cos\theta_{an_i} - \cos(\theta_{ap} - \beta))})$$

where θ_{ap} is the angle between e^{X_a} and e^{X_p}; θ_{an_i} is the angle between e^{X_a} and $e^{X_{n_i}}$. β is the margin hyper-parameter, which imposes the distance between negative pair to be larger than β. Finally, s acts like a scaling factor.

Additionally, Yu and Tao (2019) also introduced the intra-pair variance loss, which was theoretically proven to mitigate the intra-pair variation and improve the generalizability. In MTS, we use a weighted combination of both tuplet margin and intra-pair variance as our loss function. The formulation of the latter one is:

$$\begin{aligned}\mathcal{L}_{pos} &= \mathbb{E}[(1-\epsilon)\,\mathbb{E}[\cos\theta_{ap}] - \cos\theta_{ap}]_+^2 \\ \mathcal{L}_{neg} &= \mathbb{E}[\cos\theta_{an} - (1+\epsilon)\,\mathbb{E}[\cos\theta_{an}]_+^2 \\ \mathcal{L}_{\text{intra-pair}} &= \mathcal{L}_{pos} + \mathcal{L}_{neg}\end{aligned}$$

where $[\cdot]_+ = \max(0, \cdot)$.

As pointed out by Hermans et al. (2017); Wu et al. (2017), training these siamese neural networks raises a couple of issues regarding easy/uninformative examples bias. In fact, if we keep feeding random pairs, more easy ones are included and prevent models from training. Hence, a hard mining strategy becomes crucial for avoiding learning from such redundant pairs. In MTS, we adapt the multi-similarity mining from Wang et al. (2019), which identifies a sample's hard pairs using its neighbors.

Given a pre-defined threshold ϵ, we select the negative pairs if they have the cosine similarity greater than the hardest positive pair, minus ϵ. For instance, let X_a be a statement, which has its positive and negative sets of statements denoted by $\mathcal{P}_{X_a}$ and $\mathcal{N}_{X_a}$, respectively. A negative pair of statements $\{X_a, X_n\}$ is chosen if:

$$\text{cosine}(\mathbf{e}^{X_a}, \mathbf{e}^{X_n}) \geq \min_{X_i \in \mathcal{P}_{X_a}} \text{cosine}(\mathbf{e}^{X_a}, \mathbf{e}^{X_i}) - \epsilon$$

Such pairs are referred to as hard negative pairs, we carry out a similar process to form hard positive pairs. If a positive pair $\{X_a, X_p\}$ is selected, then:

$$\text{cosine}(\mathbf{e}^{X_a}, \mathbf{e}^{X_p}) \leq \max_{X_i \in \mathcal{N}_{X_a}} \text{cosine}(\mathbf{e}^{X_a}, \mathbf{e}^{X_i}) + \epsilon$$

4.6 Inference

At inference time, we pair up the arguments and key points that debate on a topic under the same stance. Afterward, we compute the matching score based on the angle between their embeddings. For instance, an argument A and key point K will have a matching score of:

$$\begin{aligned}\text{score}(\mathbf{e}^A, \mathbf{e}^K) &= 1 - \mathcal{D}_{\text{cosine}}(\mathbf{e}^A, \mathbf{e}^K) \\ &= \cos(\mathbf{e}^A, \mathbf{e}^K)\end{aligned}$$

The right-hand side function squashes the score into the probability interval of $[0, 1)$ and compatible with the presented loss function in section 4.5.

5 Experiment

To verify the effectiveness of the Matching The Statements model, we conduct extensive experiments on the ArgKP-2021 (Bar-Haim et al., 2020) dataset and compare the performance of MTS against baselines.

5.1 ArgKP-2021 Dataset

ArgKP-2021 (Bar-Haim et al., 2020), the data set used in the Quantitative Summarization – Key Point Analysis Shared Task, is split into training and development sets with the ratio of $24:4$. The training set is composed of 5583 arguments and 207 key points while those figures in the development set are 932 and 36. Each argument could be matched to one or more key points, yet the latter ones account for a small proportion of the data, as stated in section 4.1. The texts presented in ArgKP-2021 are relatively short, with approximately 18.22 ± 7.76 by words or 108.20 ± 43.51 by characters.

5.2 Evaluation protocol

For evaluation, only the most likely key point is chosen for each argument based on the predicted scores. These pairs are then sorted by their matching scores in descending order, and only the first half of them are included in the assessment. According to Friedman et al. (2021), there are two metrics used in Track 1, namely relaxed and strict mean Average Precision (mAP):

$$\textbf{Precision} = \frac{\text{True Positive}}{\text{True Positive} + \text{False Positive}}$$

Since there are some argument-key point pairs in the ArgKP-2021 dataset that have indecisive annotations (i.e. their label is neither matched nor non-matched): in the relaxed mAP evaluation, these pairs are considered as matched whereas strict mAP treats them as non-matched pairs.

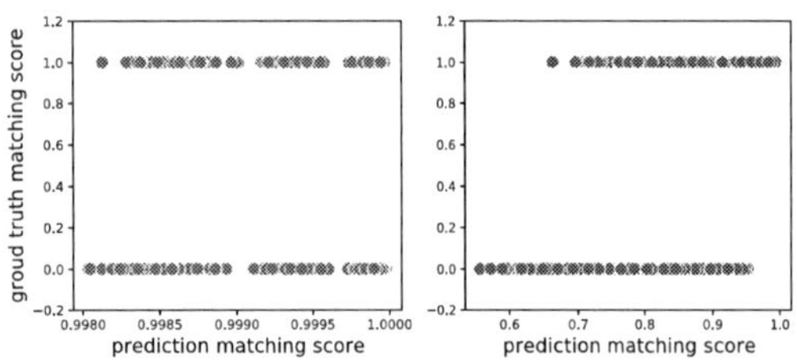

Figure 3: Statement representation before (left) and after (right) training.

5.3 Embeddings quality

Figure 3 depicts the qualitative representation learning result of MTS before and after training. In the beginning, the similarity scores between matched/non-match key point-argument pairs are extremely high (≈ 0.999). That means, almost all the statements are projected into a small region of the embedding space, and it is difficult to derive a cut-off threshold to get rid of the non-matching pairs.

Therefore, the mean Average Precision scores when we directly use the untrained model with RoBERTa backbone are relatively low. Though, our training procedure improves the model's distinguishability and reduces the collapsed representation phenomenon. Indeed, the similarity scores at this point are stretched out and the mAP scores significantly increase (strict mAP $0.45 \rightarrow 0.84$; relaxed mAP $0.62 \rightarrow 0.94$).

5.4 Baselines

For performance benchmarking, we implement two different baselines and their variations, namely Simple Argument-Key point matching (SimAKP)

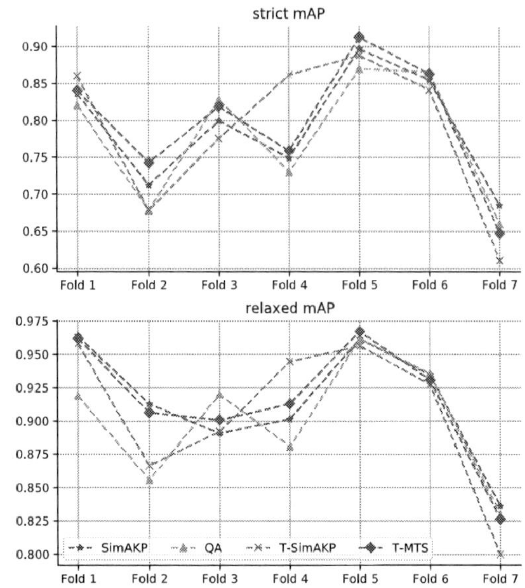

Figure 4: Mean Average Precision scores over 7 folds. The "T-" prefix denotes the models that use triplet loss (Dong and Shen, 2018) while the rest are trained with the contrastive loss (Chopra et al., 2005).

and Question Answering-liked Argument-Key point matching (QA) models. We construct a sampling strategy in an online manner: in each mini-batch, we select the hardest positive/negative pairs according to the method discussed in Section 4.5 to compute the loss.

Simple Argument-Key point matching: The architecture of SimAKP is the same as MTS with the main difference in the data preparation. Instead of clustering similar statements, SimAKP simply performs pair-wise classification on the ArgKP-2021 dataset. Equivalently, each input to the SimAKP model consists of an argument-key point pair. This approach will not make use of the analogous nature of these claims that matched with the same key point.

Question Answering-liked Argument-Key point matching: Inspired by the Question Answering, we format the arguments and key points fed to the RoBERTa model in order to incorporate the context into statements as below:

[CLS] Topic [SEP] [SEP] Statement [SEP]

[CLS] Topic [SEP] [SEP] Key point [SEP]

where [CLS] and [SEP] are two special tokens.

In particular, obtained outputs of RoBERTa model with the above inputs are then concatenated with the stance representations to produce a tensor with shape (batch size, $N + 3072$), which is fed to a fully connected layer to embed the semantic meaning of each individual statement.

5.5 Results

To facilitate evaluation, we set up a 7-fold cross-validation, each contains 24 topics for training and 4 topics for development. The train-dev split in Track 1 of Quantitative Summarization – Key Point Analysis Shared Task is replicated in fold 1.

As can be seen in Figure 4, we observe that our proposed MTS (we use triplet loss for a fair comparison) consistently outperforms other baselines in both mAP scores (higher is better). It achieved competitive scores on all splits, except fold 7. The reason is that the number of labeled argument-key point pairs of the development set in this part is the smallest among 7 folds, and there are substantial drops in terms of performance for all baselines.

Model	strict mAP	relaxed mAP
SimAKP	0.790 ± 0.072	0.914 ± 0.041
SimAKP w.o mining	0.783 ± 0.074	0.917 ± 0.037
T-SimAKP	0.788 ± 0.098	0.906 ± 0.054
T-SimAKP w.o mining	0.782 ± 0.101	0.901 ± 0.076

Table 1: The effect of hard sample mining in baselines.

We also examine the impact of hard negative mining in Table 1, the baselines are compared against themselves when using the hard mining strategy (i.e. avoid learning the embeddings of trivial samples). With the employment of hard mining, there is an improvement in performance for most baselines. Except for a small decrease in terms of relaxed mAP in SimAKP, both contrastive and triplet loss Simple Argument-Key point matching models have an average increase of 0.005% in mAP scores.

5.6 Differential Analysis

To provide insight analysis in the setting of Matching The Statements, we therefore create four different setups: original MTS, MTS with batch normalization (Ioffe and Szegedy, 2015) immediately after context integration layer, MTS without mining strategy, and triplet-loss MTS. Although tuplet margin loss has an up/down weighting hard/easy samples mechanism, we find that MTS with multi-similarity mining (Wang et al., 2019) performed best during the exploratory phase.

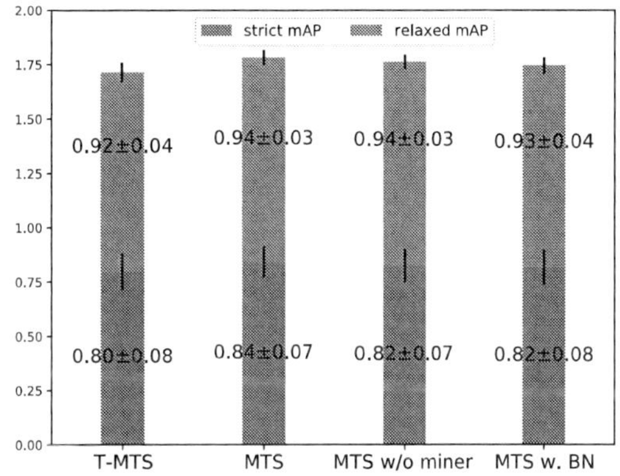

Figure 5: Switching off different setups shows that each component of the original MTS's setting contributes to its performance.

Figure 5 summarizes the average score for all setups. Overall, MTS performs similarly or better than its variants (without multi-similarity mining or adding a batch normalization layer). Replacing triplet loss with tuplet margin loss helps to boost both strict mAP and relaxed mAP by 0.2. Eventually, in an attempt to produce a consistent and accurate prediction on the test dataset, an ensemble of 4/7 best models from splits was used for final submission. As shown in Table 2, among the performances of the top-10 team, our proposed model achieved the third position in terms of strict mAP, 7th position in relaxed mAP and 4th overall.

#	Team	strict mAP	relaxed mAP
1	mspl	0.908 (2)	0.972 (3)
2	heinrichreimer	0.912 (1)	0.967 (5)
3	vund	0.878 (4)	0.968 (4)
4	**HKL (ours)**	**0.896 (3)**	**0.963 (7)**
5	sohanpatnaik	0.872 (5)	0.966 (6)
6	fengdoudou	0.853 (10)	0.98 (2)
7	mozhiwen	0.833 (12)	0.985 (1)
8	Fibelkorn	0.869 (6	0.952 (10)
8	emanuele.c	0.868 (7)	0.956 (9)
10	niksss	0.858 (8)	0.95 (11)

Table 2: Leaderboard of the Track 1 Quantitative Summarization – Key Point Analysis.

5.6.1 BERT embeddings

Here, we showcase the benefit of taking the concatenation of the last four hidden state layers of the [CLS] token as the aggregate representation for the whole document. The first part of Table 3 is a clear

Embedding	strict mAP	relaxed mAP	#Param
Sum all tokens	0.834 ± 0.065	0.938 ± 0.037	
Mean all tokens	0.796 ± 0.068	0.916 ± 0.034	125M
[CLS] last hidden layer	0.823 ± 0.072	0.937 ± 0.038	
[CLS] 4 hidden layers	$\mathbf{0.840 \pm 0.071}$	$\mathbf{0.941 \pm 0.034}$	126M
LUKE	0.808 ± 0.096	0.926 ± 0.056	276M
ALBERT	0.748 ± 0.071	0.879 ± 0.044	13M
MPNet	0.839 ± 0.059	0.940 ± 0.029	111M
DistilBERT	0.724 ± 0.065	0.864 ± 0.058	68M
BERT (uncased)	0.746 ± 0.062	0.888 ± 0.035	110M
BERT (cased)	0.752 ± 0.073	0.883 ± 0.057	

Table 3: Comparison between different embedding strategies and pre-trained language models. In this experiment, we report the result of the base version.

proof for this advantage, using only the last hidden layer of [CLS] can hurt the overall performance. Likewise, the mean-pooling or summing up the token embeddings has worse results, compared to our method.

To show the generality and applicability of our proposed model, we retain the MTS configuration when experimenting with other transformers-based backbones, such as: BERT (Devlin et al., 2018), ALBERT (Lan et al., 2019), DistilBERT (Sanh et al., 2019), LUKE (Yamada et al., 2020) or MPNet (Song et al., 2020). According to the second part of Table 3, among six pre-trained language models, MPNet yields a comparable result with RoBERTa (≈ 0.84 & 0.94) while requiring 10% less number of parameters. We also note that, the increase in model size of Language Understanding with Knowledge-based Embeddings (LUKE) compared with RoBERTa results in unexpected performance reduction.

5.6.2 Stance effect

Up till now, we have almost finished the needed experiments to examine the effectiveness of our methodology. In this subsection, we further investigate the importance of the stance factor in building the MTS model by posing a question: *"How good is MTS when it has to predict the implicit relation between claims and topic"*. Since the topic information is incorporated in encoding the statements, so perhaps it is sufficient to learn meaningful representations, without explicitly providing the stance information.

By discarding the stance-involved components in MTS 2, the averaged result in 7 folds conceivably degrades to 0.741 ± 0.094 in strict mAP but rises up to 0.952 ± 0.019 in relaxed mAP. This is because each argument now can be matched with key points that have different stances. According to this exploration, an open challenge for future research is finding a better way to comprehend statements within a topic (i.e. let the model infer the stance itself). For instance, one could consider employing the attention mechanism between a topic and its arguments and key points to characterize the relationship between them.

6 Conclusion

In this paper, we present an efficient key point matching method based on supervised contrastive learning. We suppose that clustering the statements will be beneficial for the model training, and empirically verify this conclusion in the experiments. In addition, we found a simple and effective technique to encode these statements, and thus yields superior performance. In terms of model architecture, the components are carefully designed to ensure productivity. Results on Track 1 of Quantitative Summarization – Key Point Analysis show our method is a conceptually simple approach yet achieves promising performance.

References

Stefanos Angelidis and Mirella Lapata. 2018. Summarizing opinions: Aspect extraction meets sentiment prediction and they are both weakly supervised. In *Proceedings of the 2018 Conference on Empirical Methods in Natural Language Processing*, pages 3675–3686, Brussels, Belgium. Association for Computational Linguistics.

Roy Bar-Haim, Lilach Eden, Roni Friedman, Yoav Kantor, Dan Lahav, and Noam Slonim. 2020. From arguments to key points: Towards automatic argument summarization. In *Proceedings of the 58th Annual Meeting of the Association for Computational Linguistics*, pages 4029–4039, Online. Association for Computational Linguistics.

Piotr Bojanowski, Edouard Grave, Armand Joulin, and Tomas Mikolov. 2017. Enriching word vectors with subword information. *Transactions of the Association for Computational Linguistics*, 5:135–146.

Arthur Brazinskas, Mirella Lapata, and Ivan Titov. 2019. Unsupervised multi-document opinion summarization as copycat-review generation. *arXiv preprint arXiv:1911.02247*.

Daniel Cer, Yinfei Yang, Sheng-yi Kong, Nan Hua, Nicole Limtiaco, Rhomni St John, Noah Constant, Mario Guajardo-Céspedes, Steve Yuan, Chris Tar, et al. 2018. Universal sentence encoder. *arXiv preprint arXiv:1803.11175*.

Sumit Chopra, Raia Hadsell, and Yann LeCun. 2005. Learning a similarity metric discriminatively, with application to face verification. In *2005 IEEE Computer Society Conference on Computer Vision and Pattern Recognition (CVPR'05)*, volume 1, pages 539–546. IEEE.

Alexis Conneau, Douwe Kiela, Holger Schwenk, Loïc Barrault, and Antoine Bordes. 2017. Supervised learning of universal sentence representations from natural language inference data. In *Proceedings of the 2017 Conference on Empirical Methods in Natural Language Processing*, pages 670–680, Copenhagen, Denmark. Association for Computational Linguistics.

Jacob Devlin, Ming-Wei Chang, Kenton Lee, and Kristina Toutanova. 2018. Bert: Pre-training of deep bidirectional transformers for language understanding. *arXiv preprint arXiv:1810.04805*.

Xingping Dong and Jianbing Shen. 2018. Triplet loss in siamese network for object tracking. In *Proceedings of the European conference on computer vision (ECCV)*, pages 459–474.

Alexander Fabbri, Irene Li, Tianwei She, Suyi Li, and Dragomir Radev. 2019. Multi news: A large-scale multi-document summarization dataset and abstractive hierarchical model. In *Proceedings of the 57th Annual Meeting of the Association for Computational Linguistics*, pages 1074–1084, Florence, Italy. Association for Computational Linguistics.

Roni Friedman, Lena Dankin, Yoav Katz, Yufang Hou, and Noam Slonim. 2021. Overview of kpa-2021 shared task: Key point based quantitative summarization. In *Proceedings of the 8th Workshop on Argumentation Mining*. Association for Computational Linguistics.

Kavita Ganesan, ChengXiang Zhai, and Jiawei Han. 2010. Opinosis: A graph based approach to abstractive summarization of highly redundant opinions. In *Proceedings of the 23rd International Conference on Computational Linguistics (Coling 2010)*, pages 340–348, Beijing, China. Coling 2010 Organizing Committee.

Tianyu Gao, Xingcheng Yao, and Danqi Chen. 2021. Simcse: Simple contrastive learning of sentence embeddings. *arXiv preprint arXiv:2104.08821*.

Yixiao Ge, Dapeng Chen, and Hongsheng Li. 2020. Mutual mean-teaching: Pseudo label refinery for unsupervised domain adaptation on person re-identification. *arXiv preprint arXiv:2001.01526*.

Jiafeng Guo, Yixing Fan, Qingyao Ai, and W Bruce Croft. 2016. A deep relevance matching model for ad-hoc retrieval. In *Proceedings of the 25th ACM international on conference on information and knowledge management*, pages 55–64.

Alexander Hermans, Lucas Beyer, and Bastian Leibe. 2017. In defense of the triplet loss for person re-identification. *arXiv preprint arXiv:1703.07737*.

Po-Sen Huang, Xiaodong He, Jianfeng Gao, Li Deng, Alex Acero, and Larry Heck. 2013. Learning deep structured semantic models for web search using clickthrough data. In *Proceedings of the 22nd ACM international conference on Information & Knowledge Management*, pages 2333–2338.

Sergey Ioffe and Christian Szegedy. 2015. Batch normalization: Accelerating deep network training by reducing internal covariate shift. In *International conference on machine learning*, pages 448–456. PMLR.

Masaru Isonuma, Junichiro Mori, Danushka Bollegala, and Ichiro Sakata. 2021. Unsupervised abstractive opinion summarization by generating sentences with tree-structured topic guidance. *arXiv preprint arXiv:2106.08007*.

Jyun-Yu Jiang, Mingyang Zhang, Cheng Li, Michael Bendersky, Nadav Golbandi, and Marc Najork. 2019. Semantic text matching for long-form documents. In *The World Wide Web Conference*, pages 795–806.

Zhenzhong Lan, Mingda Chen, Sebastian Goodman, Kevin Gimpel, Piyush Sharma, and Radu Soricut. 2019. Albert: A lite bert for self-supervised learning of language representations. *arXiv preprint arXiv:1909.11942*.

Danqi Liao. 2021. Sentence embeddings using supervised contrastive learning. *arXiv preprint arXiv:2106.04791*.

Peter J Liu, Mohammad Saleh, Etienne Pot, Ben Goodrich, Ryan Sepassi, Lukasz Kaiser, and Noam Shazeer. 2018. Generating wikipedia by summarizing long sequences. *arXiv preprint arXiv:1801.10198*.

Yinhan Liu, Myle Ott, Naman Goyal, Jingfei Du, Mandar Joshi, Danqi Chen, Omer Levy, Mike Lewis, Luke Zettlemoyer, and Veselin Stoyanov. 2019. Roberta: A robustly optimized bert pretraining approach. *arXiv preprint arXiv:1907.11692*.

Jeffrey Pennington, Richard Socher, and Christopher Manning. 2014. GloVe: Global vectors for word representation. In *Proceedings of the 2014 Conference on Empirical Methods in Natural Language Processing (EMNLP)*, pages 1532–1543, Doha, Qatar. Association for Computational Linguistics.

Nils Reimers and Iryna Gurevych. 2019. Sentence-BERT: Sentence embeddings using Siamese BERT-networks. In *Proceedings of the 2019 Conference on Empirical Methods in Natural Language Processing and the 9th International Joint Conference on Natural Language Processing (EMNLP-IJCNLP)*, pages 3982–3992, Hong Kong, China. Association for Computational Linguistics.

Victor Sanh, Lysandre Debut, Julien Chaumond, and Thomas Wolf. 2019. Distilbert, a distilled version of bert: smaller, faster, cheaper and lighter. *arXiv preprint arXiv:1910.01108*.

Kaitao Song, Xu Tan, Tao Qin, Jianfeng Lu, and Tie-Yan Liu. 2020. Mpnet: Masked and permuted pre-training for language understanding. *arXiv preprint arXiv:2004.09297*.

Chi Sun, Xipeng Qiu, Yige Xu, and Xuanjing Huang. 2019. How to fine-tune bert for text classification? In *China National Conference on Chinese Computational Linguistics*, pages 194–206. Springer.

Xun Wang, Xintong Han, Weilin Huang, Dengke Dong, and Matthew R Scott. 2019. Multi-similarity loss with general pair weighting for deep metric learning. In *Proceedings of the IEEE/CVF Conference on Computer Vision and Pattern Recognition*, pages 5022–5030.

Chao-Yuan Wu, R Manmatha, Alexander J Smola, and Philipp Krahenbuhl. 2017. Sampling matters in deep embedding learning. In *Proceedings of the IEEE International Conference on Computer Vision*, pages 2840–2848.

Ikuya Yamada, Akari Asai, Hiroyuki Shindo, Hideaki Takeda, and Yuji Matsumoto. 2020. Luke: deep contextualized entity representations with entity-aware self-attention. *arXiv preprint arXiv:2010.01057*.

Yuanmeng Yan, Rumei Li, Sirui Wang, Fuzheng Zhang, Wei Wu, and Weiran Xu. 2021. Consert: A contrastive framework for self-supervised sentence representation transfer. *arXiv preprint arXiv:2105.11741*.

Liu Yang, Mingyang Zhang, Cheng Li, Michael Bendersky, and Marc Najork. 2020. Beyond 512 tokens: Siamese multi-depth transformer-based hierarchical encoder for long-form document matching. In *Proceedings of the 29th ACM International Conference on Information & Knowledge Management*, pages 1725–1734.

Yi Yang, Wen-tau Yih, and Christopher Meek. 2015. WikiQA: A challenge dataset for open-domain question answering. In *Proceedings of the 2015 Conference on Empirical Methods in Natural Language Processing*, pages 2013–2018, Lisbon, Portugal. Association for Computational Linguistics.

Baosheng Yu and Dacheng Tao. 2019. Deep metric learning with tuplet margin loss. In *Proceedings of the IEEE/CVF International Conference on Computer Vision*, pages 6490–6499.

Xiao Zhang, Yixiao Ge, Yu Qiao, and Hongsheng Li. 2021. Refining pseudo labels with clustering consensus over generations for unsupervised object reidentification. In *Proceedings of the IEEE/CVF Conference on Computer Vision and Pattern Recognition*, pages 3436–3445.

Ming Zhong, Pengfei Liu, Yiran Chen, Danqing Wang, Xipeng Qiu, and Xuanjing Huang. 2020. Extractive summarization as text matching. In *Proceedings of the 58th Annual Meeting of the Association for Computational Linguistics*, pages 6197–6208, Online. Association for Computational Linguistics.

Modern Talking in Key Point Analysis: Key Point Matching using Pretrained Encoders

Jan Heinrich Reimer and **Thi Kim Hanh Luu** and **Max Henze** and **Yamen Ajjour**
Martin Luther University Halle-Wittenberg, Germany
{jan.reimer,thi.luu,max.henze}@student.uni-halle.de
yamen.ajjour@informatik.uni-halle.de

Abstract

We contribute to the ArgMining 2021 shared task on Quantitative Summarization and Key Point Analysis with two approaches for argument key point matching. For key point matching the task is to decide if a short key point matches the content of an argument with the same topic and stance towards the topic. We approach this task in two ways: First, we develop a simple rule-based baseline matcher by computing token overlap after removing stop words, stemming, and adding synonyms/antonyms. Second, we fine-tune pretrained BERT and RoBERTa language models as a regression classifier for only a single epoch. We manually examine errors of our proposed matcher models and find that long arguments are harder to classify. Our fine-tuned RoBERTa-Base model achieves a mean average precision score of 0.913, the best score for strict labels of all participating teams.

1 Introduction

Arguments influence our decisions in many places of our daily life (Bar-Haim et al., 2020a). But with the increasingly larger amount of information found on the Web[1] and more effective argument mining, people often need to summarize arguments (Lawrence and Reed, 2019; Bar-Haim et al., 2020a). Bar-Haim et al. (2020a) see matching key points to arguments as an intermediate step towards automatically generating argumentative summaries (Section 2). The ArgMining 2021 shared task on Quantitative Summarization and Key Point Analysis (Friedman et al., 2021) is the first task on key point matching, which is an important step towards summarizing arguments. By matching arguments with a pre-defined set of key points, an argumentative text can be summarized using the prevalence of the key points in it. Different approaches of matching argument key point pairs, here called matchers, should be proposed and discussed. Given an argument and a key point, a matcher should return a real value between 0 and 1 which represents the extent to which the argument matches the key point.[2] For evaluating different argument key point matchers, the shared task organizers uses mean average precision evaluation as a metric (Friedman et al., 2021) to evaluate the approaches and publish the ArgKP-2021 benchmark dataset (Section 3) to compare matchers (Bar-Haim et al., 2020a).

Pretrained language models like BERT and RoBERTa are nowadays becoming standard approaches to tackle various Natural Language Processing tasks (Devlin et al., 2019; Liu et al., 2019). Because of their extensive pretraining, often fine-tuning these language models with even a small task-specific dataset can achieve state-of-the-art performance (Devlin et al., 2019). As the ArgKP-2021 dataset (Bar-Haim et al., 2020a) used in the ArgMining 2021 shared task on Quantitative Summarization is relatively small (24 083 labelled pairs), we decide to fine-tune BERT and RoBERTa language models rather than train a neural classifier from scratch (Section 4).

Contrasting this neural approach, we introduce a simple rule-based baseline matcher that compares preprocessed tokens of each argument to the tokens of each key point (Section 4). For the baseline, we compute token overlap after removing stop words, adding synonyms and antonyms, and stemming the tokens from both argument and key point using the NLTK toolkit (Bird and Loper, 2004).

Our fine-tuned RoBERTa-Base matcher achieves a mean average precision score of up to 0.967 and ranks second in the shared task's leaderboard (Section 5). In a manual error analysis, we find that the imbalanced ArgKP-2021 dataset causes neural models to predict non-matching argument key

[1] https://internetlivestats.com/

[2] https://2021.argmining.org/shared_task_ibm.html

Proceedings of The 8th Workshop on Argument Mining, pages 175–183
Punta Cana, Dominican Republic, November 10–11, 2021.

point pairs more precisely than matching pairs (Section 6). We further observe a tendency that large length differences between arguments and key points can cause errors. To encourage researchers to train more robust argument key point matchers, we release our source code under a free license.

2 Related Work

Similar tasks to key point analysis include clustering arguments (Reimers et al., 2019; Ajjour et al., 2019), detecting similar arguments in a pairwise fashion (Misra et al., 2016) and matching arguments to generic-arguments (Naderi and Hirst, 2017). Using points to summarize arguments were approached by Egan et al. (2016) on online discussion. Points were extracted by using the verbs and their syntactic arguments and are then clustered together to deliver a summary of the discussion.

Key point analysis is the task of matching a given argument with one or more pre-defined key points (Bar-Haim et al., 2020a). To develop models for the task, Bar-Haim et al. (2020a) introduced a dataset (ArgKP-2021) which contains 24 093 argument key point pairs on 28 topics. Each argument and key point is labeled manually as `match` or `no-match`. The authors experimented with several unsupervised and supervised approaches to perform the task in a cross-topic experimental setting. BERT (Devlin et al., 2019) performed the best in their experiments by reaching an F1 score of 0.68.

In a later work, Bar-Haim et al. (2020b) develop a summarization approach for online discussions that uses key point analysis. The summrization approach takes as input a set of comments on a given topic and extracts a set of representative key points from them. The output of the summarization approach is the set of extracts key points together with the count of matched comments for each key point. In its essence, the summarization approach uses a matching model that gives a score for a given comment and key point or a pair of key points. For matching models, Bar-Haim et al. (2020b) compare different variants of BERT (Devlin et al., 2019). Among the tested models, ALBERT (Lan et al., 2019) performed the best with an F1 score 0.809, but RoBERTa (Liu et al., 2019) were chosen for key point extraction at the end, which is 6 times faster than ALBERT and still achieves an F1 score of 0.773.

Our approaches for the key point analysis are based on BERT and RoBERTa. BERT stands for Bidirectional Encoder Representations from Transformers and is an open-source bidirectional language representation model published by Google (Devlin et al., 2019). BERT is pre-trained over unlabeled text to learn a language representation and can be fine-tuned on downstream tasks. During pre-training, BERT is trained on two unsupervised tasks: Masked Language Model and Next Structure Prediction. RoBERTa is an improved variant of BERT that is introduced by Facebook in 2019 (Liu et al., 2019). Liu et al. (2019) modified BERT by using a larger training data size of 160GB of uncompressed text, more compute power, larger batch-training size, and optimized hyperparameters. In comparison to BERT, pre-training tasks for RoBERTa were done with full-length sentences and include only Masked Language Model while applying different masks in each training epoch (dynamic masking). RoBERTa outperforms BERT on all 9 GLUE tasks in the single-task setting and 4 out of 9 tasks in the ensembles setting (Wang et al., 2018; Liu et al., 2019).

3 Data

The dataset used in the ArgMining 2021 shared task on Quantitative Summarization and Key Point Analysis is the ArgKP-2021 dataset (Bar-Haim et al., 2020a) which consists of 24 083 argument and key point pairs labeled as matching/non-matching. They all belong to one of 28 controversial topics, for example: "Assisted suicide should be a criminal offence". Every key point and argument pair is annotated with its stance towards the topic.

The training split of the ArgKP-2021 dataset has 5 583 arguments belonging to 207 key points within 24 topics. This leaves the validation split with 932 arguments and 36 key points for 4 topics. Friedman et al. (2021) complement the ArgKP-2021 dataset's training and validation split with a test split that is used to evaluate submissions to the shared task. The test split contains 723 arguments with 33 key points from 3 topics.

3.1 Characteristics

Here, we do qualitative and quantative analyses of the ArgKP-2021 dataset. Table 1 shows examples of argument key point pairs from the ArgKP-2021 dataset (Bar-Haim et al., 2020a). In pair A from Table 1, the argument matches the given key point.

Table 1: Examples of argument key point pairs from the ArgKP-2021 dataset (Bar-Haim et al., 2020a)

#	Argument	Key point
A	child actors can be overworked and they can miss out on their education.	Being a performer harms the child's education
B	as long as nuclear weapons exist, the entire world has to worry about nations deciding to fire them at another or terrorists getting hold of them and causing disaster	Nuclear weapons can fall into the wrong hands
C	'people reach their limit when it comes to their quality of life and should be able to end their suffering. this can be done with little or no suffering by assistance and the person is able to say good bye.	Assisted suicide reduces suffering

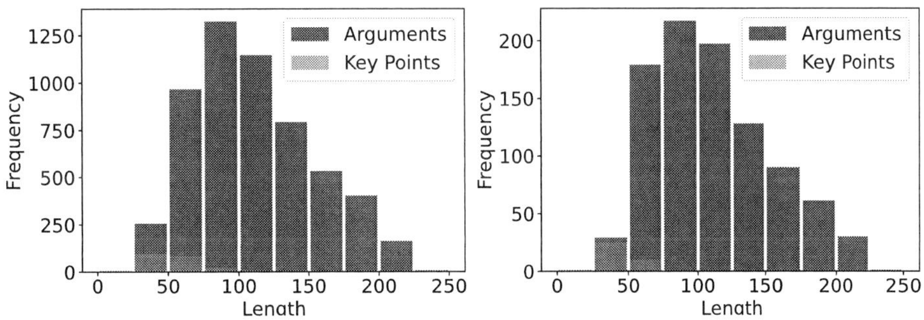

Figure 1: Lengths in characters for arguments and key points from the training and development set.

Both sentences discuss children actors and their education. The word "actors" is not explicitly used in the key point but is semantically similar to the word "performer". Such lexical variation can be opposed by using WordNet (Miller, 1995) to find synonyms and antonyms.

Pair B in Table 1 is a harder example, since the argument matches the key point but are expressed differently. The key point makes usage of "wrong hands" as figurative meaning for "nations" and "terrorists" from the argument. In comparison to pair A, the linguistic variation in pair B goes beyond finding synonyms and requires a deep understanding of the semantics of the argument and key point.

Figure 1 shows the average length of the arguments and key points in the training and developments splits. As shown, the arguments in the ArgKP-2021 dataset are substantially longer than key points. In the training set, the average length of arguments is 109 characters. Compared to that, key points are on average only half as long (52 characters). In the validation set, the key points have an average length of 41 characters and therefore key points are shorter than those in the training set. The average length of arguments remains almost the same at 108 characters. The proportion of arguments that are 67 characters longer than key points constitute 39 % of the training set and 44 % of the validation set. We can see that there are more short key points in the validation set. This length difference might be a challenge for the models in key point matching (Section 6). Pair C is an example of an argument and key point pair with a large length difference.

All in all, we identify the following major difficulties in matching key points to arguments: semantically similar words, meaning understanding, and the length difference between the arguments and key points. In the following section, we approach the first two problems while developing our baseline and approaches. In Section 6, we analyze the errors made by our approaches with regard to the length difference between the arguments and key points.

4 Approach

To match key points to arguments, we propose two different approaches. First, we discuss a simple yet effective baseline measuring token overlap between key points and arguments. Second, to improve upon this simple baseline, we introduce an approach based on BERT and RoBERTa (Devlin et al., 2019; Liu et al., 2019). We fine-tune both language models in standard configuration with only minor changes highlighted below.

4.1 Token Overlap Baseline

To be able to compare more sophisticated matchers, we first propose a very simple token overlap baseline using preprocessed tokens from each argument and key point, as parsed by the NLTK toolkit (Bird and Loper, 2004). In general, key points summarize ideas of their matched arguments. Our intuition, therefore, is that certain words or tokens from an argument are also likely to be present in its matched key points. Rather than using completely new words for summarization of arguments, a human would tend to reuse important words from the argument. For example, in the argument and key point pair C from Table 1 both, the argument and key point, contain the token "suffering".

We can further increase the token overlap between arguments and key points by preprocessing their tokens as following: First, we remove stop words for reducing noise within all arguments. Initially, this can seem counterproductive because with fewer words the highest possible overlap would also decrease and therefore could lead to worse performance. However, a lot of arguments and key points contain functional words like "the", "and" or "as". Removing these results in sentences that contain more specific information and thus leads to less confusion with the token overlap matcher. As a second preprocessing step, we reduce tokens to their corresponding stems by applying stemming using the Snowball stemmer (Porter, 1980). We expect the token overlap matcher to be able to generalize more when comparing tokens. For example, the words "assistance" and "assisted" from the above example (Table 1, C) are both stemmed to "assist" with the Snowball stemmer. Consequently, stemming creates an overlap between different forms of the same word and, for instance, increases the probability that an argument containing "assistance" is associated with a key point containing "assisted". Last, we increase generalization for token overlap even further by supplementing the set of tokens with synonyms and antonyms (Miller, 1995). This step should also increase the chance of overlapping tokens.

To compute the similarity between an argument and a key point, let tokens_a be the set of preprocessed tokens from an argument a and tokens_k the set of tokens from a key point k. We calculate the set of overlapping tokens like this:

$$\text{overlap}_{a,k} = \{t : t \in \text{tokens}_a \land t \in \text{tokens}_k\} \quad (1)$$

The token overlap matcher returns matching scores based on the overlap size weighted against the minimum size of either the argument or the key point:

$$\text{score}_{a,k} = \frac{|\text{overlap}_{a,k}|}{\min\{|\text{tokens}_a|, |\text{tokens}_k|\}} \quad (2)$$

That is, pairs with a higher proportion of tokens that appear both in the argument as well as in the key point are classified with a higher matching score.

4.2 Transformers Fine-tuning

To improve upon this simple token overlap baseline, we fine-tune BERT and RoBERTa Transformer models for classifying argument key point matches (Devlin et al., 2019; Liu et al., 2019). While BERT is pretrained on a very large document corpus (16GB of raw data), RoBERTa is pretrained on an even larger corpus (160GB). Thus RoBERTa models can be fine-tuned on higher end task performance (Liu et al., 2019). We tokenize both the arguments and the key points with BERT's default WordPiece tokenizer and the resulting sequences are trimmed to 512 tokens for both models. We then fine-tune the BERT-Base and RoBERTa-Base variants in the standard sentence-pair regression setting using the Simple Transformers library.[3] The input to the models is formatted as [CLS] argument [SEP] key point [SEP] for BERT and <s> argument </s></s> key point </s> for RoBERTa respectively. For classification, we interpret the regression output value as the probability of an argument matching a key point. That is, the training labels are always 0 or 1, depending on whether the corresponding pair in the training set matches or not. Both model variants contain 12 hidden layers with a hidden size of 768 and 12 attention heads. We train each of the two models for one single epoch at a learning rate of $\eta = 2 \cdot 10^{-5}$. We use an AdamW optimizer with $\beta = (0.9, 0.999)$ and zero weight decay (Loshchilov and Hutter, 2019). The optimizer is warmed up with a ratio of 6 % of the training data, and we fine-tune both models with

[3] https://simpletransformers.ai/

the binary cross-entropy loss. We explore three ways of handling argument key point pairs in the training set with missing ground-truth label. In the first way, we remove those pairs completely from the traning dataset. In the second and third ways, we assume all the arguments and key points with missing labels to be either a `match` or `no-match`. By comparing the effectiveness of the models, we find that the first way lead to the best effectiveness on the validation set. Similarly, we experiment with textual data augmentation[4] (swapping synonyms, randomly omitting words) to increase the amount of training data, leading to no improvement on validation scores either. Thus, for the submitted model, we consider only training pairs that have an associated ground-truth label and do not oversample. We don't restrict the models output to the interval $[0, 1]$—like we did for the baseline—, as the shared task did not mention constraints on the score value that should be returned by a matcher.

5 Results

Submissions to the ArgMining 2021 shared task on Quantitative Summarization and Key Point Analysis are evaluated with respect to mean average precision (Friedman et al., 2021). The organizers calculate the score by pairing each argument with the best matching key point according to the predicted matching probabilities. Within each topic-stance combination, only 50 % of the arguments with the highest predicted matching score are then considered for evaluation. The task organizers claim that this removal of 50 % of the pairs is necessary because some arguments do not match any of the key points, which would influence mean average precision negatively (Friedman et al., 2021). For the remaining argument key point pairs in each topic-stance combination, the average precision is calculated and the final score is computed as the mean of all average precision scores.

The task organizers consider two evaluation settings: strict and relaxed. Both settings are based on the ground-truth labels from the ArgKP-2021 dataset (Bar-Haim et al., 2020a). The two evaluation settings are created to account for argument key point pairs in the ArgKP-2021 with undecided labels (i.e. not enough agreement between annotators). In the strict setting, the shared task organizers consider those undecided pairs as `no-match`. In the relaxed setting, however, the shared task organizers consider the undecided pairs as `match` (Friedman et al., 2021). The mean average precision score is then calculated in the two settings based on the ground-truth labels and the derived labels for the undecided pairs. We stress that in this complex evaluation setup, the mean average precision score in the relaxed setting would favor assuming matches in case of model uncertainty. In comparison, in the strict setting mean average precision would favor assuming `no-match` between an argument and key point. However, we find that because only the most probable matching key point is being considered for evaluation, this effect is minor. The evaluation score in general favors matchers that can match a single key point for each argument with high precision. It is however not important if a matcher does predict non-matches with high certainty.

5.1 Discussion

In Table 2, we report mean average precision in the strict and relaxed settings of the training, validation, and test set in the ArgKP-2021 dataset. We complement the mean average precision scores by adding precision and recall scores of the `match` label, both in the strict and relaxed setting. To calculate precision and recall, we label an argument and key point pair as `match` if their score is higher than 0.5 and as `no-match` otherwise. To aggregate results of the strict and relaxed settings, we also report the average score of the two variants. The reported scores should allow for automated and unbiased evaluation of our models and easier comparison with competitive approaches. We report all 27 scores for the token overlap baseline model as well as for the fine-tuned BERT-Base and RoBERTa-Base models. To make our results more comparable, we add a second baseline, where matches between arguments and key points of same topic and stance are predicted with uniform random probability. That random baseline represents a worst-case matcher and any weak matcher should exceed its evaluation scores.

The token overlap baseline achieves a mean average precision of 0.483 in the strict setting and 0.575 in the relaxed setting on the test set. Thus, it is nearly twice as good as a random matcher with respect to mean average precision. Even though this baseline has reasonably good scores on all datasets, we are concerned about the large discrepancies between its scores on the validation set and the train-

[4]https://github.com/makcedward/nlpaug

Table 2: Performance of the random and token overlap baseline, BERT-Base, and RoBERTa-Base models with respect to mean average precision (mAP), precision (P), and recall (R) of the match label. Precision and recall are calculated by deriving boolean labels from the matching scores with a threshold of 0.5 for all approaches. We report scores for the training, validation, and test set in the strict and relaxed label settings, as well as the averages of the two settings. The best result per set is highlighted **bold**.

Approach	**Strict**			**Relaxed**			**Average**		
	mAP	P	R	mAP	P	R	mAP	P	R
Training set									
Random	0.260	0.173	0.500	0.409	0.330	0.501	0.335	0.252	0.501
Token Overlap	0.541	0.269	0.323	0.653	0.435	0.275	0.597	0.352	0.299
BERT-Base	0.889	**0.703**	**0.864**	**0.981**	**0.936**	**0.607**	0.935	**0.819**	**0.736**
RoBERTa-Base	**0.915**	0.702	0.820	0.979	0.927	0.572	**0.947**	0.814	0.696
Validation set									
Random	0.232	0.180	0.523	0.430	0.364	0.524	0.331	0.272	0.524
Token Overlap	0.643	0.219	0.390	0.802	0.416	0.366	0.722	0.317	0.378
BERT-Base	0.717	0.397	**0.802**	0.928	0.648	**0.649**	0.822	0.522	**0.725**
RoBERTa-Base	**0.879**	**0.567**	0.799	**0.984**	**0.816**	0.569	**0.932**	**0.692**	0.684
Test set									
Random	0.237	0.150	0.545	0.355	0.286	0.549	0.296	0.218	0.547
Token Overlap	0.483	0.232	0.225	0.575	0.350	0.178	0.529	0.291	0.201
BERT-Base	0.827	0.326	**0.848**	0.940	0.526	**0.721**	0.883	0.426	**0.784**
RoBERTa-Base	**0.913**	**0.490**	0.741	**0.967**	**0.716**	0.569	**0.940**	**0.603**	0.655

ing and test dataset. The rather simple baseline captures the similarity between an argument and a key point on the token level and might be sensative against more complicated parphrases.

Both fine-tuned matchers outperform the baselines by a large margin. While the BERT-Base matcher achieves higher relaxed mean average precision on the training set than the RoBERTa-Base matcher, the RoBERTa-Base matcher is overall better than BERT, especially with strict labels. The RoBERTa-Base matcher achieves a mean average precision of 0.913 in the strict setting on the test set, and 0.967 in the relaxed setting. As these scores on the test set are nearly as high as on the training set, we argue that RoBERTa is a more robust language model and generalizes better than BERT. Also the RoBERTa-Base matcher performs better in terms of precision, while the BERT-Base matcher is better with respect to recall for all dataset splits in both the strict and relaxed settings.

6 Error Analysis

To find errors of the two trained matchers, BERT-Base and RoBERTa-Base, in Figure 2 we show histograms of predicted match scores with respect to ground-truth labels. Both matchers classify most pairs correctly, which can be seen because the histogram spikes around 0 for the true `no-match` label and around 1 for the true `match` label. We also observe that predictions on the training set are closer to the true label than on the development set for both RoBERTa-Base and BERT-Base. Even though we expect any machine-learned matcher to perform better on training data than on validation data, we see this as a room for improvement with better generalization. We notice that in Figures 2a and 2c both approaches predict non-matching argument key point pairs better than matching key points. This effect is likely to occur because of the higher amount of non-matching pairs provided in the training dataset. Most arguments match with only a few or even just a single key point. But nonetheless each argument is compared to all other key points; hence, the underlying data to learn from is imbalanced (Barandela et al., 2004). Even though experiments with using textual data augmentation or simple oversampling to balance the dataset were unsuccessful (Dietterich, 1995), more advanced oversampling or undersampling approaches could possibly resolve this issue. We further identify that the predicted matching scores of BERT-Base are spread a bit more than scores from RoBERTa-Base.

In Figure 2b, we observe that the BERT-Base matcher falsely predicts certain non-matching pairs

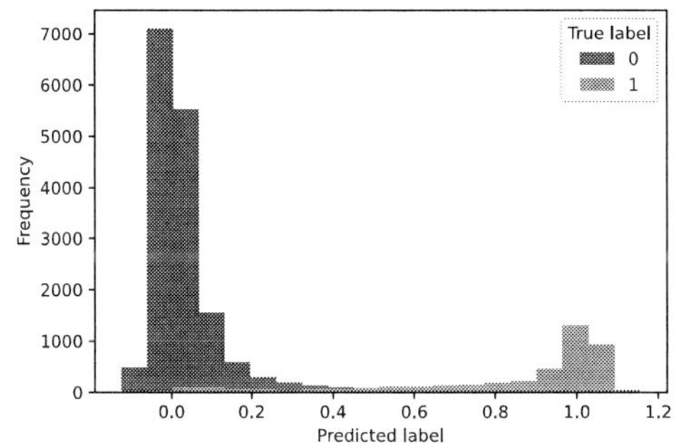

(a) Predictions with BERT-Base on the training set.

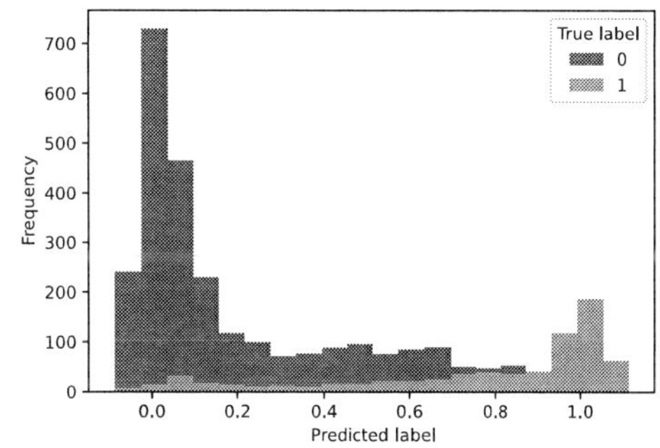

(b) Predictions with BERT-Base on the validation set.

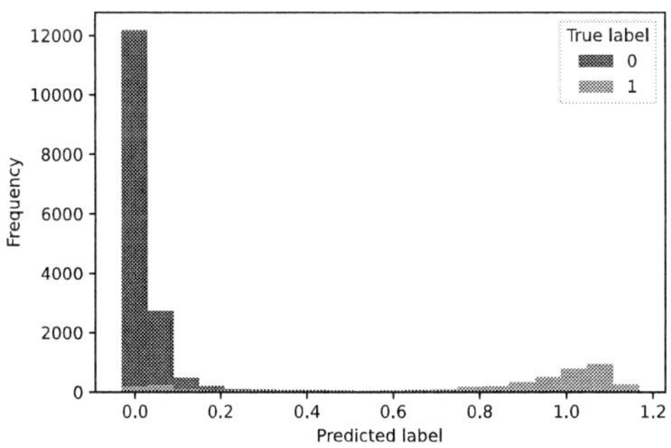

(c) Predictions with RoBERTa-Base on the training set.

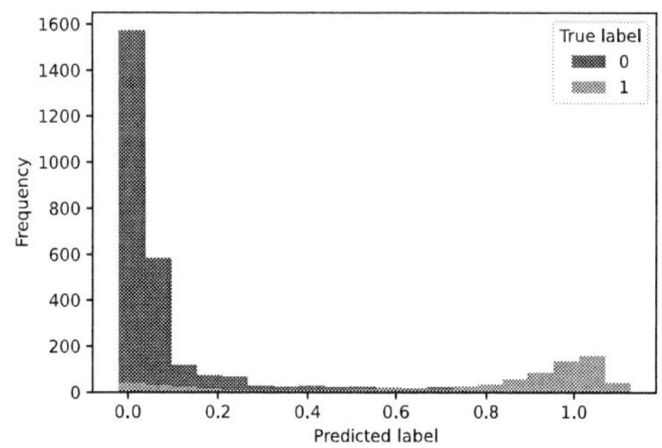

(d) Predictions with RoBERTa-Base on the validation set.

Figure 2: Histograms of predicted labels on the training and validation sets for argument key point pairs with the BERT-Base and RoBERTa-Base classifiers. For good classifiers, predicted labels should approximately equal the true label (0 or 1).

Table 3: Examples of argument key point pairs from the ArgKP-2021 dataset (Bar-Haim et al., 2020a) where the predicted score is off the ground truth label (True) with either the BERT-Base or RoBERTa-Base matcher.

#	**Argument**	**Key point**	**True**	**BERT**	**RoBERTa**
D	School uniforms can be less comfortable than students' regular clothes.	School uniforms are expensive	0	0.48	0.03
E	affirmative action discriminates the majority, preventing skilled workers from gaining employment over someone less qualified but considered to be a member of a protected minority group.	Affirmative action reduces quality	1	-0.05	0.03

with scores around 0.5. An example of such uncertain pair is the argument key point pair D from Table 3. This argument which is in the training dataset has no matching key points. For this argument, the BERT-Base matcher has not learned well how to classify matches for that type of argument, and therefore predicts a neutral score of 0.48. However, the RoBERTa-Base matcher does not make that error.

Both, the BERT-Base matcher and RoBERTa-Base falsely predict some argument key point pairs as `no-match` that are in fact labelled as a `match`. For example, it seems to be difficult to predict a `match` for the argument key point pair E from Table 3. The argument from the example is longer than most arguments and especially much longer than the key point (431 % more characters). It might be more challenging to reduce such longer arguments, that contain more complex information, to very compact key points. We confirm that observation by comparing the squared classification error with respect to the absolute difference between argument and key point lengths.

7 Conclusion and Future Work

We approach the practical problem of matching arguments with short key points with the goal of summarizing arguments. Although our token overlap baseline approach is very simple, it achieves a mean average precision of up to 0.575 on the test set, nearly double the score of a random matcher. The baseline approach is straightforward to implement but can not eliminate the problem of context understanding. RoBERTa-Base and BERT-Base have achieved good performance, because they can overcome the context understanding challenge. Our fine-tuned RoBERTa-Base model also performed better than BERT-Base in this task and scores a mean average precision of up to 0.967. With strict ground truth labels it achieves a mean average precision score of 0.913 on the test set, which is the best score of the participating teams in the shared task. This again shows the importance of architecture, training objectives, and hyperparameter selection.

7.1 Future Work

In Section 3, we observed that transformer models tend to misclassify argument key point pairs if the argument and key point largely differ in length. As an extension to our approach, we propose to combine transformer models with the overlap baseline in an ensemble. Another possible improvement are recent improvements in language models (Sun et al., 2021). If a language model is even more robust than, for example, RoBERTa, we expect a fine-tuned matcher to outperform the RoBERTa-Base matcher as well.

References

Yamen Ajjour, Milad Alshomary, Henning Wachsmuth, and Benno Stein. 2019. Modeling frames in argumentation. In *Proceedings of the 2019 Conference on Empirical Methods in Natural Language Processing and the 9th International Joint Conference on Natural Language Processing (EMNLP-IJCNLP)*, pages 2915–2925.

Roy Bar-Haim, Lilach Eden, Roni Friedman, Yoav Kantor, Dan Lahav, and Noam Slonim. 2020a. From arguments to key points: Towards automatic argument summarization. In *Proceedings of the 58th Annual Meeting of the Association for Computational Linguistics, ACL 2020, Online, July 5-10, 2020*, pages 4029–4039. Association for Computational Linguistics.

Roy Bar-Haim, Yoav Kantor, Lilach Eden, Roni Friedman, Dan Lahav, and Noam Slonim. 2020b. Quantitative argument summarization and beyond: Cross-domain key point analysis. In *Proceedings of the 2020 Conference on Empirical Methods in Natural Language Processing, EMNLP 2020, Online, November 16-20, 2020*, pages 39–49. Association for Computational Linguistics.

Ricardo Barandela, Rosa Maria Valdovinos, José Salvador Sánchez, and Francesc J. Ferri. 2004. The imbalanced training sample problem: Under or over sampling? In *Structural, Syntactic, and Statistical Pattern Recognition, Joint IAPR International Workshops, SSPR 2004 and SPR 2004, Lisbon, Portugal, August 18-20, 2004 Proceedings*, volume 3138 of *Lecture Notes in Computer Science*, page 806. Springer.

Steven Bird and Edward Loper. 2004. NLTK: the natural language toolkit. In *Proceedings of the 42nd Annual Meeting of the Association for Computational Linguistics, Barcelona, Spain, July 21-26, 2004 - Poster and Demonstration*. ACL.

Jacob Devlin, Ming-Wei Chang, Kenton Lee, and Kristina Toutanova. 2019. BERT: pre-training of deep bidirectional transformers for language understanding. In *Proceedings of the 2019 Conference of the North American Chapter of the Association for Computational Linguistics: Human Language Technologies, NAACL-HLT 2019, Minneapolis, MN, USA, June 2-7, 2019, Volume 1 (Long and Short Papers)*, pages 4171–4186. Association for Computational Linguistics.

Thomas G. Dietterich. 1995. Overfitting and undercomputing in machine learning. *ACM Comput. Surv.*, 27(3):326–327.

Charlie Egan, Advaith Siddharthan, and Adam Wyner. 2016. Summarising the points made in online political debates. In *Proceedings of the Third Workshop on Argument Mining (ArgMining2016)*, pages 134–143.

Roni Friedman, Lena Dankin, Yoav Katz, Yufang Hou, and Noam Slonim. 2021. Overview of kpa-2021 shared task: Key point based quantitative summarization. In *Proceedings of the 8th Workshop on Argumentation Mining*. Association for Computational Linguistics.

Zhenzhong Lan, Mingda Chen, Sebastian Goodman, Kevin Gimpel, Piyush Sharma, and Radu Soricut. 2019. Albert: A lite bert for self-supervised learning of language representations. *arXiv preprint arXiv:1909.11942*.

John Lawrence and Chris Reed. 2019. Argument mining: A survey. *Comput. Linguistics*, 45(4):765–818.

Yinhan Liu, Myle Ott, Naman Goyal, Jingfei Du, Mandar Joshi, Danqi Chen, Omer Levy, Mike Lewis, Luke Zettlemoyer, and Veselin Stoyanov. 2019. Roberta: A robustly optimized BERT pretraining approach. *CoRR*, abs/1907.11692.

Ilya Loshchilov and Frank Hutter. 2019. Decoupled weight decay regularization. *CoRR*, abs/1711.05101.

George A Miller. 1995. Wordnet: a lexical database for english. *Communications of the ACM*, 38(11):39–41.

Amita Misra, Brian Ecker, and Marilyn Walker. 2016. Measuring the similarity of sentential arguments in dialogue. In *Proceedings of the 17th Annual Meeting of the Special Interest Group on Discourse and Dialogue*, pages 276–287, Los Angeles. Association for Computational Linguistics.

Nona Naderi and Graeme Hirst. 2017. Classifying Frames at the Sentence Level in News Articles. In *Proceedings of Recent Advances in Natural Language Processing*, pages 536–542.

Martin F Porter. 1980. An algorithm for suffix stripping. *Program*.

Nils Reimers, Benjamin Schiller, Tilman Beck, Johannes Daxenberger, Christian Stab, and Iryna Gurevych. 2019. Classification and clustering of arguments with contextualized word embeddings. *arXiv preprint arXiv:1906.09821*.

Yu Sun, Shuohuan Wang, Shikun Feng, Siyu Ding, Chao Pang, Junyuan Shang, Jiaxiang Liu, Xuyi Chen, Yanbin Zhao, Yuxiang Lu, Weixin Liu, Zhihua Wu, Weibao Gong, Jianzhong Liang, Zhizhou Shang, Peng Sun, Wei Liu, Xuan Ouyang, Dianhai Yu, Hao Tian, Hua Wu, and Haifeng Wang. 2021. ERNIE 3.0: Large-scale knowledge enhanced pre-training for language understanding and generation. *CoRR*, abs/2107.02137.

Alex Wang, Amanpreet Singh, Julian Michael, Felix Hill, Omer Levy, and Samuel R. Bowman. 2018. GLUE: A multi-task benchmark and analysis platform for natural language understanding. In *Proceedings of the Workshop: Analyzing and Interpreting Neural Networks for NLP, BlackboxNLP@EMNLP 2018, Brussels, Belgium, November 1, 2018*, pages 353–355. Association for Computational Linguistics.

Key Point Analysis via Contrastive Learning and Extractive Argument Summarization

Milad Alshomary † **Timon Gurke** † **Shahbaz Syed** ‡ **Philipp Heinisch** ⋆

Maximilian Splietḧover † **Philipp Cimiano** ⋆ **Martin Potthast** ‡ **Henning Wachsmuth** †

†Paderborn University, Germany, `milad.alshomary@upb.de`
‡Leipzig University, Germany, `<first>.<last>@uni-leipzig.de`
⋆Bielefeld University, Germany, `<first>.<last>@uni-bielefeld.de`

Abstract

Key point analysis is the task of extracting a set of concise and high-level statements from a given collection of arguments, representing the gist of these arguments. This paper presents our proposed approach to the Key Point Analysis shared task, collocated with the 8th Workshop on Argument Mining. The approach integrates two complementary components. One component employs contrastive learning via a siamese neural network for matching arguments to key points; the other is a graph-based extractive summarization model for generating key points. In both automatic and manual evaluation, our approach was ranked best among all submissions to the shared task.

1 Introduction

Informed decision-making on a controversial issue usually requires considering several pro and con arguments. To answer the question "Is organic food healthier?", for example, people may query a search engine that retrieves arguments from diverse sources such as news editorials, debate portals, and social media discussions, which can then be compared and weighed. However, given the constant stream of digital information, this process may be time-intensive and overwhelming. Search engines and similar support systems may therefore benefit from employing argument summarization, that is, the generated summaries may aid the decision-making by helping users quickly choose relevant arguments with a specific stance towards the topic.

Argument summarization has been tackled both for single documents (Syed et al., 2020) and multiple documents (Bhatia et al., 2014; Egan et al., 2016). A specific multi-document scenario introduced by Bar-Haim et al. (2020a) is *key point analysis* where the goal is to map a collection of arguments to a set of salient key points (say, high-level arguments) to provide a quantitative summary of these arguments.

The Key Point Analysis (KPA) shared task by Friedman et al. (2021)[1] invited systems for two complementary subtasks: *matching arguments to key points* and *generating key points from a given set of arguments* (Section 3). As part of this shared task, we present an approach with two complementary components, one for each subtask. For key point matching, we propose a model that learns a semantic embedding space where instances that match are closer to each other while non-matching instances are further away from each other. We learn to embed instances by utilizing a contrastive loss function in a siamese neural network (Bromley et al., 1994). For the key point generation, we present a graph-based extractive summarization approach similar to the work of Alshomary et al. (2020a). It utilizes a PageRank variant to rank sentences in the input arguments by quality and predicts the top-ranked sentences to be key points. In an additional experiment, we also investigated an approach that performs aspect identification on arguments, followed by aspect clustering to ensure diversity. Finally, arguments with the best coverage of these diverse aspects are extracted as key points.

Our approaches yielded the top performance among all submissions to the shared task in both quantitative and qualitative evaluation conducted by the organizers of the shared task (Section 5).[2].

2 Related Work

In summarization, arguments are relatively understudied compared to other document types such as news articles or scientific literature, but a few approaches have come up in the last years.

In an extractive manner, argument mining has been employed to identify the main claim as the summary of an argument (Petasis and Karkaletsis,

[1]https://2021.argmining.org/shared_task_ibm, last accessed: 2021-08-08

[2]The code is available under https://github.com/webis-de/ArgMining-21

Proceedings of The 8th Workshop on Argument Mining, pages 184–189
Punta Cana, Dominican Republic, November 10–11, 2021.

2016; Daxenberger et al., 2017). Wang and Ling (2016) used a sequence-to-sequence model for the abstractive summarization of arguments from online debate portals. A complementary task of generating conclusions as informative argument summaries was introduced by Syed et al. (2021). Similar to Alshomary et al. (2020b) who inferred a conclusion's target with a triplet neural network, we rely on contrastive learning here, using a siamese network though. Also, we build upon ideas of Alshomary et al. (2020a) who proposed a graph-based model using PageRank (Page et al., 1999) that extracts the argument's conclusion and the main supporting reason as an extractive summary. All these works represent the single-document summarization paradigm where only one argument is summarized at a time, whereas the given shared task is a multi-document summarization setting.

The first approaches to multi-document argument summarization aimed to identify the main points of online discussions. Among these, Egan et al. (2016) grouped verb frames into pattern clusters that serve as input to a structured summarization pipeline, whereas Misra et al. (2016) proposed a more condensed approach by directly extracting argumentative sentences, summarized by similarity clustering. Bar-Haim et al. (2020a) continued this line of research by introducing the notion of *key points* and contributing the ArgsKP corpus, a collection of arguments mapped to manually-created key points. These key points are concise and self-contained sentences that capture the gist of the arguments. Later, Bar-Haim et al. (2020b) proposed a quantitative argument summarization framework that automatically extracts key points from a set of arguments. Building upon this research, our approach aims to increase the quality of such generated key points, including a strong relation identifier between arguments and key points.

3 Task Description

In the context of computational argumentation, Bar-Haim et al. (2020a) introduced the notion of a *key point* as a high-level argument that resembles a natural language summary of a collection of more descriptive arguments. Specifically, the authors defined a good key point as being "general enough to match a significant portion of the arguments, yet informative enough to make a useful summary." In this context, the KPA shared task consists of two subtasks as described below:

1. *Key point matching.* Given a set of arguments on a certain topic that are grouped by their stance and a set of key points, assign each argument to a key point.
2. *Key point generation and matching.* Given a set of arguments on a certain topic that are grouped by their stance, first generate five to ten key points summarizing the arguments. Then, match each argument in the set to the generated key points (as in the previous track).

Data We start from the dataset provided by the organizers as described in Friedman et al. (2021). The dataset contains 28 controversial topics, with 6515 arguments and a total of 243 key points. For each argument, its stance towards the topic as well as a quality score are given. Each topic is represented by at least three key points, with at least one key point per stance and at least three arguments matched to a key point. From the given arguments, 4.7% are unmatched, 67.5% belong to a single key point, and 5.0% belong to multiple key points. The remaining 22.8% of the arguments have ambiguous labels, meaning that the annotators could not agree on a correct matching to the key points. The final dataset contains 24,093 argument-key point pairs, of which 20.7% are labeled as matching. To develop our approach, we use the split as provided by the organizers with 24 topics for training, four topics for validation, and three topics for testing.

4 Approach

Our approach consists of two components, each corresponding to one subtask of the KPA shared task. The first subtask of matching arguments to key points is modeled as a contrastive learning task using a siamese neural network. The second subtask requires generating key points for a collection of arguments and then matching them to the arguments. We investigated two models for this subtask: One is a graph-based extractive summarization model utilizing PageRank (Page et al., 1999) to extract sentences representing the key points; the other identifies aspects from the arguments and selects the most representative sentences that maximize the coverage of these aspects as the key points.

4.1 Key Point Matching

Conceptually, we consider pairs of arguments and key points that are close to each other in a semantic embedding space as possible candidates for matching. Furthermore, we seek to transform this space

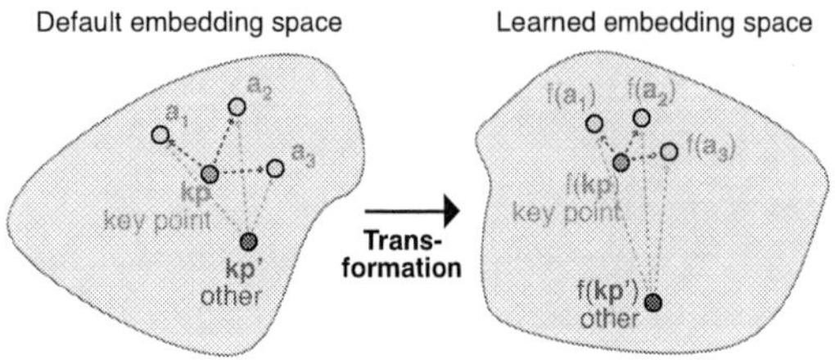

Figure 1: We learn to transform an embedding space into a new space in which matching pairs of key point and argument (e.g., kp and a_1) are closer to each other, and the distance between non-matching pairs (e.g., kp' and a_1) is larger. For simplicity, kp and kp' each represent a concatenation of key point and topic.

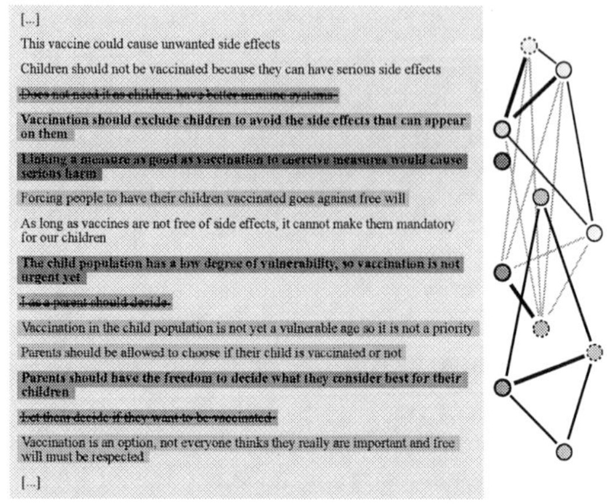

Figure 2: Example graph of our key point generation approach. Nodes with high saturation are considered to be key points (bold text). Nodes with dashed lines have lower argument quality. Edge thickness represents similarity between two nodes. Notice that the shown arguments do not reflect the view of the authors.

into a new embedding space where matching pairs are closer and the non-matching ones are more distant from each other (Figure 1). To do so, we utilize a siamese neural network with a contrastive loss function.

Specifically, in the training phase, the input is a topic along with a key point, an argument, and a label (matching or not). First, we use a pretrained language model to encode the tokens of the argument as well as those of the concatenation of the topic and the key point. Then, we pass their embeddings through a siamese neural network, which is a mean-pooling layer that aggregates the token embeddings of each input, resulting in two sentence-level embeddings. We compute the contrastive loss using these embeddings as follows:

$$\mathcal{L} = -y \cdot \log(\hat{y}) + (1-y) \cdot \log(1-\hat{y})$$

where $\hat{y}$ is the cosine similarity of the embeddings, and y reflects whether a pair matches (1) or not (0).

4.2 Key Point Generation

Our primary model for key point generation is a graph-based extractive summarization model. Additionally, we also investigate clustering the aspects of the given collection of arguments.

Graph-based Summarization Following the work of Alshomary et al. (2020a), we first construct an undirected graph with the arguments' sentences as nodes. As a filtering step, we compute argument quality scores for each sentence as Toledo et al. (2019) and exclude low-quality arguments from the graph. Next, we employ our key point matching model (Section 4.1) to compute the edge weight between two nodes as the pairwise matching score of the corresponding sentences. Only nodes with a score above a defined threshold are connected via an edge. An example graph is sketched in Figure 2. Finally, we use a variant of PageRank (Page et al., 1999) to compute an importance score $P(s_i)$ for each sentence s_i as follows:

$$P(s_i) = (1-d) \cdot \sum_{s_j \neq s_i} \frac{match(s_i, s_j)}{\sum_{s_k \neq s_j} match(s_j, s_k)} P(s_j) + d \cdot \frac{qual(s_i)}{\sum_{s_k} qual(s_k)} \quad (1)$$

where d is a damping factor that can be configured to bias the algorithm towards the argument quality score $qual$ or the matching score $match$. To ensure diversity, we iterate through the ranked list of sentences (in descending order), adding a sentence to the final set of key points if its maximum matching score with the already selected candidates is below a certain threshold.

Aspect Clustering Extracting key points is conceptually similar to identifying aspects (Bar-Haim et al., 2020a), which inspired our clustering approach that selects representative sentences from multiple aspect clusters as the final key points. We employ the tagger of Schiller et al. (2021) to extract the arguments' aspects (on average, 2.1 aspects per argument). To tackle the lack of diversity, we follow Heinisch and Cimiano (2021) and create k diverse aspect clusters by projecting the extracted aspect phrases to an embedding space. Next, we model the candidate selection of argument sentences as the set cover problem. Specifically, the

Approach	R-1	R-2	R-L
Graph-based Summarization	**19.8**	3.5	**18.0**
Aspect Clustering	18.9	**4.7**	17.1

Table 1: ROUGE scores on the test set for our two approaches to key point generation.

final set of key points summarizing the arguments for a given topic and stance maximizes the coverage of the set of arguments' aspects. To this end, we apply greedy approximation for selecting our candidates, where an argument sentence is chosen if it covers the maximum number of unique aspect clusters while having the smallest overlap with the clusters covered by the already selected candidates. Also, to avoid redundant key points, we compute its semantic similarity to the already selected candidates in each candidate selection step, and we add it to the final set if its score is below a certain threshold.

5 Experiments and Evaluation

In the following, we present implementation details of our two components, and we report on their quantitative and qualitative results.

5.1 Key Point Matching

We employed RoBERTa-large (Liu and Lapata, 2019) for encoding the tokens of the two inputs of key point matching to the siamese neural network, which acts as a mean-pooling layer and projects the encoder outputs (matrix of token embeddings) into a sentence embedding of size 768. We used Sentence-BERT (Reimers and Gurevych, 2019) to train our model for 10 epochs, with batch size 32, and maximum input length of 70, leaving all other parameters to their defaults.

For automatic evaluation, we computed both strict and relaxed mean Average Precision (mAP) following Friedman et al. (2021). In cases where there is no majority label for matching, the relaxed mAP considers them to be a match while the strict mAP considers them as not matching. In the development phase, we trained our model on the training split and evaluated on the validation split provided by the organizers. The strict and relaxed mAP on the validation set were 0.84 and 0.96 respectively. For the final submission, we did a five-fold cross validation on the combined data (training and validation splits) creating an ensemble for the matching (as per the mean score).

5.2 Key Point Generation

For the **graph-based summarization model**, we employed Spacy (Honnibal et al., 2020) to split the arguments into sentences. Similar to (Bar-Haim et al., 2020b), only sentences with a minimum of 5 and a maximum of 20 tokens, and not starting with a pronoun, were used for building the graph. Argument quality scores for each sentence were obtained from Project Debater's API (Toledo et al., 2019)[3]. We selected the thresholds for the parameters *d*, *qual* and *match* in Equation 1 as 0.2, 0.8 and 0.4 respectively, optimizing for ROUGE (Lin, 2004). In particular, we computed ROUGE-L between the ground-truth key points and the top 10 ranked sentences as our predictions, averaged over all the topic and stance combinations in the training split. We excluded sentences with a matching score higher than 0.8 with the selected candidates to minimize redundancy.

For **aspect clustering**, we created 15 clusters per topic and stance combination. After greedy approximation of the candidate sentences, we removed redundant ones using a threshold of 0.65 for the normalized BERTScore (Zhang et al., 2020) with the previously selected candidates.

Comparison of both approaches To select our primary approach for key point generation, we first performed an automatic evaluation of the aforementioned models on the test set using ROUGE (Table 1). Additionally, we performed a manual evaluation via pairwise comparison of the extracted key points for both models for a given topic and stance.

Examples of key points from both the models are shown in Table 2. The key points from graph-based summarization model are relatively longer. This also improves their informativeness, matching findings of Syed et al. (2021). For the aspect clustering, we observe that the key points are more focused on specific aspects such as "disease" (for Pro) and "effectiveness" (for Con). In a real-world application, this may provide the flexibility to choose key points by aspects of interest to the end-user, especially with further improvement of aspect tagger by avoiding non-essential extracted phrases as "mandatory". Hence, given the task of generating a quantitative summary of a collection of arguments, we believe that the graph-based summary provides

[3]Available under: https://early-access-program.debater.res.ibm.com/

Topic	Stance	Graph-based Summarization	Aspect Clustering
Routine child vaccinations should be mandatory	Pro	(1) Child vaccinations should be mandatory to provide decent health care to all. (2) Vaccines help children grow up healthy and avoid dangerous diseases. (3) Child vaccinations should be mandatory so our children will be safe and protected.	(1) Child vaccination is needed for children, they get sick too. (2) Routine child vaccinations should be mandatory to prevent the disease. (3) Yes as they protect children from life threatening and highly infectious diseases.
Routine child vaccinations should be mandatory	Con	(1) Vaccination should exclude children to avoid the side effects that can appear on them. (2) Parents should have the freedom to decide what they consider best for their children. (3) The child population has a low degree of vulnerability, so vaccination is not urgent yet.	(1) Child vaccination shouldn't be mandatory because the virus isn't effective in children. (2) Child vaccinations should not be mandatory because vaccines are expensive. (3) It has not been 100% proven if the vaccine is effective.

Table 2: Examples of keypoints from our proposed approaches. Only the top three key points are shown for brevity.

	KP Matching	KP Generation		
Approach	mAP/Rank	Rel.	Rep.	Pol.
bar_h	0.885/1	2	1	1
mspl (ours)	0.818/2	2	1	2
sohanpat	0.491/3	4	4	2
peratham	0.443/4	1	3	4

Table 3: Final evaluation results of both tracks, comparing our approach (mspl) to the top two submitted approaches, along with Bar-Haim et al. (2020b) approach (bar_h). The generated key points were ranked in terms of how relevant (Rel.) and representative (Rep.) of the input arguments, as well as their polarity (Pol.)

a more comprehensive overview and chose this as our preferred approach for key point generation.

5.3 Shared Task's Evaluation Results

In key point matching, our approach obtained a strict mAP of 0.789 and a relaxed mAP of 0.927 on the test set, the best result among all participating approaches. For the second track, in addition to evaluating the key point matching task, the shared task organizers manually evaluated the generated key points through a crowdsourcing study in which submitted approaches were ranked according to the quality of their generated key points. Table 3 presents the evaluation results of the top three submitted approaches, along with the reference approach of Bar-Haim et al. (2020b). Among the submitted approaches, our approach was ranked the best in both the key point generation task as well as the key point matching task. For complete details on the evaluation, we refer to the task organizers' report (Friedman et al., 2021).

6 Conclusion

This paper has presented a framework to tackle the key point analysis of arguments. For matching arguments to key points, we achieved the best performance in the KPA shared task via contrastive learning. For key point generation, we developed a graph-based extractive summarization model that output informative key points of high quality for a collection of arguments. We see abstractive key point generation as part of our future work.

References

Milad Alshomary, Nick Düsterhus, and Henning Wachsmuth. 2020a. Extractive snippet generation for arguments. In *Proceedings of the 43rd International ACM SIGIR conference on research and development in Information Retrieval, SIGIR 2020, Virtual Event, China, July 25-30, 2020*, pages 1969–1972. ACM.

Milad Alshomary, Shahbaz Syed, Martin Potthast, and Henning Wachsmuth. 2020b. Target inference in argument conclusion generation. In *Proceedings of the 58th Annual Meeting of the Association for Computational Linguistics, ACL 2020, Online, July 5-10, 2020*, pages 4334–4345. Association for Computational Linguistics.

Roy Bar-Haim, Lilach Eden, Roni Friedman, Yoav Kantor, Dan Lahav, and Noam Slonim. 2020a. From arguments to key points: Towards automatic argument summarization. In *Proceedings of the 58th Annual Meeting of the Association for Computational Linguistics*, pages 4029–4039. Association for Computational Linguistics.

Roy Bar-Haim, Yoav Kantor, Lilach Eden, Roni Friedman, Dan Lahav, and Noam Slonim. 2020b. Quantitative argument summarization and beyond: Cross-domain key point analysis. In *Proceedings of the*

2020 Conference on Empirical Methods in Natural Language Processing, EMNLP 2020, Online, November 16-20, 2020, pages 39–49. Association for Computational Linguistics.

Sumit Bhatia, Prakhar Biyani, and Prasenjit Mitra. 2014. Summarizing online forum discussions - can dialog acts of individual messages help? In *Proceedings of the 2014 Conference on Empirical Methods in Natural Language Processing, EMNLP 2014, October 25-29, 2014, Doha, Qatar, A meeting of SIGDAT, a Special Interest Group of the ACL*, pages 2127–2131. ACL.

Jane Bromley, Isabelle Guyon, Yann LeCun, Eduard Säckinger, and Roopak Shah. 1994. Signature verification using a "siamese" time delay neural network. In *Advances in neural information processing systems*, pages 737–744.

Johannes Daxenberger, Steffen Eger, Ivan Habernal, Christian Stab, and Iryna Gurevych. 2017. What is the essence of a claim? cross-domain claim identification. In *Proceedings of the 2017 Conference on Empirical Methods in Natural Language Processing*, pages 2055–2066, Copenhagen, Denmark. Association for Computational Linguistics.

Charlie Egan, Advaith Siddharthan, and Adam Z. Wyner. 2016. Summarising the points made in online political debates. In *Proceedings of the Third Workshop on Argument Mining, hosted by the 54th Annual Meeting of the Association for Computational Linguistics, ArgMining@ACL 2016, August 12, Berlin, Germany*. The Association for Computer Linguistics.

Roni Friedman, Lena Dankin, Yoav Katz, Yufang Hou, and Noam Slonim. 2021. Overview of KPA-2021 shared task: Key point based quantitative summarization.

Philipp Heinisch and Philipp Cimiano. 2021. A multitask approach to argument frame classification at variable granularity levels. *it - Information Technology*, 63(1):59–72.

Matthew Honnibal, Ines Montani, Sofie Van Landeghem, and Adriane Boyd. 2020. spaCy: Industrial-strength Natural Language Processing in Python.

Chin-Yew Lin. 2004. ROUGE: A package for automatic evaluation of summaries. In *Text Summarization Branches Out*, pages 74–81, Barcelona, Spain. Association for Computational Linguistics.

Yang Liu and Mirella Lapata. 2019. Text summarization with pretrained encoders. In *Proceedings of the 2019 Conference on Empirical Methods in Natural Language Processing and the 9th International Joint Conference on Natural Language Processing (EMNLP-IJCNLP)*, pages 3730–3740, Hong Kong, China. Association for Computational Linguistics.

Amita Misra, Brian Ecker, and Marilyn Walker. 2016. Measuring the similarity of sentential arguments in dialogue. In *Proceedings of the 17th Annual Meeting of the Special Interest Group on Discourse and Dialogue*, pages 276–287, Los Angeles. Association for Computational Linguistics.

Lawrence Page, Sergey Brin, Rajeev Motwani, and Terry Winograd. 1999. The pageRank citation ranking: Bringing order to the web. Technical report, Stanford InfoLab.

Georgios Petasis and Vangelis Karkaletsis. 2016. Identifying argument components through textrank. In *Proceedings of the Third Workshop on Argument Mining, hosted by the 54th Annual Meeting of the Association for Computational Linguistics, ArgMining@ACL 2016, August 12, Berlin, Germany*.

Nils Reimers and Iryna Gurevych. 2019. Sentence-bert: Sentence embeddings using siamese bert-networks. In *Proceedings of the 2019 Conference on Empirical Methods in Natural Language Processing*. Association for Computational Linguistics.

Benjamin Schiller, Johannes Daxenberger, and Iryna Gurevych. 2021. Aspect-controlled neural argument generation. In *Proceedings of the 2021 Conference of the North American Chapter of the Association for Computational Linguistics: Human Language Technologies, NAACL-HLT 2021, Online, June 6-11, 2021*, pages 380–396. Association for Computational Linguistics.

Shahbaz Syed, Roxanne El Baff, Johannes Kiesel, Khalid Al Khatib, Benno Stein, and Martin Potthast. 2020. News editorials: Towards summarizing long argumentative texts. In *Proceedings of the 28th International Conference on Computational Linguistics, COLING 2020, Barcelona, Spain (Online), December 8-13, 2020*, pages 5384–5396. International Committee on Computational Linguistics.

Shahbaz Syed, Khalid Al Khatib, Milad Alshomary, Henning Wachsmuth, and Martin Potthast. 2021. Generating informative conclusions for argumentative texts. *CoRR*, abs/2106.01064.

Assaf Toledo, Shai Gretz, Edo Cohen-Karlik, Roni Friedman, Elad Venezian, Dan Lahav, Michal Jacovi, Ranit Aharonov, and Noam Slonim. 2019. Automatic argument quality assessment-new datasets and methods. In *Proceedings of the 2019 Conference on Empirical Methods in Natural Language Processing and the 9th International Joint Conference on Natural Language Processing (EMNLP-IJCNLP)*, pages 5625–5635.

Lu Wang and Wang Ling. 2016. Neural network-based abstract generation for opinions and arguments. In *Proceedings of the 2016 Conference of the North American Chapter of the Association for Computational Linguistics: Human Language Technologies*, pages 47–57, San Diego, California. Association for Computational Linguistics.

Tianyi Zhang, Varsha Kishore, Felix Wu, Kilian Q. Weinberger, and Yoav Artzi. 2020. Bertscore: Evaluating text generation with bert. In *International Conference on Learning Representations*.

Key Point Matching with Transformers

Emanuele Cosenza
University of Pisa, Italy
e.cosenza3@studenti.unipi.it

Abstract

Key point analysis (KPA) has been proposed as a way to summarize arguments with short-sized pieces of text termed key points. This work aims at describing a solution for the Track 1 of the KPA 2021 shared task, analyzing different methodologies for the specific problem of key point matching, which consists in finding a reasonable mapping from arguments to key points. The analysis will focus on transformer based architectures, experimentally investigating the effectiveness of variants specifically tailored to the task.

1 Introduction

In the context of natural language processing, text summarization is the act of creating a concise summary of a given text. This is particularly useful when the text at hand represents arguments, i.e. opinions, about a certain topic. An example is that of political debates, in which politicians express opinions concerning the subject matter. Another scenario is that of e-commerce sites, where users can write reviews about different items. In both cases, a third party can greatly benefit from a summary of the arguments in order to make effective decisions.

In recent years, there have been several attempts to automatize the summarization of arguments in a meaningful way. The first works focused on clustering, by which arguments are assigned to clusters based on different notions of relatedness (e.g. semantic similarity) between pairs of arguments (Reimers et al., 2019; Ajjour et al., 2019; Misra et al., 2016). Unfortunately, with this methodology the actual summary of the arguments had to be compiled manually by analyzing the contents of the clusters. More recently, Bar-Haim et al. (2020a) proposed to transform the summarization problem into what has been named key point analysis (KPA). Given a certain topic of discussion, arguments are summarized by matching them to a short list of high-level summaries, called *key points*. This allows a quantitative approach to summarization, in which the saliency of a key point (i.e. the degree of matched arguments) gives a hint of the underlying nature of the arguments. Even though Bar-Haim et al. (2020a) have shown that a domain expert can create meaningful key points for a topic even without looking at the arguments, the final goal of this field would be to generate the key points and match them with the respective arguments without human intervention. With this goal in mind, the KPA 2021 shared task [1] (Friedman et al., 2021) poses two problems to its participants: a key point matching subtask (Track 1) and a key point generation subtask (Track 2). This paper describes a solution to the key point matching subtask, in which key points are given and the goal is to match them with the appropriate arguments. The problem is framed as a classification task and the paper will focus on analyzing different transformer based models with different possible variants.

All experiments are executed on a Nvidia Tesla P100 with limited access. The computational limitations have influenced many design choices and results of the paper.

2 KPA 2021 shared task: data and evaluation metrics

As training data, the proponents shared the *ArgKP* dataset (Bar-Haim et al., 2020a) divided into training and development sets, containing respectively 24 and 4 debate topics of various nature and arguments mined from the internet. The dataset contains 24,093 `<argument, key point>` pairs. Each pair is associated with the concerned topic, presented as a short-sized text, and the stance towards the topic (+1 for the pro side, -1 for the con side). A binary label (1 for a match, 0 otherwise) is

[1] `https://github.com/IBM/KPA_2021_shared_task`

Proceedings of The 8th Workshop on Argument Mining, pages 190–199
Punta Cana, Dominican Republic, November 10–11, 2021.

assigned only to <argument, key point> pairs under the same stance towards the topic, noting that arguments and key points having opposite stance automatically constitute a mismatch. At the end of the competition, the task organizers have also released an external test set containing 3 topics, totalling 3426 pairs, to be used for the final evaluation and ranking of participants.

Not every feasible pair appears in the labeled data. A pair appears in the dataset as a match or a mismatch if, respectively, more than 60% or less than 15% of the original annotators labeled it as matching. All the other pairs are not included in the dataset. Intuitively, this ensures that the pairs are not labeled ambiguously whenever there was no net agreement between the annotators. Even if the dataset is constructed like so, in the evaluation phase of the task the final model will be queried on all possible pairs including the unlabeled ones, testing the system's ability to deal with uncertainty. In fact, the model will have to output, for each argument, a match score in [0, 1] for each of the key points under the same topic and in the same stance towards the topic.

The task is evaluated by the average rank of the *strict* and the *relaxed* mean Average Precisions (mAP), where the ranks are intended as the final positions of the two values in the rankings of the competition. The mAP, which is the mean of the precision values of the model at different recalls, is chosen as a metric since it gives a summary of the recall-precision curve without having to choose a specific classification threshold. Given the match scores output by a model on a certain dataset, the strict and relaxed mAP values are computed as follows. First, each argument is paired with the highest scoring key point. Then, half of the lowest matching pairs are discarded. This is done to avoid evaluating the model on arguments with no matching key points. At this point, precision values and therefore mAP values can be computed on the remaining pairs based on the labeled data. Note, however, that a pair can have a high match score but no labels in the dataset because of its ambiguity. In this case, the pair can arbitrarily be considered a match or a mismatch. This results in the computation of two different mAP scores: a strict mAP, for which absent pairs are considered a match, and a relaxed mAP, for which the pairs are considered a mismatch. The final values are computed by taking the macro-average of strict and relaxed mAP values for each topic/stance combination.

3 Methodological survey

Assigning a match score to an <argument, key point> pair can be considered as a text classification task where the problem is to determine the probability that the pair is a match. In recent years, transfer learning through fine-tuning of pretrained transformers such as BERT (Devlin et al., 2018) have dramatically improved results on a variety of NLP tasks, including classification. Furthermore, transformer based architectures are particularly suited for the task of sentence pair classification. In fact, many of these models are pretrained on tasks such as next sentence prediction (NSP) and sentence order prediction (SOP), which require the model to take in pairs of sentences or segments and to classify them accordingly. This implies that the *ArgKP* dataset can be easily adapted to these models. Moreover, since the models have already learned how to process and internally represent sentences, one would expect to see good results also in the context of key point matching. For these reasons, this work focuses on transformers. This is not a limiting decision, since there are many transformers architectures to test and many possible variants for each model. In literature, previous works related to KPA (Bar-Haim et al., 2020a,b) already report results for 4 transformer based models, namely BERT (Devlin et al., 2018), XLNet (Yang et al., 2019), RoBERTa (Liu et al., 2019) and ALBERT (Lan et al., 2019), considering only their largest versions. For each model, only classification metrics such as accuracy, precision, recall and F1 scores are reported. This work aims at expanding the analysis by studying the behavior of the models under the metrics of the competition and by experimentally evaluating new variants. In particular, to allow a comparison with the state of the art, the same 4 transformers are analyzed also here, extending the investigation to smaller versions of the models and to other variants that will be described later on. Smaller models are not expected to be superior to the larger versions. Nonetheless, they are included in the study to give a reference point regarding their performance on the task of key point matching.

Key point matching can also be considered as an instantiation of a natural language inference (NLI) task (Dagan et al., 2013), where the problem is to determine whether the key point logically follows from the argument (or viceversa). However, fine-tuning models pretrained on NLI datasets already showed no improvement in literature (Bar-Haim et al., 2020a). Because of this and of the additional computational burden caused by pretraining on large NLI datasets, this variant is avoided.

Besides basic transformers, this work includes SBERT (Reimers and Gurevych, 2019), a sentence embedding transformer model. SBERT produces semantically meaningful sentence embeddings, which means that semantically similar sentences are close in the vector space. SBERT has been used alone, without fine-tuning, computing the cosine similarity between arguments and key points embeddings. Furthermore, it has also been used in one of the variants, feeding its outputs to the linear top-layer of the transformer based models to see if adding information about semantically meaningful sentence embeddings yields an increase in the performance.

BERT, XLNet, RoBERTa and ALBERT have been downloaded through the huggingface library (Wolf et al., 2020), while SBERT has been downloaded through the Sentence-Transformers Python framework, choosing the `paraphrase-mpnet-base-v2` model since it has the best performance on a variety of different tasks. BERT is uncased. XLNet and RoBERTa are cased since no uncased versions have been released for them. For each transformer other than SBERT and ALBERT, both `base` and `large` versions have been tested. For what concerns ALBERT, `albert-base-v2` has been used for the smaller version, while `albert-xxlarge-v1` has been chosen for the larger version since it is generally better than `albert-xxlarge-v2` on downstream tasks.

A thorough analysis should have included also RNNs and CNNs. In fact, arguments and key points are generally short-sized and simpler models may actually work better in this context. However, given the non negligible computational limitations of this work, discarding these and other valuable models allowed for the exploration of a greater number of transformer based architectures and variants.

4 Data preprocessing and analysis

Since the training data shared by the organizers is split into a training (TR) and a validation set (VL), an internal test set (TS) split had to be extracted from the TR in order to assess the performance of the final model. In order not to allow different `<argument, key point>` pairs under the same topic to be spread between different splits, the TS has been extracted from the TR by doing a topic based division. The final internal TS contains 3 topics with a total of 3164 pairs, while the final TR and VL contain respectively 21 and 4 topics with a total of 17471 and 3458 pairs.

Arguments are mined from the internet and even if they have been originally filtered, their quality can vary a lot throughout the dataset. They sometimes contain misspellings and an informal use of symbols (e.g. slash between words). Even if there is evidence of the fact that BERT based models can suffer from natural adversarial instances such as typos (Sun et al., 2020), the quality of the dataset has not been improved for the sake of simplicity.

As mentioned earlier in the paper, for each `<argument, key point>` pair the dataset also contains the concerned topic and the stance towards it. Adding the topic to the input of the model is useful especially when neither the argument nor the key point contains enough information about the context of discourse. In previous works, the topic has not been included in the inputs and therefore its utility will be tested in one of the variants presented later. When the topic is considered, it is simply prepended to the concerned argument and the input to the model therefore becomes `<topic+argument, kp>`. Notice, however, that topics are always written in the affirmative form as in *"Kids should be wearing uniforms at school"*. When the stance towards the topic is negative, in order not to fool the model by giving it contradictory information, the topic should be expressed in its negative form. One way to do this would be to encode the stance as a binary input to the linear output layers. Here, instead, affirmative topic are simply transformed into their negative form in order to exploit the encoding capabilities of the transformers. Transforming an affirmation to a negation is not a trivial task, but fortunately the topics contained in the dataset and in the external TS are all in the form SUBJECT + *should* or *is* + REST. This allows to just add *not* after *should* or *is* in order to complete the transfor-

mation, noting that, in order to make the system generalizable, one would have to develop a fully working affirmative-to-negative module. The alternative to this would have been to encode the stance as a binary input to the models.
Arguments appear in the dataset in all lower case, all caps (a very small portion) and a mixture of both. Arguably, in the context of key point matching, a cased analyis of the text would not be much useful. For this reason, `uncased` models have been used when possible, transforming the text to lowercase before processing it. All text is tokenized and transformed to lowercase by relying on the different tokenizers provided by each transformer. Finally, each <`arg, kp`> pair is transformed by the tokenizer as follows: `[cls] arg [sep] kp [sep]`.

5 Models and variants

In the model selection phase, BERT, ALBERT, ROBERTA, XLNet and SBERT are all tested with the following modalities. For each model except SBERT, the representations computed by the transformers are fed to a single linear layer with two output logits. A softmax layer is then used at evaluation time to compute the final match probability. Each model except SBERT can have multiple possible configurations corresponding to different variants of the basic models. This work focuses on three main variants. First, one can decide whether to inform or not the model about the topic with the modalities shown in the previous section. Second, the final contextualized representations output by the transformers can be computed in a number of different ways as in Devlin et al. (2018). This was allowed since the best representation usually depends on the particular task at issue. One can decide to just take the `[cls]` token representation or to get a final vector by applying a pooling operation to the hidden representations of the transformer. Three pooling options are available: average of the last layer (`avg_last`), average of the second last layer (`avg_2ndlast`), average of the sum of the last four layers (`avg_sumlast4`). Finally, one can choose to concatenate the 768-dimensional SBERT embeddings of the two input segments to the representation output by the transformer. This was allowed to see if adding information about semantically meaningful sentence embeddings would help the models in the classification task.

6 Training procedure and model selection

6.1 Metrics

Before training, an evaluation metric had to be defined in order to make the model selection possible. The metric should follow the one used in the competition so to favor models that can potentially place high in the final rankings. As explained earlier, the metrics involved in the competition are the strict and relaxed mAP scores. More specifically, the final rank of a system is determined by the average of the ranks of the strict and relaxed mAP values. For this reason, the average of the two scores, indicated from now on with Avg mAP, has been used as the metric. Notice that this is not the same thing as the average of the ranks. Still, this is a reasonable way give importance to both scores. Furthermore, a model with a high Avg mAP is also likely to have a high average rank. When computing the Avg mAP, the strict and relaxed mAP scores have been determined with the already outlined procedure used by the organizers.

Even if the task does not require the models to compute the actual classification labels, for the sake of completeness, classification metrics such as accuracy, precision, recall and F1 scores have been computed both on the TR and the VL. Computing classification labels from match scores can be done in multiple ways as shown in Bar-Haim et al. (2020a). It can be done locally, considering just the single score of a pair, or globally, taking into account all the match scores between an argument and the key points. Since this problem was not the focus of the paper, only two simple local methods have been evaluated. In the first one, a match score is trivially transformed using a threshold of 0.5. In the second one, the threshold is learned and is chosen to maximize the F1 score on the TR. Since the learned threshold often generalizes worse than the fixed one, it is not considered in the discussion and related results are shown in Appendix A.

6.2 Training

All models are fine-tuned end to end without freezing the transformers, using Adam as the optimizer and cross entropy loss as the loss function. The hyperparameters of the models are fixed before the model selection, following when possible the configurations employed in the papers of the respective transformers. The dropout rate of the transformers is always the default one (0.1). In the final linear layer, dropout is always set to 0.1. Also, the maximum number of epochs e is always 3 and checkpoints are saved in each epoch whenever the cross entropy loss on the VL reaches a new minimum. The number of epochs was found by manually checking the convergence of the models during the preliminary phase of the study. The batch size b is set to 32. When training smaller models a fixed learning rate is used. For the largest models, which show no convergence with a constant learning rate, a learning rate schedule is used following the original papers. The same warm up and linear decay schedules are used for each model. The duration of the warm up phase was found by trying different values and by checking if the models converged. At the end, the number of training steps of the warm up phase was heuristically computed as $\frac{1}{5}$ of the total training steps $\frac{|TR|}{b}e$, which amounts to around 300 steps.

6.3 Model selection

For computational reasons, the model selection procedure has been divided into two phases. The procedure is suboptimal but it nonetheless gives a hint of what is the appropriate model for the task. For the same reason, instead of a robust cross-validation procedure, hold-out validation is executed in both phases. Given the relatively high number of models to be tested and the long training time of transformers, cross-validation would have been unfeasible with the computational limitations of this work. In the first phase, the chosen models (both small and large) are all trained and validated with their basic configurations, which are the ones that use the `cls` token representation, no topic and no concatenation of SBERT embeddings. Then, the best model on the VL, i.e. the one that has the highest Avg mAP score, is selected for the second phase. In this phase, the selected model is trained again on the same data splits in a grid search with 16 different configurations. At the end, the model with the best configuration on VL is chosen as the final system and is used for the evaluation on the internal and external TS.
Given the limited access to the used machine, all results are obtained with a single random seed, without averaging multiple runs.

6.4 Results

Results on TR and VL of the first phase of the model selection are shown in Table 1. As already mentioned, training is executed only on labeled data, while results are computed also on all possible `<arg, kp>` pairs. In the table, strict and relaxed mAP values computed on all possible pairs are shown on VL but not on TR. This is done to avoid showing TR results on data which the model has never seen during training. The table also contains the average of strict and relaxed mAP. This is the metric used to select the best model. SBERT, the only unsupervised model in the analysis, is the worst model as expected and serves as a baseline for the other models. However, even if the model is not fine-tuned for the task, the results are not so far from those of the fine-tuned models in terms of Avg mAP. This is remarkable, given that the sentence embeddings and the cosine similarity scores can be computed in a matter of seconds without any training process. RoBERTa, on the other hand, is the best of the models in terms of Avg mAP with ALBERT as a close second. Table 2 shows the classification metrics on TR and VL for the same models. The results are similar to those reported in Bar-Haim et al. (2020a). ALBERT is the best model under all metrics except for the recall, while SBERT is the worst one with a very low precision, showing its weaknesses as an unsupervised model. Even if RoBERTa managed to beat the other models under the specified metrics, ALBERT may be better overall for the task of key point matching when considering non ambiguous data. However, given the results of this first model selection, RoBERTa was selected for the second phase.

Results on both TR and VL for the second phase of the model selection are shown in Table 3. Remember that with the employed hold-out validation procedure results may be non representative of the actual performance of the models. Nonetheless, analyzing the general behavior of the different variants may give an idea about their effectiveness. Variants exploiting the topic show an average increase of more than 0.02 in the Avg mAP, indicating that including the topic in the input actually helped. On the other hand, there are no clear winners among the different pooling methods. On average, `avg_last` was the best, while `cls` was the worst. Similarly, the concatenation of the SBERT embeddings did not make much difference and on average they actually caused a

Model	Type	TR	VL				
		Loss	Loss	mAP (S)	mAP (R)	Avg mAP	Time (TR)
SBERT	`paraphrase-mpnet-base-v2`	0.743	0.729	0.759	0.904	0.831	-
BERT	`base-uncased`	0.115	0.409	0.817	0.964	0.891	00:06:10
	`large-uncased`	0.127	0.389	0.765	0.95	0.857	00:20:41
XLNet	`base-cased`	0.27	0.302	0.779	0.94	0.86	00:09:41
	`large-cased`	0.207	0.333	0.767	0.945	0.856	00:27:38
RoBERTa	`base`	0.153	0.271	0.823	0.954	0.889	00:06:17
	`large`	**0.057**	0.226	**0.884**	**0.995**	**0.939**	00:21:17
ALBERT	`base-v2`	0.134	0.298	0.762	0.926	0.844	00:06:33
	`xxlarge-v1`	0.09	**0.223**	0.879	0.992	0.935	02:03:37

Table 1: Results and training times of transformer based models on TR and VL in the first phase of the model selection. (S) = strict, (R) = relaxed, Loss = cross entropy loss. Avg mAP is the average between strict and relaxed mAP.

	Model	Type	Accuracy	Precision	Recall	F1
TR	SBERT	`paraphrase-mpnet-base-v2`	0.455	0.261	0.888	0.403
	BERT	`bert-base-uncased`	0.963	0.911	0.909	0.91
		`bert-large-uncased`	0.96	0.911	0.893	0.902
	XLNet	`xlnet-base-cased`	0.894	0.753	0.73	0.741
		`xlnet-large-cased`	0.918	0.839	0.75	0.792
	RoBERTa	`roberta-base`	0.945	0.929	0.793	0.856
		`roberta-large`	**0.98**	**0.981**	0.919	**0.949**
	ALBERT	`albert-base-v2`	0.956	0.968	0.813	0.884
		`albert-xxlarge-v1`	0.971	0.926	**0.937**	0.931
VL	SBERT	`paraphrase-mpnet-base-v2`	0.488	0.284	0.921	0.434
	BERT	`bert-base-uncased`	0.82	0.554	0.82	0.661
		`bert-large-uncased`	0.824	0.561	0.813	0.664
	XLNet	`xlnet-base-cased`	0.891	**0.771**	0.695	0.731
		`xlnet-large-cased`	0.865	0.676	0.709	0.692
	RoBERTa	`roberta-base`	0.896	0.764	0.745	0.754
		`roberta-large`	0.912	0.744	0.894	0.812
	ALBERT	`albert-base-v2`	0.89	0.727	0.774	0.75
		`albert-xxlarge-v1`	**0.918**	0.749	**0.925**	**0.828**

Table 2: Classification results on TR and VL with classification threshold set to 0.5 in the first phase of the model selection.

slight degradation of the performance. Finally, the model with the best Avg mAP score was the one exploiting the `[cls]` token representation, the topic and the SBERT embeddings. This is the final model used for the evaluation on the internal and external TS. Table 4 shows its results under the classification metrics on TR and VL.

7 Test set results and analysis

Having chosen the best model on the VL, the last phase consisted of its assessment on the internal and external TS. Results on both internal and external TS with a reference to previous results on VL are shown in Table 5. Under the chosen metrics, the performance of the model on the internal TS is remarkably higher than on the VL, showing an increase of about 2% in the avg mAP caused by a sharp increase in the strict mAP. Compared to the results on the VL, the model seems to behave well also on the external TS, showing only a slight decrease in the avg mAP. Table 6 shows classification metrics on VL, internal and external TS. On the internal TS, the model still gives good results, improving the F1 score of the VL. On the other hand, the model drastically loses its precision on the external TS while having a high recall, which indicates that the model tended to match the pairs

SBERT	Topic	Pooling	TR	VL			
			Loss	Loss	mAP (S)	mAP (R)	Avg mAP
N	N	cls	0.057	0.226	0.884	0.995	0.939
N	N	avg_last	0.061	0.242	0.868	0.979	0.924
N	N	avg_2ndlast	0.109	0.259	0.869	0.995	0.932
N	N	avg_sumlast4	0.053	0.281	0.881	0.993	0.937
N	Y	cls	0.132	0.205	0.896	0.995	0.945
N	Y	avg_last	0.115	0.212	0.897	0.995	0.946
N	Y	avg_2ndlast	0.043	0.219	0.889	**0.998**	0.943
N	Y	avg_sumlast4	0.049	0.317	0.885	0.991	0.938
Y	N	cls	0.211	0.251	0.789	0.961	0.875
Y	N	avg_last	0.119	0.207	0.877	0.995	0.936
Y	N	avg_2ndlast	0.117	**0.197**	0.872	0.991	0.931
Y	N	avg_sumlast4	0.118	0.249	0.837	0.978	0.907
Y	Y	cls	**0.036**	0.262	**0.901**	**0.998**	**0.949**
Y	Y	avg_last	0.133	0.261	0.882	0.99	0.936
Y	Y	avg_2ndlast	0.052	0.285	0.872	0.995	0.933
Y	Y	avg_sumlast4	0.096	0.236	0.868	0.992	0.93

Table 3: Results of RoBERTa and variants on TR and VL in the second phase of the model selection. SBERT indicates whether SBERT embeddings are concatenated to the transformer outputs before feeding them to the final linear layer. Topic specifies if the topic is being given as input to the model. Pooling indicates the type of pooling employed to get the final contextualized representation from the transformer. (S) = strict, (R) = relaxed, Loss = cross entropy loss. Avg mAP is the average between strict and relaxed mAPs.

	Accuracy	Precision	Recall	F1
TR	0.990	0.978	0.973	0.976
VL	0.907	0.725	0.911	0.807

Table 4: Classification metrics on TR and VL for the best model of the second phase of the model selection. The classification threshold is set to 0.5.

too often. This, together with the model selection results, indicates that the used metrics may favor models which do not perform necessarily well on non ambiguous labeled data.

8 Error analysis

To complete the study, errors on the external TS have been analyzed manually in order to try to understand the weaknesses of the model. To avoid choosing a particular threshold for the classification labeling, only the pairs which the model was most confident about have been considered for the study.

Since the final model has a low precision, most of the analysis focused on the pairs labeled with 0 that have been wrongly matched. What emerged was that, at first glance, many of these pairs seemed to be matching also for a human. For humans, a reasonable match score can be assigned only after seeing all the possible key points and the general distribution of the arguments. To show an example, consider the following topic, argument and key point in order: *"Routine child vaccinations should be mandatory"*, *"Child vaccination should be mandatory to prevent children from spreading the virus"*, *"Routine child vaccinations are necessary to protect others"*. The argument seems to be matching the key point to a high degree. Let us now introduce a key point that actually matches the argument: *"Routine child vaccinations should be mandatory to prevent virus/disease spreading"*. The argument seems to be matching this second key point more than the first one. The score assigment can be also influenced

	Loss	mAP (S)	mAP (R)	Avg mAP
VL	0.262	0.901	0.998	0.949
Internal TS	0.208	0.940	0.996	0.968
External TS	0.366	0.900	0.977	0.939

Table 5: Results of the final model on VL, internal TS and external TS. mAP (with no letters) is computed with labeled data only. (S) = strict, (R) = relaxed, Loss = cross entropy loss. Avg mAP is the average between strict and relaxed mAP.

	Accuracy	Precision	Recall	F1
VL	0.907	0.725	0.911	0.807
Internal TS	0.929	0.796	0.868	0.830
External TS	0.883	0.585	0.933	0.719

Table 6: Classification metrics on VL, internal TS and external TS of the final model. The classification threshold is set to 0.5.

by the nature of the other arguments. If the arguments generally happen to match key points in a strict way, one may end up assigning lower scores to looser but still matching pairs. This indicates that, perhaps, the model should be informed about the existence of other key points and arguments to assign the scores in a reasonable way.

Other more subtle errors are caused by the model wrongly associating different terms coming from the same semantic field. Consider for example the following topic, argument and key point: *"The USA is not a good country to live in"*, *"The USA is a bad country to live in because some people are aggressive"*, *"The US is xenophobic/racist"*. Here, the model is fooled by the semantic similarity between aggressiveness and xenophobia/racism. More specifically, since transformer based models are pretrained focusing only on the co-occurrence of words, the model is not aware of the actual logical relationship between them. Consequently, it can not know that someone who is aggressive is not necessarily xenophobic or racist.

Lastly, some errors depend on the bad quality of the arguments and of the labeling. Consider the following triple: *"The USA is not a good country to live in"*, *"Not because it is a country with many restrictions for immigrants."*, *"The US is xenophobic/racist"*. The model correctly assigns a low score to the input. However, the pair is labeled with a 1, indicating that the annotator interpreted the initial *"Not"* as a mining mistake.

9 Conclusions

Key point analysis is a promising way to summarize a large number of arguments about a certain topic. In this paper, which describes a solution for the Track 1 of the KPA 2021 shared task, the specific problem of assigning match scores to `<argument, key point>` pairs was tackled by framing it as a text classification task, focusing on different state of the art transformer-based architectures and variants specifically tailored to the problem. The analysis included a number of different transformers, namely BERT, XLNet, RoBERTa and ALBERT, as well as sentence embedding transformers, such as SBERT. After a lightweight model selection procedure, RoBERTa managed to beat the other models under the metrics imposed by the competition. Informing the model about the topic (appropriately modified based on the stance) has been beneficial for the overall performance. On the other hand, supplying the model with information about the semantic similarity between arguments and key points through SBERT embeddings gave no particular advantage. Similarly, changing the type of pooling of the transformer's hidden representations did not result in any notable difference. After the evaluation on the external TS, the model maintained a good behavior under the specified metrics, which take into account ambiguous non-labeled data, while getting a low precision on non-ambiguous data, showing that the metrics may favor imprecise models. Lastly, the final error analysis showed how the classification problem as formulated in the paper may be underspecified and that the model should also be informed about the existence of other key points and arguments. Moreover, particular errors highlighted the intrinsic weaknesses of transformer based models in the task of key point matching.

Many choices and results of this work have been determined by computational limitations. With more computational power, one could improve the model selection by employing a robust cross-validation procedure and by testing other valuable architectures. Finally, as suggested by the error analysis, an interesting direction in the key point matching related research would be to experiment with models that take information regarding multiple key points and arguments when computing a match score for a single <`argument, key point`> pair.

References

Yamen Ajjour, Milad Alshomary, Henning Wachsmuth, and Benno Stein. 2019. Modeling frames in argumentation. In *Proceedings of the 2019 Conference on Empirical Methods in Natural Language Processing and the 9th International Joint Conference on Natural Language Processing (EMNLP-IJCNLP)*, pages 2922–2932, Hong Kong, China. Association for Computational Linguistics.

Roy Bar-Haim, Lilach Eden, Roni Friedman, Yoav Kantor, Dan Lahav, and Noam Slonim. 2020a. From arguments to key points: Towards automatic argument summarization. In *Proceedings of the 58th Annual Meeting of the Association for Computational Linguistics*, pages 4029–4039, Online. Association for Computational Linguistics.

Roy Bar-Haim, Yoav Kantor, Lilach Eden, Roni Friedman, Dan Lahav, and Noam Slonim. 2020b. Quantitative argument summarization and beyond: Cross-domain key point analysis. *arXiv preprint arXiv:2010.05369*.

Ido Dagan, Dan Roth, Mark Sammons, and Fabio Massimo Zanzotto. 2013. Recognizing textual entailment: Models and applications. *Synthesis Lectures on Human Language Technologies*, 6(4):1–220.

Jacob Devlin, Ming-Wei Chang, Kenton Lee, and Kristina Toutanova. 2018. Bert: Pre-training of deep bidirectional transformers for language understanding. *arXiv preprint arXiv:1810.04805*.

Roni Friedman, Lena Dankin, Yoav Katz, Yufang Hou, and Noam Slonim. 2021. Overview of kpa-2021 shared task: Key point based quantitative summarization. In *Proceedings of the 8th Workshop on Argumentation Mining*. Association for Computational Linguistics.

Zhenzhong Lan, Mingda Chen, Sebastian Goodman, Kevin Gimpel, Piyush Sharma, and Radu Soricut. 2019. Albert: A lite bert for self-supervised learning of language representations. *arXiv preprint arXiv:1909.11942*.

Yinhan Liu, Myle Ott, Naman Goyal, Jingfei Du, Mandar Joshi, Danqi Chen, Omer Levy, Mike Lewis, Luke Zettlemoyer, and Veselin Stoyanov. 2019. Roberta: A robustly optimized bert pretraining approach. *arXiv preprint arXiv:1907.11692*.

Amita Misra, Brian Ecker, and Marilyn Walker. 2016. Measuring the similarity of sentential arguments in dialogue. In *Proceedings of the 17th Annual Meeting of the Special Interest Group on Discourse and Dialogue*, pages 276–287, Los Angeles. Association for Computational Linguistics.

Nils Reimers and Iryna Gurevych. 2019. Sentence-bert: Sentence embeddings using siamese bert-networks. *arXiv preprint arXiv:1908.10084*.

Nils Reimers, Benjamin Schiller, Tilman Beck, Johannes Daxenberger, Christian Stab, and Iryna Gurevych. 2019. Classification and clustering of arguments with contextualized word embeddings. In *Proceedings of the 57th Annual Meeting of the Association for Computational Linguistics*, pages 567–578, Florence, Italy. Association for Computational Linguistics.

Lichao Sun, Kazuma Hashimoto, Wenpeng Yin, Akari Asai, Jia Li, Philip Yu, and Caiming Xiong. 2020. Adv-bert: Bert is not robust on misspellings! generating nature adversarial samples on bert. *arXiv preprint arXiv:2003.04985*.

Thomas Wolf, Lysandre Debut, Victor Sanh, Julien Chaumond, Clement Delangue, Anthony Moi, Pierric Cistac, Tim Rault, Rémi Louf, Morgan Funtowicz, Joe Davison, Sam Shleifer, Patrick von Platen, Clara Ma, Yacine Jernite, Julien Plu, Canwen Xu, Teven Le Scao, Sylvain Gugger, Mariama Drame, Quentin Lhoest, and Alexander M. Rush. 2020. Transformers: State-of-the-art natural language processing. In *Proceedings of the 2020 Conference on Empirical Methods in Natural Language Processing: System Demonstrations*, pages 38–45, Online. Association for Computational Linguistics.

Zhilin Yang, Zihang Dai, Yiming Yang, Jaime Carbonell, Russ R Salakhutdinov, and Quoc V Le. 2019. Xlnet: Generalized autoregressive pretraining for language understanding. *Advances in neural information processing systems*, 32.

A Classification results with F1 maximizer classification threshold

	Model	Type	Th	Accuracy	Precision	Recall	F1
TR	SBERT	paraphrase-mpnet-base-v2	0.666	0.749	0.418	0.535	0.470
	BERT	bert-base-uncased	0.459	0.963	0.906	0.918	0.912
		bert-large-uncased	0.443	0.96	0.901	0.904	0.903
	XLNet	xlnet-base-cased	0.498	0.894	0.752	0.731	0.742
		xlnet-large-cased	0.376	0.916	0.791	0.806	0.798
	RoBERTa	roberta-base	0.315	0.948	0.877	0.869	0.873
		roberta-large	0.264	0.983	0.958	0.959	0.958
	ALBERT	albert-base-v2	0.132	0.966	0.92	0.914	0.917
		albert-xxlarge-v1	0.697	0.974	0.95	0.923	0.936
VL	SBERT	paraphrase-mpnet-base-v2	0.666	0.744	0.430	0.619	0.508
	BERT	bert-base-uncased	0.459	0.814	0.542	0.836	0.658
		bert-large-uncased	0.443	0.815	0.544	0.827	0.656
	XLNet	xlnet-base-cased	0.498	0.89	0.768	0.695	0.73
		xlnet-large-cased	0.376	0.851	0.625	0.757	0.685
	RoBERTa	roberta-base	0.315	0.87	0.654	0.829	0.731
		roberta-large	0.264	0.866	0.626	0.927	0.748
	ALBERT	albert-base-v2	0.132	0.847	0.602	0.835	0.7
		albert-xxlarge-v1	0.697	0.929	0.799	0.889	0.842

Table 7: Classification results on TR and VL with F1 score optimizing classification threshold in the first phase of the model selection.

Team Enigma at ArgMining-EMNLP 2021: Leveraging Pre-trained Language Models for Key Point Matching

Manav Nitin Kapadnis*, **Sohan Patnaik***,
Siba Smarak Panigrahi*, **Varun Madhavan***, **Abhilash Nandy**
Indian Institute of Technology Kharagpur
{iammanavk, sohanpatnaik106, sibasmarak.p, varun.m.iitkgp, nandyabhilash}@gmail.com

Abstract

We present the system description for our submission towards the Key Point Analysis Shared Task at ArgMining 2021. Track 1 of the shared task requires participants to develop methods to predict the match score between each pair of arguments and keypoints, provided they belong to the same topic under the same stance. We leveraged existing state of the art pre-trained language models along with incorporating additional data and features extracted from the inputs (topics, key points, and arguments) to improve performance. We were able to achieve *mAP* strict and *mAP* relaxed score of 0.872 and 0.966 respectively in the evaluation phase, securing 5th place[1] on the leaderboard. In the post evaluation phase, we achieved a *mAP* strict and *mAP* relaxed score of 0.921 and 0.982 respectively. All the codes to generate reproducible results on our models are available on Github[2].

1 Introduction

The Quantitative Summarization - Key Point Analysis (KPA) Shared Task requires participants to identify the keypoints in a given corpus. Formally, given an input corpus of relatively short, opinionated texts focused on a particular topic, KPA aims to identify the most prominent keypoints in the corpus. Hence the goal is to condense free-form text into a set of concise bullet points using a well-defined quantitative framework. In track 1, given a debatable topic, a set of keypoints per stance, and a set of crowd arguments supporting or contesting the topic, participants must report for each argument the corresponding match score for each keypoint under the same stance towards the topic. In track 2, we are required to build a language model that would generate keypoints given a set of arguments and a topic and finally find the match score of that particular keypoint with the argument. We mainly focused on the first track.

We frame the task of identifying the most prominent keypoints as a sentence similarity task, obtaining the most similar keypoints corresponding to a given argument.

2 Related Work

Sentence similarity is gaining much attention in the research community due to its versatility in various natural language applications such as text summarization (Abujar et al., 2019), question answering (Ashok et al., 2020), sentiment analysis (Khamphakdee and Seresangtakul, 2021) and plagarisim detection (Lo and Simard, 2019). Two major approaches to quantitatively measure similarity have been proposed -

- **Lexical similarity**, as the name suggests, is a measure of the extent or degree of lexicon overlap between two given sentences, ignoring the semantics of the lexicons.
- **Semantic similarity** takes into account the meaning or semantics of the sentences. Deep Learning based approaches are typically leveraged to create dense representations of sentences, which are then compared using statistical methods like cosine similarity.

Since the *ArgKP-2021* dataset (Friedman et al., 2021) contains crowd arguments for or against a particular stance, naturally, we expect some paraphrasing in the arguments put forth by different people. This indicates that semantic similarity would be an appropriate measure of similarity. However, we observe the problem of semantic drift (Jansen, 2018) in keypoint - argument pairs. Hence, we add additional lexical overlap and syntactic parse based features to improve performance (details on the features can be found in Section 4).

*Equal contribution.

[1] All results and leaderboard standings are reported using the default evaluation method (explained in section 5)

[2] https://github.com/manavkapadnis/Enigma_ArgMining

Proceedings of The 8th Workshop on Argument Mining, pages 200–205
Punta Cana, Dominican Republic, November 10–11, 2021.

3 Dataset Description

The *ArgKP-2021* dataset (Friedman et al., 2021) which was the main dataset used for the shared task consists of approximately 27,520 argument/keypoint pairs for 31 controversial topics. Each of the pairs is labeled as matching or non-matching, along with a stance towards the topic. The train data comprises of 5583 arguments and 207 keypoints, the validation data comprises of 932 arguments and 36 keypoints and the test data comprises of 723 arguments and 33 keypoints.
Additionally, since external datasets were permitted, we experimented with two more datasets i.e., the IBM Rank 30k dataset (Gretz et al., 2019) and the Semantic Textual Similarity or STS dataset (Cer et al., 2017) (described in section 4.5) to train our model before fine-tuning on the *ArgKP-2021* dataset. The *STS* dataset comprises of 8020 pairs of sentences, whereas the IBM Rank 30k dataset comprises of 30497 pairs of arguments and keypoints.

4 Implementation Details

In this section, we elaborate on our experiments and methodology to find the best-performing models. The section is organized to describe the addition of dependency parsing features in Section 4.2, parts of speech features in Section 4.3, Tf-idf features in Section 4.4, and the use of external datasets in Section 4.5.

4.1 Baseline Transformer Model Architecture

In recent work, Transformer (Vaswani et al., 2017) based pre-trained language models like BERT (Devlin et al., 2019), RoBERTa (Liu et al., 2019), BART (Lewis et al., 2019), and DeBERTa (He et al., 2021), have proven to be very powerful in learning robust context-based representations of lexicons and applying these to achieve state of the art performance on a variety of downstream tasks.

We leverage these models for learning contextual representations of a keypoint - argument pair. The keypoints and arguments are individually concatenated, along with the topic (in the same order) for additional context information. We then obtain the contextual representation of this triplet and concatenate to it an encoded feature vector of additional features (one of Dependency Parse based features, Parts-of-Speech based features, and Tf-idf vectors). This concatenated vector was then passed through dense layers and a sigmoid activation to get a final similarity score in the desired range of $[0, 1]$, as shown in Figure 1.

4.2 Dependency Parsing Features

To capture the syntactic structure of the sentences, we added the dependency parse tree of the sentence as an additional feature.

To obtain the same, we used the open-source tool *spacy* [3]. The dependency features are then label encoded according to descending order of occurrences. Consider three unique dependency features in all the concatenated sentences of the original dataset, namely, 'aux', 'amod', and 'nsubj'. Let 'aux', 'nsubj', and 'amod' be the descending order of count in the dataset, then 'aux' is encoded as one, 'nsubj' as two and 'amod' is encoded as three. All the names of unique features can be found in the supplementary material.

These encoded dependency features are then concatenated to the output of the transformer model and passed to subsequent layers as shown in Figure 1.

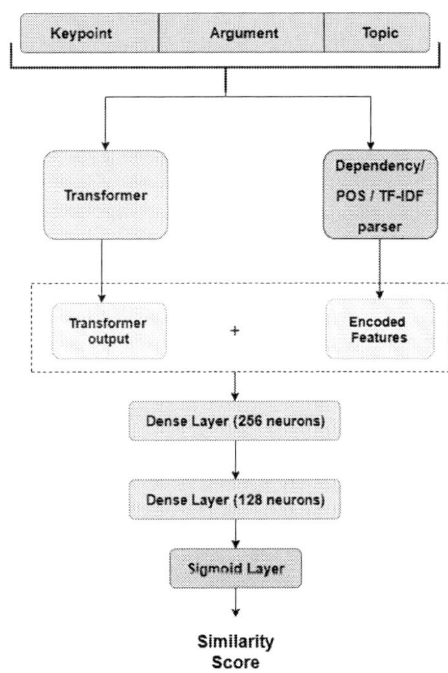

Figure 1: Model Architecture ("+" implies concatenation)

4.3 Parts of Speech Features

With a similar motive as before, i.e., to better capture the syntactic structure of the sentences, we

[3] https://spacy.io/

experimented with Part-Of-Speech (POS) Features as well.

As before, we used the open-source tool *Spacy* to obtain POS labels for each lexicon, which were then label encoded according to descending order of occurrences. The encoded feature vector is then concatenated to the output of the transformer model and fed to the subsequent layers.

4.4 Tf-idf features

In addition to semantic overlap, we wished to see if adding lexical overlap-based features would improve the ability of the model to identify similar sentences. To this end, we obtained the Tf-idf vector of the (keypoint, argument, topic) triplet (with padding). As before, the encoded feature vector is then concatenated to the output of the transformer model and fed further to the subsequent layers.

4.5 External Datasets

We further tried to experiment with sentence similarity pre-training task on two additional datasets. The two datasets used were the STS benchmark dataset and the IBM Debater® - IBM Rank 30k dataset.

For the STS dataset, we normalized the target similarity score to bring the scores between 0 and 1. No additional preprocessing was done to the text. The two input sentences were concatenated into a single sentence and then directly fed to the model. We trained our model on STS dataset for 6 epochs and on the main dataset for 3 epochs.

For the IBM Rank 30k dataset, we used the MACE (Hovy et al., 2013) Probability score as the target column, which signifies the argument quality score for the corresponding topic. This is analogous to our approach for main task, wherein we output a similarity score for each argument-keypoint pair. No preprocessing was done to the text, the argument and topic were concatenated into a single sentence and then fed to the model. We trained our model on the IBM Rank 30k dataset for 3 epochs and on the main dataset for 3 epochs.

Due to resource constraints, we were not able to perform pre-training on both the additional datasets one after another.

5 Results and Discussions

After we had concluded our experiments, a new evaluation method was proposed by organizers, which removes the positive bias towards a system that predict less true positives in high confidence. In the default evaluation metric a perfect recall is attained only when all positive ground truth labels are predicted, whereas the new method allows a perfect recall score when the top 50% of the predictions (ranked by confidence) are positive. However, since we had completed all our experiments at this point, it was not feasible to rerun all our experiments in the given time frame. Hence we have reported all our results according to the default evaluation method.

Among all the transformer models without the use of external datasets, we found BART-large to perform best, along with DeBERTa-large with Tf-idf as additional features, achieving the best *mAP* strict and *mAP* relaxed score of 0.909, 0.982 and 0.911, 0.987 respectively. All the reported results are averaged over three seeds.

Table 1 describes our experiments with different Transformer-based contextual language models without using any additional features. Recent improvements to the state-of-the-art in contextual language models in BART and DeBERTa perform significantly better than BERT. Further, BART is pre-trained using various self-supervised objectives such as token masking, sentence permutation, document rotation, token deletion and text infilling, unlike other models that mostly use either masked language modelling or next sentence prediction. In our opinion, the tasks of sentence permutation and document rotation help the model get a better understanding of context at the sentence level, and thus, are helpful when considering the keypoint matching task. We also observe that the *large* version of the models, trained on more data with more parameters, perform significantly better than the *base* versions, as expected.

Model	mAP Strict	mAP Relaxed
BERT-base	0.804 ± 0.037	0.910 ± 0.050
RoBERTa-base	0.826 ± 0.051	0.930 ± 0.032
BART-base	0.824 ± 0.030	0.908 ± 0.020
DeBERTa-base	0.894 ± 0.020	0.973 ± 0.015
BERT-large	0.821 ± 0.025	0.924 ± 0.006
RoBERTa-large	0.892 ± 0.003	0.970 ± 0.015
BART-large	$\mathbf{0.909 \pm 0.011}$	$\mathbf{0.982 \pm 0.003}$
DeBERTa-large	0.889 ± 0.030	0.979 ± 0.010

Table 1: Results of Transformer models

Table 2 shows the best performing results obtained by concatenating one of the following - Dependency Parse features, POS features, and Tf-idf features. We note that out of the three feature vectors methods, Tf-idf features performs the best. Tf-idf gives a relation/measure of lexical overlap between the argument and keypoint, whereas the other features (POS and Dependency Parse) just expand on the sentence structures of the argument and the keypoint, without expressing the relation between the same. Thus it is observed that Tf-idf performs better than the other two feature vectors. In table 2, we report the best-performing transformer-based models for each feature vector. Detailed results (each transformer model with each feature) can be found in the Appendix which is present in the supplementary material. We could not perform combination of all the syntactic features due to limited GPU memory availability.

Feature	Best Model	mAP Strict	mAP Relaxed
Dep[4]	BART-large	0.868 ± 0.023	0.977 ± 0.015
POS[5]	BART-large	0.906 ± 0.011	0.987 ± 0.005
Tf-idf	DeBERTa-large	**0.911 ± 0.005**	**0.987 ± 0.008**

Table 2: Results with Additional Features

Table 3 shows the outcome of training on additional datasets such as the STS and the IBM Rank 30k dataset without using any feature vectors. We find that the best performing scores using both these datasets are almost equal and are achieved by the same BART-large model architecture. Thus training on additional datasets led to a substantial increase in both *mAP* strict and *mAP* relaxed scores. The best results of pre-training on the additional datasets were almost similar, which might be because the ground truth scores in both the datasets effectively reflect the semantic overlap between two sentences (i.e., if two sentences of a data sample are semantically similar, they would have a higher score, and vice versa), thus making the datasets similar to one another.

We also tried adding feature vectors plus training on additional datasets[6], but there was no significant change in the performance than the existing results. Transformers themselves are able to learn syntactic and semantic features on their own during the training process (Clark et al., 2019). Adding these features only increases redundancy, as a result of which the performance of the model isn't affected much. This observation could also be seen in the difference in the results of table 1 and 2.

[4]Encoded dependency features (section 4.2)

[5]Encoded parts of speech features (section 4.3)

[6]The results of these experiments can be found in Appendix available in the supplementary material.

Complete results of these experiments can be found in the Appendix available in the supplementary material.

Model	Additional Dataset	mAP Strict	mAP Relaxed
BERT-large	STS	0.818 ± 0.045	0.933 ± 0.016
RoBERTa-large	STS	0.905 ± 0.007	**0.986 ± 0.004**
BART-large	STS	**0.920 ± 0.005**	0.967 ± 0.036
DeBERTa-large	STS	0.912 ± 0.004	0.983 ± 0.003
BERT-large	IBM Rank 30k	0.793 ± 0.029	0.914 ± 0.019
RoBERTa-large	IBM Rank 30k	0.872 ± 0.006	0.974 ± 0.003
BART-large	IBM Rank 30k	**0.921 ± 0.018**	**0.982 ± 0.002**
DeBERTa-large	IBM Rank 30k	0.894 ± 0.017	0.982 ± 0.008

Table 3: Results with pretraining on additional datasets

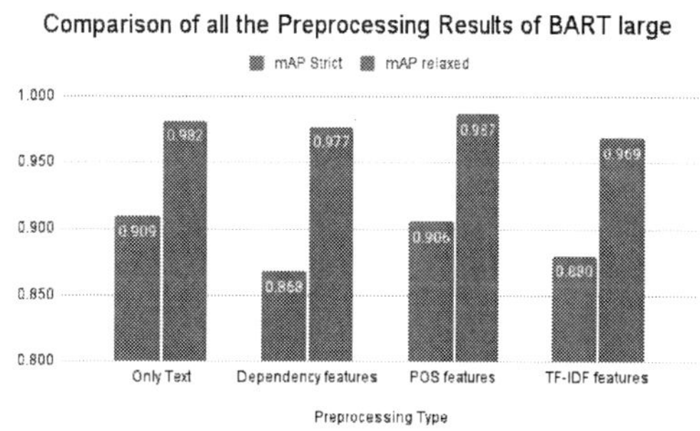

Figure 2: All preprocessing methods with BART large

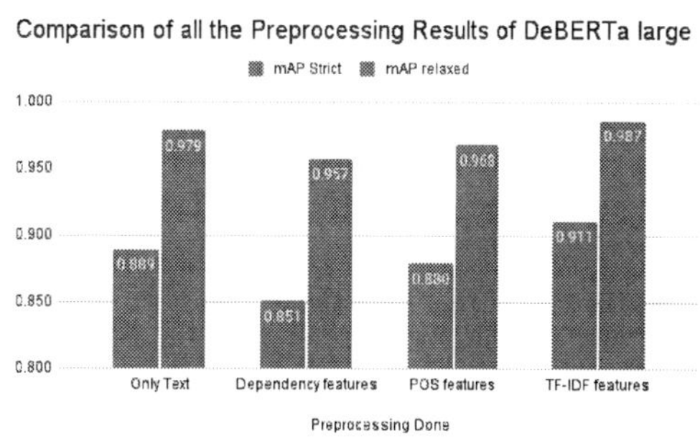

Figure 3: All preprocessing methods with DeBERTa large

In Figures 2 and 3, we plot the results of the best-performing transformer-based models using different feature vectors.

6 Ablation Study

We designed different settings to compare and validate our approach and its performance. This section consists of results on excluding of topics from input in Section 6.1, incorporating average of hidden states before feeding to dense layers in Section 6.2, and boosting in Section 6.3. Since we obtain best results with BART-large and DeBERTa-large with Tf-idf features, thus the following ablation study is done with these class of models.

6.1 Exclusion of topic from input

We incorporate the combination of keypoints and arguments as input to the pre-trained language models to analyze the importance of the topic towards generating the matching score. Comparing Table 1 and Table 4, incorporating topic provides more context in the input, thus improving both *mAP* strict score and *mAP* relaxed score.

Model	mAP Strict	mAP Relaxed
BART-base	0.803 ± 0.028	0.898 ± 0.015
DeBERTa-base	0.823 ± 0.030	0.922 ± 0.012
BART-large	$\mathbf{0.880 \pm 0.006}$	$\mathbf{0.946 \pm 0.010}$
DeBERTa-large	0.874 ± 0.025	0.946 ± 0.027

Table 4: Results with input as keypoint plus argument

6.2 Average of hidden states

We average the last two and the last three hidden states of the pre-trained language model. The average hidden states were then fed into the dense layers to obtain the match score. It can be observed that for both BART-large and DeBERTa-large, the performance decreases as we incorporate more hidden states for the output. The intuition behind this observation can be attributed to the fact that task-specific information encoded in hidden states is less as compared to the last layer, resulting in decreased performance. The results are shown in Table 5.

Model	No. of Hidden States	mAP Strict	mAP Relaxed
BART-large	2	0.868 ± 0.016	0.941 ± 0.004
DeBERTa-large	2	$\mathbf{0.871 \pm 0.039}$	$\mathbf{0.949 \pm 0.015}$
BART-large	3	0.837 ± 0.020	0.933 ± 0.012
DeBERTa-large	3	0.850 ± 0.014	0.934 ± 0.022

Table 5: Results with average of hidden states

6.3 Boosting

We implemented the AdaBoost algorithm by considering our baseline transformer architecture as the base model for this sequential paradigm. BART-large and DeBERTa-large were the transformers used for this study. The first base model was trained with the whole training set, whereas the other four models were trained by sampling data points from a probability distribution. Initially, all the data points were assigned an equal probability. However, the distribution was updated in a way such that the erroneous data points for the previous base models were given a higher probability to be sampled.

The top $10,000$ most probable data points were sampled for each base model except for the first one. It can be observed from Table 1 and Table 6 that for DeBERTa large model, the *mAP* Strict has indeed been boosted from 0.889 to 0.904. The results are mentioned in Table 6.

Model	mAP Strict	mAP Relaxed
BART-large	0.832 ± 0.020	0.960 ± 0.010
DeBERTa-large	$\mathbf{0.904 \pm 0.021}$	$\mathbf{0.973 \pm 0.017}$

Table 6: Boosting Results on Transformer model

7 Conclusion

In this work, we used Pre-trained Language Models (PLMs) to predict the match score for each argument and keypoint pair under the same stance towards the topic. We observed the state-of-the-art PLMs such as BART and DeBERTa perform the best compared to other models. We further improve the performance with additional datasets (IBM Rank 30k and STS) to perform additional pre-training (with sentence similarity) before fine-tuning on ArgKP-2021 dataset. We experimented with POS, Dependency and Tf-idf features to evaluate the addition of extra syntactic features. We support the selection of our final models with various ablation studies. It would be a good future direction to generate appropriate explanations from concatenated input and propose methods to use explanations in the training process.

8 Acknowledgements

We would like to thank the organizers Roni Friedman-Melamed, Lena Dankin, Yufang Hou, and Noam Slonim for holding this shared task. It was a great learning experience for us. We would also like to thank our fellow participants at ArgMining 2021; we look forward to learning more about their approaches and interacting with them at EMNLP. Finally, we would like to extend a big thanks to makers and maintainers of the exemplary HuggingFace (Wolf et al., 2020) repository, without which most of our research would have been impossible.

References

Sheikh Abujar, Mahmudul Hasan, and Syed Akhter Hossain. 2019. Sentence similarity estimation for text summarization using deep learning. In *Proceedings of the 2nd International Conference on Data Engineering and Communication Technology*, pages 155–164, Singapore. Springer Singapore.

Aishwarya Ashok, Ganapathy Natarajan, Ramez Elmasri, and Laurel Smith-Stvan. 2020. SimsterQ: A similarity based clustering approach to opinion question answering. In *Proceedings of The 3rd Workshop on e-Commerce and NLP*, pages 69–76, Seattle, WA, USA. Association for Computational Linguistics.

Daniel Cer, Mona Diab, Eneko Agirre, Iñigo Lopez-Gazpio, and Lucia Specia. 2017. Semeval-2017 task 1: Semantic textual similarity multilingual and crosslingual focused evaluation. In *Proceedings of the 11th International Workshop on Semantic Evaluation (SemEval-2017)*, pages 1–14.

Kevin Clark, Urvashi Khandelwal, Omer Levy, and Christopher D. Manning. 2019. What does bert look at? an analysis of bert's attention.

Jacob Devlin, Ming-Wei Chang, Kenton Lee, and Kristina Toutanova. 2019. BERT: Pre-training of deep bidirectional transformers for language understanding. In *Proceedings of the 2019 Conference of the North American Chapter of the Association for Computational Linguistics: Human Language Technologies, Volume 1 (Long and Short Papers)*, pages 4171–4186, Minneapolis, Minnesota. Association for Computational Linguistics.

Roni Friedman, Lena Dankin, Yoav Katz, Yufang Hou, and Noam Slonim. 2021. Overview of kpa- 2021 shared task: Key point based quantitative summarization. In *Proceedings of the 8th Workshop on Argumentation Mining. Association for Computational Linguistics.*

Shai Gretz, Roni Friedman, Edo Cohen-Karlik, Assaf Toledo, Dan Lahav, Ranit Aharonov, and Noam Slonim. 2019. A large-scale dataset for argument quality ranking: Construction and analysis.

Pengcheng He, Xiaodong Liu, Jianfeng Gao, and Weizhu Chen. 2021. Deberta: Decoding-enhanced bert with disentangled attention.

Dirk Hovy, Taylor Berg-Kirkpatrick, Ashish Vaswani, and Eduard Hovy. 2013. Learning whom to trust with MACE. In *Proceedings of the 2013 Conference of the North American Chapter of the Association for Computational Linguistics: Human Language Technologies*, pages 1120–1130, Atlanta, Georgia. Association for Computational Linguistics.

Peter Jansen. 2018. Multi-hop inference for sentence-level TextGraphs: How challenging is meaningfully combining information for science question answering? In *Proceedings of the Twelfth Workshop on Graph-Based Methods for Natural Language Processing (TextGraphs-12)*, pages 12–17, New Orleans, Louisiana, USA. Association for Computational Linguistics.

Nattawat Khamphakdee and Pusadee Seresangtakul. 2021. A framework for constructing thai sentiment corpus using the cosine similarity technique. In *2021 13th International Conference on Knowledge and Smart Technology (KST)*, pages 202–207.

Mike Lewis, Yinhan Liu, Naman Goyal, Marjan Ghazvininejad, Abdelrahman Mohamed, Omer Levy, Ves Stoyanov, and Luke Zettlemoyer. 2019. Bart: Denoising sequence-to-sequence pre-training for natural language generation, translation, and comprehension.

Yinhan Liu, Myle Ott, Naman Goyal, Jingfei Du, Mandar Joshi, Danqi Chen, Omer Levy, Mike Lewis, Luke Zettlemoyer, and Veselin Stoyanov. 2019. Roberta: A robustly optimized bert pretraining approach.

Chi-kiu Lo and Michel Simard. 2019. Fully unsupervised crosslingual semantic textual similarity metric based on BERT for identifying parallel data. In *Proceedings of the 23rd Conference on Computational Natural Language Learning (CoNLL)*, pages 206–215, Hong Kong, China. Association for Computational Linguistics.

Ashish Vaswani, Noam Shazeer, Niki Parmar, Jakob Uszkoreit, Llion Jones, Aidan N. Gomez, Lukasz Kaiser, and Illia Polosukhin. 2017. Attention is all you need.

Thomas Wolf, Lysandre Debut, Victor Sanh, Julien Chaumond, Clement Delangue, Anthony Moi, Pierric Cistac, Tim Rault, Rémi Louf, Morgan Funtowicz, Joe Davison, Sam Shleifer, Patrick von Platen, Clara Ma, Yacine Jernite, Julien Plu, Canwen Xu, Teven Le Scao, Sylvain Gugger, Mariama Drame, Quentin Lhoest, and Alexander M. Rush. 2020. Huggingface's transformers: State-of-the-art natural language processing.

Association for Computational Linguistics
209 N. Eighth Street
Stroudsburg, Pennsylvania 18360

ISBN 978-1-7138-9174-1
9 781713 891741

CURRAN ASSOCIATES INC.
proceedings.com